Lecture Notes in Computer Science 1598

Edited by G. Goos, J. Hartmanis and J. van Leeuwen

T0238812

Springer
Berlin
Heidelberg
New York
Barcelona
Hong Kong
London
Milan
Paris
Singapore
Tokyo

Riccardo Poli Peter Nordin
William B. Langdon Terence C. Fogarty (Eds.)

Genetic Programming

Second European Workshop, EuroGP'99
Göteborg, Sweden, May 26-27, 1999
Proceedings

 Springer

Volume Editors

Riccardo Poli
University of Birmingham, School of Computer Science
Egdbaston, Birmingham B15 2TT, UK
E-mail: R.Poli@cs.bham.ac.uk

Peter Nordin
Chalmers University of Technology, Department of Physical Resource Theory
S-412 96 Göteborg, Sweden
E-mail: nordin@fy.chalmers.se

William B. Langdon
Centrum voor Wiskunde en Informatic
Kruislaan 413, 1098 SJ Amsterdam, The Netherlands
E-mail: W.B.Langdon@cwi.nl

Terence C. Fogarty
Napier University
219 Colinton Road, Edinburgh EH14 1DJ, UK
E-mail: tcf@dcs.napier.ac.uk

Cataloging-in-Publication data applied for

Die Deutsche Bibliothek - CIP-Einheitsaufnahme

Genetic programming : second European workshop ; proceedings /
EuroGP '99, Göteborg, Sweden, May 26 - 27, 1999. Riccardo Poli ...
(ed.). - Berlin ; Heidelberg ; New York ; Barcelona ; Hong Kong ;
London ; Milan ; Paris ; Singapore ; Tokyo : Springer, 1999
  (Lecture notes in computer science ; Vol. 1598)
  ISBN 3-540-65899-8

CR Subject Classification (1998): D.1, F.1, I.5, J.3

ISSN 0302-9743
ISBN 3-540-65899-8 Springer-Verlag Berlin Heidelberg New York

© Springer-Verlag Berlin Heidelberg 1999
Printed in Germany

Typesetting: Camera-ready by author
SPIN: 10704745   06/3142 – 5 4 3 2 1 0   Printed on acid-free paper

Preface

Genetic Programming (GP) is a powerful set of techniques, inspired by natural selection and genetic inheritance, which allows the automatic production of computer programs.

GP, as a method of developing software, is radically different from current software engineering practice. Potentially, in GP, the domain experts, instead of trying to transfer their knowledge to computer programmers, can create programs by directly specifying how they should behave. This is done either by selecting the examples from which GP must learn and generalise, or by grading intermediate solutions. There is great hope in the field that this process of non-mediated automatic knowledge elicitation will dramatically reduce costs and development time while increasing the effectiveness of the programs developed. This hope is corroborated by the success obtained by GP on a large number of difficult problems like automatic design, pattern recognition, robotic control, synthesis of neural networks, symbolic regression, music and picture generation, and many others.

GP as a field was founded by John Koza at the beginning of the 1990s, and has grown exponentially since then. GP is now a separate, very successful branch of its parent field, Evolutionary Computation. More than 1000 papers have been published over the last ten years in GP, with the number still growing quickly. Since 1996, GP has had its own annual international conference held in the United States of America, which is now the largest conference devoted to Evolutionary Computation, and its own European event, EuroGP.

This volume contains the proceedings of EuroGP'99, the Second European Workshop on Genetic Programming, held at the University of Göteborg, Sweden, on 26 and 27 May 1999. EuroGP'99 followed EuroGP'98, which took place in Paris in April 1998. The aim of these events was to give European and non-European researchers in the area of genetic programming, as well as people from industry and commerce, an opportunity to present their latest research and discuss current developments and applications. EuroGP'99 was sponsored by EvoNet, the Network of Excellence in Evolutionary Computation, as one of the activities of EvoGP, the EvoNet working group on genetic programming. The workshop was held in conjunction with three other major European events: EvoRobot'99, the second European workshop on evolutionary robotics, held on 28 and 29 May; EvoIASP'99, the first European workshop on evolutionary image analysis and signal processing, held on 28 May; and EuroECTel'99, the first European workshop on evolutionary telecommunications, held on 29 May.

Twenty-three papers were accepted for publication in this volume and for presentation at the workshop (twelve for oral presentation, eleven as posters). Many of these are by internationally recognised researchers in genetic programming and evolutionary computation, all are of a high quality. This has been ensured by an international programme committee including not only the main

GP experts in Europe but also most of the leading GP researchers from around the world. We are extremely grateful to them for their quick and thorough work, which has allowed us to provide three independent anonymous reviews for each paper submitted despite the limited time available. With such a high-quality international programme committee, with the tutorial given by John Koza, the founder of GP, with the invited speech by David B. Fogel and with authors coming from ten different countries, we believe that the workshop and these proceedings represent a cross section of the best genetic programming research in Europe and in the rest of the world.

May 1999   Riccardo Poli, Peter Nordin
                        William B. Langdon, and Terence C. Fogarty

Organization

EuroGP'99 is organized by EvoGP, the EvoNet Working Group on Genetic Programming.

Organizing Committee

Program co-chair:	Riccardo Poli (University of Birmingham, UK)
Program co-chair:	Peter Nordin (Chalmers University of Technology, Sweden)
Publication chair:	Terence C. Fogarty (Napier University, UK)
Publicity chair:	William B. Langdon (CWI, The Netherlands)
Local co-chair:	Mats Nordahl (Chalmers University of Technology, Sweden)
Local co-chair:	Kristian Lindgren (Chalmers University of Technology, Sweden)

Program Committee

Lee Altenberg, University of Hawaii at Manoa, USA
Peter Angeline, Natural Selection, New York, USA
Wolfgang Banzhaf, University of Dortmund, Germany
Tobias Blickle, Saarbruecken, Germany
Marco Dorigo, Free University of Brussels, Belgium
Gusz Eiben, University of Leiden, The Netherlands
Terence C. Fogarty, Napier University, UK
James A. Foster, University of Idaho, USA
Frederic Gruau, CWI, The Netherlands
Tom Haynes, Wichita State University, USA
Hitoshi Iba, University of Tokyo, Japan
W. B. Langdon, CWI, The Netherlands
Kristian Lindgren, Chalmers University of Technology, Sweden
Evelyne Lutton, INRIA, France
Nic McPhee, University of Minnesota, USA
Jean-Arcady Meyer, Ecole Normale Superieure, France
Mats Nordahl, Chalmers University of Technology Sweden
Peter Nordin, Chalmers University of Technology, Sweden
Una-May O'Reilly, Massachusetts Institute of Technology, USA
Riccardo Poli, The University of Birmingham, UK
Conor Ryan, University of Limerick, Ireland
Justinian Rosca, Siemens, USA
Marc Schoenauer, Ecole Polytechnique, France

Michele Sebag, Ecole Polytechnique, France
Terry Soule, St. Cloud State University, USA
Andrea Tettamanzi, Genetica, Italy
Marco Tomassini, Universite de Lausanne, Switzerland
Hans-Michael Voigt, GFaI Berlin, Germany
Byoung-Tak Zhang, Seoul National University, Korea

Sponsoring Institutions

Chalmers University of Technology and Göteborg University, Sweden
EvoNet: the Network of Excellence in Evolutionary Computing

Table of Contents

Posters

Boolean Functions Fitness Spaces

W. B. Langdon[1] and R. Poli[2]

[1] Centrum voor Wiskunde en Informatica
Kruislaan 413, NL-1098 SJ Amsterdam
bill@cwi.nl
http://www.cwi.nl/~bill
Tel: +31 20 592 4093, Fax: +31 20 592 4199
[2] School of Computer Science, The University of Birmingham
Birmingham B15 2TT
R.Poli@cs.bham.ac.uk
http://www.cs.bham.ac.uk/~rmp

Abstract. We investigate the distribution of performance of the Boolean functions of 3 Boolean inputs (particularly that of the parity functions), the always-on-6 and even-6 parity functions. We use enumeration, uniform Monte-Carlo random sampling and sampling random full trees. As expected XOR dramatically changes the fitness distributions. In all cases once some minimum size threshold has been exceeded, the distribution of performance is approximately independent of program size. However the distribution of the performance of full trees is different from that of asymmetric trees and varies with tree depth.

1 Introduction

Our investigations of the artificial ant following the Santa Fe trail [6] suggests that, provided programs are big enough, the distribution of program fitnesses is roughly independent of their size. That is if we pick a program of a certain size at random its as likely to perform as well as another program of a different size also chosen at random (provided both exceed some threshold size). If this is generally true then as the size of the search space grows approximately exponentially as we allow longer programs then so to does the number of programs with a certain level of performance. Therefore while a search space with no size or depth limits will be infinite it will contain an infinite number of solutions!

We test this result from the Ant problem on a range of other problems. In Sect. 2 we describe the Boolean problems. Section 3 describes how we measure the performance spaces of these problems and gives our results. The ramped-half-and-half method [2, page 93] is commonly used to generate the initial population in genetic programming (GP). Half the random programs generated by it are full. Therefore we also explicitly consider the subspace of full trees. This is followed by a discussion of these results and their implications (Sect. 4) and our conclusions (Sect. 5).

R. Poli et al. (Eds.): EuroGP'99, LNCS 1598, pp. 1–14, 1999.
© Springer-Verlag Berlin Heidelberg 1999

2   Boolean Functions

The Boolean functions have often been used as benchmark problems. The program trees we will consider are composed of n terminals (D0, D1, ... D_{n-1}) which are the Boolean inputs to the program and the Boolean logic functions AND, OR, NAND and NOR [2]. These are sufficient to construct any Boolean function but we shall also investigate including the exclusive-or function (XOR) which is asymmetric. Note [2] required all the functions to have the same arity, this is not required in our approach. The fitness of each tree is given by evaluating it as a logical expression for each of the 2^n possible combinations of D_n inputs. Its fitness is the number of fitness cases when its output agrees with that of the target Boolean function.

There are $n^{(l+1)/2}|F|^{(l-1)/2} \times \frac{(l-1)!}{((l+1)/2)!((l-1)/2)!}$ different trees of size l [2, page 213] [1]. $|F|$ is four (or five if XOR is included). (Note this formula is simple as each function (internal node) has two arguments). The number of programs rises rapidly (approximately exponentially) with increasing program size l (see Figs. 1 and 2). Of course if no bounds are placed on the size or depth of programs then the number of them is unbounded, i.e. the search space is infinite.

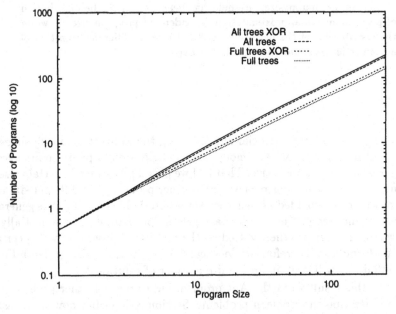

Fig. 1. Size of 3-Input Boolean Function Search Spaces (note log log scale)

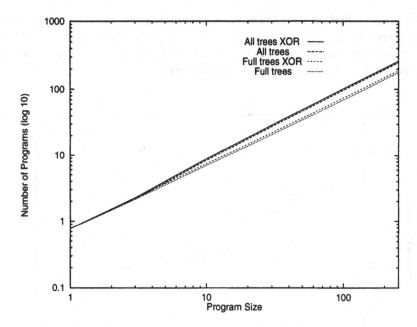

Fig. 2. Size of 6-Input Boolean Function Search Spaces (note log log scale)

3 Boolean Program Spaces

3.1 3 Input Boolean Program Spaces

Recall that the fitness of a program is determined by the closeness of the function the program actually implements and the target function. E.g if the program implements function 0 (always return false) its fitness when searching for 3 input rule 150 (3-even parity) is 4, since it gets half of the 8 test cases right. That is for each target function there is a fixed simple mapping between the function implement by a program and the program's fitness. So the functionality of a trial solution readily gives its fitness on all the Boolean problems. Therefore by considering the distribution of the functionality of each point in the search space, we can consider simultaneously the fitness distribution of all of the Boolean functions.

In this section we consider all the Boolean functions for $n = 3$. There are 256 of them but they can be split into 80 equivalence classes. Functions are equivalent if permuting their inputs can produce the same functionality. By symmetry members of the same equivalence class will occur in the same numbers in the search space. Therefore we need only consider one representative function from each class [2, page 215].

Figure 3 shows the number of examples of each function found when 10 million trees of size 41 were created at random. (The 80 equivalence classes are ordered along the x-axis in order of decreasing frequency). As expected there is good agreement with [2, Table 9.3]. Figure 4 shows similar plots for a wide range of sizes. (Data for trees of size 1, 3, 5, 7, 9, 11 and 13 were gathered by evaluating every tree of that size, whereas data for larger trees was gathered by randomly sampling 10 million programs for each size. C++ code to generate random programs is available via ftp://ftp.cs.bham.ac.uk /pub/authors/W.B.Langdon/gp-code/rand_tree.cc).

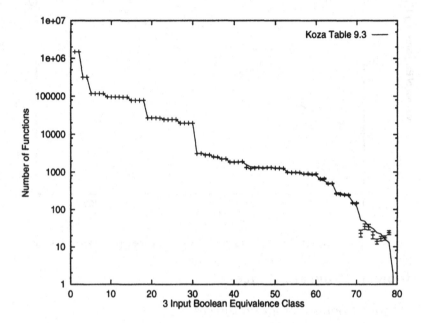

Fig. 3. Number of functions of size 41 in each equivalence class

Figure 4 shows a certain minimum size is required before the problem can be solved and that the minimum size depends on the difficulty of the problem. Once this threshold size is exceeded the proportion of programs which belong to the equivalence class grows rapidly to a stable value which appears to be more-or-less independent of program size. Figure 5 shows these characteristics are retained if we extend the function set to include XOR. (Adding XOR to the function set greatly extends the search space and so enumerating all trees of size 13 is no longer feasible, therefore data for size 13 was produced by random sampling). Note adding the asymmetric XOR function radically changes the program space. In particular, as might be expected, the two parity functions (equivalence classes 79 and 80) are much more prevalent. Also the range of frequencies is much reduced. For example 68 of the 80 equivalence classes have frequencies between 0.1/256 and 10/256 rather than 28 with the standard function set.

While Figs. 4 and 5 can be used to estimate the fitness space of each three input Boolean function across the whole space, there are some interesting parts of these spaces where certain functions are more concentrated than elsewhere. Figure 6 plots the proportion of full trees of different depths which implement the parity functions. It is clear there are far more parity functions amongst

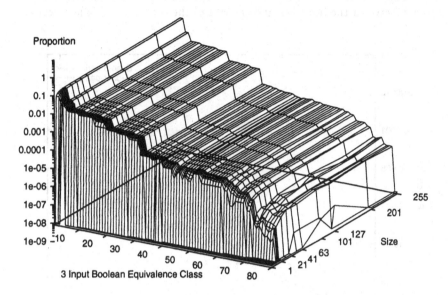

Fig. 4. Proportion of functions in each equivalence class

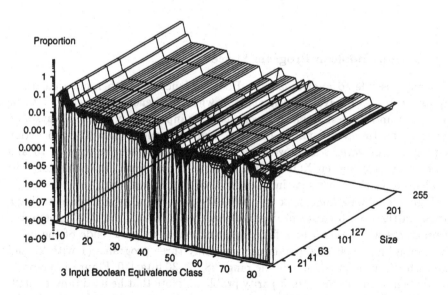

Fig. 5. Proportion of functions in each equivalence class with XOR in function set

the full trees than there are on average. When XOR is added to the function set, see Fig. 7, there are again a higher proportion of parity functions but the difference between the full trees and the rest of the search space is less dramatic.

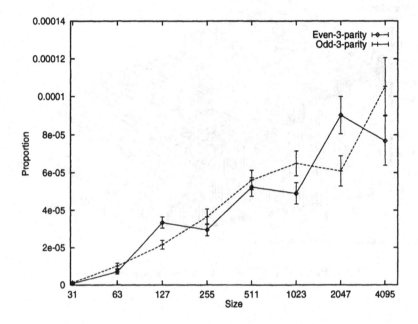

Fig. 6. 3 input parity functions in full trees

3.2   6 Input Boolean Program Spaces

It is not possible to analyse all the Boolean functions with more than three inputs. Instead we have concentrated on what are generally considered to be the easiest and hardest Boolean functions of six inputs. Namely the always-on-6 function and the even-6 parity function. Figures 8 and 9 show the proportion of programs of various sizes with each of the possible scores. Figures 10 and 11 show the same when XOR is added to the function set. It is clear all four problems have the same near independence of fitness from size.

Figure 9 shows a huge peak with 90% of points in the search space having a fitness on the even-6 parity problem of exactly half marks, i.e. 32. The number of programs with other scores falls exponentially away either side of the peak. Even sampling 10,000,000 points per size, only three programs (1 with 27 and two with 37) were found outside the range 28 ... 36 hits. [10, Figure 4.1] reports similar behaviour on the even-5-parity problem. (Note that he used ramped-half-and-half, only sampled 16,000 programs and did not consider variation of the fitness distribution with size). He reports that the fitness distribution for the even-5-parity problem are even more tightly grouped in a range of 5 values. This

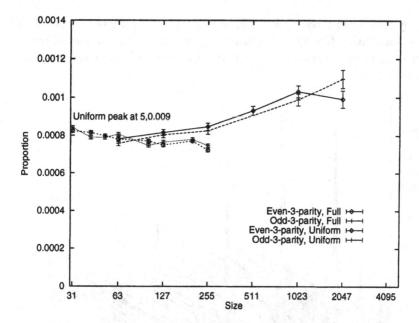

Fig. 7. Proportion of 3 input parity functions in full trees with XOR

could be due to the smaller study size but allowing for this, the comparable range for even-6 parity still spans 7 values. Looking at the short programs in Fig. 9 shows they have an even tighter distribution of fitness. If this is also true for the even-5 parity problem then the range reported in [10] will be due to the larger of the trees he sampled, particularly the full trees. It seems reasonable to suggest that the difference between a range of fitness values reported by [10] on the even-5 parity problem (5) and that we find on the even-6 parity problem (7 or 9) is indeed due to the peak in the fitness distribution being wider, rather than an artifact of the bias inherent in ramped-half-and-half.

The fitness distribution of the even-6 parity problem is much tighter than that of the binomial distribution that would be produced by selecting Boolean functions uniformly at random from the 2^{2^n} available. I.e. centred on $\frac{n}{2}$ with variance of $\frac{n}{4}$ [10, page 62]. The measured variance is only 0.12 rather than 1.5. Such a tight fitness distribution and in particular the absence of a high fitness tail suggests that the problem will be hard for any adaptive algorithm.

As expected adding XOR to the function set greatly increases the even-6 parity fitness distribution's width and it retains its near independence of program size (see Fig. 11). The standard deviation is now 0.92 rather than 0.34. However the more dramatic effect of the wider distribution is the number of solutions (i.e. programs scoring 64 hits) is now measurable and is about 2×10^{-7}.

Figure 8 shows the distribution of number of trues returned is a saw toothed curve. The proportion of programs which have one of the odd scores on the always-on-6 problem is about 0.3%. The proportion which have an even score, not divisible by four, is about 1%, scores divisible by 4 about 2%, those by 8 3%, those by 16 6% and those by 32 10%. Note the central peak in the even-6 parity fitness distribution (see Fig. 9) is not solely due to a large number of programs which implement always-on-6 or always-off-6. Only 18.6% of programs are of these two types.

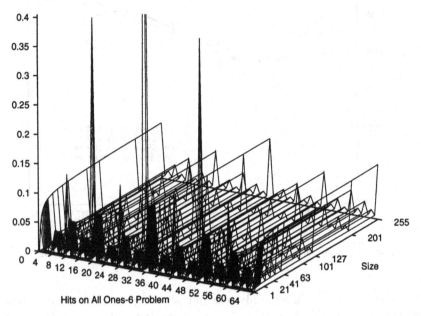

Fig. 8. Number of ones returned by 6-input Boolean functions (note linear scale)

Figure 10 shows the distribution of number of trues returned when XOR is added to the function set is a little changed (cf. Fig. 8) but retains its saw toothed appearance and near independence of program size.

3.3   Even-6 Parity and Always-On-6 Full Trees

Restricting our search to just the full trees yields a similar fitness distribution for the even-6 parity problem, see Fig. 13. However the distribution of fitness values is considerably wider with a range of 25–38 (twice that for the whole search space) and a standard deviation of 0.68. Adding XOR to the function set (see Fig. 15) further widens the distribution (the standard deviation becomes 1.8). Even when including XOR, solutions are so rare that their proportion is difficult to estimate accurately. Given this the proportion of solutions in the full trees appears to be the same as in the rest of the search space (with the same program size) despite an overall spreading of the fitness distribution. (The only even-6 parity programs found by random search through full trees contained either 15 or 31 nodes). Both with XOR and without the distribution of hits on the even-6 parity problem returned by full trees shows some dependence on depth of tree but this is much less dramatic than is the case with the three

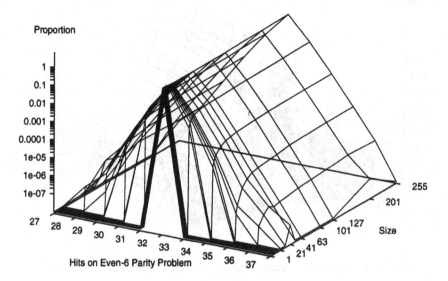

Fig. 9. Even-6 parity program space

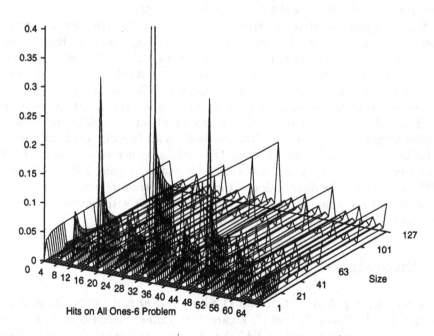

Fig. 10. Number of ones returned by 6-input Boolean functions, XOR included (note linear scale)

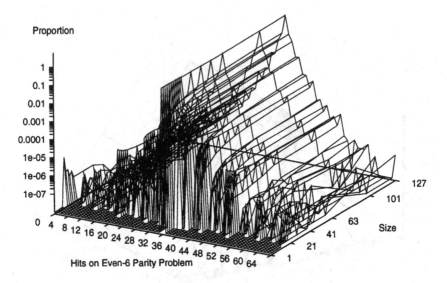

Fig. 11. Even-6 parity program space, including XOR in function set

input parity functions, see Figs. 6 and 7. However, as with asymmetric trees, this appears to die away as the programs become bigger.

Searching just the full trees yields a similar fitness distribution for the always-on-6 problem as for the whole search space (compare Figs. 8 and 12). However the peaks corresponding to functions returning true multiples of 4, 8, 16 or 32 times are now far less prominent and instead always-on-6 itself and its compliment, always-off-6, now dominate and together represent 35% of all trees, compared to 18% when considering asymmetric trees as well. Also the troughs at odd numbers of hits are also less prominent, each representing about 0.5% rather than about 0.3% of all programs. Adding XOR to the function set (see Fig. 14) has the effect of further smoothing the distribution. The peaks at either extreme are now 8% with a typical odd values near 32 being 1.4% and even being 1.8%. Both with XOR and without the distribution of the number of trues returned by full trees shows some dependence on depth of tree. However, as with even-6 parity, this appears to fade away as the programs become bigger.

4   Discussion

If we compare Fig. 4, 5, 8, 9, 10 and 11 with a similar plot for the artificial ant problem on the Santa Fe trail [6, Figure 2] and other plots for all 2, 3 and 4 Boolean functions composed on NAND gates and a continuous domain problem [5], we see in all cases a certain minimum size is required before any solutions with a certain functionality exist, and that this threshold increases with the difficulty of the functionality. Once this threshold size is exceeded the proportion

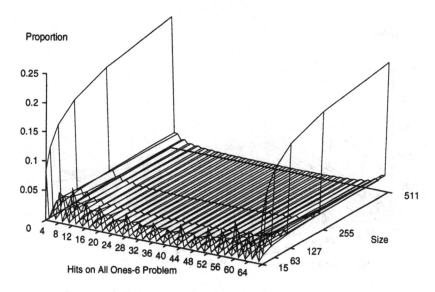

Fig. 12. Number of ones returned by 6-input full trees (note linear scale)

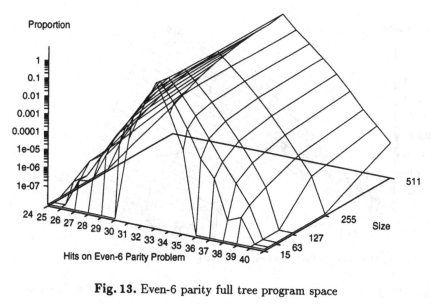

Fig. 13. Even-6 parity full tree program space

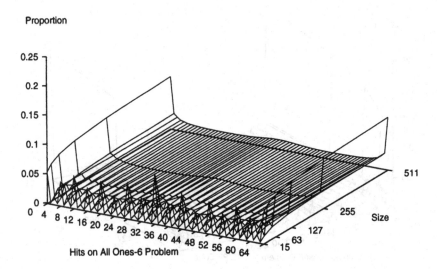

Fig. 14. Number of ones returned by 6-input full trees, XOR included (note linear scale)

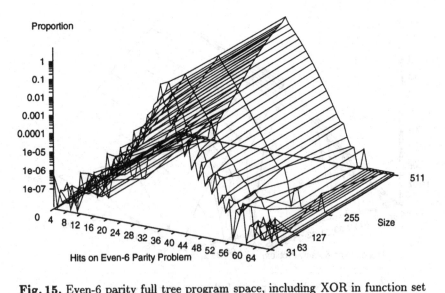

Fig. 15. Even-6 parity full tree program space, including XOR in function set

of programs grows rapidly to a stable value which appears to be more-or-less independent of program size. Conversely the proportion of the search space which implements easy functionality starts high and then falls with increasing program size, again converging to a stable value which is more-or-less independent of further increases in program size. We have demonstrated this property on the 256 3-input Boolean functions, four 6-input Boolean functions as well as the Ant problem. We expect this property to hold in many cases, indeed it can be proved in special cases [7], however demonstrating it on 261 problems (66344 including work in progress) is not sufficient to prove it holds in general. But it does add experimental weight to some of our claims about the nature of program fitness landscapes and their influence on the bloating phenomena [8].

On average half the random trees sampled using the ramped-half-and-half method [2, page 93] are full. Therefore, particularly if the depth parameter is increased beyond the usual 6 (equivalent to maximum size of 63), the chances of finding at random both the even-3 and the odd-3 parity functions are considerably higher using it than using uniform search. In contrast ramped-half-and-half is less likely to find solutions to the Santa Fe ant trail problem than uniform search (see [6, Table 3]). This suggests that the best method to use to create the initial random population is problem dependent.

In [2, Chapter 9] GP performance is shown not to be the same as random search. Indeed in the case of all but a few of the simplest problems which both GP and random search easily solve, GP performance is shown to be superior to random search. [2, Chapter 9] treats in detail all the 256 Boolean functions with 3 bit inputs. (See also [4] and [3]). When [2, page 211] compares the performance of GP with random search on these problems it explicitly assumes that programs of one size (41) are typical of the whole search space. In Sect. 3.1 we have verified this assumption. It should be noted that the subspaces consisting of short trees or full trees are not typical of the whole space. In particular full trees are much more likely to implement one of the parity functions than asymmetric trees which form most of the search space. In the presence of code bloat where programs increase in size, the use of a depth limit (rather than size limit) may encourage the formation of full trees of the maximum permitted depth and so ease the solution of problems in which full trees contain a higher proportion of solutions while a size limit will discourage the formation of full trees and so may help in problems where the density of solutions is lower in full trees.

If we are right and the density of solutions changes little with program size then there is no intrinsic advantage in searching programs longer than the threshold. Of course, in general, we will not know in advance where the threshold is. Also it may be that some search techniques perform better with longer programs, perhaps because together they encourage the formation of smoother more correlated or easier to search fitness landscapes [9]. However in practice searching at longer sizes is liable to be more expensive both in terms of memory and also time (since commonly the CPU time to perform each fitness evaluation rises in proportion to program size).

5 Conclusions

In three very different classes of problems (the Ant, Boolean and symbolic regression problems) we have now shown that the fitness space is in a gross manner independent of program size. In general the number of programs of a given size grows approximately exponentially with that size. Thus the number of programs with a particular fitness score or level of performance also grows exponentially, in particular the number of solutions also grows exponentially.

References

1. Laurent Alonso and Rene Schott. *Random Generation of Trees*. Kluwer Academic Publishers, 1995.
2. John R. Koza. *Genetic Programming: On the Programming of Computers by Means of Natural Selection*. MIT Press, Cambridge, MA, USA, 1992.
3. John R. Koza. A response to the ML-95 paper entitled "Hill climbing beats genetic search on a boolean circuit synthesis of Koza's". Distributed 11 July 1995 at the 1995 International Machine Learning Conference in Tahoe City, California, USA, 11 July 1995.
4. Kevin J. Lang. Hill climbing beats genetic search on a boolean circuit synthesis of Koza's. In *Proceedings of the Twelfth International Conference on Machine Learning*, Tahoe City, California, USA, July 1995. Morgan Kaufmann.
5. W. B. Langdon. Scaling of program tree fitness spaces. 31 January 1999.
6. W. B. Langdon and R. Poli. Why ants are hard. In John R. Koza, Wolfgang Banzhaf, Kumar Chellapilla, Kalyanmoy Deb, Marco Dorigo, David B. Fogel, Max H. Garzon, David E. Goldberg, Hitoshi Iba, and Rick Riolo, editors, *Genetic Programming 1998: Proceedings of the Third Annual Conference*, pages 193–201, University of Wisconsin, Madison, Wisconsin, USA, 22-25 July 1998. Morgan Kaufmann.
7. W. B. Langdon and R. Poli. Why "building blocks" don't work on parity problems. Technical Report CSRP-98-17, University of Birmingham, School of Computer Science, 13 July 1998.
8. W. B. Langdon, T. Soule, R. Poli, and J. A. Foster. The evolution of size and shape. In Lee Spector, W. B. Langdon, Una-May O'Reilly, and Peter J. Angeline, editors, *Advances in Genetic Programming 3*, chapter 8. MIT Press, Cambridge, MA, USA, 1999. Forthcoming.
9. Riccardo Poli and William B. Langdon. On the search properties of different crossover operators in genetic programming. In John R. Koza, Wolfgang Banzhaf, Kumar Chellapilla, Kalyanmoy Deb, Marco Dorigo, David B. Fogel, Max H. Garzon, David E. Goldberg, Hitoshi Iba, and Rick Riolo, editors, *Genetic Programming 1998: Proceedings of the Third Annual Conference*, pages 293–301, University of Wisconsin, Madison, Wisconsin, USA, 22-25 July 1998. Morgan Kaufmann.
10. Justinian P. Rosca. *Hierarchical Learning with Procedural Abstraction Mechanisms*. PhD thesis, University of Rochester, Rochester, NY 14627, February 1997.

Meta-Evolution in Graph GP

Wolfgang Kantschik[1,2], Peter Dittrich[1],
Markus Brameier[1], and Wolfgang Banzhaf[1,2]

[1] Dept. of Computer Science, University of Dortmund, Dortmund, Germany
[2] Informatik Centrum Dortmund (ICD), Dortmund, Germany

Abstract. In this contribution we investigate the evolution of operators for Genetic Programming by means of Genetic Programming. Meta-evolution of recombination operators in graph-based GP is applied and compared to other methods for the variation of recombination operators in graph-based GP. We demonstrate that a straightforward application of recombination operators onto themselves does not work well. After introducing an additional level of recombination operators (the meta level) which are recombining a pool of recombination operators, even self-recombination on the additional level becomes feasible. We show that the overall performance of this system is better than in other variants of graph GP. As a test problem we use speaker recognition.

1 Introduction to Graph GP

The representations of programs used in Genetic Programming can be classified into three major groups by their underlying structure which directs the program flow: 1) tree-based [Koz92,Koz94], 2) linear-based [Nor94,BNKF98], and 3) graph-based [TV96] representations. Graph-based GP is defined as a GP system where the program flow during the interpretation/execution of an individual is directed by a graph.

For our system we use the structure that has been introduced by Teller in [TV96]. We refer to the representation of Teller when we talk about graph GP. In the literature one can find either systems using graph-like structures, for instance Poli's PDGP (parallel distributed GP [Pol96] or the MIP (multiple interacting programs) system developed by Angeline [Ang98]. The main difference between these approaches and the approach by Teller is that edges in the graph-like programs of PDGP and MIPs denote data flow whereas edges in the graph programs of Teller denote program flow.

In *graph-based* GP each program p is represented by a directed graph of N_p nodes. Each node can have up to N_p outgoing edges. Each node in the program has two parts, *action* and *branching decision*. The *action* part is either a constant or a function that will be executed when the node is reached during the interpretation of the program. The environment of a program consists of an indexed memory and a stack, both of which are used to transfer data among the nodes. An action function could therefore get its inputs from the stack and could push its output back onto the stack. After the action of a node is executed,

R. Poli et al. (Eds.): EuroGP'99, LNCS 1598, pp. 15–28, 1999.

an outgoing edge is selected according to the branching decision. This decision is made by a *branching function* which determines the edge to the next node, while using the information held on the top of the stack, in memory or in the *branching constant* of each node. Hence, not all nodes of a graph are necessarily visited during an interpretation. Figure 1 shows the structure of a node.

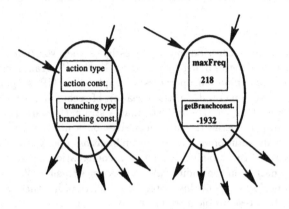

Fig. 1. The structure of a node in a graph-based GP program (left) and an example node (right).

Each program has two special nodes, a *start* and a *stop node*. The start node is always the first node to be executed when the interpretation of a program begins. After the stop node is reached, its action is executed and the program halts. Since the graph structure inherently allows loops and recursion, it is possible that the stop node is never reached during the interpretation. In order to avoid that a program runs forever it is terminated after a certain *time threshold* is reached. In our system the time threshold is implemented as a fixed maximum number of nodes which can be executed during the interpretation.

1.1   Recombination of Graph-based Programs

The crossover operation combines the genetic material of two parent programs by swapping certain program parts. Each node of a parent p is labeled by a fixed index $i \in \{1, \ldots, N_p\}$. The following algorithm for the recombination of graphs is applied for recombination [TV96]:

1. Mark some nodes in both parents which will be exchanged.
   (Here, this operation will be performed either by a random selection of nodes or by a "smart" or "meta" operator to be explained below.)
2. Label all edges as *external* which are connecting marked nodes with unmarked nodes and all edges which are connecting unmarked nodes with marked nodes.

3. Replace the nodes of a parent by the marked nodes of the other parent. A marked node with index i replaces a node with the same index in the other parent. If the target parent p does not contain a node with index i, then the node gets a new index $N_p + 1$ and will be added to the parent p.
4. Modify all *external edges* in a parent so that they point to randomly selected nodes of the same parent which have not been exchanged.

The method assures that all edges are connected in the two child graphs and that valid graphs are generated. Figure 2 shows an example of this crossover method.

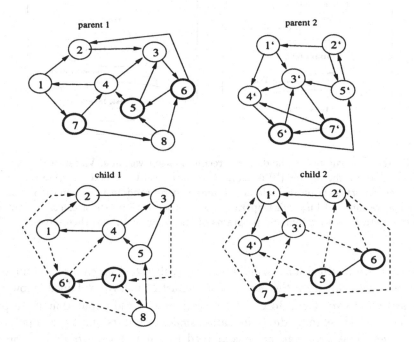

Fig. 2. Crossover-operation of two graph-based programs.

2   Levels of Evolution

The focus of this contribution is the meta-evolution of genetic recombination-like variation operators. This is done by expressing (recombination) operators as graph programs that may undergo their own evolution, possibly using the same methods. In order to compare different approaches we consider four variants (Fig. 3):

Variant (a) "task random": This is the conventional GP approach, where individuals are recombined by exchanging randomly chosen sub-components. There is only one population of individuals that should solve the desired task,

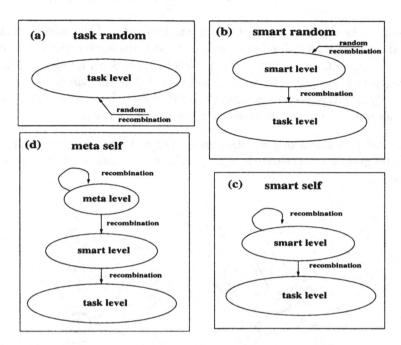

Fig. 3. System structure of the different recombination variants. Variant (a) a conventional GP approach, variant (b) is using the smart level to recombine programs of the task level. Smart level individuals are recombined by random recombination. Variant (c) is like variant (b) but smart operators are recombined by themselves. Variant (d) uses the meta level to recombine programs of the smart level and themselves.

here, speaker identification. Its individuals are called *task programs* to distinguish them from individuals of the higher level (smart or meta), explained below.

Variant (b) "smart random": In this variant a second population of GP programs exists. These individuals are called *smart operators* and their population *smart level*. Task programs are recombined by smart operators [Tel96]. Smart operators, in turn, are recombined by a random recombination as in variant (a).

Variant (c) "smart self": Like variant (b) but smart operators are recombined by themselves.

Variant (d) "meta self": Like variant (b) but smart operators are recombined by meta operators. Meta operators form a third population (*meta level*) and are recombined by themselves.

The following sections describe the task, smart and meta levels in more detail.

3   The Task Level

The task level consists of a population of task programs which should solve the desired test problem, a speaker identification problem [RS86a,RS86b,FSD97].

Therefore, a task program p_{task} represents a mapping

$$p_{task} : Input \rightarrow [min, max] \tag{1}$$

where *Input* represents the set of spoken word smaples (see below).

3.1   Fitness Function on Task Level

The speaker identification problem considered in this study is to identify one person out of a set of four persons based on speech samples.

The raw sound data was sampled at 22 kHz in 16 bit format. A fast Fourier transformation has been done on a 20 msec window, which was weighted using a Hamming window. Windows were overlapping by 50 %. A spectral vector of dimension 32 was computed out of these FFT spectral vectors by using a triangle filter. The spectral vectors for the different word groups and speakers were received by the task programs as inputs to identify whether a given input (a word group of one speaker) belongs to the specific class (speaker) or not. The input data for one identification task consist of one to five different words form each class, i.e., the task program has to identify a speaker based on a speech sample of less than 5 seconds.

The return value of an individual is a number between $min = -10000$ and $max = 10000$. The normalized return value is interpreted as a measure of probability. If the return value is high and the individual is associated with class i, then the input sample is identified as belonging to class i. By combining the identification result of programs associated with different classes it is possible to identify the speaker for a given input.

The fitness $Fit(p_{task})$ of a task program p_{task} associated with class i on the fitness cases C, is computed as

$$Fit(p_{task}) = \sum_{e \in C_i} ((n_C - 1) * r(p_{task}, e)) - \sum_{e \notin C_i} r(p_{task}, e) \tag{2}$$

where $r(p, e)$ is the return value of program p executed with input e, $C_i \subset C$ is the subset of the fitness cases containing only samples class i, and n_C is the number of classes. The return value of a positive classification is multiplied with $(n_C - 1)$ so it is possible for an individual to get a positive fitness value even though it makes false classifications. This is done because for each class there are $(n_C - 1)$ times more negative example during the fitness evaluation then positive examples.

Each individual gets n_C fitness values, one fitness value for each class. So it is possible to evolve individuals for the different classes in one pool. For the recombination the pool is divided in subpools, so that the best individuals for each class are found in the subpools. After the recombination all subpools are merged to one pool.

3.2   Representation and Operator Set on Task Level

On each level programs are represented as graphs. On the task level programs need the ability to examine input data (spectral vectors) in sufficient detail in order to perform their task. Therefore they use various functions which operate directly on the input vectors. These function can read the values at a special position in the input sample, compare two values of the input data, or calculate the average or difference of some input values. The programs have no opportunity to store a vector of the input data to compare it later to other input. In other words, programs have to identify a speaker without the use of reference vectors. This distinguishes the method from classical solutions for the speaker identification problem. Stack and indexed memory only store one-dimensional real values during the execution of program. Task programs use the action function set shown in Tab. 1

function name	description of action function (task level)
$+,-,*,/$	arithmetic functions
$<,>,=$	comparison functions
readFrequency	reads the value of a given frequency and spectral vector.
maxFreq	returns the frequency and value with the maximal value of a given spectral vector.
minFreq	returns the frequency and value with the minimal value of a given spectral vector.
interMaxFreq	returns the spectral vector number and value of a given frequency with the maximal frequency value of 6 following spectral vectors.
interMinFreq	returns the spectral vector number and value of a given frequency with the minimal frequency value of 6 following spectral vectors.
countFreq	returns the number of spectral vector which have a frequency value equal x.
frameAverage	returns the average frequency value of a given spectral vector.
interAverage	returns the average frequency value of a given frequency of a variable number of spectral vectors.
variance	returns the average variance value of a given spectral vector.
interVariance	returns the average variance value of a given frequency of a variable number of spectral vectors.
smallerFreq	returns the smaller value of two given frequency of one spectral vectors.
greaterFreq	returns the greater value of two given frequency of one spectral vectors.

Table 1. Action functions (operators, non-terminals) at task level.

3.3 Variation and Selection on Task Level

The selection method on the task level is a $(\mu + \lambda)$-strategy [Sch96]. The variation method depends on the variant: **Variant (a)** uses random recombination and applies random mutation to 5 % of the programs in the pool after the recombination. During the mutation maximal 5 % of the program nodes will be mutated. **Variants (b)-(d)** use recombination by randomly chosen smart operators from the smart level. Mutation is only performed by an explicit mutate instruction as part of the smart operator set in smart programs (see below and Tab. 2).

4 The Smart Level

Smart operators[1] [Tel96] should enable the GP system to find a good and suitable recombination method automatically. Therefore, a smart operator p_{smart} represents a mapping

$$p_{smart} : P \times P \to P \times P \qquad (3)$$

where P is the set of all programs (task or smart operators).

4.1 Fitness Function on Smart Level

The goal of the smart operators with respect to the task level population is to maximize the fitness of task programs. Smart operators and task programs co-evolve. A smart operator is tested by allowing it to actually perform a recombination of task programs. Its fitness value is a function of the relative fitness of the task programs it recombines (parents) and the fitness of programs it produces as descendants (children). To compute this fitness in a generation-based evolutionary algorithm the relative fitness increase a smart operator is able to cause on task programs during a generation is accumulated by using Ω (see step 4c) in the following algorithm. The fitness value is than computed in step 6 of the algorithm. The algorithm represents a loop of one generation during which λ task programs are generated.

1. Reset counters:
   $\forall p \in P : \Omega(p) \leftarrow 0, m(p) \leftarrow 0, n(p) \leftarrow 0$.
2. Select two parents $p_{task}^{(p1)}, p_{task}^{(p2)}$ from the task level and a smart operator p_{smart} from the smart level, randomly.
3. Create two offsprings by applying the smart operator on parents:

$$(p_{task}^{(c1)}, p_{task}^{(c2)}) = p_{smart}(p_{task}^{(p1)}, p_{task}^{(p2)}).$$

4. FOR $j = 1$ TO 2 DO
   (a) Let $n(p_{smart}) \leftarrow n(p_{smart}) + 1$

---

[1] Simply called "operator" by Edmonds [Edm98].

(b) Let $f_{cj} = Fit_{task}(p_{task}^{(cj)})$ and $f_{pj} = Fit_{task}(p_{task}^{(pj)})$ be the fitness of a child and its corresponding parent, respectively.

(c) If f_{cj} (child) is better than f_{pj} (parent) then let

$$\Omega(p_{smart}) \leftarrow \Omega(p_{smart}) + \frac{f_{cj} + f_{max}}{f_{pj} + f_{max}} - 1,$$

$$m(p_{smart}) \leftarrow m(p_{smart}) + 1.$$

where f_{max} is the maximal fitness a program can reach,

5. GOTO 2 UNTIL λ task programs are created to form the next generation.
6. The fitness of a smart operator is defined by

$$Fit_{smart}(p_{smart}) = \frac{m(p_{smart})}{n(p_{smart})} * \Omega(p_{smart}).$$

This means that a smart operator is good, if the children (at least one) have a better fitness than the parents.

4.2   Representation and Operator Set on Smart Level

A smart operator recombines two given programs by creating subsets which is achieved by marking some nodes in both parents according to step 1 of the recombination algorithm in Sec. 1.1. To perform this task the smart operator needs the ability to examine its input programs in sufficient detail. Therefore we provide the *special action functions* shown in Tab. 2.

During the execution of a smart operator the environment contains an additional elements the *current node*, this is the program node the smart operator currently works with. The smart operator executes its graph-program at first on parent $p_{task}^{(p1)}$ and then independently on $p_{task}^{(p2)}$. After the smart operator has been executed, the new child programs will be created by exchanging the marked nodes according to the algorithm in Sec. 1.1. If a parent has no marked node, the smart operator receives fitness 0 and a random crossover is executed.

The smart operators used for this study also mark a subset of nodes to be mutated after the recombination. So the recombination process of a smart operator is a combination of a crossover and a mutation operation.

4.3   Variation and Selection on Smart Level

The selection method on the smart level is rank proportional. The variation method depends on the variant: **Variant (a)** does not use the smart level. **Variant (b)** uses random recombination for smart operators and applies random mutation of some nodes after recombination. **Variant (c)** uses recombination by choosing the best programs from the same level (smart level). Mutation is only performed by an explicit mutate instruction in the smart operators. **Variant (d)** uses recombination by randomly chosen programs from the meta level. Mutation is performed by an explicit mutate instruction in meta operators.

function name	description of action function (smart and meta level)
pickRand	Picks at random a new *current node* which is not member of the *set*.
pickNode	Picks a specific node to be the new current node.
pickChild	Picks node pointed to by an edge of the current node to be the new current node.
addCurrent	Adds current node to set.
addChild	Adds children of current node to set.
delCurrent	Deletes current node form set.
delChild	Deletes children of current node from set.
randSet	Makes set be a random set of nodes.
setSize	Returns size of set.
progSize	Returns size of program.
nodeAction	Returns action of current node.
nodeConst	Returns constant of current node.
nodeOutgrad	Returns out grade (number of out going edges) of current node.
nodeBAction	Returns branching action of current node.
nodeBConst	Returns branching constant of current node.
mutate	Marks a specific node and a specific part of the node to be mutated after recombination.

Table 2. Action functions at smart and meta level.

5   The Meta Level

Until now we have described a system with two levels, the *task level* and the *smart level*. The task programs at the task level are evolved to solve the given problem. Those at the smart level are evolved to perform recombination at the task level. One of the most obvious issues of the smart level is the question how the smart operators should be evolved.

New meta operators are introduced because self-recombination (Variant (c)) does not work on the smart level (a result stated in [Tel96] and confirmed in Fig. 4 below). However, there is the chance that it works if a next level (the meta level) of evolution is introduced. Why should this be possible?

The reasoning might go as such: The goal of smart operators is to find a good recombination for programs on the task level and not for the smart level. Smart operators have a different structure than task programs. Therefore it is possible that a good smart operator for a task program has a low performance in recombining smart operators. Teller uses the *random* recombination for smart operators because empirically tests have shown that *self* recombination does not work at the smart level.

5.1   Fitness Function and Representation on Meta Level

To allow the self-recombination on the meta level (Variant (d)) the meta level uses the same fitness function as the smart level (see Sec. 4.1). It also uses the same representation and operator set as the smart level (see Sec. 4.2).

5.2   Variation and Selection on Meta Level

The selection method on the meta level is rank proportional. The variation method depends on the variant: **Variants (a)-(c)** do not use the meta level. **Variant (d)** recombines meta operators by choosing the best programs from the same level (meta level) as recombination operators. Mutation is only performed by an explicit mutate instruction in the meta operators.

6   Test Problem Results

In this section we describe the effects of the four variants (a) *task random*, (b) *smart random*, (c) *smart self*, and (d) *meta self* recombination.

In this study the task level contains 400 programs and the maximum number of nodes for each program is 600. The smart population contains 100 operators and the maximum number of nodes is 300. The meta population contains 50 operators with the same structure as the smart operators. The fitness cases consist of 15 sound examples for each speaker. In each generation the programs are tested with 6 randomly chosen examples from each speaker.

The task level uses a truncation or $(\mu+\lambda)$ selection [Sch96] with $\mu = 100$ and $\lambda = 300$, the smart and meta pools use a *rank proportional* selection method, like Teller [TV96]. All plots in this section are based on averages over 30 runs.

Figure 4 shows the progression of the fitness values using the different recombination variants. The figure shows the advantage of *smart random* and *meta self* recombination over *task random* and *smart self* recombination. The results also confirm that self-recombination on the smart level does not work [Tel96] and that self-recombination on the meta level works in our test case. This result indicates that smart operators use a different recombination scheme than meta operators. An interesting result is that meta recombination produces, on average, fitter individuals than smart recombination although the operators use the same operator set.

6.1   Diversity

For measuring the diversity during evolution we define a simple measure of diversity, called *I-O diversity*. The diversity measure is based on the *I-O distance*, which describes the difference of the result values r, between two individuals, for a given set of input data:

Definition 1 (I-O Distance).
    Let $\mathcal{E}$ be a finite set of input data, then the I-O distance $d(p, p')$ between the individuals $p, p' \in P$ is defined by

$$d(p, p') = \sum_{e \in \mathcal{E}} \begin{cases} 1 & \text{if } r(p, e) \neq r(p', e), \\ 0 & \text{otherwise.} \end{cases} \tag{4}$$

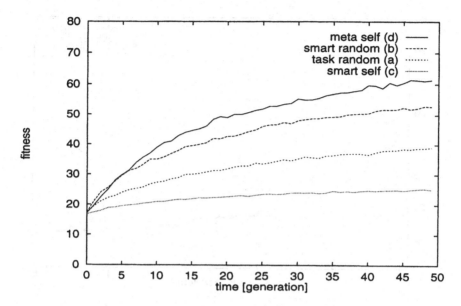

Fig. 4. These curves show the average fitness value of the best 20 individuals at the task level for four recombination variants in percent of maximum fitness. Each curve is an average over 30 runs. The order of the curves according to fitness in generation 50 is significant.

Definition 2 (I-O Diversity).

Let S be a population of individuals out of P and d : P × P → ℕ⁰ be the I-O distance. The I-O diversity 𝒟(S) is then defined as

$$\mathcal{D}(S) = \sum_{p \in S} \sum_{p' \in S} d(p, p').$$ (5)

A high *I-O diversity* value means that the results for a given input are different between different individuals.

Figure 5 indicates that recombination with smart operators uses a different recombination scheme than the random recombination, because the diversity of the random recombination decreases slower than the diversity with smart operators. An interesting aspect of this figure is that the diversity of *meta self* recombination shows the same diversity behavior as *smart random* and *smart self* recombination although they create on average individuals with poor fitness values.

6.2   Mutation Rate

Another interesting aspect of the smart and meta operators is their ability to select explicitly nodes for mutation by using the *special action function* which marks a node to be mutated. Thus, the mutation rate depends on the smart and meta operators and is therefore subject to evolution and changes over time. The

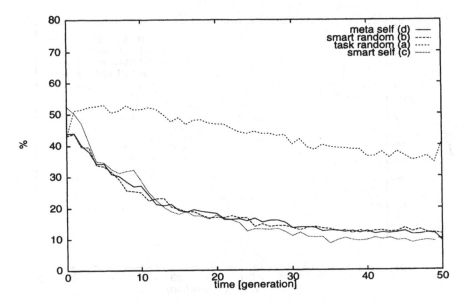

Fig. 5. I-O diversity in percent of the task level for the different recombination variants. The lower three curves can not be discriminated significantly.

mutation rate of the task level actually defines how often the smart operators use this special operation during the crossover operation in a generation. Figure 6 shows the mutation rate of the task level over the course of generations. The mutation rate for random recombination is 5 % over all generations. The mutation rate for self-recombination is zero during all runs. This mean that no operator uses the possibility to mutate an individual even though it could. The mutation rate in each run starts at about zero. This can be an indication that mutation becomes more important during the evolution. An interesting aspect is that, although smart and meta-recombination result in different mutation rates, the I-O diversity of the individuals is rather the same.

7   Summary and Outlook

We haver investigated a system which used smart and meta-recombination to find a better recombination scheme. We have shown that it is possible to create a GP system which does not use a fixed recombination operator, and that such a system can create individuals with better fitness.

The most significant results are: GP programs can be used to perform a crossover operation. In our test case *self* recombination at the level of smart operators does not work well. *Self* recombination at the level of meta operator works. Smart and meta-recombination could find a recombination scheme which is better than random recombination. To say whether these are general phenomena more experiments have to be run on a varity of test cases. We are currently

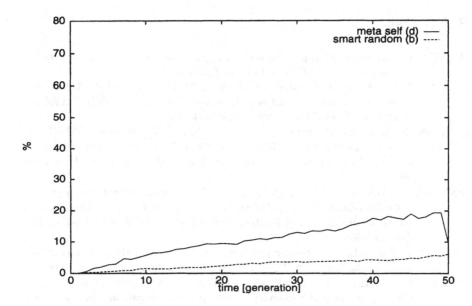

Fig. 6. Average mutation rate at the task level with smart and meta recombination. The mutation rate during self-recombination is zero in all runs.

testing meta-evolution with different representation and different levels by using the SYSGP system [BDKB98].

Meta-evolution has long been applied in evolutionary algorithms [Sch77], [Bäc97]. For example, in evolution strategies (ES) [Sch96] parameters are used which determine the variance and covariance of a generalized n-dimensional normal distribution for mutations. The strategy parameters themselves are adapted during the optimization process. Only the operators used for adaptation are fixed. In our system, the variation of an object on the meta level alters the way how other objects on the meta level are modified, because the object will subsequently interact with others. This "strange loop" and the relation of self-adaption in classical evolutionary algorithms to self-modifying programs should also be investigated in the future.

Acknowledgment

Support has been provided by the DFG (Deutsche Forschungsgemeinschaft), under grant Ba 1042/5-2 and under grant B2 in the Sonderforschungsbereich SFB 531.

Supplement Material

To ensure reproducibility more detailed information, complete source code, raw experimental data are available from:

`http://ls11-www.cs.uni-dortmund.de/gp/meta`

References

[Ang98]   P.J. Angeline. Multiple interacting programs: A representation for evolving complex behaviors. *Cybernetics and Systems*, 1998.

[Bäc97]   Th. Bäck. Self-adaptation. In Th. Bäck, D. B. Fogel, and Z. Michalewicz, editors, *Handbook of Evolutionary Computation*, page C7.1. IOP Publishing, Bristol and Oxford Univ. Press, New York, 1997.

[BDKB98] M. Brameier, P. Dittrich, W. Kantschik, and W. Banzhaf. SYSGP - A C++ library of different GP variants. Technical Report Internal Report of SFB 531,ISSN 1433-3325, Fachbereich Informatik, Universität Dortmund, 1998.

[BNKF98] W. Banzhaf, P. Nordin, R. Keller, and F. Francone. *Genetic Programming – An Introduction On the Automatic Evolution of Computer Programs and its Applications.* Morgan Kaufmann, San Francisco and dpunkt.verlag, Heidelberg, 1998.

[Edm98]   B. Edmonds. Meta-genetic programming: Co-evolving the operators of variation. CPM Report 98-32, Manchester Metropolitan University, 1998.

[FSD97]   R.A. Finan, A.T. Sapeluk, and R.I. Damper. VQ score normalisation for text-dependent and text-independent speaker recognition. In *Audio- and Video-based Biometric Person Authentication*, pages 211–218. First International Conference, AVBPA'97, 1997.

[Koz92]   J. Koza. *Genetic Programming.* MIT Press, 1992.

[Koz94]   J. Koza. *Genetic Programming II.* MIT Press, 1994.

[Nor94]   J. P. Nordin. *A Compiling Genetic Programming System that Directly Manipulates the Machinecode.* Cambridge, MIT Press, 1994.

[Pol96]   R. Poli. Some steps towards a form of parallel distributed genetic programming. In *The 1st Online Workshop on Soft Computing (WSC1)*, http://www.bioele.nuee.nagoya-u.ac.jp/wsc1/, 19–30 August 1996. Nagoya University, Japan.

[RS86a]   A.E. Rosenberg and F.K. Soong. Evaluation of a vector quantization talker recognition system in text independent and text dependent modes. *Proc. ICASSP*, pages 873– 876, 1986.

[RS86b]   A.E. Rosenberg and F.K. Soong. On the use of instantaneous and transitional spectral information in speaker recognition. *Proc. ICASSP*, pages 877– 880, 1986.

[Sch77]   H.-P. Schwefel. *Numerische Optimierung von Computer-Modellen mittels der Evolutionsstrategie (Inderdisciplinary Systems Research 26).* Birkhäuser, Basel, 1977.

[Sch96]   H.-P. Schwefel. *Evolution and Optimum Seeking.* John Wiley & Sons, Inc., 1996.

[Tel96]   A. Teller. Evolving programmers: The co-evolution of intelligent recombination operators. In P. Angeline and K. Kinnear, editors, *Advances in Genetic Programming II.* MIT Press, 1996.

[TV96]   A. Teller and M. Veloso. Pado: A new learning architecture for object recognition. In *Symbolic Visual Learning*, pages 81 –116. Oxford University Press, 1996.

Busy Beaver – The Influence of Representation

Penousal Machado[1,2], Francisco B. Pereira[1,2],

Amílcar Cardoso[1], and Ernesto Costa[1]

[1] Centro de Informática e Sistemas da Universidade de Coimbra, Departamento de
Engenharia Informática, Polo II, 3030 Coimbra, Portugal
{ machado, xico, amilcar, ernesto}@dei.uc.pt
[2] Instituto Superior de Engenharia de Coimbra, Quinta da Nora, 3030 Coimbra, Portugal

Abstract. The Busy Beaver is an interesting theoretical problem proposed by
Rado in 1962, in the context of the existence of non computable functions. In
this paper we propose an evolutionary approach to this problem. We will focus
on the representational issues, proposing alternative ways of codifying and
interpreting Turing Machines, designed to take advantage of the existence of
sets of equivalent Turing Machines. The experimental results show that these
alternatives provide improvement over the „standard" genetic codification.

1 Introduction

One of the most important results of theoretical computer science deals with the
existence of non computable functions. This fact can be easily established showing
that there are functions, which are not Turing computable: there are more functions
than Turing Machines to compute them.

In 1962 Tibor Rado proposed one such function based on what is known today as
the „Busy Beaver Game or Problem" [8]. It can be described as follows: Suppose a
Turing Machine (TM) with a two way infinite tape and a tape alphabet = {blank, 1}.
The question Rado asked was: What is the maximum number of 1's that can be
written by an N-State[1] halting TM when started on a blank tape? This number, which
is function of the number of states, is denoted by $\Sigma(N)$. A machine that produces
$\Sigma(N)$ non-blank cells is called a Busy Beaver (BB).

The problem with $\Sigma(N)$ is that it grows faster than any computable function, i.e.,
$\Sigma(N)$ is non computable. Some values for $\Sigma(N)$, and the corresponding TM's are
known today for small values of N. We have, for instance, $\Sigma(1)= 1$, $\Sigma(2)= 4$, $\Sigma(3)= 6$,
$\Sigma(4)= 13$. As the number of states increases the problem becomes harder, and, for
N>= 5, we have several candidates (or contenders) which set lower bounds on the
value of $\Sigma(N)$. This is partially due to the fact that there is neither a general, nor a
particular theory about the structure of a BB. The only available technique for finding
such machines is to perform an exhaustive search over the space of all N-state TM.

---

[1] N does not include the final state.

R. Poli et al. (Eds.): EuroGP'99, LNCS 1598, pp. 29–38, 1999.
© Springer-Verlag Berlin Heidelberg 1999

Due to these difficulties, the Busy Beaver problem has attracted the attention of many researchers and several contests were organised trying to produce the best candidates. The techniques used perform a partial search on the solution space, looking for TM which produce the best lower bound for the value of $\Sigma(N)$. Some of the best contenders were obtained be Marxen [6] (e.g., he found a 5 state TM that writes 4098 1's in 47,176,870 transitions). His approach involves enumeration and simulation of all N-state TMs, using several techniques to reduce the number of inspected machines, accelerate simulation and determine non-termination. In his search for BB(5) he only left 0.3% of the TMs undecided. Marxen also found the best BB(6) contender that writes 95,524,079 1's in approximately 8.7e15 transitions.

In the original setting, the problem was defined for 5-tuple TMs. With this definition, machines, given a current state and the symbol being scanned in the tape, write a symbol over it, enter a new state and move the read/write head left or right. One of the main variants consists in considering 4-tuple TM. The main difference from the others is that, during the transition to a new state, a TM either writes a new symbol to the tape or moves the head (both actions are not simultaneously allowed).

In our research, we focus on the 4-tuple TMs variant. Although the dimension of the search space remains unchanged, this type of TMs allows faster simulation. The best contenders perform a substantially smaller number of transitions than their 5-tuple counterparts (e.g. the best 4-tuple BB(6) contender writes 21 1's in 125 transitions). We use an evolutionary approach, which has already proved to be extremely effective. In a recent work [7], we presented new best lower bounds for 4-tuple BB(7) and BB(8), showing that $\Sigma(7)>=102$ and that $\Sigma(8)>=384$. If we compare these results with previous best candidates ($\Sigma(7)>=37[5]$ and $\Sigma(8)>=84$), it clear that our approach can bring significant improvements. These new lower bounds were found in less than one day, using a 300 MHz Pentium II computer. Only (8.5e-11)% of the search space was evaluated.

In this paper, we will focus our attention on representational issues. We will propose and study three different representations for TMs. The results achieved prove that this is a very important issue when searching for good BB candidates. We will use BB(6) as a testbed for the proposed representations. Our goal is to determine which representation allows us to find this solution in a consistent way.

The paper as the following structure: Section 2 comprises a formal definition of five and four tuple TM, and the specification of the rules of the BB problem for each of these variants. In Section 3 we present three ways of representing and interpreting TMs. Section 4 relates to the simulation and evaluation of TMs. In Section 5 we present the experimental results, which are analysed in Section 6. Finally in Section 7 we state overall conclusion and suggest some directions for future work.

2 Problem Definition

A deterministic TM can be specified by a sextuple $(Q,\Pi,\Gamma,\delta,s,f)$, where[9]:
- Q is a finite set of states
- Π is an alphabet of input symbols
- Γ is an alphabet of tape symbols

- δ is the transition function
- s in Q is the start state
- f in Q is the final state.

The transition function can assume several forms, the most usual one is:

$$\delta: Q \times \Gamma \rightarrow Q \times \Gamma \times \{L, R\}$$

where L denotes move left and R move right. Machines with a transition function with this format are called 5-tuple TMs. A common variation consists in considering a transition function of the form:

$$\delta: Q \times \Gamma \rightarrow Q \times \{\Gamma \cup \{L, R\}\}$$

Machines of this type are known as 4-tuple TMs. When performing a transition, a 5-tuple TM will write a symbol on the tape, move the head left or right and enter a new state. A 4-tuple TM either writes a new symbol on the tape or moves its head, before entering the new state.

The original definition, proposed by Rado [8], considered deterministic 5-tuple TMs with N+1 states (N states and an anonymous halt state). The tape alphabet has two symbols, $\Gamma = \{blank, 1\}$, and the input alphabets has one, $\Pi = \{1\}$.

The productivity of a TM is defined as the number of 1's present, on the initially blank tape, when the machine halts. Machines that do not halt have productivity zero. $\Sigma(N)$ is defined as the maximum productivity that can be achieved by a N-state TM. This TM is called a Busy Beaver.

In the 4-tuple variant productivity is usually defined as the length of the sequence of ones produced by the TM when started on a blank tape, and halting when scanning the leftmost one of the sequence, with the rest of the tape blank. Machines that do not halt, or, that halt on another configuration, have productivity zero [1]. Thus, accordingly to these rules in the 4-tuple variant, the machine must halt when reading a 1, this 1 must be the leftmost of a string of 1s and, with the exception of this string, the tape must be blank.

3 Representation

Genetic Algorithms (GAs) are probabilistic search procedures based on the principles of natural selection and genetics [3]. They have been used to solve hard problems (those with a huge and multimodal space to search). Typically they only need to explore a small portion of the space. In simple terms, GAs iteratively evolve a population, that is set of solutions' candidates (points of the search space, called individuals) using genetic operators, until some conditions are met. They start from a random generated set of potential solutions. Each individual is defined by its chromosome.

As stated before, a 4-tuple TM can be defined by a sextuple $(Q, \Pi, \Gamma, \delta, s, f)$. Without loss of generality, we can consider $Q = \{1, 2, ..., N, N+1\}$, set 1 as the initial state and N+1 as the final one. Since $\Pi = \{1\}$ and $\Gamma = \{blank, 1\}$, we only need to represent the transition function, $\delta: Q \times \{blank, 1\} \rightarrow Q \times \{L, R, blank, 1\}$. Fig.1 shows a 4-tuple TM and its transition table.

In our approach, the chromosome of each individual will be represented trough a binary string with the following format:

The encoding of each *New State* requires three bits and the encoding of each *Action* requires two bits. This gives 10 bits per state and thus 10*N bits to represent an N state 4-tuple TMs.

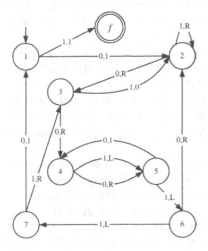

δ	By blank		By one	
State	New State	Action	New State	Action
1	2	1	f	1
2	3	R	2	R
3	4	R	2	0
4	5	R	5	L
5	4	1	6	L
6	2	R	7	L
7	1	1	3	R

Fig. 1. A seven state 4-tuple TM and its corresponding transition table. The blank symbol is represented by 0. This machine is the best known 4-tuple BB(7) candidate [7], it writes 102 1s in 4955 transitions.

It is clear that there are several TMs that exhibit the same behaviour, this machines can be considered equivalent. If we could construct sets of machines with equivalent behaviour we would only need to run one of the machines of the set. The most important of these equivalent classes is known as the *Tree Normal Form* (TNF) [6]. Using a TNF representation ensures that machines differing only in the naming of the states or in transition that never are used, are represented in the same way. We can convert a machine to its TNF by running the machine and numbering the states in the order that they are visited. States that were never visited and unused transitions are deleted. It would be nice to represent the machines in the TNF. Unfortunately, to convert a machine to its TNF (or to know if it is in TNF) we have to run it. There are two possibilities to be considered:
- Directly decoding the chromosome to a TM, and thus not taking advantage of equivalence classes.
- Interpret the machine codified in the chromosome, as if it was in TNF. This can be achieved by using the algorithm presented in Fig.2.

```
Mark all transitions as undefined
Mark all the states as not-visited
Visited_states ← 0
Defined_transitions ← 0
CState ← 1        //Current State
While (CState ≠ Halting State) and
        (Limit number of transitions not reached)
      Read the symbol on the tape to CSymbol
      If the transition (δ:CStatexCSymbol) is undefined
        Mark it as defined
        Increase the number of defined transitions
        If the Current State is not-visited
          Mark it as visited
          Increase the number of visited states
        If state (δ:CStatexCSymbol→Q)>(Visited_states+1)
          Set (δ:CStatexCSymbol→Q) to Visited_states
        If this is the last undefined transition
          Set (δ:CStatexCSymbol→Q) to Halting State
      Perform the action indicated by (δ:CStatexCSymbol)
      //i.e. move the head or write a symbol on the tape
      Set Cstate to (δ:CStatexCSymbol→Q)
```

Fig. 2. During the process of simulation of the TM we can choose to interpret it as if it where in the Tree Normal Form. The simulation process ends when the machine reaches its halting state, or when a predefined number of transitions is met (this will be explained in Section 4).

A further possibility is to code back the changes induced by the TNF interpretation of the machine, i.e. modify the original chromosome to one with the machine in TNF format. Thus, we have three different options for the representation and interpretation of TMs: using a standard representation (*Standard*), use a tree normal form interpretation of the machine (*TNF*), or the TNF interpretation combined with back coding of the resulting phenotype (*Backcoding*).

In Fig. 3 we highlight the differences between these alternatives. From the original genotype we can construct a TM trough standard interpretation. Alternatively, we can use a TNF interpretation of the genotype, which leads to a different phenotype. The changes introduced by TNF interpretation can be coded back to the chromosome, and thus directly passed to the descendants.

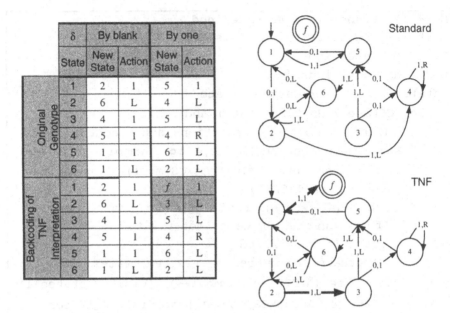

Fig. 3. The original genotype, presented in the upper half the table, can be mapped to two different phenotypes (TMs) as a result of using standard or TNF interpretation. The transitions modified by TNF are represented in bold. These changes can be coded back to the genotype. The lower half of the table shows the result of this operation (altered fields depicted in gray).

4 Simulation and Evaluation

The evaluation phase involves the interpretation of each chromosome and simulation of the resulting TM. Due to the Halting Problem we must establish a limit for the number of transitions. Machines that don't halt before this limit are considered non-halting TMs. We keep track of the maximum number of transitions (MaxT) made by a TM before halting and set the limit of transitions to ten times this number. Thus, when the GA finds a machine halting after a number of transitions higher than MaxT the limit is increased.

To assign fitness we consider the following factors [7], in decreasing order of importance:
1. Halting before reaching the predefined limit for the number of transitions.
2. Accordance to the rules [1].
3. Productivity.
4. Number of used transitions.
5. Number of steps made before halting.

This seems to yield better results than using the productivity, alone, as fitness function [7]. The idea is to establish and explore the differences between „bad" individuals, e.g., a machine that never leaves state 1 is considered worse than one that goes trough all the states, even if they have the same productivity.

5 Experimental Results

The experiments were performed using GALLOPS 3.2 [2]. The parameters of the GA were the following: Number of Evaluations={40 000 000}; Population Size={100, 500};Two-point crossover restricted to gene boundaries; Crossover rate=70%; Single point mutation; Mutation rate={1%,5%,10%}; Elitist strategy; Tournament selection; Tournament size={2,5}. Each experiment was repeated thirty times with the same initial conditions and different random seeds.

A brief perusal of the result graphs in Fig.4 shows that *TNF* and *BackCoding* clearly outperform *Standard* interpretation. It is also visible that *TNF* is usually better than *BackCoding*, although in a lesser scale. Another interesting result is the need for a fairly high mutation rate. The results achieved when using a 1% mutation rate are clearly worse than when using 5% or 10% mutation rates. The difference between 5 and 10% mutation rates is less significant, though 5% gives better results. Tendentiously, small populations perform better.

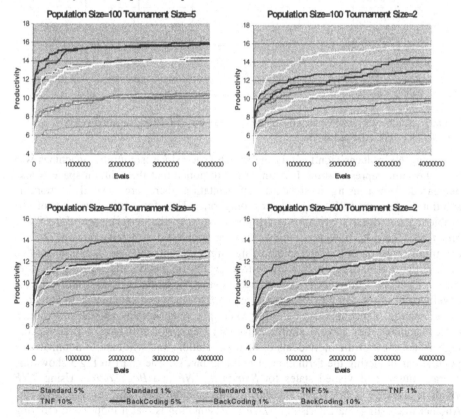

Fig. 4. The charts show the number of ones written by the best individual. The results are the average of series of 30 runs.

6 Analysis of the Results

In Table 1 we indicate the number of times that the best 4-tuple BB(6) candidate (21 1s in 125 transitions) was found. This table confirms and emphasizes the results shown in the previous section. Using a *Standard* representation the GA only reached the maximum once in 360 runs. This result is in accordance to the ones presented in [4] for the 5-Tuple BB(4), showing that the busy beaver can be a complex problem, and that the space is difficult to search by an evolutionary approach when using standard representation. When using *TNF* the maximum was reached 17 times, approximately twice as much as when using *BackCoding*.

		Standard				TNF				BackCoding			
	Pop. Size	100		500		100		500		100		500	
	Tour. Size	2	5	2	5	2	5	2	5	2	5	2	5
Mutation	1%												
	5%					1	6	2			4	1	
	10%			1		4	3	1				2	
				1		5	9	3			4	3	
Totals		1				14		3		4		3	
		1					17				7		

Table 1. Number of runs in which the maximum was reached. Blank cells indicate that none of the 30 runs reached the maximum.

Using *TNF* reduces significantly the search space since isomorphic machines will have the same representation. It is important to notice that the solution space is also decreased. When using a standard representation there are several isomorphic solutions while in *TNF* these became only one. Therefore, this reduction of the problem space doesn't explain the difference between the performance of *TNF* and *Standard*. There is, however, another type of problem space reduction in *TNF*. A careful observation of the interpretation algorithm presented in Fig. 2, will reveal that in *TNF* the machines are only allowed to enter the final state after visiting all other states. Thus, in *TNF*, machines that halt always visit all the states, allowing the development of the complex behaviour, required to find good candidates. In *Standard* representation, a machine can halt after visiting a small number of states. Although these machines may have a simple behaviour, they will still have a fitness score higher than most of the individuals of their generation, and will tend to dominate the populations hindering the formation of building blocks. The chart in Fig.5 shows the average number of visited states for *Standard*, *TNF* and *BackCoding*. Using *TNF* yields an average of 5.5 while *Standard* representation only achieves a 4.6 average. Another interesting characteristic of *TNF* representation is that it induces an ordering of the states. States that are directly connected have a higher probability of being close in the chromosome[2]. Thus, there is a higher similarity between genotype neighbourhood and phenotype neighbourhood.

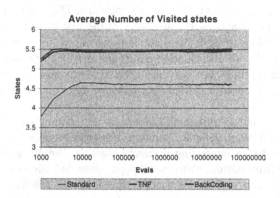

Fig. 5. Average number of visited states

The difference in the performance of *TNF* and *BackCoding* is less visible, and only becomes clear when considering the results in Table 1. With *BackCoding,* changes in the TM produced by *TNF* simulation are coded back to the genotype and directly passed to the descendants. This reduces the diversity of the population, which may explain the difference in the results.

Mutation plays an important role in the evolutionary process. The charts show that BB requires a high mutation rate. With 1% mutation rate the best candidate was never found. It is perceptible both on the charts and on Table 1 that 5% mutation rate is slightly better than 10%. The need for high mutation rates is an interesting result by itself, and may indicate that the fitness landscape is highly irregular and hard to sample.

An interesting and „hidden" difference between *TNF* and *BackCoding* is that *TNF* allows the accumulation of neutral mutations. Consider that we have a chromosome whose gene value for *New State* of the transition of state two by blank is 3; admit also that, when this transition is first used, state three was not yet visited. The alteration of this value to 6 won't produce any changes in the phenotype, since the *TNF* interpretation would still consider it as a transition to state 3. These neutral mutations may become effective, sometime later, due to other alterations of the chromosome. With *BackCoding* the transfer of the phenotype to the genotype eliminates neutral mutations.

7 Conclusions and Further Work

In this paper we explored the importance of representation and interpretation, in the search for good candidates for BB(6) using an evolutionary approach. We proposed

---

[2]E.g. In *Standard* representation we can jump directly from state 1 to state 6. In *TNF* this is only possible if states 2 through 5 have already been visited.

an alternative interpretation of the standard TM representation, *TNF*. We also considered the possibility of back coding this interpretation to the genotype. In order to assess the performance of the different representations we conducted a comprehensive set of experiments. The results show that *TNF* clearly outperforms the standard representation, enabling the discovery of the best candidate for BB(6). The addition of back coding to TNF does not improve the results. Preliminary results indicate that this results are extensible to BB(7) and BB(8). The combination of TNF with a fitness function that explores the differences between bad machines makes evolutionary computation an excellent approach to find good candidates for the BB problem.

As future work we intend to include and test several learning models. The addition of non-standard high level genetic operators, designed to take advantage of TNF representation may be an interesting research direction. We are also considering a distributed GA implementation, with several populations and migration mechanisms.

To attack BB(9) and higher, we need to speed up the simulation of the TMs. Among the possibilities are: using macro-transitions, avoiding evaluation of equivalent machines and early detection of non-halting machines [6].

Acknowledgments

This work was partially funded by the Portuguese Ministry of Science and Technology, under Program PRAXIS XXI.

References

1. Boolos, G., and Jeffrey, R. (1995). *Computability and Logic*, Cambridge University Press.
2. Goodman, E. (1996). GALOPPS (Release 3.2 – July, 1996), The Genetic Algorithm Optimized for Portability and Parallelism System, Technical Report #96-07-01, Michigan State University.
3. Holland, J. (1975) *Adaptation in Natural and Artificial Systems*, Univ. of Michigan Press.
4. Jones, T., Rawlins, G. (1993) Reverse HillClimbing, Genetic Algorithms and the Busy Beaver Problem, In Forrest, S. (Ed.), *Genetic Algorithms: Proceedings of the Fifth International Conference (ICGA-93)*. San Mateo, CA: Morgan Kaufmann, pp 70-75.
5. Lally, A., Reineke, J., and Weader, J. (1997). An Abstract Representation of Busy Beaver Candidate Turing Machines.
6. Marxen, H. Buntrock, J. (1990). Attacking Busy Beaver 5, *Bulletin of the European Association for Theorethical Computer Science*, Vol 40.
7. Pereira, F. B., Machado, P., Costa, E. and Cardoso, A. (1999). Busy Beaver: An Evolutionary Approach. To be published in the *Proceedings of the 2nd Symposium on Artificial Intelligence (CIMAF-99)*, Havana, Cuba.
8. Rado, T. (1962) On non-computable functions, *The Bell System Technical Journal*, vol. 41, no. 3, pp.877-884.
9. Wood, D. (1987). *Theory of Computation*, Harper & Row, Publishers.

Smooth Uniform Crossover with Smooth Point Mutation in Genetic Programming: A Preliminary Study

J. Page, R. Poli, and W.B. Langdon

School of Computer Science, University of Birmingham
Birmingham B15 2TT, UK
{J.Page,R.Poli,W.B.Langdon}@cs.bham.ac.uk

Abstract. In this paper we examine the behaviour of the uniform crossover and point mutation GP operators [12] on the even-n-parity problem for $n = 3, 4, 6$ and present a novel representation of function nodes, designed to allow the search operators to make smaller movements around the solution space. Using this representation, performance on the even-6-parity problem is improved by three orders of magnitude relative to the estimate given for standard GP in [5].

1 Introduction

Although a mutation operator is defined, the canonical form of Genetic Programming (GP) [4] relies almost exclusively on the crossover operator for exploring the solution space. GP crossover selects a random subtree from one parent program and splices it to a random location in another, affording GP the ability to search a space of arbitrary-sized programs. Its insensitivity to position in cutting and splicing (aside of satisfying constraints on tree depth), combined with the fact that multiple instances of function nodes are generally distributed throughout each tree, make it extremely unlikely that a function will be eliminated from the population altogether. In contrast to genetic algorithms (GAs), GP does not generally require a mutation operator to reintroduce information eliminated by selection, and many GP runs use crossover alone.

More recently, however, crossover has come under a certain amount of criticism. Since the standard form is applied to tree-based representations, most randomly selected crossover points are located towards the leaves, an effect that becomes increasingly pronounced as tree size increases [8] [12]. Furthermore, trees tend to increase rapidly in size as a GP run progresses – a phenomenon referred to in the literature as bloat (e.g. [4], [1]). Soule and Foster [16] argue that this bias towards selecting lower branches as crossover points further exacerbates the increase in program size.

The tendency of crossover to exchange subtrees located towards the leaves led Poli to argue [9] and prove [12] that GP crossover is essentially a local search operator, sampling at best only points in the immediate vicinity of the solution space occupied by the parent donating the root node. In contrast, most GA

R. Poli et al. (Eds.): EuroGP'99, LNCS 1598, pp. 39–48, 1999.

crossover operators combine genetic material from each parent in roughly equal quantities. Early in a GA run, when genetic diversity is high, two randomly selected parents will probably be quite different from each other, with the result that the offspring may little resemble either. As the population begins to converge, an increasing number of locations on the bitstring will be identical in both parents and the offspring produced are therefore genotypically quite similar. We may therefore say that GA crossover moves from being a global to a local search operator as the run progresses. This is a desirable property since global search early in the run allows an efficient exploration of the search space and an identification of promising areas, whilst local search later in the run affords the fine-tuning of imperfect solutions. GP crossover, however, rapidly becomes a local search operator such that individuals behave essentially as local hill-climbers and the population thus become susceptible to convergence on local optima.

These observations led Poli and Langdon to develop two GA-inspired crossover operators for GP: one-point crossover [10] [11] [13] and uniform crossover [12]. Poli and Langdon have presented theoretical results indicating that, given a sufficiently diverse initial population, both operators proceed from a global to local exploration of the search space as the run progresses [12].

In this paper, we build on the work reported in [12] by introducing a novel representation of function nodes that allows GP uniform crossover (GPUX) to perform more finely-grained, directed movements around the solution space. We refer to GPUX operating on this representation as *smooth uniform crossover* (GPSUX), and the representation itself as *sub-symbolic node representation*. The remainder of the paper is organised as follows. The next section describes uniform crossover, and a mutation operator - point mutation, in detail. We then describe the sub-symbolic node representation and the manner in which uniform crossover acts upon it. We compare GPUX, GPSUX and an implementation of standard GP on the even-3-parity, even-4-parity and even-6-parity induction problems and show that GPSUX performs extremely favourably. We conclude with a discussion of these results and suggest some future work.

2   Uniform Crossover and Point Mutation

GP Uniform crossover (GPUX)[12], as the name suggests, is a GP operator inspired by the GA operator of the same name [17]. GA uniform crossover (GAUX) constructs offspring on a bitwise basis, copying each allele from each parent with a 50% probability. Thus the information at each gene location is equally likely to have come from either parent and on average each parent donates 50% of its genetic material. The whole operation, of course, relies on the fact that all the chromosomes in the population are of the same structure (i.e. linear bit strings) and the same length. No such assumption can be made in GP since the parent trees will almost always contain unequal numbers of nodes and be structurally dissimilar.

GP uniform crossover [12] begins with the observation that many parse trees are at least partially structurally similar. This means that if we start at the root

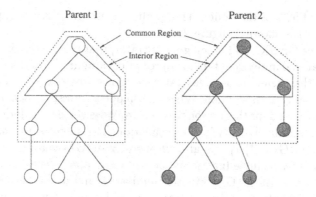

Fig. 1. Two parental parse trees prior to uniform crossover

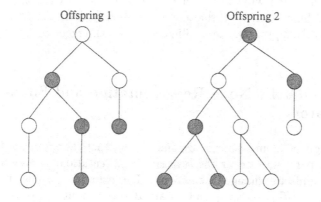

Fig. 2. Offspring trees after uniform crossover

node and work our way down each tree, we can frequently go some way before finding function nodes of differing arity at the same locations. Furthermore we can swap every node up to this point with its counterpart in the other tree without altering the structure of either. Working down from the root node, we can define two regions of a pair of trees as follows. Any node in one tree having a corresponding node at the same location in the other is said to be located within the *common region*. Those pairs of nodes within the common region that have the same arity are referred to as *interior*. The interior nodes and common region of two trees is illustrated in figure 1. Note that the common region necessarily subsumes the interior nodes. The uniform crossover algorithm is then as follows. Once the interior nodes have been identified, the parent trees are both copied. Interior nodes are selected for crossover with some probability p_c. Crossover involves exchanging the selected nodes between the trees, with those nodes not selected for crossover remaining unaffected. Non-interior nodes within the common region can also be crossed, but in this case the nodes and their subtrees are swapped. Nodes outside the common region are not considered. As in GA uniform crossover, the value of p_c is generally set to 0.5, resulting in an exchange of 50% of the nodes. The result of uniform crossover applied to the trees in figure 1 is shown in figure 2.

GPUX, like GAUX, is a homologous operator, that is it preserves the position of genetic material in the genotype. As a result of sampling error, this can in both cases lead to the phenomenon of lexical convergence whereby a sub-optimal gene becomes fixed at a given location. When this happens, crossover cannot introduce the optimal gene and for this reason it is generally desirable to include a mutation operator to maintain diversity in the population. The operator we use here – GP point mutation (GPPM)[7] – is also inspired by its GA counterpart (GAPM). GPPM substitutes a single function node with a randomly selected replacement of the same arity. As in GAPM, the number of mutations performed on an individual is a function of the program size and a user-defined mutation rate parameter. Since in GP program lengths vary, this means that larger programs undergoing mutation will, on average, be perturbed to a greater degree than smaller ones. Since such perturbations are generally detrimental to the fitness of a highly-evolved program, this will generate an emergent parsimony pressure [10].

3   Sub-Symbolic Node Representation and Smooth Operators

Whilst a single point mutation is the smallest syntactical operation that can be applied to a parse tree under the standard representation, it may nevertheless result in a significant change in behaviour. For example, consider the following subtree: (AND T_1 T_2) where T_1 and T_2 are Boolean input terminals. If the AND node is replaced with NAND (and bear in mind that with the standard Boolean function set of {AND, OR, NAND, NOR } the probability of this is $\frac{1}{3}$, assuming the mutation operator replaces the original with a different node), the value returned by the subtree will be altered in all the fitness cases. Controlling this means addressing the mechanism used to replace the node. Our solution is simple. We begin by noting that a Boolean function of arity n can be represented as a truth table (bit-string) of length 2^n, specifying its return value on each of the 2^n possible inputs. Thus AND may be represented as 1000, OR as 1110. We refer to this representation as *sub-symbolic* because the representation, and hence the behaviour, of a function node can be modified slightly during the course of a GP run. For example, flipping a single bit will alter the behaviour of the node for just one of its possible input combinations.

We can define a point mutation operator which works in exactly this manner – a single randomly-selected bit is flipped in a single randomly-selected node. Since GPUX is homologous, we can extend it to use a GA crossover operator on the nodes at reproduction (in the experiments reported here we use GAUX). The crossover operation is illustrated in figure 3. When a pair of interior nodes are selected for crossover, GA uniform crossover is applied to their binary representations. In other words, the bits specifying each node's function are swapped with probability 0.5. Clearly such an operator interpolates the behaviour of the

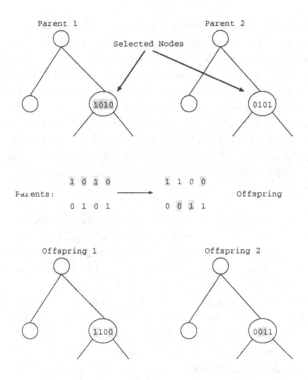

Fig. 3. Uniform crossover on the sub-symbolic representation. In this example, the two central bits of the selected nodes are exchanged to generate the offspring

parents' corresponding nodes, rather than exchanging nodes in their entirety. The sub-symbolic node representation allows GP to move around the solution space in a smoother, more controlled manner and hence we refer to these versions of the operators as *smooth uniform crossover* (GPSUX) and *smooth point mutation* GPSPM.

One feature of the sub-symbolic representation of Boolean function nodes is that it necessarily incorporates all 2^n nodes of arity n into its function set. This is in contrast to the reduced function set normally used for Boolean classification problems. We further discuss the effects of this in the next section.

4   Experimental Set-up

In this paper we demonstrate an implementation of GPSUX and GPSPM on the even-3-, even-4- and even-6-parity problems. Our function set was restricted to diadic Boolean functions. Unconstrained, the GPSUX and GPSPM operators can potentially generate any of the 16 arity 2 Boolean functions and for this reason we included them all in the standard representation function set. Such a set will undoubtedly contain a number of extraneous functions (always-on and always-off being the most obvious examples), although what effect, if any, they have on performance is poorly understood. Rosca [15] notes that increasing the size of the function set from 4 to 8 increases the fitness diversity of randomly generated trees on the even-5-parity problem, but that this effect is slightly reduced when the size is further increased to 16 functions. Koza [4] examined the effects of extraneous functions on a number of problems including the 6-multiplexer and found performance using set sizes of less than 6 to be superior to that using larger sets, with the complete set {NAND} performing best of all. However, the choice of additional function is likely to be of crucial importance. For example, the addition of the EQ (even-2-parity) function to the standard set of {AND, OR, NAND, NOR} dramatically improves standard GP's performance on the even-6-parity problem [6].

The other parameters of our runs are summarised in Table 1. Pilot studies suggested that the sub-symbolic representation was quite capable of solving the problem with a population of just 50, but we used 200 too to give standard GP a fighting chance. Note that every individual in the population was subjected to mutation (although an elitist strategy was used in the event of a decrease in fitness of the best of generation individual) and that mutation probability in the case of point mutation therefore refers to the probability that a single node will be mutated. In the case of standard mutation, a single random subtree was spliced to a random node of each tree with a probability of 0.1. At 0.3, the crossover rate is significantly lower than that used in most standard GP runs and is based on the results of a number of pilot studies using the sub-symbolic representation, and on evidence from the literature suggesting that low crossover and high mutation rates are beneficial when small populations are used in GP [3]. It was used in all the conditions to ensure validity of comparison. Finally, the initial tree depth value of 7 counts the root node as node 0 such that, with ramped half-and-half population initialisation, the largest individual in the initial population contained 511 nodes.

Population sizes	50 and 200
Crossover probability	0.3
Mutation probability	0.1
Tournament size	7
Max. initial tree depth	7
Initialisation method	ramped
Max. tree depth	17
Maximum generations	80
Number of runs per condition	50

Table 1. Experimental Parameters for even-n-parity problems

5   Results

We compared performance of standard GP without ADFs, GP using the GPUX and GPPM operators and GP using the GPSUX and GPSPM operators on the even-n-parity problem for $n = 3, 4, 6$. We would have liked to have studied GPUX and GPPM in isolation, but the lexical convergence associated with GPUX means that some mutation is necessary to maintain population diversity. However, we did examine the GPPM and GPSPM operators in isolation for the standard and fine-grain representations. Tables 2, 3 and 4 show the minimum effort (fitness evaluations) required to find a solution with 99% probability [4], the average complexity (number of nodes) of the correct solutions, and the percentage of runs on which a correct solution was found for each of the three problems.

Operators	Population size	Fitness evaluations	Complexity	Success Rate
Standard GP	50	5,550	742	32%
Standard GP	200	2,400	156	76%
GPUX, GPPM	50	850	67	92%
GPUX, GPPM	200	2,000	66	100%
GPPM only	50	1,050	72	98%
GPPM only	200	1,400	59	100%
GPSUX, GPSPM	50	900	72	94%
GPSUX, GPSPM	200	600	43	100%
GPSPM only	50	600	56	100%
GPSPM only	200	600	48	100%

Table 2. Minimum effort, average complexity of correct solutions and percentage of runs on which a correct solution was found for the even-3-parity problem

Operators	Population size	Fitness evaluations	Complexity	Success Rate
Standard GP	50	11,250	428	12%
Standard GP	200	19,000	568	68%
GPUX, GPPM	50	4,200	84	88%
GPUX, GPPM	200	6,000	49	98%
GPPM only	50	4,200	68	80%
GPPM only	200	6,000	49	98%
GPSUX, GPSPM	50	2,250	82	92%
GPSUX, GPSPM	200	2,200	56	100%
GPSPM only	50	2,250	76	98%
GPSPM only	200	8,400	49	98%

Table 3. Minimum effort, average complexity of correct solutions and percentage of runs on which a correct solution was found for the even-4-parity problem

Operators	Population size	Fitness evaluations	Complexity	Success Rate
Standard GP	50	No solution found	N/A	0%
Standard GP	200	No solution found	N/A	0%
GPUX, GPPM	50	34,850	38	36%
GPUX, GPPM	200	127,600	40	60%
GPPM only	50	35,550	43	44%
GPPM only	200	71,400	51	82%
GPSUX, GPSPM	50	17,000	49	62%
GPSUX, GPSPM	200	19,200	53	80%
GPSPM only	50	16,200	59	67%
GPSPM only	200	18,400	42	82%

Table 4. Minimum effort, average complexity of correct solutions and percentage of runs on which a correct solution was found for the even-6-parity problem

Given the small population sizes, the unusual parameter settings and the test function, it is unsurprising that standard GP failed to find a solution on the even-6-parity problem – its poor performance on this problem is well known [5] [2]. Koza reports that the effort required for GP *with* ADFs to solve the even-6-parity problem is 1,344,000 [5]. Gathercole and Ross [3] did not estimate the effort required for their limited-error fitness approach to solving the task, but did report that it required 2500 generations to find a solution with a population size of 400 (i.e. 1,000,000 individuals evaluated). Standard GP's performance on the even-3-parity and even-4-parity problems, however, compares favourably with other results reported using the standard function set of {OR, AND, NOR, NAND}. Koza [5] reports efforts of 96,000 and 384,000 fitness evaluations for the even-3-parity and even-4-parity problems respectively. We believe this to be due to the faciliting effect engendered by the inclusion of the EQ and XOR functions [6]. The other conditions fared considerably better and compare favourably with other algorithms reported in the literature, particularly on the even-6-parity problem.

The performance of GPUX with GPPM seems to be 3 to 5 times better than that of standard GP. We believe this to be due to the ability of the GPUX operator to perform global search [12].

The complexity of the solutions is also surprisingly low. Since GPUX, GPPM, GPSUX and GPSPM cannot increase tree depth beyond that of the largest tree created at initialisation, the bloating observed in the standard GP runs cannot occur. Nevertheless, the average solution sizes are all well short of the maximum possible (511 nodes in this case), confirming that mutating on a per node basis generates a counter-pressure against increased program size, since parsimonious solutions are still found in the absence of the uniform crossover operator.

Clearly, the sub-symbolic node representation with GPSUX and GPSPM further enhances the performance of GP, typically by a factor of 2 on the even-4 and even-6-parity problem. We believe that this is because this allows GP to make smoother movements around the solution space, although further analytical work is necessary to confirm this.

The GPPM and GPSPM operators also performed well on their own. In many conditions mutation alone performed the same as or better than when it was used with crossover. However, pilot studies on higher-order versions of the parity problem suggested that better performance could be achieved using uniform crossover as well, indicating that the performance of mutation alone is mainly a result of the relative simplicity of the lower-order parity problems (for a discussion of the work on higher-order parity problems see [14]).

6   Conclusions

In this paper we have demonstrated the application of two alternative search operators for GP – point mutation and uniform crossover. We have also described a simple representation for function nodes and shown that the combined approach produces a considerable improvement in performance on the even-n-parity problem, particularly for $n = 6$. This improvement appears to be due to a combination of two factors: the global search property of the GPUX operator and the finer granularity of the sub-symbolic representation which allows GP to make smaller, directed movements around the solution space. Of these, the former has been established theoretically [12]. Further work is required to confirm the latter.

Of course, we have only demonstrated the success of the sub-symbolic node representation on a single problem. Furthermore, certain regularities associated with the parity problems may have contributed to the encouraging results reported here. However, we are confident that the approach can be generalised to other problems and other representations. If our assumptions concerning the benefits that can be accrued from increasing the granularity of the search space and allowing the operators to make use of this increase are correct, there is good reason to expect that the approach will also succeed when applied to other problems. Future work will address this.

References

1. Tobias Blickle and Lothar Thiele. Genetic programming and redundancy. In J. Hopf, editor, *Genetic Algorithms within the Framework of Evolutionary Computation (Workshop at KI-94, Saarbrücken)*, pages 33–38, Im Stadtwald, Building 44, D-66123 Saarbrücken, Germany, 1994. Max-Planck-Institut für Informatik (MPI-I-94-241).
2. Chris Gathercole and Peter Ross. The MAX problem for genetic programming - highlighting an adverse interaction between the crossover operator and a restriction on tree depth. Technical report, Department of Artificial Intelligence, University of Edinburgh, 80 South Bridge, Edinburgh, EH1 1HN, UK, 1995.
3. Chris Gathercole and Peter Ross. Tackling the boolean even N parity problem with genetic programming and limited-error fitness. In John R. Koza, Kalyanmoy Deb, Marco Dorigo, David B. Fogel, Max Garzon, Hitoshi Iba, and Rick L. Riolo, editors, *Genetic Programming 1997: Proceedings of the Second Annual Conference*, pages 119–127, Stanford University, CA, USA, 13-16 July 1997. Morgan Kaufmann.

4. John R. Koza. *Genetic Programming: On the Programming of Computers by Means of Natural Selection.* MIT Press, Cambridge, MA, USA, 1992.
5. John R. Koza. *Genetic Programming II: Automatic Discovery of Reusable Programs.* MIT Press, Cambridge Massachusetts, May 1994.
6. W. B. Langdon and R. Poli. Boolean functions fitness spaces. In R. Poli, P. Nordin, W. B. Langdon, and T. Fogarty, editors, *Proceedings of the Second European Workshop on Genetic Programming – EuroGP'99*, Goteborg, May 1999. Springer-Verlag.
7. Ben McKay, Mark J. Willis, and Geoffrey W. Barton. Using a tree structured genetic algorithm to perform symbolic regression. In A. M. S. Zalzala, editor, *First International Conference on Genetic Algorithms in Engineering Systems: Innovations and Applications, GALESIA*, volume 414, pages 487–492, Sheffield, UK, 12-14 September 1995. IEE.
8. Una-May O'Reilly and Franz Oppacher. Hybridized crossover-based search techniques for program discovery. In *Proceedings of the 1995 World Conference on Evolutionary Computation*, volume 2, page 573, Perth, Australia, 29 November - 1 December 1995. IEEE Press.
9. Riccardo Poli. Is crossover a local search operator? Position paper at the Workshop on Evolutionary Computation with Variable Size Representation at ICGA-97, 20 July 1997.
10. Riccardo Poli and W. B. Langdon. Genetic programming with one-point crossover. In P. K. Chawdhry, R. Roy, and R. K. Pant, editors, *Soft Computing in Engineering Design and Manufacturing*, pages 180–189. Springer-Verlag London, 23-27 June 1997.
11. Riccardo Poli and W. B. Langdon. A new schema theory for genetic programming with one-point crossover and point mutation. In John R. Koza, Kalyanmoy Deb, Marco Dorigo, David B. Fogel, Max Garzon, Hitoshi Iba, and Rick L. Riolo, editors, *Genetic Programming 1997: Proceedings of the Second Annual Conference*, pages 278–285, Stanford University, CA, USA, 13-16 July 1997. Morgan Kaufmann.
12. Riccardo Poli and William B. Langdon. On the search properties of different crossover operators in genetic programming. In John R. Koza, Wolfgang Banzhaf, Kumar Chellapilla, Kalyanmoy Deb, Marco Dorigo, David B. Fogel, Max H. Garzon, David E. Goldberg, Hitoshi Iba, and Rick Riolo, editors, *Genetic Programming 1998: Proceedings of the Third Annual Conference*, pages 293–301, University of Wisconsin, Madison, Wisconsin, USA, 22-25 July 1998. Morgan Kaufmann.
13. Riccardo Poli and William B. Langdon. Schema theory for genetic programming with one-point crossover and point mutation. *Evolutionary Computation*, 6(3):231–252, 1998.
14. Riccardo Poli, Jonathan Page, and William B. Langdon. Solving even-12, -13, -15, -17, -20 and -22 boolean parity problems using sub-machine code GP with smooth uniform crossover, smooth point mutation and demes. Technical Report CSRP-99-2, University of Birmingham, School of Computer Science, January 1999.
15. Justinian P. Rosca. *Hierarchical Learning with Procedural Abstraction Mechanisms.* PhD thesis, University of Rochester, Rochester, NY 14627, February 1997.
16. Terence Soule and James A. Foster. Removal bias: a new cause of code growth in tree based evolutionary programming. In *1998 IEEE International Conference on Evolutionary Computation*, pages 781–186, Anchorage, Alaska, USA, 5-9 May 1998. IEEE Press.
17. G. Syswerda. Uniform crossover in genetic algorithms. In J. Schaffer, editor, *Proceedings of the Third International Conference on Genetic ALgorithms*. MOrgan Kaufmann, 1989.

Phenotype Plasticity in Genetic Programming: A Comparison of Darwinian and Lamarckian Inheritance Schemes

Anna Esparcia-Alcázar* and Ken Sharman

Department of Electronics & Electrical Engineering
University of Glasgow, Scotland, UK
aesparcia@ieee.org, kenshar@elec.gla.ac.uk

Abstract We consider a form of *phenotype plasticity* in Genetic Programming (GP). This takes the form of a set of real-valued numerical parameters associated with each individual, an optimisation (or learning) algorithm for adapting their values, and an inheritance strategy for propagating learned parameter values to offspring. We show that plastic GP has significant benefits including faster evolution and adaptation in changing environments compared with non-plastic GP. The paper also considers the differences between Darwinian and Lamarckian inheritance schemes and shows that the former is superior in dynamic environments.

1 Introduction

In this paper we introduce a plastic phenotype variant of standard GP which enables individuals to employ adaptive learning procedures at the level of the phenotype. The motivation for this follows from observations of higher animals in nature. We provide phenotype plasticity by augmenting standard GP with a set of numerical parameters (or *node gains*) attached to each individual. The combination of the GP tree structure and the values of these parameters determines the function computed by each individual. The parameter values for a particular individual are determined by an optimisation algorithm (simulated annealing, SA) and a set of training data. This can be viewed as a form of on-line adaptive learning.

The overall strategy , labelled *node gain GP+SA*, is similar to the development of many higher animals. Such development arises when the genotype specifies only certain components of the phenotype (e.g. its physical structure), and where the remaining phenotype components or behaviours are learned during the individual's lifetime. This two-stage strategy is apparently very successful in nature and, as we show in this paper, enables similar benefits in artificial evolution.

We also investigate inheritance schemes for the parameters learned by an individual. In particular, we consider the two classical evolutionary paradigms

---

* presently with the Industrial Control Centre, University of Strathclyde, Glasgow, Scotland

R. Poli et al. (Eds.): EuroGP'99, LNCS 1598, pp. 49–64, 1999.
© Springer-Verlag Berlin Heidelberg 1999

of Darwinian and Lamarckian inheritance in the context of plastic GP. In the former, the parameter values are not transmitted from parent to offspring during evolution and each new individual re-learns its own parameters values from scratch (possibly guided by its parent or peers). In the latter scheme, learned parameter values are transmitted directly from parents to children whereupon they may undergo further adaptation. We show that the two schemes lead to similar performance when the environment is static and the fitness function is unchanging over time. However, in a dynamic environment with a time-varying fitness function we observe that the Darwinian scheme is superior.

The paper is structured as follows. In Sect. 2 we outline the motivation for developing plastic GP and point out the benefits that might be expected. Sect. 3 focuses on the relationships between learning (acquisition of knowledge) and adaptation (adjustment to suit different conditions). We first consider the learning processes found in nature and how these may be exploited in artificial evolution. We then proceed to discuss the simulation of learning in artificial systems, outlining some of the existing approaches and pointing out some of their shortcomings. In Sect. 4 we present the details of our plastic GP approach, while in Sect. 5 we describe the differences between Darwinian and Lamarckian inheritance schemes. The simulated annealing learning algorithm is briefly described in Sect. 6. In Sect. 7 we present the results of some experiments designed to investigate the performance of plastic GP compared to non-plastic GP, and to compare the different inheritance schemes. Several performance measures are presented as is a statistical analysis of the overall results. Our conclusions are presented in Sect. 8.

2   Motivation

A characteristic of higher animals is that they are born dumb. Consequently, they require to undergo a process of learning during their early development before they are able to operate autonomously at their full potential. Whilst this learning effort is obviously costly in various ways, the end benefits are significant, as the natural world shows clearly. Motivated by this observation, we have developed an analogous strategy for artificial evolution using GP. We refer to this as *plastic* GP. This approach makes a clear distinction between the genotype (GP tree structures) and the phenotype (the actual function computed by the GP). In conventional GP, there is a direct relationship between the genotype and the phenotype. This is not the case in plastic GP where certain components of the phenotype are independent of the genotype. Consequently, there are many phenotypes that can be grown from the same genotype. The genotype to phenotype mapping is flexible or plastic.

Phenotype plasticity is important for two main reasons. Firstly, a plastic phenotype is far more adaptive than a non-plastic one. An organism can learn new behaviour in a dynamic environment. The second reason why plasticity is important stems from the fact that certain phenotypic characteristics (or behaviours) are impossible or at least extremely difficult to specify at the level of the genotype. Consider, for example, the problem of encoding complex skills such as reading, mathematical reasoning, or song writing in human DNA sequences. Nature has discovered that such complexity is best learned and not defined by the genotype. Note however that the genotype still has the important role of defining the organism's *capacity* for learning such complex skills.

3 Natural and artificial learning

3.1 Analogies

Atmar [2] defines natural learning as the selective retention of behaviours that have been accumulated through stochastic trial and error. It is a process inherent to and indistinguishable from evolution itself. Following this definition, three forms of learning can be observed in natural evolution:

Phylogenetic learning, where the learned knowledge is stored in the species genetic code; the time scale of this process is the lifetime of a species.

Sociogenetic learning, where the knowledge is stored in the form of social culture; the time scale is the lifetime of a group.

Ontogenetic learning, where the knowledge is stored in an individual's memory; the time scale is the lifetime of the individual.

The first type of learning, phylogenetic learning, is implicit in the Genetic Programming algorithm. Attempts have also been made at modelling the second type of learning by providing GP with a notion of culture e.g. [13]. This paper will be concerned with the simulation of the third type, ontogenetic learning, which from now on will be referred to simply as learning. The key idea is to provide each individual with the opportunity to adapt to its environment and modify its behaviour accordingly.

Individual learning affects the whole population in various ways. For instance it has been postulated [1] that one effect is the decrease in the reproduction rate, as time devoted to learning cannot be spent in reproduction[1]. More importantly, learning can also influence evolution. The process by which learning assists the integration of genetic components of behaviours into the gene pool has been termed *Baldwin effect* [11, 3, 8, 1, 12].

The effect of learning in fixed environments is a speed up in the search for the optimum, because instead of a phylogenetic (and possibly blind) search for an optimal genotype, the optimal phenotype can be found via an ontogenetic ("directed") search. However, the main advantage of learning comes in variable environments. From the individual's point of view, learning allows it to adapt to the new environment and therefore increases its chances to survive under the modified conditions. From the population's point of view, it is claimed that learning maintains genotypic diversity [1] during evolution. As a consequence, there will be a higher probability that at least some of the genotypes will have a high fitness after the environment changes, than in the case where only few

---

[1] While you sit there reading this paper, other people are breeding

genotypes were present before the change took place. Hence, the risk of extinction of the species is minimised.

3.2 Simulating learning

Many attempts have been made at artificially modelling the natural learning processes, both to gain insight into the learning process itself [11, 3, 8, 1, 12] or to exploit its potential benefits when applied to engineering problems [4, 10]. Most of these models involve significant simplifications of the complexity of natural learning.

In our case the simplifications are as follows. First, the individual learns at no cost to itself. The cost to the user is the increase in computational time required to produce a given number of individuals. But, from an engineering point of view, this is irrelevant if less "births" are needed to reach a solution. Second, the amount of effort an individual devotes to learning is controlled externally: it is neither congenital to the individual nor controlled by it. This issue can be addressed by modifying the implementation such that the amount of learning effort is regulated by a "learning gene". Another interesting development would be to run the simulation in parallel and allow the individuals to learn or reproduce "at will". These concerns are left for future study.

4   Basic details of Adaptive GP

Let $\underline{n} \in \aleph$ be a syntactically correct vector of nodes[2] and let $\underline{g} \in \mathcal{G}$ be a vector of gains. Define the function $\ell(\underline{v})$ to be the number of elements in a vector $\underline{v}$. An individual genotype $\underline{h} \in \mathcal{H}$ can be represented as the pair of vectors

$$\underline{h} = \langle \underline{n}, \underline{g} \rangle \quad : \quad \ell(\underline{n}) = \ell(\underline{g}) \tag{1}$$

We now proceed to define a GP phenotype. Let $\underline{e} \in \mathcal{E}$ be the environment in which a GP individual operates. In the context of Digital Signal Processing, the environment is the input data sequence and the training output (if required).

The *fitness function*, $f \in \mathcal{F}$, is

$$f \quad : \mathcal{H} \times \mathcal{E} \longrightarrow \quad [0,1] \tag{2}$$

Let ω be a *learning algorithm*:

$$\omega : \mathcal{H} \times \mathcal{E} \times \mathcal{F} \longrightarrow \mathcal{G} \tag{3}$$

The above learning algorithm produces a new set of gain values for a given individual and fitness function in a particular environment.

We further define a *reproduction function* as

$$r \quad : \quad \mathcal{H} \times \mathcal{H} \longrightarrow \mathcal{H} \tag{4}$$

---

[2] i.e. a tree [6]. The vectorial notation lends itself to easier mathematical treatment.

or, alternatively, as

$$r \quad : \quad \aleph \times \aleph \longrightarrow \aleph \tag{5}$$

depending on whether or not the learned gain values are inherited during cross/-over (details given in Sect. 5).

Hence, before learning we have

$$f = (\underline{h}, \underline{e}) = f\left(\langle \underline{n}, \underline{g} \rangle \ \underline{e}\right) \tag{6}$$

and after learning

$$f(\underline{h}', \underline{e}_2) \tag{7}$$

where

$$\underline{h}' = \langle \underline{n}, \omega(\underline{h}, \underline{e}_1, f) \rangle \tag{8}$$

where $\underline{e}_1$ is the environment used for learning and $\underline{e}_2$ is the environment where the individual will operate afterwards.

Finally, an individual phenotype $p \in \mathcal{P}$ is represented as the 4–tuple:

$$\underline{p} = \langle \ \underline{h}, \ f, \ \omega, \ r \ \rangle \tag{9}$$

5   Darwinism vs. Lamarckism

In standard GP evolution takes place following Darwinian rules. Darwinian evolution is a two-step process, taking place as follows, [9]

1. **random** genetic variations take place, caused by recombination and mutation only
2. selection (natural or artificial) favours the survival of the fittest, or rather, the **culling of the less fit** [2], among these variants.

The former implies that individual learning does not affect the genetic material and therefore cannot be inherited.

On the other hand, another classical theory of evolution, Lamarckism, is essentially a theory of *directed variation*. In the face of an environmental change, an organism would react by incorporating preferentially favourable genetic information, which would then be transmitted to offspring. The latter, also known as "inheritance of acquired characters", has taken over the meaning of the word Lamarckism and it is also the definition that we will use here.

Although Lamarckian evolution (in any of its meanings) has not been observed in biological history[3], it can be said that the evolution of human culture (or learning in higher mammals and other animals) is Lamarckian in character: knowledge is transmitted from one generation to another.

---

[3] Although genetic changes can be due to exposure to radiation or chemical agents, these changes are random, not directed. [9]

Lamarckian evolution is implemented in the GP+SA system by allowing the annealed node gains to be inherited by the offspring. In Darwinian evolution, the gains are set to 1 or initialised with random values before the annealing takes place and are not inherited.

Let T_1 and T_2 be two trees selected for crossover, with lengths ℓ and m respectively, and whose expressions are:

$$T_1 \equiv \begin{cases} \underline{n}_1 = \{n_{1,0} \quad n_{1,1} \quad \cdots \quad n_{1,(\ell-2)} \quad n_{1,(\ell-1)}\} \\ \underline{g}_1 = \{g_{1,0} \quad g_{1,1} \quad \cdots \quad g_{1,(\ell-2)} \quad g_{1,(\ell-1)}\} \end{cases} \tag{10}$$

$$T_2 \equiv \begin{cases} \underline{n}_2 = \{n_{2,0} \quad n_{2,1} \quad \cdots \quad n_{2,(m-2)} \quad n_{2,(m-1)}\} \\ \underline{g}_2 = \{g_{2,0} \quad g_{2,1} \quad \cdots \quad g_{2,(m-2)} \quad g_{2,(m-1)}\} \end{cases} \tag{11}$$

Let us assume that T_1 is acting as the "mother" and T_2 as the "father"; this means T_1 provides the root of the tree and T_2 the branch to swap. Further assume that the crossover points are i, $0 \le i < \ell$, for T_1 and j, $0 \le j < m$, for T_2. Let the subtrees starting at i and j comprehend all the nodes up to p and q in their respective trees. The result of the crossover, $T_{1\times2}$, is a tree of length $\ell - p + q$, whose expression is:

$$T_{1\times2} \equiv$$

$$\begin{cases} \underline{n}_{1\times2} = \{ n_{1,0} \cdots n_{1,(i-1)} \, n_{2,j} \cdots n_{2,(j+q-1)} \, n_{1,(i+p)} \cdots n_{1,(\ell-1)}\} \\ \underline{g}_{1\times2} = \{ g_{1,0} \cdots g_{1,(i-1)} \, g_{2,j} \cdots g_{2,(j+q-1)} \, g_{1,(i+p)} \cdots g_{1,(\ell-1)}\} \end{cases} \tag{12}$$

The gain vector $\underline{g}_{1\times2}$ has components inherited from T_1 and T_2. In an alternative scheme, the components of $\underline{g}_{1\times2}$ would be set to 1 or initialised with random values. These two ways of proceeding are labelled here *Lamarckian* and *Darwinian learning schemes* respectively.

Using the notation given in section 4, the Darwinian learning scheme implies defining the reproduction function r as follows

$$r = r(\underline{n}) \tag{13}$$

i.e. r is only a function of the node vector $\underline{n}$, as in Eqn. 5. On the other hand, in Lamarckian evolution

$$r = r(\underline{n}, \, \omega(\underline{h}, \underline{e}, f)) \tag{14}$$

r is a function of the genotype $\underline{h}$ modified by the learning function ω in the environment $\underline{e}$, as in Eqn. 4

6   Learning by Simulated Annealing

The main characteristics of a Simulated Annealing algorithm are as follows:

- a perturbation–generating probability distribution.

- an acceptance/rejection probability distribution.
- a cooling schedule (or temperature variation law)

Details are given in Table 6.

The SA algorithm for expression trees works as follows:

1. Initialise parameters T_0 , maxTrials, trials, n_{max}, n
2. Perturb the gain vector $g(i)$ to get $\underline{g}(i)$
3. Evaluate the fitness, $f(i)$ using the perturbed gain vector $\underline{g}(i)$
4. If $f(i) \geq f(i)$ then accept the perturbation: $\underline{g}(i+1) = \underline{g}(i)$ and continue
   else accept the perturbation with probability p and continue;
5. If trials $>$ maxTrials then trials $= 0$
   else trials++ and go back to step 2
6. Reduce the temperature T according to annealing schedule
7. If $n < n_{max}$ then n++ and go back to step 2.

7 Experimental analysis

7.1 Four methods

This section provides results obtained by four different methods. The first one is the standard GP algorithm, in which the gains are fixed and equal to 1. This is referred to as **NGNL** (no gains - no learning). The other three methods employ node gains, whose values are initialised at random in the first population.

In the second method studied the gain values remain fixed (save in the case of a random mutation) and thus are inherited by the offspring. This is labelled **RGNL** (random gains - no learning). The remaining two methods employ learning of the gains. In the **Darwinian learning** scheme the gains are also initialised at random for every individual that is born and then subjected to annealing. In **Lamarckian learning** the annealed gains of the parents are inherited by the offspring, which then undergo their own annealing process.

The four methods will be applied to three channel equalisation problems. For background on this problem and the application of GP to it the reader is referred to [6, 7]. The GP and SA settings for these experiments are shown in Table 6.

7.2 Fixed environments

Overview Strictly speaking a fixed environment would be one in which the population has reached equilibrium, i.e. the average fitness remains constant. When tackling engineering problems, however, the behaviour in the equilibrium is not usually observed. The concern in these cases is finding an optimal solution; hence, the process is stopped once it is considered that no further improvement can be achieved.

In the particular case of the experiments discussed here we are interested in both the solutions and the evolutionary process itself. A fixed environment will then be defined as a GP run of the channel equalisation problem in which the unknown channel does not change for the duration of the run. The run proceeds for up to a given number of node evaluations (as explained below) regardless of whether or not a suitable solution has been found or equilibrium has been reached.

Two cases are studied: a linear channel (LC1) and a nonlinear one (NLC). The difference equations for these channels are

$$y_n = x_n + 0.9 \cdot x_{n-1} + n_n \tag{15}$$

for LC1 and

$$p_n = x_n + 0.6 \cdot x_{n-1} + 0.5 \cdot p_{n-1} \tag{16}$$

$$y_n = p_n + 0.15 \cdot p_{n-2} + n_n \tag{17}$$

for NLC, where x_n and y_n are the inputs to the channel and equaliser respectively at instant n and n_n is the additive white Gaussian noise.

Study of the performance The study of the performance can be divided into two aspects. The first one is related to how well the solutions obtained perform with unseen data, i.e. the generalisation ability. The second aspect is the success rate.

In order to test the generalisation ability of the Darwinian and Lamarckian learning schemes, each experiment was run a number of times using 70 samples (of which the first 20 were rejected for the fitness calculation as transient). The termination criterion for evolution was a number of node evaluations equal or exceeding a given limit (1e8 for LC1, 3e8 for NLC).

The solutions were tested with a further 10100 samples (of which the first 100 are rejected) to obtain a fitness value and a bit-error-rate. These two values themselves provide a measure of "how good" the solutions are.

The fitness in the test was also compared with the one obtained during evolution and the discrepancy measured as follows:

$$d = \frac{1}{N} \sum_N \left(\text{fitness}_{\text{test}} - \text{fitness}_{\text{after evolution}} \right)^2 \tag{18}$$

where N is the number of runs. This gives an idea of how well the fitness during evolution can predict the subsequent behaviour of the solutions obtained by each method, therefore being a measure of reliability. The averages of these values are given in Tables 1 and 2.

These results show that, on average, Darwinian learning outperforms the other methods, the differences being more noticeable in the case of NLC, which is a more difficult problem. On the other hand, the discrepancy in LC1 is lower for Lamarckian learning, whereas in NLC the lowest value corresponds to Darwinian learning; both results show that learning methods generalise better than non learning ones.

Table1. Comparison of results (averages of 50 runs for LC1)

	fitness (in test)	BER (in test)	fitness (after evolution)	discrepancy d
Darwinian	0.9765	0	0.9825	0.0018
Lamarckian	0.9679	0.00806	0.9704	0.0002
RGNL	0.9731	0.00006	0.9890	0.0037
NGNL	0.8231	0.03045	0.8933	0.0487

Table2. Comparison of results (averages of 24 runs for NLC)

	fitness (in test)	BER (in test)	fitness (after evolution)	discrepancy d
Darwinian	0.9620	0.00564	0.9816	0.0013
Lamarckian	0.9261	0.01071	0.9620	0.0052
RGNL	0.7418	0.02920	0.9655	0.2090
NGNL	0.8049	0.10371	0.9303	0.0336

The second aspect in measuring the performance is the success rate. This is given by the ratio of successful runs over the total number of runs. We define a successful run as one in which the fitness of the best solution measured during the evolution is greater than an arbitrary value, here chosen as 0.9. The values are shown in Table 4.

Darwinian learning maintains the advantage because it has both high success rates and low discrepancies. RGNL has higher success rates than Lamarckian learning, but on the other hand, as shown in the previous tables, it also has a greater discrepancy, which makes its solutions less reliable.

7.3 Variable environments

Overview A variable environment is one in which the unknown channel is modified during the run.

The implementation of this is as follows. Evolution proceeds as explained in the previous section for LC1, up to 10^8 node evaluations approximately. Then a new set of data is generated for the modified channel LC2. LC2 has the same structure as LC1 but one of its coefficients is slightly different in absolute value and has opposite sign. The difference equation for LC2 is

$$y_n = x_n - 0.99 \cdot x_{n-1} \tag{19}$$

The population is then re-evaluated and re-annealed and evolution continues for approximately up to $3 \cdot 10^8$ node evaluations.

Study of the performance The solutions are tested as explained before with 10100 samples generated for the channel LC2. A comparison of the solution performances is given in table 3.

Darwinian learning maintains the advantage, both in fitness and reliability, clearly over RGNL and NGNL and slightly over Lamarckian learning.

Table3. Comparison of results in a variable environment. Averages of 51 runs for LC1 $\longrightarrow$ LC2

	fitness (in test)	BER (in test)	fitness (after evolution)	discrepancy d
Darwinian	0.9078	0.002047	0.9592	0.0030
Lamarckian	0.8930	0.001986	0.9606	0.0208
RGNL	0.8296	0.038525	0.9146	0.0313
NGNL	0.6062	0.195249	0.7719	0.1242

When studying the success rates given in Table 4 it can be observed that the Darwinian learning scheme has a slightly lower probability of success than Lamarckian learning. Nevertheless, the performance of the solutions obtained by this method is higher due to the low discrepancy.

Table4. Success rates

| | fixed environment | | variable environment |
	LC1 (50 runs)	NLC (24 runs)	LC1 $\longrightarrow$ LC2 (51 runs)
Darwinian	1	0.92	0.9608
Lamarckian	0.96	0.83	0.9804
RGNL	1	0.92	0.8431
NGNL	0.78	0.76	0.5882

7.4 Analysis

The results obtained in previous sections are analysed statistically by means of a **Kruskal-Wallis test**. This is a multiple comparison non parametric test [5], which means the k populations compared are not assumed to have normal distributions. Briefly, the hypotheses tested are as follows:

H_0 : All of the k populations compared are identical

H_a : At least one of the populations tends to yield larger observations than at least one of the other populations (i.e. the k populations do not have identical means)

For a confidence level of 0.01 the result of the test for all three cases studied was rejection of H_0. A procedure was then employed to determine which pairs of populations tended to differ. The results, for the same confidence level, are summarised in Table 5.

Table5. Multiple comparisons with the Kruskal-Wallis test. The symbol $=$ indicates that the value of the statistic is below the critical, hence the two distributions compared cannot be distinguished. The symbol $\neq$ indicates a value of the statistic above the critical and two different distributions.

Methods		LC1	NLC	LC1→LC2
Critical values		26.57	19.67	25.85
Darwinian	Lamarckian	0.68 (=)	9.89 (=)	0.67 (=)
Darwinian	RGNL	16.71(=)	23.23 ($\neq$)	29.78 ($\neq$)
Darwinian	NGNL	54.79 ($\neq$)	30.45 ($\neq$)	74.92 ($\neq$)
Lamarckian	RGNL	17.39 (=)	13.33 (=)	30.45 ($\neq$)
Lamarckian	NGNL	14.11 ($\neq$)	20.56 ($\neq$)	75.59 ($\neq$)
RGNL	NGNL	71.50 ($\neq$)	7.23 (=)	45.14 ($\neq$)

The conclusion is that, for this confidence level, the Darwinian and Lamarck/-ian learning schemes cannot be distinguished. In the case of LC1, RGNL cannot be distinguished from either the Darwinian or Lamarckian learning schemes. For NLC the test is inconclusive.

7.5 Influence of learning on evolution.

To trace the influence of learning on evolution a new variable is introduced: the fitness at birth or *fab*. The statistics of the *fab* will be compared to those of the fitness after learning, or *fit*. With no learning, *fit* = *fab*. We are interested in the variations in the distributions of *fit* and *fab* as the run proceeds.

For this study 24 runs were performed for Darwinian and Lamarckian learning and RGNL with the set up shown in Table 6.

In this case the emphasis is not placed on the solution but on the evolutionary process itself and therefore the experiments run for a longer time. In practise the termination criterion for evolution is a number of node evaluations greater than or equal to $3 \cdot 10^8$.

The distributions for LC1 are shown in Figs. 1 and 2. The distributions for NLC showed similar results and are not displayed to avoid repetition.

It can be seen that the *fit* distribution moves to the right as the run proceeds. This displacement is slowest in Darwinian learning and fastest in RGNL. In more difficult problems we have observed that the fit distribution in RGNL doesn't reach the higher values of the scale. Instead, it gets "stuck" at suboptimal values.

The *fab* distribution shows an increasing peak at zero in Darwinian learning. This means that individuals that can learn are selectively preferred to those that are naturally fit. The opposite occurs in Lamarckian learning: the *fab* distributions are displaced towards the right, as would be expected.

In both cases the displacement of the *fab* distributions is much slower than that of the *fit* for RGNL (remember that for RGNL *fit* = *fab*). This shows how the presence of learning slows down the evolution of the genotype.

7.6   Further comments: Extending the analogy

A number of limitations apply to our simulations other than those pointed out in Sect. 3.2, in particular:

- all individuals have the same probability of learning (equal to 1)
- the maximum number of annealing iterations is fixed
- in the experiment with varying environment, the unknown channel is modified only once.

It would be of great interest to relax these constraints, as well as, as already mentioned, letting the individuals "decide" on their own learning and parallelise the simulation. Further work will aim at achieving these objectives, which would be easily incorporated in the implementation.

8   Conclusions

In complex engineering problems an adaptation algorithm is required to optimise the values of parameters, here called node gains. By drawing an analogy between such an adaptation algorithm and the learning process in nature, one is able to envisage the way in which individual adaptation affects the whole system.

A step beyond the natural analogy is the introduction of Lamarckian inheritance, which is easily implemented in the node gain GP+SA system.

The learning algorithm is implemented by means of Simulated Annealing. This offers a number of possibilities in the selection of parameters and different schedules used, in contrast with the GP algorithm which is somewhat more rigid.

Introducing SA in the node gain GP system provides a faster way of finding solutions to engineering problems and a more robust one in the case of variable environments.

Applying a learning algorithm might not be advisable in all cases. Two general decision rules as per when to employ learning can be given :

- when the performance of a system is sensitive to parameter variations; for instance, when a wrong selection of parameters can make a system unstable
- when environmental changes are expected; for instance in equalisation in mobile systems, where the unknown channel is constantly varying.

Two possible learning schemes for GP have been addressed here, namely Darwinian and Lamarckian. It has been shown that, in the examples presented, using node gains and learning provides better results than those obtained by standard GP. Furthermore, the use of learning improved the performance in the two more complex problems addressed.

A measure of the generalisation ability has been introduced which shows that overfitting is not a problem in any of the learning schemes presented; on the contrary, both generalise better than the non learning methods. This might be due to the fact that the solutions obtained with any of the learning schemes tend to be smaller than those obtained without learning. Further analysis is required to prove this point.

The statistical tests taken do not allow us to conclude whether the Darwinian scheme performs better or worse than the Lamarckian one. However, the former appears to be intuitively the more robust of the two, thus more indicated for a wider variety of problems.

References

1. RW Anderson. Learning and evolution: A quantitative genetics approach. *Journal of Theoretical Biology*, 175:89–101, 1995.
2. Wirt Atmar. Notes on the simulation of evolution. *IEEE Trans. on Neural Networks*, 5(1):130–147, January 1994.
3. RK Belew. Evolution, learning and culture: computational metaphors for adaptive algorithms. *Complex Systems*, 4:11–49, 1990.
4. EJW Boers, MV Borst, and IG Sprinkhuizen–Kuyper. Evolving artificial neural networks using the baldwin effect. In DW Pearson, NC Steele, and RF Albrecht, editors, *Artificial Neural Nets and Genetic Algorithms. Proceedings of the International Conference*, Springer Verlag, 1995.
5. W Conover. *Practical Non-Parametric Statistics*. John Wiley & sons, 2nd edition, 1980.
6. AI Esparcia-Alcázar. *Genetic Programming for Adaptive Digital Signal processing*. PhD thesis, University of Glasgow, Scotland, UK, 1998.
7. AI Esparcia-Alcázar and KC Sharman. Some applications of genetic programming in digital signal processing. In *Late Breaking Papers at the GP'96 conference*, pages 24–31, Stanford University, USA, July 1996.
8. RM French and A Messinger. Genes, phenes and the Baldwin effect: Learning and evolution in a simulated population. In R Brooks and P Maes, editors, *Artificial Life IV*, pages 277–282. MIT Press, Cambridge, MA, 1994.
9. SJ Gould. *The panda's thumb*. W.W. Norton & Co., 1980.
10. F Gruau and D Whitley. Adding learning to the cellular development of neural networks: evolution and the baldwin effect. *Evolutionary Computation*, 3:213–233, 1993.
11. GE Hinton and SJ Nowlan. How learning can guide evolution. *Complex Systems*, 1:495–502, 1987.
12. D Parisi and S Nolfi. The influence of learning on evolution. In RK Belew and M Mitchell, editors, *Adaptive individuals in evolving populations*, pages 419–428. Addison-Wesley, 1996.
13. L Spector and S Luke. Cultural transmission of information in genetic programming. In JR Koza, D Goldberg, D Fogel, and RL Riolo, editors, *Genetic Programming 1996: Proceedings of the First Annual Conference*, pages 209–214, Stanford University, USA, July 1996.

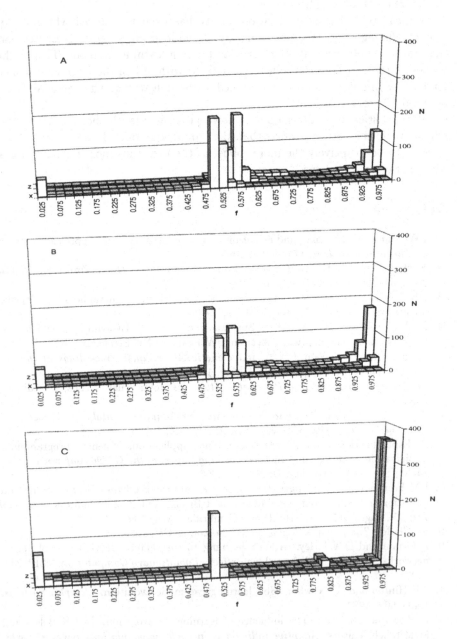

Figure1. Evolution of the *fit* (or fitness after learning, where applicable) for the Darwinian (top), Lamarckian (middle) and RGNL (bottom) methods. Averaged histograms for initial, middle and final stages of the run.

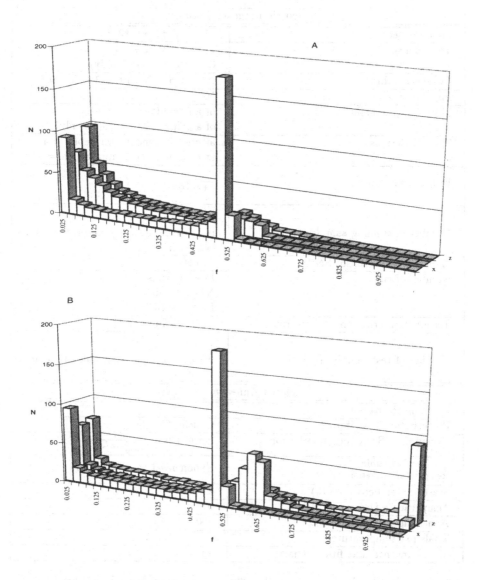

Figure2. Evolution of the *fab* (fitness at birth) for Darwinian (top) and Lamarckian (bottom) learning. Averaged histograms for initial, middle and final stages of the run.

Table6. GP and SA settings

Genetic Program Settings	
Function set	+ − * / +1 −1 *2 /2
Terminal set §	1 X0...X3 Y1 Y2 C0...C6 C7...C255 (NGNL only)
Constant Table	0.1 0.5 2 10 -1 3 0.7
Population size	500
Mutation probability	of a node: 0.01 of a gain: 0, 0.01 (RGNL only)
Size restrictions	at creation: maximum depth = 4 at crossover: maximum depth = 6
Fitness function †	$\frac{1}{1+MSE}$ $0 \le f \le 1$
Number of training samples (e_1)	70 the first 20 are not considered for fitness calculation.
Signal to Noise Ratio (SNR)	30 dB
Number of runs	LC1: 50 runs NLC: 24 runs LC1 $\longrightarrow$ LC2: 51 runs
Termination criterion for each run	node evaluations ¶
Number of test samples (e_2)	10100 the first 100 are not considered for fitness calculation.
Simulated Annealing Settings	
Learning Probability	1
Perturbation Distribution	Cauchy $C(0,1)$
Acceptance/Rejection Distribution	Fermi-Dirac : $\frac{1}{\exp\frac{-\Delta I}{T}+1}$
Cooling Schedule (temperature variation law)	Exponential : $T = \alpha^n \cdot T_0$
Starting Temperature (T_0)	2
Temperature Decay (α)	0.99
Annealing Iterations (n_{max})	400
Trials per temperature	1
Maximum invariant fitness trials	20

§XN: system input delayed by N samples; YN: system output delayed by N samples.

†Entries 7 to 255 in the constant table for NGNL are chosen at random uniformly within the interval [-1,1].

‡The MSE or mean squared error is the average of the squared differences between the expected and the obtained values of the output.

¶The node evaluations measure is similar to clock time, with the advantage that it can be used in different computers.

Sub-machine-code GP:
New Results and Extensions

Riccardo Poli

School of Computer Science
The University of Birmingham, Edgbaston
Birmingham, B15 2TT, UK
R.Poli@cs.bham.ac.uk
Phone: +44-121-414-3739

Abstract. Sub-machine-code GP (SMCGP) is a technique to speed up genetic programming (GP) and to extend its scope based on the idea of exploiting the internal parallelism of sequential CPUs. In previous work [20] we have shown examples of applications of this technique to the evolution of parallel programs and to the parallel evaluation of 32 or 64 fitness cases per program execution in Boolean classification problems. After recalling the basic features of SMCGP, in this paper we first apply this technique to the problem of evolving parallel binary multipliers. Then we describe how SMCGP can be extended to process multiple fitness cases per program execution in continuous symbolic regression problems where inputs and outputs are real-valued numbers, reporting experimental results on a quartic polynomial approximation task.

1 Introduction

Genetic Programming (GP) [8, 9, 2] is usually quite demanding from the computation load and memory use point of view. So, over the years a number of ideas on how to improve GP performance have been proposed in the literature.

For example, Singleton [22] proposed a GP implementation in C++ which was several times faster than equivalent Lisp implementations. Handley [6] proposed storing a population of trees as a single directed acyclic graph obtaining considerable savings of memory and computation. Nordin proposed evolving programs in machine code form [13, 16, 14, 15], a technique which is claimed to be at least one order of magnitude faster than GP system based on higher-level languages. Other researchers (see for example [4]) have proposed to compile at runtime standard GP trees into machine code before evaluation. Speed up strategies based on intelligently reducing the number of fitness cases have been proposed [5, 24, 11]. Finally, some research has been devoted to parallel and distributed implementations of GP (see for example [1, 23, 7]).

Some of these techniques are now used in many GP implementations. This and the increased power of modern workstations make it possible run 50 generations of a typical GP benchmark problem with a population of 500 individuals

R. Poli et al. (Eds.): EuroGP'99, LNCS 1598, pp. 65–82, 1999.
© Springer-Verlag Berlin Heidelberg 1999

in perhaps ten seconds on a normal workstation. Nonetheless, the demand for more and more efficient implementations has not stopped.

Most computer users consider their machines as sequential computers. However, at a lower level of abstraction CPUs are really made up of parallel components. In this sense CPUs can be seen as Single Instruction Multiple Data (SIMD) processors. *Sub-machine-code GP* (SMCGP) is a method to exploit this form of parallelism to improve the efficiency and the range of applications of genetic programming [20]. SMCGP extends the scope of GP to the evolution of *parallel programs running on sequential computers*. These programs are faster since, thanks to the parallelism of the CPU, they perform multiple calculations in parallel during a single program evaluation. SMCGP is more efficient since, in some domains, it allows the evaluation of multiple fitness cases per program execution. In [20] we showed that on Boolean classification problems nearly 2 orders of magnitude speedups can be achieved. In this paper we apply SMCGP to the problem of evolving parallel binary multipliers and extend SMCGP to process multiple fitness cases per program execution in continuous symbolic regression problems where inputs and outputs are real-valued numbers.

The paper is organised as follows. In Section 2 we describe the basic principles behind SMCGP and we provide examples on how the technique can be used to evaluate multiple fitness cases per program execution in Boolean classification problems and to evolve parallel programs which exploit the CPU's internal parallelism. In Section 3 we describe a new application of SMCGP to the evolution of parallel 2-bit multipliers. In Section 4, we describe how sub-machine-code GP can be extended to allow the parallel evaluation of multiple fitness cases in continuous symbolic regression problems. In the same section we report the results of the application of this SMCGP extension to a quartic polynomial approximation task. We discuss the advantages and disadvantage of SMCGP and draw some conclusions in Section 5.

2   Sub-machine-code GP

In a CPU some instructions are performed in parallel and independently for all the bits in the operands. For example, if the operands are two words containing the integers 193 (binary 00000000000000000000000011000001, assuming a 32-bit CPU) and 252 (binary 00000000000000000000000011111100), a bitwise AND operation on a modern CPU will produce a word containing the integer 192 (binary 00000000000000000000000011000000) in a single clock tick. The CPU will perform the operation by concurrently activating 32 different AND gates within as many slices of the arithmetic logic unit. So, logically in this operation the CPU can be seen as a SIMD processor made up of 32 1-bit processors. In other instructions the CPU's 1-bit processors can be imagined to interact through communication channels; in shift operation, for example, where each processor sends data to one of its neighbours. Some operations in the CPU are executed simultaneously by all 1-bit processors. Those requiring interaction between the 1-bit processors may require multiple clock ticks. Nonetheless, as far as the user is concerned the CPU's 1-bit processors run in parallel, since the results of the operation of all processors become available at the same time.

All this powerful parallelism inside our CPUs has been ignored by most of the GP community so far, perhaps because many of us are not used to think in term of bits, nibbles, carries, registers, etc. The most notable exception to this is the work of Peter Nordin [13, 16, 14, 15] which exploits the CPU is its entirety in some problems (for example, in [13] complete Swedish words were coded into 32 bit integers which were processed in parallel for classification purposes).

Sub-machine-code GP exploits the CPU's internal parallelism to obtain faster and more expressive forms of GP. This is obtained as follows:

- The function set includes operations which exploit the parallelism of the CPU, e.g. bitwise Boolean operations, shift operations, etc.
- The terminal set includes integer input variables and constants. These are interpreted as bit vectors where each bit represents the input to a different 1-bit processor. For example, the integer constant 192 (binary 000000000000 00000000000011000000) is seen as a 1 by the 1-bit processors acting on bits 7 and 8. It is seen as a 0 by all other 1-bit processors.
- The integer result produced by the evaluation of a program is interpreted as a bit vector. Each bit of this vector represents the result of a different 1-bit processor.

Since most programming languages include operations which use directly the corresponding machine code operations, it is possible to exploit the parallel nature of the CPU in most languages. This means that any GP system can potentially be used to do sub-machine code GP.

An ideal application for SMCGP is to evaluate multiple fitness cases in parallel. Boolean induction problems lend themselves naturally to this use of sub-machine-code GP, leading to 1.5 to 1.8 orders of magnitude speedups (for 32 and 64 bit machines, respectively). We explored this idea in detail in [20]. In the following subsection we recall the main points.

2.1   Simultaneous Evaluation of Multiple Boolean Fitness Cases

In Boolean classification problems sub-machine-code GP can be used to evaluate multiple fitness cases in parallel. The approach is as follows: a) bitwise Boolean functions are used, b) before each program execution the input variables need to initialised so as to pass a *different fitness case* to each of the different 1-bit processors of the CPU, c) the output integers produced by a program are converted into binary form and each of their bits is interpreted as the output for a different fitness case.

For example, let us assume that we want to evolve a program implementing the XOR function. The truth table of this function is:

x1 x2	x1 XOR x2
0 0	0
1 0	1
0 1	1
1 1	0

Let us further assume that we are using a function set including bitwise AND, OR, and NOT, a terminal set {x1,x2}, and a fitness function which measures the number of bits in the rightmost column of the truth table correctly classified by each program. Then we can evaluate the fitness of a program in one program execution by loading the values 5 (binary 0101) into x1 and 3 (binary 0011) into x2 and then executing the program. The values assigned to the terminals are integers obtained by converting into decimal the corresponding bit columns of the truth table. The value returned by the program represents the program's attempt to fit the rightmost bit column in the truth table. So, by measuring the Hamming distance between the two, we obtain a program's fitness. For example, if we run the program (AND (NOT x1) (OR x1 x2)), it first performs the bitwise negation of x1, obtaining 10 (binary 1010), then it computes the bitwise disjunction of x1 and x2, obtaining 7 (binary 0111). Finally the two results are conjoined obtaining 3 (binary 0010). If we compare (bitwise) this number with the desired output, 6, representing the binary number in the rightmost column in the truth table (0110), the comparison indicates that the program (AND (NOT x1) (OR x1 x2)) has a fitness of 3. This is obtained with only one execution of the program.

In general using SMCGP all the fitness cases associated to the problem of inducing a Boolean function of n arguments can be evaluated with a *single program execution* for $n \leq 5$ on 32 bit machines, and $n \leq 6$ on 64 bit machines. For bigger values of n the 2^n fitness cases can be evaluated in blocks of 32 or 64 [20, appendix]. Since this can be done with almost any programming language, this technique can lead to 1.5 to 1.8 orders of magnitude speedups.

Because of the overheads associated to the packing of the bits to be assigned to the input variables and the unpacking of the result the speedup factors achieved in practice are to be expected to be slightly lower than 32 or 64. However, these overheads can be very small. Indeed in [20] we reported speedups of 31 times for a 32-bit machine. More recently running a C SMCGP implementation on a 64-bit 400MHz machine we have measured an average evaluation time per fitness case of $1.37\mu s$, corresponding to 1.3 primitives per CPU cycle!

2.2 Evolution of Parallel Programs for the CPU

The CPU 1-bit processors must always execute the same program. Nonetheless it is still possible for them to perform different computations. This can be achieved by passing constants with different bits set to different processors.

For example, let us consider a 2-bit CPU which is computing a bitwise AND between a variable **x** and the constant 2 (binary 10), and suppose that **x** is either 0 (binary 00) or 3 (binary 11). In these conditions, the first 1-bit processor will perform (AND x 1) and will therefore return a copy the first bit in **x**, i.e. it will compute the identity function. The second 1-bit processor will instead compute (AND x 0) which is always false, so it will return the constant 0 whatever the value of the second bit in x.

This idea can be exploited to evolve parallel programs for the CPU using SMCGP. To do so it is sufficient to: a) use bitwise operations in the function set, b) use a range of constants in the terminal set which can excite differently different 1-bit processors in the CPU, c) use variables in the terminal set whose bits are either *all* 0 or *all* 1, d) unpack the output. Note that this approach is the exact dual of the one used in the parallel evaluation of fitness cases described in the previous subsection. Here we use different bit configurations for the constants and identical bit configurations for the variables (i.e. variables can only take the binary values 000....0 or 111....1). There we did the opposite.

In [20] we applied sub-machine-code GP to the problems of evolving parallel programs implementing 1-bit and 2-bit adders with and without carry. We also used SMCGP to evolve parallel character recognition programs. In the next section we will demonstrate the idea on another problem: the evolution of parallel 2-bit multipliers.

3   Evolution of Parallel 2-bit Multipliers

A 2-bit multiplier has four inputs: x1 and x2 which represent the least significant bit and the most significant bit of the first operand, respectively, and x3 and x4 which represent the second operand. The multiplier has four outputs, r1, r2, r3 and r4, which represent the result of the multiplication. The truth table for a 2-bit multiplier is the following:

x1	x2	x3	x4	r1	r2	r3	r4
0	0	0	0	0	0	0	0
1	0	0	0	0	0	0	0
0	1	0	0	0	0	0	0
1	1	0	0	0	0	0	0
0	0	1	0	0	0	0	0
1	0	1	0	1	0	0	0
0	1	1	0	0	1	0	0
1	1	1	0	1	1	0	0
0	0	0	1	0	0	0	0
1	0	0	1	0	1	0	0
0	1	0	1	0	0	1	0
1	1	0	1	0	1	1	0
0	0	1	1	0	0	0	0
1	0	1	1	1	1	0	0
0	1	1	1	0	1	1	0
1	1	1	1	1	0	0	1

By exploiting the parallelism in the CPU it is possible to compute r1, r2, r3 and r4 simultaneously. This can be done by slicing the output of a *single* program into its component bits and interpreting the first four of them as r1, r2, r3 and r4. Of course to do this it is necessary to include in the program appropriate constants which can excite differently different parallel components of the CPU.

Solving the multiplier problem by hand would already be difficult if one could use four separate program trees to compute r1, r2, r3 and r4. However, designing a parallel program to do that would be really challenging. Fortunately, this can easily be done by evolution using sub-machine-code GP.

To do that we used the function set {AND, OR, NOT, XOR}, where all functions were implemented using bitwise operations on integers. This problem has four outputs and so requires using four 1-bit processors within the CPU. The terminal set was {x1, x2, x3, x4, R}, where x1 and x2 represent the first operand, and x3 and x4 represent the second operand. The terminal R is a random constant generator which creates integer constants in the set {0,1,...,15}. These constants allow GP to modify selectively the behaviour of different parts of the program for different 1-bit processors. The variables x1, x2, x3 and x4 took the values 0 (binary 0000) and 15 (binary 1111) depending on whether the corresponding bits of the 2-bit multiplier truth table were 0 or 1. This was done to provide the same inputs to the first four 1-bit processors of the CPU. The fitness function was the sum (over all the 16 possible combinations of inputs) of the normalised weighted sum (over all the 4 outputs) of the absolute difference between the actual output and the desired output, i.e.

$$f = \sum_{fc=1}^{16} \sum_{i=1}^{4} \frac{2^{(i-1)}}{15} \cdot |yi - ri|$$

where y1, y2, y3 and y4 are the first four bits of the integer produced by the evaluation of a program and r1, r2, r3 and r4 are the desired outputs (for fitness case fc). To promote parsimonious solutions this fitness was decreased by 0.001 times the number of nodes in a program. Except for the fitness function, no change of our standard-GP system was necessary to run sub-machine-code GP.

In our runs we used a population of 1000 individuals, 500 generations, standard subtree crossover (with uniform probability of selection of the crossover points) with crossover probability 0.9, point mutation [18, 19] with a probability of 0.03 per node, and tournament selection with tournament size 7. The random initialisation of the population was performed so as to obtain a uniform distribution of program sizes between 1 and 40 nodes. Runs were not stopped when a solution was found, allowing GP to discover additional, more parsimonious solutions.

We performed 50 independent runs with these parameters. Of these, 32 were successful. The computational effort to obtain a solution with 99% probability in repeated runs was 2,088,000 fitness evaluations. The average generation at which the first solutions were found was 275. The average structural complexity of the first solutions found was 83.7 nodes. However, by generation 500 the average size of the solutions was 36.0, with structural complexities ranging between 21 and 55 nodes.

For example, in one run a solution was found by GP at generation 298. The solution included 105 nodes. By allowing the run to continue, by generation 477 GP had simplified this solutions down to 32 nodes. The simplified solution is shown in Figure 1. As far as the bit-1 processor of the CPU (the one which com-

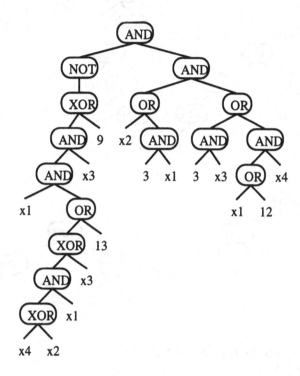

Fig. 1. A program evolved using sub-machine-code GP to solve the 2-bit multiplier problem.

putes r1) is concerned this program is equivalent to the one shown if Figure 2(a). This version of the program has been obtained by replacing all the constants in Figure 1 with bit 1 in the corresponding binary representation (e.g. 13 (binary 1101) is replaced with 1, 12 (binary 1100) with 0), and simplifying the resulting program tree. The programs "seen" by the other three 1-bit processors, shown in Figures 2(b)–(d), have been obtained in a similar fashion substituting constants with their 2nd, 3rd and 4th bits, respectively.

The two smallest solutions found by SMCGP were

```
(AND (OR x4 3) (XOR (AND (OR x2 1) (XOR 4 (AND (OR 2 x1) x3)))
                    (AND x4 (AND x1 2))))
```

and

```
(AND (XOR (AND (OR 1 x2) (XOR 4 (AND x3 (OR x1 2)))))
          (AND (AND 2 x1) x4)) (OR 3 x4))
```

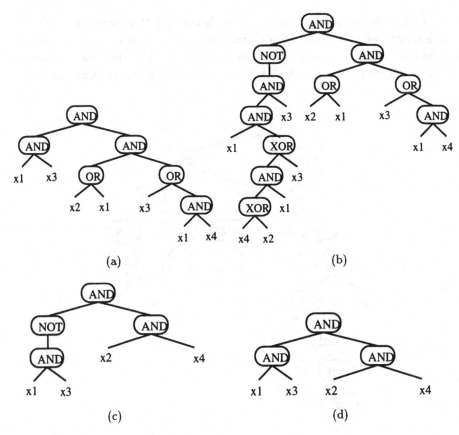

Fig. 2. Programs seen by different 1-bit processors in the CPU when executing the program in Figure 1.

These include 21 nodes, but only 10 gates each, which compares favourably with results reported in recent evolvable hardware literature [12, 3].

4   Evaluation of multiple fitness cases in continuous symbolic regression problems

In Section 2 we have seen how SMCGP can be used to evaluate multiple fitness cases in parallel in Boolean classification problems, by feeding each fitness case into a different 1-bit processor of the CPU. This is possible because in such problems the input variables can only take two values, either 0 or 1, and each operation in the function set does not require more than one 1-bit processor to be performed. In continuous symbolic regression problems, where the input variables and the program output can take a wide range of values, this is certainly not the case. If, for example, we wanted to evolve a function that fits the data points (-1.0,1.0), (-0.9,0.81), ...(1.0,1.0), obtained by sampling the polynomial $y = x^2$, using a function set $\{*,+,/,-\}$, we would normally use floating point operators and floating point representations for the terminals (e.g. for the variable x and some random constants). Since such operations and representation require the use of all slices of the CPU, it seems quite difficult to use a form of SMCGP based on a floating point representation to speed up the evaluation of programs in continuous symbolic regression problems. However, this can easily be done using a different representation for reals, the fixed point representation, which allows SMCGP to parallelise the evaluation of fitness cases in continuous domains too, although to a more limited extent than in discrete domains and with some compromises.

4.1 SMCGP with fixed point representations

Fixed point representations are widely used in digital signal processing and have been used in the GA literature to represent reals within binary chromosomes (see for example [21]). The basic idea is to discretise the range in which the variables are allowed to vary and then to represent each possible discrete value with an integer, by properly offsetting, scaling and truncating/rounding such a value. For example, if a variable x is allowed to vary in the range [1,10], one could discretise such a range with a resolution 0.1 transforming it into the set $\{1.0,1.1,1.2...,10.0\}$. Then it would be possible to represent each discrete value x_d with the integer $(x_d - 1)/0.1$. Normally the resolution is selected on the basis of the number of bits one wants to allocate to represent the integers resulting from the discretisation/rescaling process. For example, if one wants to represent the range $[a, b]$ using l-bit integers, the resolution will be set to $(b - a)/(2^l - 1)$.

In GAs fixed point numbers are manipulated directly at the binary level by crossover and mutation. So the only real-valued operation to be performed on fixed point numbers is their decoding from binary form. However, in signal processing a whole range of other operations like multiplication, addition, thresholding, etc. are normally performed. All these operations are basically defined as operations on integers, except that the results are properly scaled so as to represent the correct fixed point value. For example, if one wants to implement a multiplication between fixed point numbers in the range [0,1], stored as 8-bit integers, one can simply compute the product between the two integers and then divide the result by 256. (In reality things are slightly more complicated since overflows need to be properly handled.)

Standard GP could use fixed point numbers and operations on them. However, this would not lead to any performance advantage, since modern CPUs are able to perform floating point operations at virtually the same speed as integer ones. (This could still be a useful thing to do if one wanted to evolve digital signal processing algorithms to be later run on a different architecture.) On the contrary, a significant performance advantage can be achieved if one uses SMCGP in conjunction with a fixed point representation. This is because in most applications a relatively low resolution is sufficient. Therefore, it is possible to partition the 1-bit processors in the CPU into several groups, where each group processes a separate fitness case, in essentially the same way as in Section 2. For example, if one used 8-bit fixed point numbers on a 64 bit CPU, 8 fitness cases could be processed in parallel during each program execution.

Naturally there are limitations on what can be done with SMCGP in continuous domains. In fact, while there are operations, like addition on 32/64 bit integers, that are (nearly) decomposable into many smaller-scale (say 8-bit) operations performed in parallel, other operations, like multiplication, are not. The former kind of operations can be used freely in SMCGP with fixed point numbers, since their effect is nearly equivalent to performing several fixed-point operations sequentially and then assembling the result into a 32/64-bit word. The latter kind of operations cannot instead be used. This does not mean that one cannot use multiplications in SMCGP, but simply that multiplications will have to be performed sequentially. If other operations in the function set can be parallelised, the net effect of having some sequential operations can be relatively small.[1]

Other limitations are indirectly due to the features of fixed point representations. Fixed point representation with a small number of bits may be very efficient in terms of memory and effort to perform calculations. This is even more true in SMCGP with fixed point representations, since the number of fixed point calculations per node evaluation is inversely proportional to the number of bits used to represent fixed point numbers (when multiple calculations can be performed in parallel). However, using a small number of bits leads to inaccuracies of various kinds (limited resolution, underflow) which can only be reduced by increasing the number of bits used. So, in SMCGP with fixed point representations, there is a tradeoff between accuracy and speed.

We have explored these ideas in a set of experiments with a continuous symbolic regression problem: the problem of inducing a function that best fits a set of datapoints obtained by sampling a quartic polynomial. The experimental setup is described in the next section.

4.2   Quartic Polynomial Problem

The problem used in our experiments consisted in evolving a function from a set of (x_i, y_i) pairs obtained by sampling the polynomial $y(x) = x^4 + x^3 + x^2 + x + 6$ for $x \in [-1, 1]$. In the experiments we used 48 equally spaced fitness cases with $x_i = -1 + \frac{2}{47} \cdot i$ and $y_i = y(x_i)$ for $i = 0, ..., 47$.

We used a resolution of 8 bits to represent fixed point numbers and fixed point operations. This allowed us to divide the 64-bit CPU's 1-bit processors into 8 groups of 8, and, therefore, to process 8 fitness cases per program evaluation. The range in which the fixed point numbers were allowed to vary was

---

[1] Some CPUs have instructions which allow the execution of multiple integer operations on multiple data in parallel which eliminate the problem just mentioned. For example, the MMX technology of Intel CPUs allows one to partition 64-bit registers into multiple blocks of 8, 16 or 32 bits and to perform integer arithmetics on all the blocks in parallel and independently. MMX instructions can also take care of the overflows by using saturating arithmetics. However, since these features are architecture dependent, we have decided to ignore them in this work.

[0,10] which gives a resolution of approximately 0.04. The terminal set was {X, C1, C2, C3, C4, C5, C6, C7, C8}, where X is the fixed point representation of the input variable x (to which an appropriate constant was added to transform it into a positive number), and Ci's are fixed point constants represented by the following binary numbers: 00000001 (C1), 00000010 (C2), 00000100 (C3), 00001000 (C4), 00010000 (C5), 00100000 (C6), 01000000 (C7) and 10000000 (C8). The function set was {MUL, DIV, PLUS, MINUS}, where each operation is implemented to *approximate* multiplication, division, addition and subtraction of fixed point numbers, respectively. A C implementation of these operations for a 64 bit CPU is shown in Figure 3 (see [20, appendix] for a larger fragment of SMCGP code).

In the code the function run() is a simple recursive interpreter capable of handling terminals and four algebraic operations. The interpreter executes the program stored in prefix notation as a vector of bytes in the global variable program. The interpreter returns an unsigned long integer which is used for fitness evaluation. The terminal set is stored in an array of 64-bit integers (t[]). The first element of the array represents the variable X, which is set appropriately by the fitness function before calling run(). The other elements of t[] represent the fixed point constants Ci's.

The PLUS and MINUS operations are only approximately correct for two reasons. Firstly, the operations are performed without any overflow/underflow error checking, assuming arguments and results within the range [0,10]. Since the operations are performed as unsigned integer operations, this means that if one subtracts a positive number (say 5) from a slightly smaller positive number (e.g. 4.9), the result may be a large positive number (9.9) instead of the expected small negative number (-0.1). Also, if one adds two relatively large numbers, like 6 and 5, the result may be a small number (1), instead of the expected large one (11). Secondly, the operations are approximate because they are implemented so that 8 of them can be performed in parallel by different groups 1-bit processors. This requires ignoring (zeroing) the possible carries coming from other groups of 1-bit processors.

As indicated in the previous section multiplication and division operations cannot be performed in parallel by all the groups of 1-bit processors. For this reason, MUL and DIV are implemented as several fixed-point operations performed sequentially.

In the quartic polynomial problem, the interpreter (the function run()) is invoked by the fitness evaluator 6 times, i.e. once to evaluate fitness cases $i = 0, ...7$, once for fitness cases $i = 8, ..., 15$, etc. Before run() is invoked, the 8-bit fixed point representations of the x coordinates of 8 fitness cases are properly packed into a 64 bit integer which is stored in t[0]. Also, the program counter (program) is properly reset. The value returned by run() is decoded/unpacked into 8 8-bit fixed point numbers. The absolute differences between them and the y coordinates of the corresponding fitness cases are accumulated over the 6 calls of the interpreter and then divided by the number of fitness cases (48) to obtain the average program error. This is then subtracted from 10 (the maximum possible error) to obtain a fitness value.

In our runs we used the following parameters: population size 1,000 and 100,000 individuals, 50 generations, steady state GA, 50% of the individuals underwent subtree crossover, 50% underwent point mutation (with a mutation probability of 0.05 per node) [18, 19], tournament selection with tournament size 20, "grow" initialisation method with maximum initial depth of 3. We performed 50 independent runs with each population size. Runs were not stopped until generation 50.

During the runs whenever a new best-of-run individual was discovered, this was tested on a larger set of cases to measure its generalisation power. This was assessed by measuring the average error on 256 equally spaced values for the variable x in the interval [-1,1]. Since we use 8-bit fixed point numbers, this is the biggest set of different fitness cases that can possibly be generated.

4.3   Results

The results of the experiments with populations of 1,000 individuals were mixed. Runs were extremely fast lasting 4.1 seconds on average, but the quality of the resulting programs was relatively poor. Indeed, the mean absolute error over the 48 fitness cases of the best of run programs (averaged over 50 runs) was above 0.3. The behaviour of an average quality best-of-run program is shown in Figure 4. Nonetheless, in repeated runs it was possible to discover fairly good programs. The behaviour of best programs evolved using this population size is shown in Figure 5.

The results of the experiments with populations of 100,000 individuals instead were quite promising. The mean absolute error over the 48 fitness cases of the best of run programs (averaged over 50 runs) was below 0.1, and so was the generalisation (mean absolute error over the 256 generalisation cases) of the best of run programs. Figure 6 shows the behaviour of the program with the highest fitness discovered in the 50 runs, while Figure 7 shows the behaviour of the worst best-of-run program discovered. Considering the low resolution used to represent fixed point numbers (8 bit) this accuracy is remarkable.

The high generalisation achieved in these runs is probably a result of the relatively high number of fitness cases used, and of the implicit parsimony pressure created by point mutation with a fixed mutation rate per node [17]. Indeed the average size of the best-of-run programs was 36.6 nodes.

The 50 runs with a population size of 100,000 took a total of 27,006 seconds of CPU time to complete on a 400MHz DEC Alpha workstation. So, on average each run lasted 540 seconds, which corresponds to 10.8 seconds per generation and 108μs per individual. Since each individual was executed 6 times to assess its fitness, the average program execution time was 18 μs. During each program execution 8 fitness cases are evaluated, so the average fitness-case evaluation time is 2.25 μs.

Despite the presence of operations which could not be parallelised, SMCGP showed impressive performance in these experiments. The total number of nodes

```
unsigned long t[9] = {    /* ---------- TERMINAL SET ------------- */
     0x0000000000000000, /* 8 different values of X are stored here */
     0x0101010101010101, /* C1 is stored here (8 times) */
     0x0202020202020202, /* C2 */
     0x0404040404040404, /* C3 */
     0x0808080808080808, /* C4 */
     0x1010101010101010, /* C5 */
     0x2020202020202020, /* C6 */
     0x4040404040404040, /* C7 */
     0x8080808080808080};/* C8 */

#define mul(bits,mask) \          /* do a*b */
    c1 = (arg1 >> bits) & 0xff; \ /* unpack fixed point number a */
    c2 = (arg2 >> bits) & 0xff; \ /* unpack fixed point number b */
    c1 *= c2; \                   /* multiply corresp. integers */
    c1 >>= SCALE; \               /* normalise */
    c1 &= 0xff; \                 /* mask overflow bits */
    arg1 = (arg1 & mask) | ( c1 << bits); /* replace a with a*b */

#define div(bits,mask) \          /* do a/b */
    c1 = (arg1 >> bits) & 0xff; \ /* unpack fixed point number a */
    c2 = (arg2 >> bits) & 0xff; \ /* unpack fixed point number b */
    c1 <<= SCALE; \               /* prescale before division */
    c1 = c2 ? c1 / c2 : c1; \     /* divide corresp. integers */
    c1 &= 0xff; \                 /* mask overflow bits */
    arg1 = (arg1 & mask) | ( c1 << bits); /* replace a with a/b */

unsigned long run() { /* Interpreter */
  register unsigned long arg1, arg2, c1, c2;
  switch ( *program++ ) {    /* ---------- FUNCTION SET ------------- */
    case PLUS : return( ( run() + run() ) & 0xfefefefefefefefe );
    case MINUS : return( ( run() - run() ) & 0x7f7f7f7f7f7f7f7f );
    case MUL : arg1 = run(); arg2 = run();
    mul(56,0x00ffffffffffffff);
    mul(48,0xff00ffffffffffff);
    mul(40,0xffff00ffffffffff);
    mul(32,0xffffff00ffffffff);
    mul(24,0xffffffff00ffffff);
    mul(16,0xffffffffff00ffff);
    mul( 8,0xffffffffffff00ff);
    mul( 0,0xffffffffffffff00);
    return( arg1 );
    case DIV : arg1 = run(); arg2 = run();
    div(56,0x00ffffffffffffff);
    div(48,0xff00ffffffffffff);
    div(40,0xffff00ffffffffff);
    div(32,0xffffff00ffffffff);
    div(24,0xffffffff00ffffff);
    div(16,0xffffffffff00ffff);
    div( 8,0xffffffffffff00ff);
    div( 0,0xffffffffffffff00);
    return( arg1 );
    default: return( t[*(program-1)] );
  }
}
```

Fig. 3. 64-bit C implementation of the primitive set used in the quartic polynomial problem.

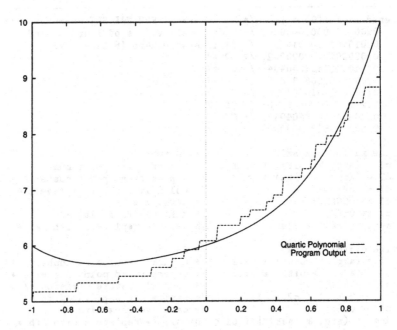

Fig. 4. Behaviour of an average quality best-of-run program evolved using sub-machine-code GP with populations of size 1,000 to solve the quartic polynomial problem.

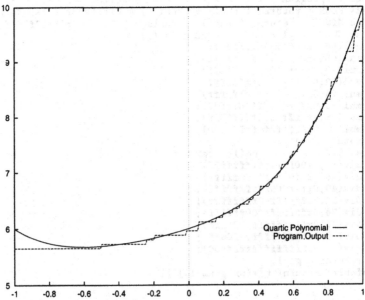

Fig. 5. Behaviour of the best best-of-run program evolved using sub-machine-code GP with populations of size 1,000 to solve the quartic polynomial problem.

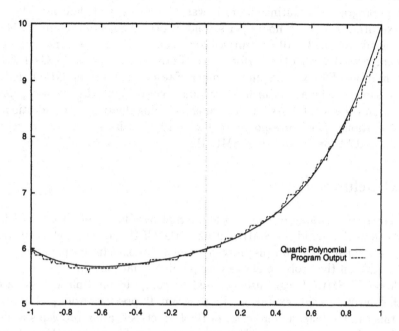

Fig. 6. Behaviour of the best program evolved using sub-machine-code GP with populations of size 100,000 to solve the quartic polynomial problem.

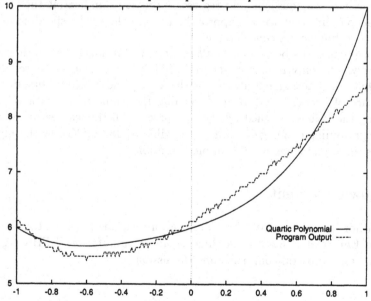

Fig. 7. Behaviour of the worst program evolved using sub-machine-code GP with populations of size 100,000 to solve the quartic polynomial problem.

evaluated during the runs was 52,404,275,616. From this we can infer that the average program size during the runs was 34.9 nodes, and that our GP system was executing 1.96×10^6 nodes per second, which, thanks to the use of SMCGP, corresponds to 15.53×10^6 primitives per second. This is a remarkable result, if one compares this with the performance of other very efficient C/C++ GP implementations. For example, in a number of tests [10, 11] using GP-QUICK [22] on the same machine on which we ran our experiments, the average primitive evaluation time was 0.8 μs for programs including floating point additions and multiplications. This corresponds to 1.25×10^6 primitives per second, which is more than 12 times slower than SMCGP.

5   Conclusions

SMCGP is a technique to exploit the internal parallelism of CPUs in GP. SMCGP can work around the SIMD nature of the CPU and evolve efficient parallel programs which solve multiple problems simultaneously. In this paper we demonstrated this on the problem of evolving parallel binary multipliers.

However, SMCGP can also be used to compute multiple fitness cases in parallel during a single execution of a program. In previous work [20] we showed how this can be done, at zero cost, in Boolean classification problems achieving speedups of up to 64 times on 64-bit processors. In this paper we have described how SMCGP can also be extended to process multiple fitness cases per program execution in continuous symbolic regression problems, indicating the limitations and tradeoffs inherent to this approach. Despite these, the speedups obtained with this technique are considerable.

All this can easily be obtained *without* any substantial change to the basic GP machinery. The only requirements to do SMCGP are a primitive set designed to exploit the internal parallelism of the CPU, and a fitness function which takes care of properly initialising/encoding the input variables and properly decoding the values returned by the interpreter. All this can easily be done in any programming language, making it possible to do SMCGP, with only minor changes, in any pre-existing GP implementation.

Acknowledgements

The author wishes to thank Nic McPhee and the members of the Evolutionary and Emergent Behaviour Intelligence and Computation (EEBIC) group at Birmingham for useful comments and discussion.

References

1. David Andre and John R. Koza. Parallel genetic programming: A scalable implementation using the transputer network architecture. In Peter J. Angeline and K. E. Kinnear, Jr., editors, *Advances in Genetic Programming 2*, chapter 16, pages 317–338. MIT Press, Cambridge, MA, USA, 1996.

2. Wolfgang Banzhaf, Peter Nordin, Robert E. Keller, and Frank D. Francone. *Genetic Programming – An Introduction; On the Automatic Evolution of Computer Programs and its Applications*. Morgan Kaufmann, dpunkt.verlag, January 1998.

3. T.C. Fogarty, J.F. Miller, and P. Thomson. Evolving digital logic circuits on Xilinx 6000 family FPGAs. In P.K. Chawdhry, R. Roy, and R.K.Pant, editors, *Soft Computing in Engineering Design and Manufacturing*, pages 299–305. Springer-Verlag, London, 1998.

4. Alex Fukunaga, Andre Stechert, and Darren Mutz. A genome compiler for high performance genetic programming. In John R. Koza, Wolfgang Banzhaf, Kumar Chellapilla, Kalyanmoy Deb, Marco Dorigo, David B. Fogel, Max H. Garzon, David E. Goldberg, Hitoshi Iba, and Rick Riolo, editors, *Genetic Programming 1998: Proceedings of the Third Annual Conference*, pages 86–94, University of Wisconsin, Madison, Wisconsin, USA, 22-25 July 1998. Morgan Kaufmann.

5. Chris Gathercole and Peter Ross. Tackling the boolean even N parity problem with genetic programming and limited-error fitness. In John R. Koza, Kalyanmoy Deb, Marco Dorigo, David B. Fogel, Max Garzon, Hitoshi Iba, and Rick L. Riolo, editors, *Genetic Programming 1997: Proceedings of the Second Annual Conference*, pages 119–127, Stanford University, CA, USA, 13-16 July 1997. Morgan Kaufmann.

6. S. Handley. On the use of a directed acyclic graph to represent a population of computer programs. In *Proceedings of the 1994 IEEE World Congress on Computational Intelligence*, pages 154–159, Orlando, Florida, USA, 27-29 June 1994. IEEE Press.

7. Hugues Juille and Jordan B. Pollack. Massively parallel genetic programming. In Peter J. Angeline and K. E. Kinnear, Jr., editors, *Advances in Genetic Programming 2*, chapter 17, pages 339–358. MIT Press, Cambridge, MA, USA, 1996.

8. John R. Koza. *Genetic Programming: On the Programming of Computers by Means of Natural Selection*. MIT Press, 1992.

9. John R. Koza. *Genetic Programming II: Automatic Discovery of Reusable Programs*. MIT Pres, Cambridge, Massachusetts, 1994.

10. W. B. Langdon and R. Poli. An analysis of the MAX problem in genetic programming. In John R. Koza, Kalyanmoy Deb, Marco Dorigo, David B. Fogel, Max Garzon, Hitoshi Iba, and Rick L. Riolo, editors, *Genetic Programming 1997: Proceedings of the Second Annual Conference*, pages 222–230, Stanford University, CA, USA, 13-16 July 1997. Morgan Kaufmann.

11. William B. Langdon. *Data Structures and Genetic Programming: Genetic Programming + Data Structures = Automatic Programming!* Kluwer, Boston, 24 April 1998.

12. J. F. Miller, P. Thomson, and T. Fogarty. Designing electronic circuits using evolutionary algorithms. arithmetic circuits: A case study. In D. Quagliarella, J. Periaux, C. Poloni, and G. Winter, editors, *Genetic Algorithms and Evolution Stategies in Engineering and Computer Science: Recent Advancements and Industrial Applications*. Wiley, 1997.

13. Peter Nordin. A compiling genetic programming system that directly manipulates the machine code. In Kenneth E. Kinnear, Jr., editor, *Advances in Genetic Programming*, chapter 14, pages 311–331. MIT Press, 1994.

14. Peter Nordin. *Evolutionary Program Induction of Binary Machine Code and its Applications*. PhD thesis, der Universitat Dortmund am Fachereich Informatik, 1997.
15. Peter Nordin. AIMGP: A formal description. In John R. Koza, editor, *Late Breaking Papers at the Genetic Programming 1998 Conference*, University of Wisconsin, Madison, Wisconsin, USA, 22-25 July 1998. Stanford University Bookstore.
16. Peter Nordin and Wolfgang Banzhaf. Evolving turing-complete programs for a register machine with self-modifying code. In L. Eshelman, editor, *Genetic Algorithms: Proceedings of the Sixth International Conference (ICGA95)*, pages 318–325, Pittsburgh, PA, USA, 15-19 July 1995. Morgan Kaufmann.
17. Riccardo Poli and W. B. Langdon. Genetic programming with one-point crossover and point mutation. Technical Report CSRP-97-13, University of Birmingham, School of Computer Science, Birmingham, B15 2TT, UK, 15 April 1997.
18. Riccardo Poli and W. B. Langdon. A new schema theory for genetic programming with one-point crossover and point mutation. In John R. Koza, Kalyanmoy Deb, Marco Dorigo, David B. Fogel, Max Garzon, Hitoshi Iba, and Rick L. Riolo, editors, *Genetic Programming 1997: Proceedings of the Second Annual Conference*, pages 278–285, Stanford University, CA, USA, 13-16 July 1997. Morgan Kaufmann.
19. Riccardo Poli and William B. Langdon. Schema theory for genetic programming with one-point crossover and point mutation. *Evolutionary Computation*, 6(3):231–252, 1998.
20. Riccardo Poli and William B Langdon. Sub-machine-code genetic programming. Technical Report CSRP-98-18, University of Birmingham, School of Computer Science, August 1998.
21. Nicol N. Schraudolph and R. K. Belew. Dynamic parameter encoding for genetic algorithms. *Machine Learning*, 9(1):9–21, 1992.
22. Andy Singleton. Genetic programming with C++. *BYTE*, pages 171–176, February 1994.
23. Kilian Stoffel and Lee Spector. High-performance, parallel, stack-based genetic programming. In John R. Koza, David E. Goldberg, David B. Fogel, and Rick L. Riolo, editors, *Genetic Programming 1996: Proceedings of the First Annual Conference*, pages 224–229, Stanford University, CA, USA, 28–31 July 1996. MIT Press.
24. Astro Teller and David Andre. Automatically choosing the number of fitness cases: The rational allocation of trials. In John R. Koza, Kalyanmoy Deb, Marco Dorigo, David B. Fogel, Max Garzon, Hitoshi Iba, and Rick L. Riolo, editors, *Genetic Programming 1997: Proceedings of the Second Annual Conference*, pages 321–328, Stanford University, CA, USA, 13-16 July 1997. Morgan Kaufmann.

Evolving Multi-line Compilable C Programs

Michael O'Neill and Conor Ryan

Dept. Of Computer Science And Information Systems
University of Limerick, Ireland
{Michael.ONeill,Conor.Ryan}@ul.ie

Abstract. We describe a Genetic Algorithm called *Grammatical Evolution* (GE) that can evolve complete programs in an arbitrary language using a variable length linear genome. The binary genome determines which production rules in a Backus Naur Form grammar definition are used in a genotype to phenotype mapping process to a program. Expressions and programs of arbitrary complexity may be evolved using this system.

Since first describing this system, GE has been applied to other problem domains, and during this time GE has undergone some evolution. This paper serves to report these changes, and also describes how we evolved multi-line C-code to solve a version of the Santa Fe Ant Trail. The results obtained are then compared to results produced by Genetic Programming, and it is found that GE outperforms GP on this problem.

1 Introduction

Grammatical Evolution (GE) is a Genetic Algorithm based system which evolves programs in any language using a Backus Naur Form (BNF) definition. Unlike Genetic Programming (GP), GE does not perform the evolutionary process on the actual programs but rather on simple binary strings. Various attempts at using BNF grammars with Genetic Programming have been made [13] [14] [4] [9] [3] with some success. We describe here a different approach to using BNF grammars for automatic programming, using a biologically inspired genotype to phenotype mapping process, where the genes are used to select production rules in a BNF grammar definition.

The original paper on GE was concerned with tackling a Symbolic Regression problem [10], and has subsequently been applied to a Symbolic Integration problem [12], and to solving Trigonometric Identities [11]. During this time it has been found that using a Steady State replacement strategy has enhanced the performance of GE.

We begin by presenting GE in its evolved state, before describing how GE was successfully applied to evolving multi-line C-code when finding a solution to the Santa Fe Trail. The results obtained whilst tackling the Santa Fe Trail are then compared to results which were produced by a GP system, and it is shown that GE outperforms GP on this problem.

R. Poli et al. (Eds.): EuroGP'99, LNCS 1598, pp. 83–92, 1999.
© Springer-Verlag Berlin Heidelberg 1999

2   Grammatical Evolution

Our system codes a set of pseudo random numbers, which are used to decide which production rule to use when a non terminal of the BNF definition has one or more possible outcomes. A description of BNF definitions is given in Appendix A, along with the definition used for the Santa Fe Trail problem described later. A chromosome in GE consists of a variable number of 8 bit binary genes, each of which encodes an integer value.

Consider an example of a BNF production rule, #5 from the BNF definition in Appendix A:

```
(5) <op> :: =    left()         (A)
             | right()          (B)
             | move()           (C)
```

In this case, the non-terminal *op* can produce one of three different results, our system takes the next available number (gene integer value) from the chromosome to decide which production to use and gets the modulus of it by the number of rules to choose from, in this case three. Each time a decision has to be made, another pseudo random number is read from the chromosome, and in this way, the system traverses the chromosome.

The genetic code of biological organisms is usually contained in a special molecule called DNA. For simplicity, consider DNA to be a string of building blocks called nucleotides, of which there are four, named A, T, G, and C, for Adenine, Tyrosine, Guanine, and Cytosine respectively. Groups of three nucleotides, called a codon, are used to specify the building blocks of proteins. These protein building blocks are known as Amino Acids, and the sequence of these Amino Acids in the protein is determined by the sequence of codons on the DNA. The sequence of Amino Acids is very important as it plays a large part in determining the final three dimensional structure of the protein, which in turn has a role to play in determining its functional properties. Proteins have a major role to play in biological organisms, such as, in metabolism, and as structural components of the body to name but a few. Figure 2 outlines the mapping process described here from Genetic Code to Phenotype in biological organisms.

In a fashion similar to natural biology the genes in GE are expressed as proteins, in our case terminals, Figure 2. These terminals can act either independently or in conjunction with other terminals [1], the physical results depending on the other terminals that are present immediately before and after a genes expression. During the genotype to phenotype mapping process it is possible for individuals to run out of genes, and in this case we wrap the individual, and reuse the genes. This is quite an unusual approach in EAs, as it is entirely possible for certain genes to be used two or more times. This technique of wrapping the individual draws inspiration from the gene overlapping phenomenon which has been observed in many organisms in nature [1]. In GE, each time the gene is expressed it will always generate the same integer, but depending on the other rules present, may have a different effect, that is, it may select a different production rule. What is crucial, however, is that each time a particular individual is mapped from its genotype to its phenotype, the same output is generated. This is because the same choices are made each time.

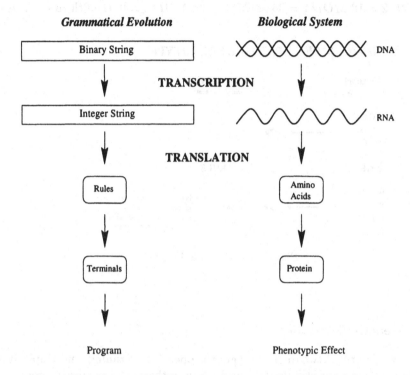

Fig. 1. The Grammatical Evolution System and a Biological System

An interesting point to note in the mapping process is that given an 8 bit binary number, each gene can represent 256 distinct integer values. However, many of these integer values can represent the same production rule, taking production rule 5 above as an example, if the current gene value was 6, then $6 \ MOD \ 3 = 0$ would select rule (A) $left()$. The same rule would be chosen if the gene value was 3, 9, 12, etc. A similar phenomenon can be observed in the genetic code of biological organisms, referred to as *Degenerate Genetic Code* [1].

There are 4^3, i.e. 64, unique combinations of nucleotides in a codon, 61 of these coding for a specific Amino Acid, the other three are special codons which delimit the end of a gene on the DNA. On average, there are three codons for every amino acid, that is more than one codon can represent the same Amino Acid. This code degeneracy has interesting implications when it comes to mutation effects. A mutation at the third codon position can often produce what is called a *silent mutation*, meaning that the Amino Acid specified will be the same as the one before the mutation event. With respect to GE this means that subtle changes in the search space (genotype) may have no effect on the solution space (phenotype). In Figure 2 we see how in the genetic code of biological organisms, the nucleotide at position three of the codon is independent of the amino acid produced (Valine) for this example. Similarly with GE it can be seen in the given example that a single bit mutation has no effect on the rule used in this case i.e. $2 \, MOD \, 2 = 18 \, MOD \, 2 = 34 \, MOD \, 2 = 66 \, MOD \, 2 = 0$, the 0th rule $< line >$.

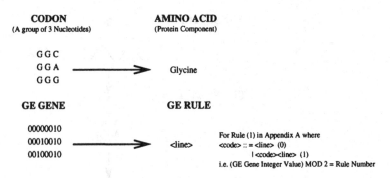

Fig. 2. Genetic Code Degeneracy

2.1   Genetic Operators

In [10] we described two distinctive genetic operators, Pruning, and Duplication. While Duplication is still used in our system in the hope that it can produce either more of a particular protein, or provide a means by which new functionality can be obtained independently of the current functionality, the Pruning operator is used to a lesser extent. As use is made of the wrapping feature, described earlier, Pruning would remove any of the introns at the end of a chromosome, thus removing potentially useful genetic material. For this reason, and the fact that introns have been shown to be beneficial in other Genetic Algorithms [8], Pruning is now applied with a much smaller probability typically 0.01.

2.2   Steady State

[12] described how a Steady State replacement mechanism was employed with GE as opposed to the previous Generational mechanism with great success. GE's performance over three problem domains was reported for both replacement mechanisms, and the results are summarised in Table 1. We believe that the Steady State replacement mechanism is better able to preserve those solutions with higher fitness, propagating them from generation to generation, whereas previously it was common for these high performing individuals to be lost to a combination of destructive crossover and mutation events, and misfortune during selection.

Table 1. Comparison of successful runs for 3 problems.

Problem Domain	% Successful	
	Steady State	Generational
Symbolic Regression	95	2
Trigonometric Identities	87	4
Symbolic Integration	87	22

3   The Problem Space

In order to show GE can produce multi-line functions the Santa Fe Ant Trail problem is tackled. The Santa Fe Ant Trail has been used as a benchmark problem in the area of Genetic Programming, and can be considered a deceptive planning problem with many local and global optima [7]. The objective is to find a computer program to control an artificial ant so that it can find all 89 pieces of food located on a non-continuous trail within a specified number of time steps. The code evolved is then executed in a loop until the number of time steps allowed has elapsed. The ant can only turn left, right, move forward one square, and may also look ahead one square in the direction it's facing to determine if that square contains a piece of food. The actions left, right, and move each take one time step to execute.

While there are many possible fitness cases to the Santa Fe Trail only one case was taken for the purposes of this experiment. The ant started in the top left hand corner of the grid facing the first piece of food on the trail. The grammar used in this problem is as given in Appendix A, note that we do not use an equivalent for $PROGN$. A summary of the problem can be seen in Table 2.

Table 2. Grammatical Evolution Tableau for the Santa Fe Trail

Objective :	Find a computer program to control an artificial ant so that it can find all 89 pieces of food located on the Santa Fe Trail.
Terminal Operators:	left(), right(), move(), food_ahead()
Fitness cases	One fitness case
Raw Fitness	Number of pieces of food before the ant times out with 615 operations.
Standardised Fitness	Total number of pieces of food less the raw fitness.
Hits	Same as raw fitness.
Wrapper	Standard productions to generate C functions
Parameters	$M = 500$, $G = 51$

4   Results

The problem was firstly tackled with GE using a population size of 500 individuals running for a maximum of 50 generations. The only fitness measure used was the number of pieces of food the ant picked up over 600 time steps. GE was successful at finding a solution to this case of the Santa Fe Trail, and indeed was capable of producing multi-line code.

It was then decided to run this problem using GP to compare it with the performance of GE. The GP system, as described in [2], uses the solutions length as a measure of fitness, as well as the number of pieces of food picked up.

During the initial runs using GP, and also with GE, it was noted that a lot of solutions picked up all but one of the pieces of food within the 600 time steps. Given a few more time steps these solutions would achieve perfect fitness in terms of the number of pieces of food picked up, so it was decided to allow the number of time steps to be increased to 615. 100 runs using each system were carried out, allowing the GP system to use the solution length as a measure of fitness, and allowing GE no such measure. A cumulative frequency measure for both of these runs can be seen in Figure 3. As can be seen performance of the two systems is on a par with each other, with GP slightly outperforming GE in the initial half of the run.

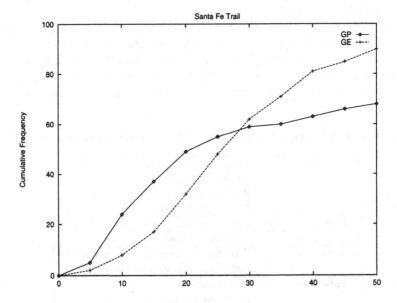

Fig. 3. GE in comparison to GP, with GP using solution length in fitness.

In order to see how the GP system would perform without the solution length as a measure of fitness, we ran 100 more runs of the GP system removing the solution length fitness measure. We felt that using solution length as a measure of fitness required a prior knowledge of the solutions length and therefore gave an unfair advantage to the GP system as GE did not use such a measure. Figure 4 shows a comparison of the cumulative frequency measure for these results with the results produced by GE. As can be seen from the figure the performance of the GP system was compromised and as a result GE outperformed GP.

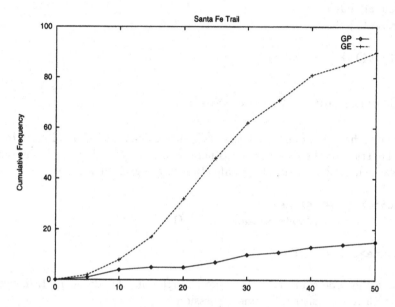

Fig. 4. GE in comparison to GP without solution length in fitness measure.

Sample solutions produced by both systems are given below.

GP example solution:

```
(PROG2 (PROG2 (IF-FOOD-AHEAD LEFT RIGHT) RIGHT) (PROG2
(IF-FOOD-AHEAD FORWARD RIGHT) (PROG2 FORWARD RIGHT)))
```

GE example solution:

```
if(food_ahead())
    { move(); }
else
    { move(); }
if(food_ahead())
    { left(); }
else
    { left(); }
if(food_ahead())
    { left(); }
```

```
else
   { right(); }
if(food_ahead())
   { right(); }
else
   { right(); }
if(food_ahead())
   { move(); }
else
   { left();}
```

5   Conclusions & Future Work

The results have demonstrated that GE successfully found a solution to the Santa Fe Trail for the case examined here, and so can produce multi-line code. This was achieved by a simple modification to the grammar namely,

```
(1) <code> :: =   <line>              (A)
                  |<code><line>       (B)

(2) <line> :: =   <expr>
```

where the code could become either a single line of code or multi-line code, where each line consisted of some expression.

On comparison with GP, it was found that GE outperformed GP for this problem. Performance of GP appeared to suffer as a result of solution bloat while GE did not. Instead of producing a single expression here, GE produces more legible multi-line code. Further analysis of solution length and its effects on the performance of GE is required.

It is now our intention to compare the performance of GE to other learning methods over some problem domains. The original purpose of GE was to produce multi-line, compilable code, in arbitrary programming languages and to this end GE has been successful to date.

A   Backus Naur Form

Backus Naur Form (BNF) is a notation for expressing the grammar of a language in the form of production rules. BNF grammars consist of terminals, which are items that can appear in the language, and non-terminals, which can be expanded into one or more terminals and non-terminals. A grammar can be represented by the tuple, $\{N, T, P, S\}$, where N is the set of non-terminals, T the set of terminals, P a set of production rules that maps the elements of N to T, and S is a start symbol which is a member of N. For example, below is the BNF used for this problem, where

$$N = \{code, line, expr, if - statement, op, if - true, if - false\}$$

$$T = \{left(), right(), move(), food\_ahead(), else, if, \{, \}, (,)\}$$

$$S =< code >$$

And P can be represented as:

(1) <code> :: = <line>   (A)
              |<code><line>   (B)

(2) <line> :: = <expr>

(3) <expr> :: = <if-statement>   (A)
              |<op>   (B)

(4) <if-statement> :: = if(food_ahead())<if-true><if-false>

(5) <op> :: =   left()   (A)
              | right()   (B)
              | move()   (C)

(6) <if-true>:={<expr>}

(7) <if-false>:=else{<expr>}

Unlike a Koza-style approach, there is no distinction made at this stage between what he describes as functions (operators in this sense) and terminals, however, this distinction is more of an implementation detail than a design issue. In GE the BNF definition is used to describe the output language produced by the system, that is, the compilable code produced will consist of elements of the terminal set T. As the BNF is a plug-in component of the system it means that, GE can produce code in any language that can be specified in the form of a BNF definition, giving the system a unique flexibility.

References

1. Elseth Gerald D., Baumgardner Kandy D. Principles of Modern Genetics. *West Publishing Company*
2. Fraser Adam, Weinbrenner Thomas. 1997. The Genetic Programming Kernel Version 0.5.2.
3. Freeman, J. J. A Linear Representation for GP using Context Free Grammars. In *Proceeding of Genetic Programming 1998*, pages 72-77. MIT Press.
4. Horner, H *A C++ class library for GP*. Vienna University of Economics.

5. Keller, R. E. & Banzhaf, W. 1996. Genetic Programming using Genotype-Phenotype Mapping from Linear Genomes into Linear Phenotypes. In *Genetic Programming 1996*, pages 116-122. MIT Press.
6. Koza, J. 1992. *Genetic Programming*. MIT Press.
7. Langdon, W. & Poli, R. Why Ant's Are Hard. In *Proceedings of Genetic Programming 1998*, pages 193-201 .
8. Levenick, James. R. Inserting Introns Improves Genetic Algorithm Success Rate: Taking a Cue from Biology. In *Proceedings of the Fourth International Conference on Genetic Algorithms 1991*, pages 123-127.
9. Paterson, N & Livesey, M. 1997. Evolving caching algorithms in C by GP. In *Genetic Programming 1997*, pages 262-267. MIT Press.
10. Ryan C., Collins J.J., O'Neill M. 1998. Grammatical Evolution: Evolving Programs for an Arbitrary Language. *Lecture Notes in Computer Science 1391, Proceedings of the First European Workshop on Genetic Programming*, pages 83-95. Springer-Verlag.
11. Ryan C., O'Neill M., Collins J.J. 1998. Grammatical Evolution: Solving Trigonometric Identities. In *Proceedings of Mendel '98: 4th International Conference on Genetic Algorithms, Optimization Problems, Fuzzy Logic, Neural Networks and Rough Sets*, pages 111-119.
12. Ryan C., O'Neill M. Grammatical Evolution: A Steady State Approach. In *Late Breaking Papers, Genetic Programming 1998*, pages 180-185.
13. Whigham, P. 1995. Grammatically-based Genetic Programming. In *Proceedings of the Workshop on Genetic Programming: From Theory to Real-World Applications*, pages 3-41. Morgan Kaufmann Pub.
14. Wong, M. and Leung, K. 1995. Applying logic grammars to induce subfunctions in genetic programming. In *Proceedings of the 1995 IEEE conference on Evolutionary Computation*, pages 737-740. USA:IEEE Press.

Genetic Programming as a Darwinian Invention Machine

John R. Koza
Section on Medical Informatics
Department of Medicine
Stanford, California 94305
koza@stanford.edu
http://www.smi.stanford.edu/people/koza/

Forrest H Bennett III
Genetic Programming Inc.
Los Altos, California 94023
forrest@evolute.com

Oscar Stiffelman
Computer Science Department
Stanford University
Stanford, California 94305
ozzie@cs.stanford.edu

ABSTRACT

Genetic programming is known to be capable of creating designs that satisfy prespecified high-level design requirements for analog electrical circuits and other complex structures. However, in the real world, it is often important that a design satisfy various non-technical requirements. One such requirement is that a design not possess the key characteristics of any previously known design. This paper shows that genetic programming can be used to generate novel solutions to a design problem so that genetic programming may be potentially used as an invention machine. This paper turns the clock back to the period just before the time (1917) when George Campbell of American Telephone and Telegraph invented and patented the design for an electrical circuit that is now known as the ladder filter. Genetic programming is used to reinvent the Campbell filter. The paper then turns the clock back to the period just before the time (1928) when Wilhelm Cauer invented and patented the elliptic filter. Genetic programming is then used to reinvent a technically equivalent filter that avoids the key characteristics of then-preexisting Campbell filter. Genetic programming can be used as an invention machine by employing a two-part fitness measure that incorporates both the degree to which an individual in the population satisfies the given technical requirements and the degree to which the individual does not possess the key characteristics of preexisting technology.

1 Introduction

Design is a major activity of practicing engineers. The design process entails the creation (synthesis) of a complex structure to satisfy user-defined requirements. Since the design process typically entails tradeoffs between competing considerations, the

R. Poli et al. (Eds.): EuroGP'99, LNCS 1598, pp. 93–108, 1999.

end product of the process is usually a satisfactory and compliant design as opposed to a perfect design. Design is usually viewed as requiring creativity and human intelligence. Consequently, the field of design is a source of challenging problems for automated techniques of machine intelligence. In particular, design problems can test whether an automated technique can produce results that are competitive with human-produced results.

Design requirements in the real world often include important non-technical considerations. For example, a practicing engineer will often be asked to create a design that does not possess the key characteristics of any previously known solution to the problem at hand. Novelty may be desirable for several reasons. Novelty enables a company to obtain patent protection for its product, to avoid infringement ("engineer around") a preexisting patent (often a competitor's patent), or simply to differentiate its product in the marketplace on the basis of its unique technology. Regardless of the motivation, avoidance of "prior art" (the term used in the patent law to describe a field's preexisting technology, whether patented or not) is often important in the real world. Avoidance of prior art is accomplished by creating a design that does not "read on" (i.e., possess the key characteristics of) the prior art. In order to be patentable, a designed entity must be both "useful" and "new."

Genetic programming is an automatic technique that is capable of creating designs. Genetic programming approaches a design problem in terms of "what needs to be done" as opposed to "how to do it". For example, genetic programming has demonstrated that it is capable of synthesizing the design of a wide variety of analog electrical circuits and other complex structures (Koza, Bennett, Andre, and Keane 1999). Genetic programming often creates novel designs because it employs a probabilistic process to evolve designs and because it is not encumbered by the preconceptions that often channel human thinking down familiar paths. Although genetic programming has demonstrated an ability to automatically create useful entities (i.e., those that satisfy technical design requirements) and although it sometimes creates novel designs, none of the previously reported efforts have addressed the issue of actively avoiding the creation of an entity that reads on prior art.

This paper demonstrates that genetic programming can be modified to automatically create designs that satisfactorily solve a given problem while simultaneously avoiding prior art. This is accomplished using an illustrative problem involving the synthesis of the design of a lowpass filter circuit. Section 2 reviews how genetic programming has been successfully applied to the problem of synthesizing the topology and sizing of electrical circuits. Section 3 states the illustrative problem. Section 4 presents the preparatory steps necessary for applying our method of synthesizing novel designs to the illustrative problem. Section 5 presents the results.

2   Automatic Creation of Circuit Topology and Sizing

Genetic programming (Koza 1992; Koza and Rice 1992) is an extension of the genetic algorithm (Holland 1975) that automatically creates computer programs to solve problems. Genetic programming is also capable of evolving multi-part programs (Koza 1994a, 1994b) consisting of a main program and one or more reusable, parametrized, hierarchically-callable automatically defined functions (subroutines). Architecture-altering operations (Koza 1995) enable genetic programming to automatically determine the number of subroutines, the number of arguments that each possesses, and the nature of the hierarchical references, if any, among the subroutines. Architecture-altering operations also enable genetic programming to automatically determine whether and how to use internal memory, iterations, and recursion in evolved programs (Koza, Bennett, Andre, and Keane 1999). Additional information on current research in genetic programming can be found in Banzhaf, Nordin, Keller, and Francone 1998; Langdon 1998; Kinnear 1994; Angeline and Kinnear 1996; Spector, Langdon, O'Reilly, and Angeline 1999; Koza, Goldberg, Fogel, and Riolo 1996; Koza, Deb, Dorigo, Fogel, Garzon, Iba, and Riolo 1997; Koza, Banzhaf, Chellapilla, Deb, Dorigo, Fogel, Garzon, Goldberg, Iba, and Riolo 1998; and Banzhaf, Poli, Schoenauer, and Fogarty 1998.

The design process for electrical circuits begins with a high-level description of the circuit's desired behavior and characteristics and entails creation of the topology and sizing of a satisfactory circuit. The *topology* of a circuit includes specifying the gross number of components in the circuit, the type of each component (e.g., a capacitor), and a *netlist* specifying where each lead of each component is to be connected. *Sizing* involves specifying the values (typically numerical) of each of the circuit's components. Until recently, there has previously been no general technique for automatically creating the topology and sizing for an analog electrical circuit from a high-level statement of the circuit's desired behavior and characteristics. In describing the design process for analog circuits, Aaserud and Nielsen (1995) observed,

> Analog designers are few and far between. In contrast to digital design, most of the analog circuits are still handcrafted by the experts or so-called 'zahs' of analog design. The design process is characterized by a combination of experience and intuition and requires a thorough knowledge of the process characteristics and the detailed specifications of the actual product.

> Analog circuit design is known to be a knowledge-intensive, multiphase, iterative task, which usually stretches over a significant period of time and is performed by designers with a large portfolio of skills. It is therefore considered by many to be a form of art rather than a science.

Genetic programming is capable of automatically creating (synthesizing) the design of both the circuit's topology and sizing from a high-level statement of a circuit's desired behavior and characteristics (Koza, Bennett, Andre, Keane, and Dunlap 1997; Koza, Bennett, Andre, and Keane 1999). The evolved circuits include lowpass, highpass, bandpass, bandstop, crossover, multiple bandpass, and asymmetric bandpass filters, amplifiers, computational circuits, a temperature-sensing circuit, a voltage reference circuit, frequency-measuring circuits, robot controller, and source identification circuits. The evolved circuits include 11 previously patented circuits.

Genetic programming can be applied to circuit design by establishing a mapping between the rooted, point-labeled trees (i.e., acyclic graphs) with ordered branches used in genetic programming and the specialized type of cyclic graphs germane to electrical circuits. The creative work of Kitano (1990) on using developmental genetic algorithms to evolve neural networks, the innovative work of Gruau (1992, 1994a, 1994b) on using genetic programming to evolve neural networks (cellular encoding), and the principles of developmental biology suggest a method for mapping trees into electrical circuits by means of a growth process that begins with a simple embryo. For electrical circuits, the embryo includes one or more modifiable wires. The embryo is embedded into a test fixture consisting of certain fixed wires that provide connectivity to the circuit's external inputs and outputs and certain fixed (hard-wired) components (such as a source resistor and a load resistor). Until the modifiable wires are modified by the developmental process, the initial circuit (consisting of an embryo embedded into a text fixture) produces only trivial output. An electrical circuit is developed by progressively applying the functions in a circuit-constructing program tree (in the population being bred by genetic programming) to the modifiable wires of the original embryo and, during the developmental process, to newly created modifiable components and modifiable wires.

The functions in the circuit-constructing program trees are divided into five categories: (1) topology-modifying functions that alter the circuit topology, (2) component-creating functions that insert components into the circuit, (3) development-controlling functions that control the development process by which the embryo and its successors is changed into a fully developed circuit, (4) arithmetic-performing functions that appear in subtrees as argument(s) to the component-creating functions and specify the numerical value of the component, and (5) automatically defined functions that enable certain substructures of the circuit to be reused (with parameterization).

An electrical circuit is created by executing the functions in a circuit-constructing program tree. The functions are progressively applied (in a breadth-first order) in a developmental process to the embryo and its successors until all of the functions in the program tree are executed. That is, the functions in the circuit-constructing program tree progressively side-effect the embryo and its successors until a fully developed circuit eventually emerges. Each branch of the program tree is created in accordance with a constrained syntactic structure. Each branch is composed of topology-modifying functions, component-creating functions, development-controlling functions, and terminals. Component-creating functions typically have one arithmetic-performing subtree, while topology-modifying functions, and development-controlling functions do not. Component-creating functions and topology-modifying functions are internal points of their branches and possess one or more arguments (construction-continuing subtrees) that continue the developmental process.

Each non-numeric function is associated with a modifiable wire or modifiable component in the developing circuit and modifies it in a specified manner. The construction-continuing subtree (if any) of a function points to a successor function or terminal in the circuit-constructing program tree. The arithmetic-performing subtree of a component-creating functions consists of a composition of arithmetic functions (addition and subtraction) and random constants (in the range -1.0 to +1.0). The arithmetic-performing subtree specifies the numerical value of a component by returning a floating-point value that is interpreted on a logarithmic scale in a range of 10 orders of magnitude (using a unit of measure appropriate for the particular type of component).

3   Statement of the Illustrative Problem

The method will be illustrated on the problem of creating the topology and sizing for a lowpass filter circuit. A simple *filter* is a one-input, one-output circuit that receives a signal and passes the frequency components of the incoming signal that lie in a specified range (called the *passband*) while suppressing the frequency components that lie in all other frequency ranges (the *stopband*) (Williams and Taylor 1995). The desired lowpass filter is to pass all frequencies below 1,000 Hertz (Hz) and suppress all frequencies above 2,000 Hz. The circuit is driven by an incoming AC voltage source with a 2 volt amplitude. The circuit is tested by a test fixture containing a 1,000 Ohm (Ω) source (internal) resistor RSOURCE and a 1,000 Ω load resistor RLOAD. There should be a sharp drop-off from 1 Volt to 0 Volts in the transitional ("don't care") region between 1,000 Hz and 2,000 Hz.

A passband voltage of exactly 1 volt and a stopband voltage of exactly 0 volts is regarded as ideal. A voltage in the passband of between 970 millivolts and 1 volt (i.e., a passband ripple of 30 millivolts or less) and a voltage in the stopband of between 0 volts and 1 millivolts (i.e., a stopband ripple of 1 millivolts or less) are regarded as acceptable. A voltage lower than 970 millivolts in the passband or above 1 millivolts in the stopband is regarded as unacceptable.

The above design goals can be satisifed by many different circuits. Figure 1 shows a 100%-compliant circuit that was evolved using genetic programming (described in chapter 25 of Koza, Bennett, Andre, and Keane 1999). This evolved circuit consists of seven inductors (L5, L10, L22, L28, L31, L25, and L13) arranged horizontally across the top of the figure "in series" with the incoming signal VSOURCE and the source resistor RSOURCE. It also contains seven capacitors (C12, C24, C30, C3, C33, C27, and C15) that are each shunted to ground.

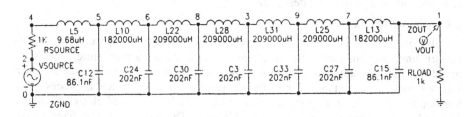

Figure 1 Seven-rung ladder lowpass filter.

This circuit has the recognizable features of the circuit for which George Campbell of American Telephone and Telegraph received U. S. patent 1,227,113 (Campbell 1917). Claim 2 of the patent covered,

> An electric wave filter consisting of a connecting line of negligible attenuation composed of a plurality of sections, each section including a capacity element and an inductance element, one of said elements of each section being in series with the line and the other in shunt across the line, said capacity and inductance elements having precomputed values dependent upon the upper limiting frequency and the lower limiting frequency of a range of frequencies it is desired to transmit without attenuation, the values of said capacity and inductance elements being so proportioned that the structure transmits with practically negligible attenuation sinusoidal currents of all frequencies lying between said two limiting frequencies, while attenuating and approximately extinguishing currents of neighboring frequencies lying outside of said limiting frequencies.

An examination of the evolved circuit of figure 1 shows that it indeed consists of "a plurality of sections." (specifically, seven). In the figure, "Each section include[es] a capacity element and an inductance element." Specifically, the first of the seven sections consists of inductor L5 and capacitor C12; the second section consists of inductor L10 and capacitor C24; and so forth. Moreover, "one of said elements of each section [is] in series with the line and the other in shunt across the line." Inductor L5 of the first section is indeed "in series with the line" and capacitor C12 is indeed "in shunt across the line." This is also true for the circuit's remaining six sections. Moreover, figure 1 here matches figure 7 of Campbell's 1917 patent. In addition, this circuit's 100% compliant frequency domain behavior confirms the fact that the values of the inductors and capacitors are such as to transmit "with practically negligible attenuation sinusoidal currents" of the passband frequencies "while attenuating and approximately extinguishing currents" of the stopband frequencies. Thus, the evolved circuit reads on claim 2 of Campbell's 1917 patent. If this patent had not long since expired, the evolved circuit would infringe on the patent.

4   Preparatory Steps

Before applying genetic programming to a problem of circuit design, seven major preparatory steps are required: (1) identify the initial circuit (test fixture and embryo) of the developmental process, (2) determine the architecture of the circuit-constructing program trees, (3) identify the primitive functions, (4) identify the terminals, (5) create the fitness measure, (6) choose control parameters, and (7) determine the termination criterion and method of result designation.

4.1   Initial Circuit

An electrical circuit is created in a developmental process by executing a circuit-constructing program tree that contains various component-creating, topology-modifying, and development-controlling functions. An initial circuit consisting of an embryo and a test fixture is the starting point of a developmental process that transforms a program tree in the population into a fully developed electrical circuit. The embryo contains at least one modifiable wire. The test fixture is a fixed (hard-wired) substructure composed of nonmodifiable wires and nonmodifiable electrical components. The test fixture provides access to the circuit's external input(s) and permits probing of the circuit's output. An embryo is embedded into the test fixture. All development occurs in the embryo.

Figure 2 shows a one-input, one-output initial circuit consisting of an embryo embedded in a test fixture. The embryo consists of two modifiable wires Z0 and Z1. The test fixture consists of an incoming signal (input to the overall circuit) in the form of voltage source VSOURCE (2 Volt peak alternating-current) between nodes 0 and 1, a source resistor RSOURCE (whose value is 1,000 Ω) between nodes 1 and 2, a nonmodifiable wire ZOUT between nodes 3 and 5, a voltage probe point VOUT (the output of the overall circuit) at node 5, a load resistor RLOAD (whose value is 1,000 Ω) between nodes 5 and 0, and a nonmodifiable wire ZGND between nodes 4 and 0.

4.2   Program Architecture

Since there is one result-producing branch in the program tree for each modifiable wire in the embryo, the architecture of each circuit-constructing program tree has two result-producing branches.

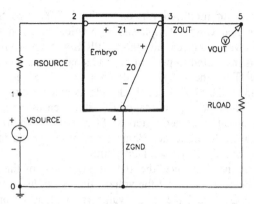

Figure 2 One-input, one-output initial circuit with two modifiable wires. **Function Set**

The function set, $\mathcal{F}_{CCS}$, for each construction-continuing subtree is

$$\mathcal{F}_{CCS} = \{C, L, SERIES, PARALLEL0, FLIP, TVIA0, ..., TVIA7, NOOP\}$$

All functions in this section are described in detail in Koza, Bennett, Andre, and Keane 1999. Briefly, the C and L functions are component-creating functions that insert an inductor or capacitor (respectively) into a developing circuit and that assign a numerical value to the inserted component. The SERIES and PARALLEL0 functions modify the topology of the developing circuit by performing a series or parallel (respectively) division. The FLIP function reverse the polarity of a component. The eight VIA functions provides direct connectivity between two points within the developing circuit via one of eight numbered layers on the imaginary printed circuit board or piece of silicon on which the circuit resides. The NOOP (No operation) function is a development-controlling function.

4.4   Terminal Set

The terminal set, $\mathcal{T}_{CCS}$, for each construction-continuing subtree is

$$\mathcal{T}_{CCS} = \{END, CUT\}.$$

Briefly, the development-controlling END function makes the modifiable wire or modifiable component with which it is associated non-modifiable (thereby ending a particular developmental path). The CUT function causes the highlighted component to be removed from the circuit.

The terminal set, $\mathcal{T}_{aps}$, for each arithmetic-performing subtree consists of

$$\mathcal{T}_{aps} = \{\Re\},$$

where $\Re$ represents floating-point random constants from -1.0 to $+1.0$.

The function set, $\mathcal{F}_{aps}$, for each arithmetic-performing subtree is,

$$\mathcal{F}_{aps} = \{+, -\}.$$

4.5   Fitness Measure

The evaluation of each individual circuit-constructing program tree in the population begins with its execution. The execution progressively applies the functions in the program tree to the embryo of the circuit, thereby creating a fully developed circuit. A netlist is created that identifies each component of the developed circuit, the nodes to which each component is connected, and the value of each component. The netlist becomes the input to our modified version of the 217,000-line SPICE (Simulation Program with Integrated Circuit Emphasis) simulation program (Quarles, Newton, Pederson, and Sangiovanni-Vincentelli 1994). SPICE then determines the behavior of the circuit. SPICE is instructed to perform an AC small signal analysis and report the output voltage VOUT in the frequency domain over five decades of frequencies (between 1 Hz and 100,000 Hz). Each decade isdivided into 20 parts (using a logarithmic scale), so that there are a total of 101 fitness cases (sampled frequencies).

The fitness of a circuit is defined in terms of two factors. The first factor measures the circuit's behavior in the frequency domain while the second factor measures the circuit's similarity to the to-be-avoided ladder filter.

The first factor is the sum, over the 101 fitness cases, of the absolute weighted deviation between the actual value of the voltage that is produced by the given circuit at the probe point VOUT and the target value for voltage (0 or 1 volts) for that frequency. Specifically, this factor is

$$F(t) = \sum_{i=0}^{100} (W(d(f_i), f_i) d(f_i))$$

where f_i is the frequency of fitness case i; $d(x)$ is the absolute value of the difference between the target and observed values at frequency x; and $W(y,x)$ is the weighting for difference y at frequency x.

The factor of the fitness measure pertaining to the circuit's frequency response does not penalize ideal voltage values, slightly penalizes acceptable voltage deviations, and heavily penalizes unacceptable voltage deviations. Specifically, if the output voltage equals the ideal value of 1.0 volt for each of the 61 points in the intended passband between 1 Hz and 1,000 Hz, the deviation is 0.0. If the voltage is between 970 millivolts and 1 volt, the absolute value of the deviation from 1 volt is weighted by a factor of 1.0. If the voltage is less than 970 millivolts, the absolute value of the deviation from 1 volt is weighted by a factor of 10.0. The deviations for each of the 35 points from 2,000 Hz to 100,000 Hz in the intended stopband are similarly weighed (by 1.0 or 10.0) based on the acceptable deviation of 1 millivolt from the ideal voltage of 0 volts. The deviations are deemed to be zero for each of the five "don't care" points between 1,000 and 2,000 Hz. The number of "hits" is defined as the number of fitness cases for which the voltage is acceptable, ideal, or that lie in the "don't care" band.

The factor of the fitness measure pertaining to similarity to the to-be-avoided ladder filter is measured in terms of the largest number of nodes and edges (circuit components) of a subgraph of the given circuit that is isomorphic to a subgraph of a template. The template is a Campbell ladder that is far larger than is needed to solve the problem at hand. As shown in figure 3, the template contains 16 shunt capacitors, 17 series inductors, the circuit's voltage source, and a source resistor.

The score is determined by a graph isomorphism algorithm (Ullman 1976, Lingas 1981) with the cost function here being based on the number of shared nodes and edges (instead of just the number of nodes). Since the graph isomorphism algorithm works with graph adjacency matrices and since circuits often contain parallel compositions of two different components, each pair of parallel components that is encountered is treated as if it were a type of component different from either a single capacitor or single inductor.

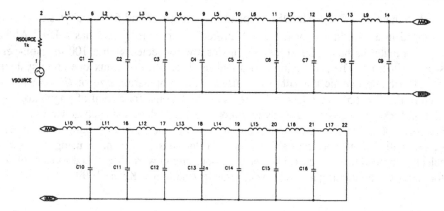

Figure 3 Campbell template.

For reference, the factor of the fitness measure pertaining to the frequency response of the 100%-compliant seven-rung ladder filter of figure 1 is 0.00784 (i.e., near zero) and its isomorphism factor is 25 (very high). The details of the calculation of the isomorphism score are found in Koza, Bennett, Andre, and Keane 1999.

A lower value of each of the above two factors of the fitness measure is better. For circuits not scoring the maximum number (101) of hits, the fitness of a circuit is the product of the two factors. For circuits scoring 101 hits (100%-compliant individuals), fitness is the number of shared nodes and edges divided by 10,000. This arrangement has the feature of almost always assigning a better (lower) fitness to any individual scoring 101 hits than to any individual scoring fewer than 101 hits.

A smaller the overall value of fitness is better. A fitness of zero is unattainable because every circuit has at least one node or edge in common with the template (even if only a single component).

Many of the random initial circuits and many that are created by crossover and mutation in subsequent generations are so pathological that the SPICE simulator cannot simulate them. These circuits receive a high penalty value of fitness (10^8) and become the worst-of-generation programs for each generation. In the run described below, 91% of the circuits in generation 0 cannot be simulated (compared to about 5% in later generations).

4.6   Control Parameters

The population size, M, is 1,950,000. The maximum size of each branch of each circuit-constructing program tree is 300 points (functions and terminals). Other control parameters are those used previously for the lowpass filter problem (Koza, Bennett, Andre, and Keane 1999, appendix D).

4.7   Termination Criterion and Results Designation

Since the goal is to generate a variety of 100%-compliant circuits for examination as to their novelty, the run was not automatically terminated upon evolution of the first 100%-compliant individual. Instead, numerous 100%-compliant circuits were harvested; and the run was manually monitored and manually terminated.

4.8   Implementation on Parallel Computer

This problem was run on a home-built Beowulf-style (Sterling, Salmon, Becker, and Savarese 1999) parallel cluster computer system consisting of 65 processing nodes (each containing a 533-MHz DEC Alpha microprocessor and 64 megabytes of RAM) arranged in a two-dimensional 5×13 toroidal mesh. The system has a DEC Alpha type computer as host. The processing nodes are connected with a 100 megabit-per-second Ethernet. The processing nodes and the host use the Linux operating system. The distributed genetic algorithm was used with a population size of $Q = 30,000$ at each of the $D = 65$ demes (semi-isolated subpopulations) for a total of population, M, of 1,950,000. Generations are asynchronous on the nodes. On each generation, four boatloads of emigrants, each consisting of $B = 2\%$ (the migration rate) of the node's subpopulation (selected probabilistically on the basis of fitness using the same selection procedure as used for the genetic operations) were dispatched to each of the four adjacent processing nodes (Koza, Bennett, Andre, and Keane 1999).

5   Results

A run starts with the random creation of an initial population (generation 0) of circuit-constructing program trees composed of the problem's functions and terminals. The best-of-generation circuit from generation 0 (figure 4a) scores 52 hits (out of 101). The fitness of this best-of-generation circuit from generation 0 is 296.5 because the factor pertaining to this circuit's frequency response is 59.30 and because this circuit's isomorphism factor is 5. The isomorphism factor is 5 because the largest number of nodes and edges of a subgraph of this circuit that is isomorphic to a subgraph of the 17-inductor, 16-capacitor template (figure 3) consists of five nodes and edges.

Figure 4a shows the behavior in the frequency domain of the best circuit of generation 0. As can be seen, the behavior of this circuit bears little resemblance to the desired lowpass filter. The horizontal axis represents the frequency of the incoming signal and ranges over five decades of frequencies between 1 Hz and 100,000 Hz on a logarithmic scale. The vertical axis represents the peak voltage of the output and ranges linearly between 0 to 1 Volts. The circuit delivers a full volt only for frequencies up to about 50 Hz. The circuit suppresses the incoming signal only for a handful of frequencies near 100,000 Hz. There is a very leisurely transition region in between. Circuits with improved fitness are evolved as the run proceeds from generation to generation.

The best-of-generation circuit from generation 16 (figure 5) has three inductors and four capacitors and scores 95 hits. Capacitors C1, C2, C3, and C4 are shunt capacitors and constitute the rungs of a ladder, while inductors L1, L4, and L3 (horizontally across the top of the figure) are the ladder's series inductors.

This circuit constitutes the rediscovery by genetic programming of the well-known ladder topology of the Campbell filter. When this circuit is compared with the template, it is assigned a high (undesirable) isomorphism factor. The overall fitness of this circuit is 32.32 because the factor pertaining to this circuit's frequency response is 2.694 and its isomorphism factor is 12.

Figure 4b shows the behavior in the frequency domain of the best circuit of generation 16. As can be seen, the behavior of this circuit bears some resemblance to the desired lowpass filter. Its transition region is more sharply defined than that of the best circuit of generation 0 (figure 4a).

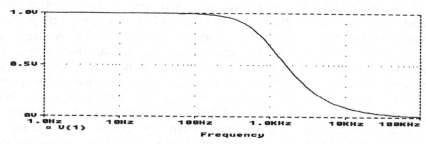

Figure 4a Frequency domain behavior of best circuit from generation 0.

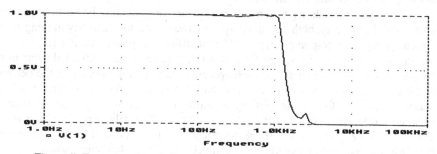

Figure 4b Frequency domain behavior of best circuit from generation 16.

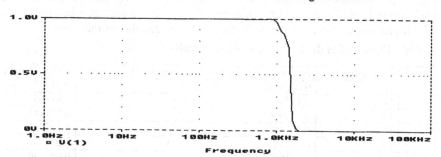

Figure 4c Frequency domain behavior of 100%-compliant circuit with elliptic topology.

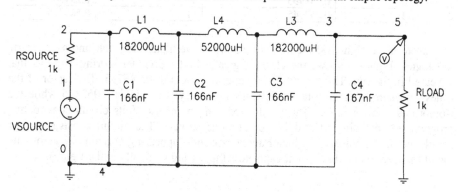

Figure 5 Best circuit of generation 16.

As the run progresses, some circuits score well primarily because of the factor pertaining to the circuit's frequency response while others score well primarily because of the isomorphism factor. For example, the fitness of one pace-setting circuit from generation 18 is 30.585. The factor of the fitness measure pertaining to this circuit's frequency response is 6.117 (not very good) but its isomorphism factor is 5 (reflecting great dissimilarity between this circuit and the 17-inductor, 16-capacitor template of figure 3). On the other hand, the fitness of another pace-setting circuit from generation 18 (in fact, the best-of-generation individual) is 11.556. The factor of the fitness measure pertaining to frequency response is 0.7704 (very good behavior in the frequency domain) but its isomorphism factor is 15 (reflecting great similarity between this circuit and the template).

As the run proceeds from generation to generation, circuits begin to appear that score well because of both the isomorphism factor and the factor pertaining to the circuit's frequency response. Eight different 100%-compliant circuits (i.e., circuits scoring 101 hits) were harvested from this run. Figure 4c shows the behavior in the frequency domain of the first 100%-compliant circuit evolved in this run; the behavior of the other seven circuits is similar. As can be seen in the figure, the circuit delivers nearly a full volt for frequencies up to 1,000 Hz; there is a very sharp drop-off between 1,000 Hz and 2,000 Hz; and the circuit effectively suppresses the output above 2,000 Hz. None of the 100%-compliant circuits harvested from this run have the ladder topology patented by Campbell in 1917. In other words, genetic programming evolved multiple novel solutions in this run to the given problem and each evolved solution avoided the prior art. Table 1 shows the factor pertaining to the circuit's frequency response, the isomorphism factor, and the overall fitness.

Table 1 Fitness of eight 100%-compliant circuits.

	Generation	Frequency response factor	Isomorphism factor	Overall fitness
1	13	0.051039	7	0.357273
2	14	0.117093	7	0.819651
3	14	0.103064	7	0.721448
4	15	0.161101	7	1.127707
5	15	0.044382	13	0.044382
6	15	0.133877	7	0.937139
7	16	0.059993	5	0.299965
8	13	0.062345	11	0.685795

Seven of the eight 100%-compliant circuits have highly irregular and asymmetric topologies. Figure 6 shows the chronologically first individual scoring 101 hits that appeared in the run. This circuit has an overall fitness of 0.685795. The factor of the fitness measure pertaining to the circuit's frequency response is 0.062345 while the isomorphism factor is 11. The result-producing branches of its circuit-constructing program tree contain 181 and 115 points, respectively. The circuit consists of four parallel compositions of an inductor and a capacitor (appearing horizontally across the top of the figure) and three shunt capacitors (appearing vertically in the figure).

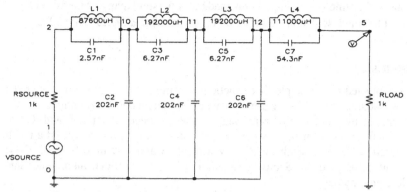

Figure 6 Evolved 100%-compliant circuit with elliptic topology.

Once genetic programming has successfully created one or more novel solutions to the given problem, a design engineer may examine them. Some may have unexpected virtues. The topology of the evolved filter of figure 6 is one form of the elliptic filter that Cauer invented and patented (Cauer 1934, 1935, 1936). The elliptic topology was invented and patented by Cauer in response to a long-standing need in the telephone industry for filters that were less expensive to manufacture. At the time of its invention by Cauer, the elliptic filter was a significant advance (both theoretically and commercially) over the prior art of their time, namely the then-known Campbell filter (and the closely related Butterworth and Chebychev filters). Specifically, for one commercially important set of specifications for the telephone industry, a fifth-order elliptic filter matches the behavior of a 17th-order Butterworth filter or an eighth-order Chebychev filter. The fifth-order elliptic filter has one less component than the eighth-order Chebychev filter. This reduction was very important in the days when filters in telephones were manufactured by individually soldering in expensive discrete components. As Van Valkenburg (1982, page 379) relates in connection with the history of the elliptic filter:

> Cauer first used his new theory in solving a filter problem for the German telephone industry. His new design achieved specifications with one less inductor than had ever been done before. The world first learned of the Cauer method not through scholarly publication but through a patent disclosure, which eventually reached the Bell Laboratories. Legend has it that the entire Mathematics Department of Bell Laboratories spent the next two weeks at the New York Public library studying elliptic functions. Cauer had studied mathematics under Hilbert at Goettingen, and so elliptic functions and their applications were familiar to him.

The elliptic topology invented and patented by Cauer was reinvented by genetic programming in this run as a consequence of the fact that the fitness measure rewarded candidate solutions that were dissimilar to the previously known Campbell filter topology. Cauer received a patent for the elliptic filter because his design satisfied the legal criteria for obtaining a U. S. patent, including the fact that it was "new" and "useful" and

> ... the differences between the subject matter sought to be patented and the prior art are such that the subject matter as a whole would [not] have been

obvious at the time the invention was made to a person having ordinary skill in the art to which said subject matter pertains. (35 *United States Code* 103a).

6   Conclusion

We have established the principle that genetic programming can automatically create designs that satisfactorily solve a problem while simultaneously avoiding prior art. The reinvention by genetic programming of the patented Campbell and Cauer topologies for filters is an instance where genetic programming has produced a result that is competitive with a result created by a creative and inventive human. These evolved results satisfy Arthur Samuel's criterion (1983) for artificial intelligence and machine learning, namely

> The aim [is] ... to get machines to exhibit behavior, which if done by humans, would be assumed to involve the use of intelligence.

References

Aaserud, O. and Nielsen, I. Ring. 1995. Trends in current analog design: A panel debate. *Analog Integrated Circuits and Signal Processing*. 7(1) 5-9.

Andre, David and Koza, John R. 1996. Parallel genetic programming: A scalable implementation using the transputer architecture. In Angeline, P. J. and Kinnear, K. E. Jr. (editors). 1996. *Advances in Genetic Programming 2*. Cambridge: MIT Press.

Angeline, Peter J. and Kinnear, Kenneth E. Jr. (editors). 1996. *Advances in Genetic Programming 2*. Cambridge, MA: The MIT Press.

Banzhaf, Wolfgang, Nordin, Peter, Keller, Robert E., and Francone, Frank D. 1998. *Genetic Programming – An Introduction*. San Francisco, CA: Morgan Kaufmann and Heidelberg: dpunkt.

Banzhaf, Wolfgang, Poli, Riccardo, Schoenauer, Marc, and Fogarty, Terence C. 1998. *Genetic Programming: First European Workshop. EuroGP'98. Paris, France, April 1998 Proceedings. Paris, France. April 1998*. Lecture Notes in Computer Science. Volume 1391. Berlin, Germany: Springer-Verlag.

Campbell, George A. 1917. *Electric Wave Filter*. Filed July 15, 1915. U. S. Patent 1,227,113. Issued May 22, 1917.

Cauer, Wilhelm. 1934. *Artificial Network*. U. S. Patent 1,958,742. Filed June 8, 1928 in Germany. Filed December 1, 1930 in United States. Issued May 15, 1934.

Cauer, Wilhelm. 1935. *Electric Wave Filter*. U. S. Patent 1,989,545. Filed June 8, 1928. Filed December 6, 1930 in United States. Issued January 29, 1935.

Cauer, Wilhelm. 1936. *Unsymmetrical Electric Wave Filter*. Filed November 10, 1932 in Germany. Filed November 23, 1933 in United States. Issued July 21, 1936.

Gruau, Frederic. 1992. *Cellular Encoding of Genetic Neural Networks*. Technical report 92-21. Laboratoire de l'Informatique du Parallélisme. Ecole Normale Supérieure de Lyon. May 1992.

Gruau, Frederic. 1994a. *Neural Network Synthesis using Cellular Encoding and the Genetic Algorithm*. PhD Thesis. Ecole Normale Supérieure de Lyon.

Gruau, Frederic. 1994b. Genetic micro programming of neural networks. In Kinnear, Kenneth E. Jr. (editor). 1994. *Advances in Genetic Programming*. Cambridge, MA: The MIT Press. Pages 495–518.

Holland, John H. 1975. *Adaptation in Natural and Artificial Systems*. Ann Arbor, MI: University of Michigan Press.

Kinnear, Kenneth E. Jr. (editor). 1994. *Advances in Genetic Programming*. Cambridge, MA: The MIT Press.

Kitano, Hiroaki. 1990. Designing neural networks using genetic algorithms with graph generation system. *Complex Systems*. 4(1990) 461–476.

Koza, John R. 1992. *Genetic Programming: On the Programming of Computers by Means of Natural Selection*. Cambridge, MA: MIT Press.

Koza, John R. 1994a. *Genetic Programming II: Automatic Discovery of Reusable Programs*. Cambridge, MA: MIT Press.

Koza, John R. 1994b. *Genetic Programming II Videotape: The Next Generation*. Cambridge, MA: MIT Press.

Koza, John R. 1995. Evolving the architecture of a multi-part program in genetic programming using architecture-altering operations. In McDonnell, John R., Reynolds, Robert G., and Fogel, David B. (editors). *Evolutionary Programming IV: Proceedings of the Fourth Annual Conference on Evolutionary Programming*. Cambridge, MA: The MIT Press. Pages 695–717.

Koza, John R., Banzhaf, Wolfgang, Chellapilla, Kumar, Deb, Kalyanmoy, Dorigo, Marco, Fogel, David B., Garzon, Max H., Goldberg, David E., Iba, Hitoshi, and Riolo, Rick. (editors). 1998. *Genetic Programming 1998: Proceedings of the Third Annual Conference*. San Francisco, CA: Morgan Kaufmann.

Koza, John R., Bennett III, Forrest H, Andre, David, and Keane, Martin A. 1999. *Genetic Programming III: Darwinian Invention and Problem Solving*. San Francisco, CA: Morgan Kaufmann.

Koza, John R., Bennett III, Forrest H, Andre, David, Keane, Martin A, and Dunlap, Frank. 1997. Automated synthesis of analog electrical circuits by means of genetic programming. *IEEE Transactions on Evolutionary Computation*. 1(2). Pages 109 – 128.

Koza, John R., Deb, Kalyanmoy, Dorigo, Marco, Fogel, David B., Garzon, Max, Iba, Hitoshi, and Riolo, Rick L. (editors). 1997. *Genetic Programming 1997: Proceedings of the Second Annual Conference* San Francisco, CA: Morgan Kaufmann.

Koza, John R., Goldberg, David E., Fogel, David B., and Riolo, Rick L. (editors). 1996. *Genetic Programming 1996: Proceedings of the First Annual Conference*. Cambridge, MA: The MIT Press.

Koza, John R., and Rice, James P. 1992. *Genetic Programming: The Movie*. Cambridge, MA: MIT Press.

Langdon, William B. 1998. *Genetic Programming and Data Structures: Genetic Programming + Data Structures = Automatic Programming!* Amsterdam: Kluwer.

Lingas, Andrzej. 1981. Certain algorithms for subgraph isomorphism problems. In Astesiano, E. and Bohm, C. (editors). *Proceedings of the. Sixth Colloquium on Trees in Algebra and Programming*. Lecture Notes on Computer Science. Springer Verlag. Volume 112. Pages 290 – 307.

Quarles, Thomas, Newton, A. R., Pederson, D. O., and Sangiovanni-Vincentelli, A. 1994. *SPICE 3 Version 3F5 User's Manual*. Department of Electrical Engineering and Computer Science, University of California. Berkeley, CA. March 1994.

Samuel, Arthur L. 1983. AI: Where it has been and where it is going. *Proceedings of the Eighth International Joint Conference on Artificial Intelligence*. Los Altos, CA: Morgan Kaufmann. Pages 1152 – 1157.

Spector, Lee, Langdon, William B., O'Reilly, Una-May, and Angeline, Peter (editors). 1999. *Advances in Genetic Programming 3*. Cambridge, MA: The MIT Press.

Sterling, Thomas L., Salmon, John, and Becker, Donald J., and Savarese. 1999. *How to Build a Beowulf: A Guide to Implementation and Application of PC Clusters*. Cambridge, MA: MIT Press.

Ullman, J. R. 1976. An algorithm for subgraph isomorphism. *Journal of the Association for Computing Machinery*. 23(1) 31 – 42. January 1976.

Williams, Arthur B. and Taylor, Fred J. 1995. *Electronic Filter Design Handbook*. Third Edition. New York, NY: McGraw-Hill.

Genetic Programming of a Goal-Keeper Control Strategy for the RoboCup Middle Size Competition

Giovanni Adorni, Stefano Cagnoni*, and Monica Mordonini

Department of Computer Engineering, University of Parma, Italy

Abstract. In this paper we describe a genetic programming approach to the design of a motion-control strategy for a goalkeeper robot created to compete in the RoboCup99, the robot soccer world championships which have been held yearly since 1997, as part of the Italian middle size robot team (ART, Azzurra Robot Team).

The evolved program sends a motion command to the robot, based on the analysis of information received from a human-coded vision sub-system. The preliminary results obtained on a simulator are encouraging. They suggest that even using very simple fitness functions and training sets including only a small sub-set of the situations that the goalkeeper is required to tackle, it is possible to evolve a complex behavior that permits the goalkeeper to perform well also in more challenging real-world conditions.

1 Introduction

The RoboCup competition [1] is aimed at fostering an interdisciplinary approach to robotics and agent-based artificial intelligence, presenting a challenge in which teams of "real" (small or middle size robot leagues) or "virtual" robots (simulator league) play soccer against one another.

In the simulator league, each team comprises eleven software clients, in communication with a central server. The server reconstructs the game, according to the commands received from the players. The server, in turn, sends back information to the players about their position, ball position and other environmental conditions that may affect the players' decisions and game strategy.

In the small size league, competition is between teams of small robots, which are controlled by an external program relying on a global vision system. The playing field size is as large as that used for table-tennis.

In the middle size league, teams of up to four fully-autonomous robots (neither central global vision systems nor external coordination systems are allowed) play on a field with a size of about $9\ m \times 5\ m$, with goals $2\ m$ wide.

---

* Address for correspondence: Stefano Cagnoni, Dept. of Computer Engineering, University of Parma, Parco Area delle Scienze 181/A, 43100 Parma, Italy, email: cagnoni@ce.unipr.it

R. Poli et al. (Eds.): EuroGP'99, LNCS 1598, pp. 109–119, 1999.
© Springer-Verlag Berlin Heidelberg 1999

Each robot, for which dimensions cannot exceed 45 *cm* for square footprints or a diameter of 50 *cm* for circular footprints, consists of several sub-systems, co-operating within the robot and providing robot-to-robot communication and coordination. The main components of a robot player are its vision/sensory sub-system, its motion-control sub-system and its communication sub-system. The sub-systems are coordinated by a software program or environment that sends or receives data and supervises the robot hardware, thus controlling the robot behavior.

The vision/sensory sub-system must be able to detect and localize the objects that are in the playing environment. These can be distinguished by their different colors: the ball (red), the field (green with white lines), the sidewalls (white), the other players (black with a purple or light-blue mark on them, depending on the team on which they are playing), the goals (striped in blue and yellow).

The communication sub-system must make it possible for the robot to send and receive messages to/from the other components of the team and, perhaps, to receive an activation signal from a remote system at the beginning of each half. This is the only signal that is allowed to be sent from human operators to the robots.

The motion-control sub-system sends commands to the engines and actuators of the robot, e.g. a kicking device or a pan/tilt camera motor.

In every middle size team at least two sorts of players must be present: a goalkeeper and up to three kickers that, in turn, can have their own specializations.

Most physical constraints that are imposed on the operation of real robots are absent in the simulated environment. Therefore, in developing simulated teams, the main focus of the research is on coordination strategies and on the study of emerging behaviors. The software architecture on which the simulation league relies [2] permits fast interaction between the players and the server.

The situation is quite different for real robots, especially if the middle size league is considered. All inputs from the outside world are received and have to be processed by the robot's own sub-systems, and are not condensed into a few chunks of information provided by the server as happens in the simulation league. A middle size robot player is a complex system that has to move in the real world and deal with real objects, so research attention has to be directed to more basic problems. Therefore, the design of a single middle size robot involves dealing with low-level tasks much more than when designing simulated players.

In this paper, we describe the use of GP to design a low-level control function for a middle size goalkeeper. Genetic programming (GP) was used, with very encouraging results, in the first two editions of the RoboCup (Nagoya 1997 and Paris 1998) to develop teams in the RoboCup simulation league [3, 4]. The evolved game strategies compared well with human-coded ones, with a balance of about 50% wins in the two tournaments.

Andre and Teller, in [4], argue that finding a good automatic-design on-line procedure for complex tasks such as the RoboCup game, besides being possible (as they have demonstrated), may overcome many problems arising from the lengthy process of tuning human-designed algorithms. The development of such methods is usually based on idealized and static models of the world, which may lead to failures when it comes to applying them to real-world situations.

In the next section of the paper the main problems that are encountered in designing a middle size league goalkeeper are summarized; in the following section, the actual GP design procedure that has been used to design the proposed control strategy is described. In the last two sections preliminary results are discussed, along with future plans for extending the goalie's skills.

2   Designing a goalkeeper for the RoboCup middle size competition

As mentioned above, the goalkeeper requirements are quite different from those of the other robot players. If we consider the vision sub-system, for example, the goalie's visual field should be as wide as possible, since it has to be directed towards the center of the playing field, while, at the same time, also keeping the part of the playing field on either side of the goal under control. For this reason, the goalie may also have a crucial role in team coordination, since it is the only player that can see almost all of the field. Therefore, it can provide team-mates with global information about the location of the ball, opponents, and about the relative positions of team-mates.

Therefore, the goalie's role and position inside the field strongly influence and constrain the design of its motion strategy.

First of all, its movements must be aimed more at intercepting the ball rather than reaching or kicking it, since it must keep close to the goal. So, the goalie will move mainly sideways in front of its goal.

Then, its movements must not extend beyond the goal boundaries, since it has to stand in front of it to defend it. Therefore, an interaction with the sensory sub-system must be provided in order for the goalie to be aware of its position relative to the goal. The goalie must also be able to reposition itself independently, without relying on the data coming from its odometers. In fact, in cases of misalignment due to sudden contacts with other players, the encoders that transduce the wheel movements cannot record such a displacement properly.

Moreover, it has to be able to perform short and rapid movements, to be able to follow even sharp deviations of the ball from its trajectory, due, for example, to a kick or to a rebound of the "body" of one of the players.

The motion-control strategy must, therefore, enable the robot to react prompt-ly to sudden changes, i.e., to exhibit a mostly-reactive behavior. The ball speed is relatively high and most computation time must be dedicated to processing the images coming from the camera system. For this reason, the specifications for the motion-control algorithm are that the input data, encoding ball position, speed and direction, must be concise and output commands must be as direct and immediately executable as possible.

These constraints require that the physical layout of the goalie be considerably different from the other players' structure. Figure 1 shows the goalie prototype we have developed to tackle such issues.

Fig. 1. The goalie prototype: the two wide-angle cameras are on the top. The front wheel, mounted in the middle of the chassis, is partially hidden by the pneumatical kick device, whose air tank is visible just above it.

The goalie is provided with a vision system based on two wide-angle cameras, that allow the visual field to be more than 180 degrees wide. Then, the two driving wheels on which the hardware platform we have used (a Pioneer robot) is based are located in the middle of the chassis, one on the front and the other on the rear. This makes translational movements more precise and accidental turns less likely. Balance is ensured by a pair of spheres, on which the robot leans, that are positioned along an axis at 90° to the wheel axis, and passing through its center (see Figure 2). Turning is possible because the two wheels can be operated independently.

The simple vision algorithm that is used returns the ball position for each frame received from the cameras. Therefore, by comparing two subsequent frames and considering the robot motion, it is also possible to deduce the instantaneous speed and direction of the ball, with respect to the goalie's position.

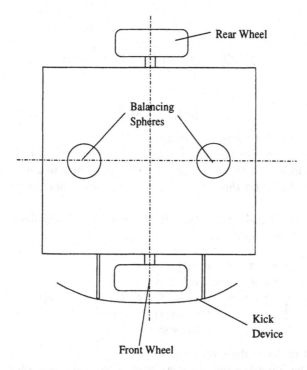

Fig. 2. Bottom view of the goalie prototype.

The motion command set used, that we term $\mathcal{M}$, is the following:
move_left or *move_right* at the maximum possible speed, *stop*, and *free_run*,
i.e., keep the same speed and direction until next command is issued;
Therefore, the strategy implies the definition of a function

$$f(\hat{x}(t,n), \hat{y}(t,n)) : \mathcal{R}^{2(n+1)} \to \mathcal{M} \tag{1}$$

where $\hat{x}(t,n), \hat{y}(t,n)$ are the sequence of the ball coordinates, with respect to
the goalie, in the $n+1$ frames acquired between time $t - n\Delta t$ and time t, Δt
being the frame acquisition interval.

3   Genetic Programming and goalkeeper control

To design function (1) using GP, it was necessary to find a suitable encoding,
satisfying the closure requirement for the function set used in evolving the program trees. As the input set consists of real numbers, we decided to encode the
set $\mathcal{M}$ of motion commands as real numbers. Consequently f was defined as
the composition of an encoding real-valued function $f'(\hat{x}(t,n), \hat{y}(t,n))$, with a
decoding function $d(f')$ that converts the output of f' into motion commands.
Thus

$$f(\hat{x}(t,n), \hat{y}(t,n)) = d(f'(\hat{x}(t,n), \hat{y}(t,n))) \tag{2}$$

where

$$f'(\hat{x}(t,n), \hat{y}(t,n), t) : \mathcal{R}^{2(n+1)} \to \mathcal{R} \tag{3}$$

and

$$d(o(t)) : \mathcal{R} \to \mathcal{M} \tag{4}$$

$o(t)$ being the encoded output command.

Intuitively, as the robot motion is supposed to be rectilinear along the x-axis, $o(t)$ could be imagined to be in some way proportional to the distance of the goalie from the ball, and therefore to be zero when the robot is aligned with the ball.

Therefore, the decoding function $d(o(t))$ was empirically designed to return a command $m(t)$ as follows:

$$m(t) = \begin{cases} move\_left & \text{if } o(t) < -40 \\ move\_right & \text{if } o(t) > 40 \\ free\_run & \text{if } (-40 \leq o(t) \leq -20 \text{ and } v(t) < 0) \text{ or} \\ & (20 \leq o(t) \leq 40 \text{ and } v(t) > 0) \\ stop & \text{otherwise.} \end{cases} \tag{5}$$

where $v(t)$ is the goalie's velocity.

We used the following set of functionals, along with two alternative sets of terminals and ephemeral random constants (ERCs) [5]:

Functional set			Terminal set 1			Terminal set 2		
Functional	Arity	Notes	Terminal	Type	Notes	Terminal	Type	Notes
+	2		V	term	*speed*	X-1	term	$x(t - \Delta t)$
−	2		D	term	*direction*	Y-1	term	$y(t - \Delta t)$
⋆	2		X	term	$x(t)$	X	term	$x(t)$
pdiv	2	*prot.division*	Y	term	$y(t)$	Y	term	$y(t)$
sin	1		R1	ERC	$[-1, 1]$	R1	ERC	$[-1, 1]$
cos	1		R2	ERC	$[0, 280]$	R2	ERC	$[0, 280]$

where x, y, expressed in *cm*, *speed*, expressed in *cm/s*, and *direction*, expressed in radians, refer to the ball position and motion with respect to the goalie, on which the origin of our reference system is set.

The GP package we used is lil-gp1.01 [6].

The genetic program relies on a simulator that builds a training set of shots, and tests each tree generated by the genetic program against it. The shot-generation procedure is parameterized, in order for the user to be able to create different training sets and different field and goalie layouts, by simply modifying some parameters. The most significant parameters are the maximum and minimum speed of the ball, the number of directions from which the shots may come, the minimum distance from which the shot can be made, the initial position of the goalie, the depth of the robot field of view, the frame rate at which the robot vision sub-system is supposed to operate.

It is also possible to simulate more realistic situations, in which the robot visual field may be occluded, e.g., by other players. In a number of frames proportional to a pre-set probability value, the robot is "blinded", and no input data made available to the control program. As a default, in these cases, the robot uses data acquired at time $t - \Delta t$ also at time t, and a default *free_run* command is issued. A further external control prevents the goalie from moving beyond the goal limits, represented by the position of the two goal posts. In the actual robot implementation, such a control is performed asynchronously using two infrared sensors that measure the depth of the free space behind the goalie, which is higher when it is standing in front of the goal.

In the simulations, a worst-case value for the frame rate of 5 frames/second was used, although the vision sub-system is actually able to work at higher rates (typically around 10 frames/second). A reasonable value for acceleration, corresponding roughly to the peak acceleration of the real robot, was set to define the equation for the robot motion, which is assumed to be uniformly accelerated until a maximum velocity value is reached.

4 Discussion

The main questions which our preliminary experiments aimed to answer were, firstly, whether GP would be able to design a solution to the problem which could be at least compared with a human-encoded one. Secondly, whether a set of very simple examples, such as the ones provided by our simulator, could be used to develop complex strategies by which more realistic and challenging situations could be tackled.

At a lower level, obviously, the usual problems that arise in designing GP applications had to be solved, such as choosing the most suitable fitness function, function set and terminal set.

Andre and Teller in [4] argue that, for complex strategy problems, such as the design of a complete simulated-league team, the genetic program performs better if a lower-level terminal set is used, avoiding any bias from some human-encoded pre-processing. The idea is that, by doing so, GP explores wider search spaces where possibly better solutions may lie, that are very far from the human-encoded ones. Therefore, we were interested in observing how the results obtained using the terminal set, in which some of the input data (ball speed and direction) derived from a pre-processing of the "raw" ball-position data, would compare with those obtained with the set in which only raw data were provided.

As the external control that keeps the goalie's position within the two posts was present, the training set only included shots directed towards the goal, in order to speed up the processing. 329 shots were generated, coming from 11 different directions (in a range varying from 15 to 165 degrees with respect to the goal line) and from distances ranging from 2 m to 3 m from the goalie, at a maximum speed of 0.5 m/s. All shots in the training set are straight shots. This choice was made considering that, in the RoboCup, the robot kicking devices are such that the ball motion is essentially straight. Therefore, possible non-straight trajectories are likely to be generated as a sequence of straight segments (e.g., a ball kicked by a player which rebounds of another one, or a ball sequentially kicked by different players in different directions). The last segment is always a straight shot, kicked relatively close to the goal. Therefore, we assume that if the goalkeeper is able to deal with close straight shots, it will be able to deal with most other plausible shots.

Two possible fitness functions were considered. The first is a very simple and basic function, whose value is directly proportional to the number of shots of the training set that score, i.e., that the goalie is not able to intercept. The second is more complex and aims to reward control programs that produce good goalie behaviors, besides limiting the number of goals scored, which remains obviously the main quality measure. Examples of such good behaviors are: being always as close as possible to the ball and/or to the center of the goal, intercepting the ball when it is as central to the goalie's position as possible, etc.

In a few test runs the simpler fitness function led to better results. Moreover, the more complex fitness function slows down the genetic program significantly, because it needs to be updated at each time step for each shot. Therefore, we adopted the simpler function for our preliminary experiments. This was mainly a practical choice, as the results obtained in a few short test runs are not significant enough to draw any certain conclusions about our choice. A small penalty term, proportional to tree depth, which is in any case lower than 1, was added to favor the development of more computationally-efficient solutions, in cases of equal performances.

Our experiments were run with a population of 200 individuals, tree depth limited to 13, with crossover rate of 0.7 and mutation rate of 0.03. The GP was run through 2000 generations. On a Pentium 200 MMX PC each run required about 20 hours of CPU time.

The results obtained were rather good. With the best program (BP1) evolved using Terminal Set 1, in which ball direction and speed are pre-computed, the simulated goalie was able to intercept 304 out of 329 shots (92.4%) in the training set. Using Terminal Set 2 the best program (BP2) intercepted 307 shots out of 329 (93.3%).

We also tested the two best programs on a much bigger set (7682 straight shots), generated by the same simulator, in which few shots of the training set were comprised. The distance from which the shots were made was kept between $2m$ and $3m$, but the direction of the shots ranged from 9 to 171 degrees. A much smaller sampling step for each parameter was used to generate the shots. BP1 had a performance of 91% while BP2 could block 92.4% of the shots.

The listings of the best programs evolved with the two terminal sets are reported below.

BP1

```
(+ J
   (+ (* (+ I
            (+ I
               (* (cos D)
                  (- D V)))) 171.23322)
      (+ (+ I
            (+ 218.53474 249.98700))
         (+ (/ 192.82038 42.74077)
            (+ (+ (+ 155.63657 190.16049) I) I)))))
```

BP2

```
(+ (+ (- (+ (cos (* I I)) J_1)
         (+ I
            (* I_1 J_1)))
      (+ (+ (+ I_1
               (* 15.91181 I_1))
            (+ I_1 I))
         (* J_1 I))) J_1)
```

where I and J are the x- and y-coordinates of the ball, expressed in cm, in the goalie-centered reference system, at time t, I_1 and J_1 are the coordinates at time $t - \Delta t$, D is the ball direction, expressed in radians, and V is the ball speed, expressed in cm/s.

If one explicits the functions implemented in BP1 and BP2, a dominant multiplicative term can be found in both programs: in BP1 its expression is $171.23 * (2I + (D - V)\cos D)$, while in BP2 $(J_1) * (2 + (I - I_1))$. As regards BP1, the term $D\cos D$ can be neglected for non-zero V or I values. The term $V\cos D$ represents the horizontal component of the ball speed: so the goalie behaviour could be described as:

"if the ball is far, move towards the ball; if the ball is near move towards where the ball is going".

As for BP2, the direction of the goalie's motion is given by $I - I_1$ (which is equivalent to the term $V\cos D$ of GP1), so the goalie will move in the same direction as the ball. If $I = I_1$ (the ball remains at the same distance from the goalie along the x-axis), the dominant term becomes $2I + 18I_1$ which means that, in that case, the goalie will move towards the ball. The term J_1 is probably used as a positive multiplicative constant, rather than for its actual meaning. It might act somehow as a "damper" for the goalie's reactions, as it tends to make the goalie less reactive when the ball is closer.

5   Conclusions and future work

Using animations obtained through a software simulator, we observed the behaviour of the goalie acting under the control of the best genetic program we obtained.

As reported above the results are preliminary, thus the following observations regard only a few experiments, and more would be required to draw final conclusions.

However, an interesting observation that can be made is that, as the shots making up the training set are all straight, a trivial solution to the optimization problem could be found: it would be sufficient to compute the intercept with the goal line of the line along which the shot is proceeding and send the goalie there as fast as possible. However, this would not be the optimum solution in real situations, in which the ball could, for example, change direction from one frame to the following one. In that case such a behavior would be too reactive and the goalie's motion could tend to become heavily oscillatory in the presence of alternate lateral movements of the ball in front of it.

A more general and reasonable strategy would imply trying to keep as close to the ball as possible at every moment. Surprisingly, since we were using a fitness in which no reward for such a behaviour was given, the strategy implemented by the above-reported fitness function was very much like this.

For example, if the goalie starting position is on the right and the shot comes from the left, the goalie tends to go to the center of the goal. So a "follow-ball" behavior is emerging, which was not explicitly learned from the training set/fitness function pair. The reason for this might reside in the fact that this is a more general and more easily implementable solution, and probably a myriad of such or of equivalent solutions are scattered around in the search space. This observation may also corroborate Andre and Teller's opinion on GP-developed strategies vs. human-encoded ones, even if the results we obtained with the two different terminal sets are almost equivalent.

Future work will extend our experiments, both in terms of their number and of population sizes. We will also try to use GP to optimize some of the "hardwired" accessory routines, such as the one controlling the goalie's re-positioning, e.g., by requiring them to be evolved as automatically-defined functions.

Acknowledgments

We wish to thank Daniele Nardi of the University of Rome "La Sapienza" and all his co-workers, for providing us with the Pioneer robot base and for their precious and continuous co-operation in the development of the goalkeeper.

We also wish to thank all other members of the "Azzurra Robot Team 1999" (ART-99), Giovanna Abelli, Carlo Bernardi and Matteo Somacher for their contribution to the project.

References

1. H. Kitano, M. Asada, Y. Kuniyoshi, I. Noda, and E. Osawa, "RoboCup: the robot world cup initiative", in *Proc. of the IJCAI-95 workshop on entertainment and AI/A Life*, 1995.
2. N. Itsuki, "Soccer server: a simulator for RoboCup", in *JSAI AI-Symposium 95: Special Session on RoboCup*, december 1995.
3. S. Luke, C. Hohn, J. Farris, G. Jackson, and J. Hendler, "Co-evolving soccer softbot team coordination with genetic programming", in *Proc. of the First International Workshop on RoboCup, IJCAI-97*. 1997, Springer-Verlag.
4. D. Andre and A. Teller, "Evolving team Darwin United", in *RoboCup-98 : Robot Soccer World Cup II*, M. Asada, Ed. 1998, Springer-Verlag.
5. J. Koza, *Genetic Programming: On the Programming of Computers by Means of Natural Selection*, MIT Press, Cambridge, 1992.
6. D. Zongker and B. Punch, *lil-gp 1.01 user's manual*, Michigan State University, 1996, available via anonymous ftp from ftp://garage.cse.msu.edu/pub/GA/lilgp.

Genetic Programming Discovers Efficient Learning Rules for the Hidden and Output Layers of Feedforward Neural Networks

Amr Radi and Riccardo Poli

School of Computer Science
The University of Birmingham
Birmingham B15 2TT, UK
{A.M.Radi,R.Poli}@cs.bham.ac.uk

Abstract. The learning method is critical for obtaining good generalisation in neural networks with limited training data. The Standard BackPropagation (SBP) training algorithm suffers from several problems such as sensitivity to the initial conditions and very slow convergence. The aim of this work is to use Genetic Programming (GP) to discover new supervised learning algorithms which can overcome some of these problems. In previous research a new learning algorithms for the output layer has been discovered using GP. By comparing this with SBP on different problems better performance was demonstrated. This paper shows that GP can also discover better learning algorithms for the hidden layers to be used in conjunction with the algorithm previously discovered. Comparing these with SBP on different problems we show they p rovide better performances. This study indicates that there exist many supervised learning algorithms better than SBP and that GP can be used to discover them.

1 Introduction

Supervised learning algorithms are by far the most frequently used methods to train artificial neural networks [13]. The Standard BackPropagation (SBP) algorithm represents a computationally effective method for the training of multilayer networks which has been applied to a number of learning tasks in science, engineering, finance and other disciplines. The SBP learning algorithm has indeed emerged as the standard algorithm for the training of multilayer networks, against which other learning algorithms are often benchmarked [25,50].

However, SBP presents several drawbacks [10,13,28,41,42,44,46]. For example, it is extremely slow, training performance is sensitive to the initial conditions, it may be trapped in local minima before converging to a solution, and oscillations may occur during learning (this usually happens when the learning rate is too high).

As a consequence, in the past few years a number of improvements to SBP have been proposed in the literature (see [44] for a survey). We will review the SBP rule and mention some of these recent improvements in Section 2.

R. Poli et al. (Eds.): EuroGP'99, LNCS 1598, pp. 120–134, 1999.
© Springer-Verlag Berlin Heidelberg 1999

All these algorithms are generally faster than the SBP rule (up to one order of magnitude) but tend to suffer from some of the problems of SBP. Efforts continue in the direction of solving these problems to produce faster supervised learning algorithms and, more importantly, to improve their reliability. However, the progress is extremely slow because any new rule has to be imagined/designed firstly (using engineering and/or mathematical principles) by a human expert and then it has to be tested extensively to verify its functionality and efficiency. In addition, scientists tend to search the space of possible learning algorithms for neural nets by using a kind of "gradient descent". So, most algorithms newly proposed are not very different from or much better than the previous ones. This way of searching may take a long time to lead to significant breakthroughs in the field. Indeed, by looking critically at the huge literature on this topic, it can be inferred that only a few really novel algorithms which demonstrate much better performance than SBP have been produced in the last 10 years [2, 3, 19, 30, 34, 35, 48].

This has led some researchers to use optimisation algorithms to explore the space of the possible learning rules. Given the limited knowledge of such a space, the tools of choice have been evolutionary algorithms [55] which, although not optimum for some domains, offer the broadest possible applicability. Very often the strategy adopted has been to use Genetic Algorithms (GAs) [16] to find the optimum parameters for prefixed classes of learning rules. The few results obtained to date are promising. We recall them in Section 3.

By using GAs, we have realised that fixing the class of rules that can be explored biases the search and prevents the evolutionary algorithm from exploring the much larger space of rules which we, humans, have not thought about. So, in line with some work by Benjio [3], which is also summarised in Section 3, we decided to use Genetic Programming (GP) [21] as this allows the direct evolution of symbolic learning rules with their coefficients (if any) rather than the simpler evolution of parameters for a fixed learning rule.

In our previous research [39, 40], GP was successful in discovering a number of learning rules for the output layers of feed-forward neural networks. Among them we found one which was better than SBP in all problems considered. This paper extends significantly that work by applying GP to the discovery of learning rules for the hidden layer.

We describe our approach in Section 4. Section 5 reports the experimental results obtained on six classes of standard benchmark problems: the parity, the encoder-decoder, the character recognition, the multiplexer, the vowel recognition, and the sonar problems. We discuss these results and draw some conclusions in Section 6.

2   Standard Backpropagation Algorithm and Recent Improvements

A multilayer perceptron is a fully connected feed-forward neural network in which an arbitrary input vector is propagated forward through the network, causing an activation vector to be produced in the output layer [13]. The network behaves like a function which maps the input vector onto an output vector. This function is determined by the connection weights of the net. The objective of SBP is to tune the weights of the network so that the network performs the desired input/output mapping. In this section we briefly recall the basic concepts of multilayer feed-forward neural networks, the SBP and some of its recent improvements. More details can be found in [42, 44].

2.1   Standard Backpropagation

Let u_i^l be the ith neuron in the lth layer (the input layer is the 0th layer and the output layer is the kth layer). Let n_l be the number of neurons in the lth layer. The weight of the connection between neuron u_j^l and neuron u_i^{l+1} is denoted by w_{ij}^l. Let $\{x_1, x_2, ..., x_m\}$ be the set of input patterns that the network is supposed to learn and let $\{t_1, t_2, ..., t_m\}$ be the corresponding target output patterns. The pairs (x_p, t_p) $p = 1, .., m$ are called training patterns. Each x_p is an n_o-dimensional vector with components x_{ip}. Each t_p is an n_k-dimensional vector with components t_{ip}.

The output o_{ip}^0 of a neuron u_i^0 in the input layer, when pattern x_p is presented, coincides with its net input net_{ip}^0 i.e. with the ith element, x_{ip}, of x_p. For the other layers, the net input net_{ip}^{l+1} of neuron u_i^{l+1} (when the input pattern x_p is presented to the network) is usually computed as follows:

$$net_{ip}^{l+1} = \sum_{j=1}^{n_l} w_{ij}^l o_{jp}^l - \theta_i^{l+1},$$

where o_{jp}^l, is the output of neuron u_j^l (usually $o_{jp}^l = O(net_{jp}^l)$ with O a non-linear activation-function) and θ_i^{l+1} is the bias of neuron u_i^{l+1}. For the sake of a homogeneous representation, in the following, the bias will be interpreted as the weights of a connection to a 'bias unit' with a constant output 1.

The error ε_{ip}^k for neuron u_i^k of the output layer for the training pair (x_p, t_p) is computed as

$$\varepsilon_{ip}^k = t_{ip} - o_{ip}^k.$$

For the hidden layers the error ε_{ip}^l is computed recursively from the errors on other layers (see [13])

The SBP rule uses these errors to adjust the weights (usually initialised randomly) in such a way that the errors gradually reduce.

The network performance can be assessed using the Total Sum of Squared (TSS) errors given by the following function:

$$E = \frac{1}{2} \sum_{p=1}^{m} \sum_{i=1}^{n_k} \varepsilon_{ip}^k{}^2.$$

The training process stops when the error E is reduced to an acceptable level, or when no further improvement is obtained.

In the batched variant of the SBP the updating of w_{ij}^l in the sth learning step (often called an "epoch") is performed according to the following equations:

$$w_{ij}^l(s+1) = w_{ij}^l(s) + \Delta w_{ij}^l(s)$$

$$\Delta w_{ij}^l(s) = \eta \frac{\partial E}{\partial w_{ij}^l(s)} = \eta \delta_{ip}^{l+1}(s) o_{jp}^l(s)$$

where $\delta_{ip}^{l+1}(s)$ refers to the error signal at neuron i in layer $l+1$ for pattern p at epoch s, which is the product of the first derivative of the activation function and the error $\varepsilon_{ip}^{l+1}(s)$, and η is a parameter called learning rate.

2.2   Improvements to SBP

Many methods have been proposed to improve generalisation performance and convergence time of SBP. Current research mostly concentrates on: the optimum setting of learning rates and momentum [5, 9, 18, 41, 46, 51–53]; the optimum setting of the initial weights [6, 24, 27]; the enhancement of the contrast in the input patterns [23, 29, 32, 49, 57]; changing the error function [1, 9, 17, 33, 45, 47]; finding optimum architectures using pruning techniques [7, 15]. In the following we will describe two speed-up methods which are relevant to the work described in the rest of the paper: the Momentum and Rprop methods.

The Momentum method implements a variable learning rate coefficient implicitly by adding to the weight change a fraction of the last weight change as follows:

$$\Delta w_{ij}^l(s) = \eta \frac{\partial E(s)}{\partial w_{ij}^l(s)} + \mu \frac{\partial E(s-1)}{\partial w_{ij}^l(s-1)}$$

where μ is a parameter called momentum. This method decreases the oscillation which may occur with large learning rates and accelerates the convergence. For a more detailed discussion see [9, 18, 51].

Rprop is one of the fastest variations of the SBP algorithm [41, 44, 56]. Rprop stands for 'Resilient backpropagation'. It is a local adaptive learning scheme, performing supervised batch learning. The basic principle of Rprop is to eliminate the harmful influence of the magnitude of the partial derivative $\frac{\partial E}{\partial w_{ij}^l}$ on the weight changes. The sign of the derivative is used to indicate the direction of the weight update while the magnitude of the weight change is exclusively determined by a weight-specific update-value $\Delta_{ij}^l(s)$ as follows

$$\Delta w_{ij}^l(s) = \begin{cases} -\Delta_{ij}^l(s) & \text{if } \frac{\partial E(s)}{\partial w_{ij}^l(s)} > 0, \\ +\Delta_{ij}^l(s) & \text{if } \frac{\partial E(s)}{\partial w_{ij}^l(s)} < 0, \\ 0 & \text{otherwise.} \end{cases}$$

The update-values $\Delta^l_{ij}(s)$ are modified according to the following equation:

$$\Delta^l_{ij}(s) = \begin{cases} \eta^+ \Delta^l_{ij}(s-1) & \text{if } \frac{\partial E(s-1)}{\partial w^l_{ij}(s-1)} \cdot \frac{\partial E(s)}{\partial w^l_{ij}(s)} > 0, \\ \eta^- \Delta^l_{ij}(s-1) & \text{if } \frac{\partial E(s-1)}{\partial w^l_{ij}(s-1)} \cdot \frac{\partial E(s)}{\partial w^l_{ij}(s)} < 0, \\ \Delta^l_{ij}(s-1) & \text{otherwise.} \end{cases}$$

where η^- and η^+ are constants such that $0 < \eta^- < 1 < \eta^+$.

The Rprop algorithm has three parameters: the initial update-value $\Delta^l_{ij}(0)$ which directly determines the size of the first weight step (default setting $\Delta^l_{ij}(0)$ = 0.1) and the limits for the step update values Δ_{max} and Δ_{min} which prevent the weights from becoming too large or too small. Typically $\Delta_{max}=50.0$ and $\Delta_{min}=0.0000001$. Convergence with Rprop is rather insensitive to the choice of these parameters. Nevertheless, for some problems it can be advantageous to allow only very cautious (namely small) steps, in order to prevent the algorithm from getting stuck too quickly in local minima. For a detailed discussion see also [41, 42].

Although the Momentum method and Rprop are considerably faster than SBP, they still suffer from same of the problems mentioned in Section 1 [11, 41].

3   Previous Work on the Evolution of Neural Network Learning Rules

A considerable amount of work has been done on the evolution of the weights and/or the topology of neural networks. See for example [20, 36–38, 54]. However only a relatively small amount of previous work has been reported on the evolution of learning rules for neural networks. Given the topology of the network, GAs have been used to find the optimum learning rules. For example, Montana [31] used GAs for training feedforward networks and created a new method of training which is similar to SBP. Chalmers [4] applied GAs to discover supervised learning rules for single-layer neural networks. He discussed the role of different kinds of connectionist systems and verified the optimality of the Delta rule, a simpler variant of SBP applicable to single-layer neural networks [43]. The author noticed that discovering more complex learning rules like the SBP using GAs is not easy because either one uses a highly complex genetic coding, or one uses a simpler coding which allows SBP as a possibility. In the first case the search space is huge, in the second case we bias the search using our own prejudices.

All the methods mentioned above are limited as they choose a fixed number of parameters and a rigid form for the learning rule. GP may be a good way of getting around the limitations inherent to fixed genetic coding which GAs suffer from. GP has been applied successfully to a large number of difficult problems like automatic design, pattern recognition, robotics control, synthesis of neural networks, symbolic regression, music and picture generation, etc. However only, one attempt to use GP to induce new learning rules for neural networks has been reported before our own work

Bengio [3] used GP to find learning rules. Bengio used the output of the input neuron o^l_{jp}, the error of the output neuron ε^{l+1}_{ip} and the first derivative of the activation function of the output neuron as terminals and algebraic operators as functions for GP. Bengio used a very strong search bias towards a certain class of SBP-like learning rules as only the ingredients to rediscover the SBP algorithm were used. GP found a better learning rule compared to the rules discovered by simulated annealing and GAs. However, the new learning rule suffered from the same problems as SBP and was only tested on a very specific problem. We will describe our approach to discovering learning rules based on GP in the next section.

4 Evolution of Neural Network Learning Rules with GP

Our work is an extension of Bengio's work with the objective to explore a larger space of rules using different parameters and different rules for the hidden and output layers. Our objective is to obtain a rule which is general like SBP but faster, more stable, and which can work in different conditions. We want to discover learning rules of the following form:

$$\Delta w^l_{ij}(s) = \begin{cases} F(w^l_{ij}, o^l_{jp}, t_{ip}, o^l_{ip}) & \text{if for the output layer,} \\ F(w^l_{ij}, o^l_{jp}, o^{l+1}_{ip}, E^l_{jp}) & \text{if for the hidden layers} \end{cases}$$

where o^l_{jp} is the output of neuron u^l_j when pattern p is presented to the network and $E^l_{jp} = \sum_i w^{l+1}_{ji} \delta^{l+1}_{ip}$, So, in our approach we used two different learning rules one for the output layer and one for the hidden layers, like in the SBP learning rule. In preliminary tests in which we tried to evolve both rules at the same time we obtain relatively poor results. This has to be attributed to the huge size of the search space and to the limited memory and CPU power of current workstations.

So, we decided to proceed in two stages. In the first stage, we used GP to evolve rules for the output layer, while the hidden layers were trained with the SBP rule (this was done in previous research [40]). In the second stage, we used GP to evolve rules for the hidden layers, while the output layer was trained with the rule discovered in the first stage. This second stage is described in this paper.

The tasks that the networks are supposed to learn with each learning rule in the population. These are described in the next section together with the functions and the terminals used by GP.

5 Experimental Results

It is not easy to perform a fair comparison between the many variants of supervised learning techniques. There are as many benchmark problems reported in the literature as there are new learning algorithms. Here, we consider six problems which have been widely used: 1) the 'exclusive or' (XOR) problem and its more general form, the N-input parity problem, 2) the family of the N-M-N encoder problems which force the network to generalise and to map input patterns into similar output activations [39], 3) the character recognition problem with 7 inputs representing the state of a 7-segment light emitting diode (LED) display and 4 outputs which represent the digits 1 to 9 binary encoded [3], 4) the display problem with 4 inputs which represent a digit from 1 to 9 in binary and 7 outputs which represent the LED configuration to visualise the digit, 5) the vowel recognition problem for independent speakers of the eleven steady state vowels of British English (for more information see [8]) where each training pattern has 10 input coefficients for each vowel and 4 outputs which represent the eleven different vowels, 6) the classification of sonar signals problem [12], where the task is to discriminate between the sonar signals (60 inputs) bounced off a metal cylinder and those bounced off a roughly cylindrical rock.

For the XOR problem, we used a three-layer network consisting of 2 input, 2 hidden, and 1 output neurons with hyperbolic tangent activation functions with output in the range [-1,1]. The weights were randomly initialised within the range [-1,1]. For the Encoder problems we used a three-layer network consisting of 10 input, 5 hidden, and 10 output neurons. Here, we used logistic activation functions with output in the range of [0,1]. For the character recognition problem we used a three-layer network consisting of 7 input, 10 hidden, and 4 output neurons. We used logistic activation functions with output in the range of [-1,1]. For the display problem we used a three-layer network consisting of 4 input, 10 hidden, and 7 output neurons. We used logistic activation functions with output in the range of [0,1]. For the vowels recognition problem we used a three-layer network consisting of 10 input, 8 hidden, and 4 output neurons with logistic activation functions with output in the range of [-1,1]. For the classification of sonar signals we used a three-layer network consisting of 60 input, 12 hidden, and 1 output neurons. We used logistic activation functions with output in the range of [-0.3,0.3] (same range as in [12]). These parameters and network topologies were determined by experimenting with different configurations (number of layers, number of hidden layers, learning rate, and range of random initial weights) and selecting the ones on which the SBP algorithm worked best. We tested each problem with 100 independent runs (i.e each run with different initial weights).

The fitness of each learning rule was computed using the TSS error E for the six problems mentioned above:

$$f = \begin{cases} \lambda(E_{max} - E) & \text{if the network does not learn,} \\ C_{max} - C_{min} & \text{otherwise} \end{cases}$$

where C_{min} is the minimum number of epochs needed for convergence and E_{max} and C_{max} are constants such that $f \geq 0$. λ is factor that makes the value of $(E_{max} - E)$ greater than $C_{max} - C_{min}$ in any condition. The value of E is measured at the maximum number of learning epochs. For the XOR, the encoder, character recognition, display, vowel recognition, and sonar signals we used 1000, 200, 500, 500, 300 and 500 epochs, respectively.

The experiments were performed using our own SBP and GP simulators. The simulators are written in POP11 and run on Digital Alpha machines with

233 MHz processors. In these conditions each GP run took six days of CPU time on average. For this reason we were able to perform only 25 GP runs for second stage. In the first stage GP discovered several rules[40]. The best is as follows:

$$NLR_o = \Delta w_{ij}^l = \eta o_{jp}^l \varepsilon_{ip}^{l+1}.$$

In all sample problems considered NLR_o is much faster than SBP even by applying both of NLR_o and SBP with Rprop. This suggests that NLR_o outperforms SBP by allowing bigger weight changes when the output of the neuron is nearly saturated

In the second stage GP was run for 500 to 1000 generations with a population size of 200 to 1000, and a crossover probability of 0.9. After applying crossover we applied subtree mutation with a probability of 0.01 to all of the population. We used the function set $\{+, -, \times\}$, and the terminal set $\{w_{ij}^l, o_{jp}^l, o_{ip}^{l+1}, E_{jp}^l, 1, 0.5, 0.1\}$. We used the "full" initialisation method with an initial maximum depth from 3 to 5 [22].

In these experiments GP was allowed to evolve learning rules for the hidden layers, while the learning rule for the output layer was NLR_o. GP discovered several rules such as

$$NLR_1 = \Delta w_{ij}^l(s) = \eta[1.5 o_{ip}^{l+1}(1 - o_{ip}^{l+1}) E_{jp}^l(o_{jp}^l - 0.5) o_{jp}^l o_{jp}^l]$$

$$NLR_2 = \Delta w_{ij}^l(s) = \eta[o_{jp}^l o_{ip}^{l+1} o_{ip}^{l+1}(1 - o_{ip}^{l+1}) E_{jp}^l + 0.1(o_{ip}^{l+1} - 0.5) o_{jp}^l]$$

$$NLR_3 = \Delta w_{ij}^l(s) = \eta[o_{jp}^l o_{ip}^{l+1}(1 - o_{ip}^{l+1}) E_{jp}^l + 0.1(o_{ip}^{l+1} - 0.55) o_{jp}^l]$$

and

$$NLR_4 = \Delta w_{ij}^l(s) = \eta[o_{jp}^l o_{ip}^{l+1}(1 - o_{ip}^{l+1}) E_{jp}^l + 0.1(o_{jp}^l - 0.55) o_{ip}^{l+1}]$$

We tested these rules on four problems obtaining the results in Tables 3 and 1. It was found that the last two rules (NLR_3 and NLR_4) are the best rules discovered in our runs. We studied them in different conditions to determine their reliability and efficiency with respect to SBP. It should be noted that for the XOR, Encoder, and Display problems the difference between the minimum and maximum number of epochs required by NLR to converge is smaller than for NLR_o although the average number of epochs for NLR_o is better on XOR and Character recognition problems. In any case this compares very favourably with the results obtained with SBP.

By looking to the last two learning rules (NLR_3 and NLR_4), we can see that they include two terms. The first one is the term: $\eta o_{jp}^l o_{ip}^{l+1}(1 - o_{ip}^{l+1}) E_{jp}^l$ which is the SBP rule in the case of logistic activation functions (which has derivative $o_{ip}^{l+1}(1 - o_{ip}^{l+1})$). This makes sense since in Encoder, display and character recognition problems, we use the logistic activation function. However, this is not beneficial for the XOR problem where we used the hyperbolic tangent activation function (which has derivative $1 - (o_{ip}^{l+1})^2$).

It is clear from the Table 3 that the convergence efficiency in the XOR problem increases by changing the term $o_{ip}^{l+1}(1 - o_{ip}^{l+1})$ into $1 - (o_{ip}^{l+1})^2$ to obtain $NLR_3(m)$ and $NLR_4(m)$.

The second term in $NLR_3(m)$ and $NLR_4(m)$ is $\eta 0.1(o_{ip}^{l+1} - 0.55)o_{jp}^l$ and $\eta 0.1(o_{jp}^l - 0.55)o_{ip}^{l+1}$, respectively. These two equations are similar to the Hebbian learning rule (HB) as explained in by Linsker [26]. A Hebbian rule for synaptic plasticity is one in which a synaptic strength is increased when pre-and post-synaptic firing are correlated, and possibly decreased when are anticorrelated [14]. The Hebb-type learning rule used by Linsker for weigh update is:

$$HB = (o_{ip}^{l+1} - k_1)(o_{jp}^l - k_2) + k_3$$

where k_1, k_2, and k_3 are constants. k_3 and either k_1 or k_2 are zero in NLR_6 and NLR_7.

So, the experiments with GP suggested that a good learning rule for the hidden layers could have the form:

$$NLR_h = \eta(\beta SBP + (1 - \beta)HB)$$

which corresponds to:

$$NLR_h = \eta[\beta o_{jp}^l o_{ip}^{l+1}(1 - o_{ip}^{l+1})E_{jp}^l + (1 - \beta)(o_{ip}^{l+1} - k_1)(o_{jp}^l - k_2)]$$

The complete learning rule is NLR_o for the output layer and NLR_h for the hidden layers.

The interest of this result is that GP suggested a NLR in which the weakness of a supervised learning rule (SBP) are removed by combining it with an unsupervised learning rule (HB).

Table 2 shows the results of the two algorithms (SBP and $NLR_o with NLR_h$) for the vowel and sonar problems. By changing the parameters of the NLR_h (β, k_1, and k_2) we found that $\beta = 0.01, k_1 = 0.5$, and $k_2 = 0$ give the best results on the vowel problem while on the sonar problem the best parameters are $\beta = 0.1, k_1 = 0.5$, and $k_2 = 0$.

The combination of NLR_o and NLR_h, which we will term NLR from now on, is very efficient and provides good performance on the six problems. So, in an other set of tests, we have decided to compare its convergence behaviour with the SBP with and without the Momentum and Rprop speed-up algorithms. Figure 1 shows the TSS error of SBP and NLR with and without Momentum on the character recognition problem. The results obtained indicate that NLR achieves its target output at the same epoch as SBP with Momentum, while NLR with Momentum converges much more quickly than the other algorithms. Also, Figure 2 shows that the NLR with Rprop outperforms SBP with Rprop in the character recognition problem. All runs used the same initial random weights.

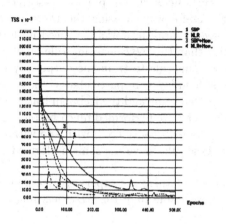

Fig. 1. Plot of the TSS error of SBP, NLR, SBP expand with Momentum, and NLR expand with Momentum in the character recognition problem.

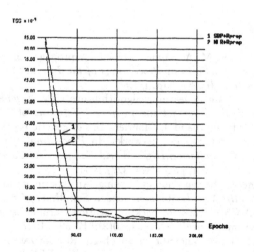

Fig. 2. Plot of the TSS error of SBP with $Rprop$ and NLR with $Rprop$ in the character recognition problem.

6   Conclusions and Future Work

In this paper we have applied GP to find new supervised learning rules for the hidden layers of neural networks. In previous researches GP has discovered for the output layer a useful way of using the Delta learning rule (originally developed for single-layer neural networks) to speed up learning. This rule has performed much better than the SBP learning rule on all the sample problems considered. Then, using this rule to train the output layer GP discovered new learning rules for the hidden layer. In particular GP has discovered a useful way of using the generalised Delta rule and the Hebbian learning rule together. These two learning rules together have performed much better than the SBP learning rule on all the sample problems considered, with and without different speed up algorithms. Whether these rules have the same performed in general remains to be seen.

This study indicates that there are supervised learning algorithms that perform better and are more stable than the SBP learning rule and that GP can discover them.

Acknowledgements

The authors wish to thank the members of the EEBIC (Evolutionary and Emergent Behaviour Intelligence and Computation) group for useful discussions and comments.

References

1. R. Ahmad and F. M. A. Salam. Error back propagation learning using the polynomial energy function. In *Proceedings of the International Joint Conference on Neural Networks, Iizuka, Japan*, 1992.
2. Pierre Baldi. Gradient learning algorithm overview: A general dynamical systems perspective. *IEEE Transactions on Neural Networks*, 6(1):182–195, Jan 1995.
3. S. Bengio, Y. Bengio, and J. Cloutier. Use of genetic programming for the search of a learning rule for neural networks. In *Proceedings of the First Conference on Evolutionary Computation,IEEE World Congress on Computational Intelligence, Orlando-Florida, USA*, pages 324–327, 1994.
4. D. J. Chalmers. The evolution of learning: An experiment in genetic connectionism. In *Connectionist Models Summer School. San Mateo, CA.*, 1990.
5. X-H Yu G-A Chen. Efficient backpropagation learning using optimal learning rate and momentum. *Neural Networks*, 10(3):517–527, 1997.
6. Vladimir Cherkassky and Robert Shepherd. Regularization effect of weight initialization in back propagation networks. In *1998 IEEE International J. Conference of Neural Networks (IJCNN'98), Anchorage, Alaska*, pages 2258–2261. IEEE, May 1998.
7. C Schittenkopf G Deco and W Brauer. Two strategies to avoid overfitting in feedforward neural networks. *Neural Networks*, 10(3):505–516, 1997.
8. D. H. Deterding. *Speaker Normalisation for Automatic Speech Recognition*. PhD thesis, University of Cambridge, 1989.

9. A. Harry Eaton and L. Tracy Oliver. Improving the convergence of the back propagation algorithm. *Neural Networks*, 5:283–288, 1992.
10. S. E. Fahlman. An empirical study of learning speed in back propagation networks. Technical report, CMU-CS-88-162, Carnegie Mellon University, Pittsburgh, PA., 1988.
11. M. Gori and A. Tesi. On the problem of local minima in backpropagation. *IEEE Transactions on PAMI*, 14(1):76–86, 1992.
12. R. P. Gorman and T.J.Sejnowski. Analysis of hidden units in a layered network trained to classify sonar targets. *Neural Networks*, 1:75–89, 1988.
13. S. Haykin. *Neural Networks: A Comprehensive Foundation*. IEEE Society Press, Macmillan College Publishing, New York 10022, 1994.
14. Donald O. Hebb. *The Organisation of Behaviour: A Neuropsychological Theory*. New York: Wiley, 1949.
15. Yoshio Hirose, Koichi Yamashit, and Shimpei Hijiya. Back propagation algorithm which varies the number of hidden units. *Neural Networks*, 4:61–66, 1991.
16. J. H. Holland. *Adaptation in Natural and Artificial Systems*. University of Michigan Press, Ann Arbor, Michigan, 1975.
17. M. J. J. Holt and S. Semnani. Convergence of back-propagation in neural networks using a log-likelihood cost function. *Electronics Letters*, 26(23):1964–1965, 1990.
18. Robert A. Jacobs. Increased rates of convergence through learning rate adaptation. *Neural Networks*, 1:295–307, 1988.
19. K. Kruschke John and R. Javier Movellan. Fast learning algorithms for neural networks. *IEEE Transactions on Circuits and Systems-II: Analogy and Digital Signal Processing*, 39(7):453–473, 1992.
20. H. Kitano. Neurogenetic learning: an integrated method of designing and training neural networks using genetic algorithms. *Physica D*, 75:225–238, 1994.
21. John R. Koza. *Genetic Programming: on the programming of computers by means of natural selection*. MIT Press, Cambridge, Massachussetts, 1992.
22. John R. Koza. *Genetic Programming II: Automatic discovery of reusable programs*. The MIT Press, Cambridge, Massachussetts, 1994.
23. John K. Kruschke and Javier R. Movellan. Benefits of gain: Speeded learning and minimal hidden layers in back propagation networks. *IEEE Transactions on Systems, Man and Cybernetics.*, 21(1), 1991.
24. T Denoeux R Lengelle. Initializing back propagation networks using prototypes. *Neural Networks*, 6(3):351–363, 1993.
25. L.E.Scales. *Introduction to non-linear optimization*. New York:Springer-Verlag, 1985.
26. R. Linsker. From basic network principles to neural architecture: Emergence of spatial-opponent cells. In *Proceedings of the National Acedemy of Science USA*, volume 83, pages 7508–7512, 1986.
27. F. A. lodewyk Wessels and Etienne Barnard. Avoiding false local minima by proper initialisation of connections. *IEEE Transactions on Neural Networks*, 3(6):899–905, 1992.
28. Howard Demuth Martin Hagan and Mark Beale. *Neural Network Design*. PWS Publishing Company, Boston, MA 02116, 96.
29. Rangachari Anand Kishan Mehrotra Chilukuri Mohan and Sanjay Ranka. An impproved algorithm for neural network classification of imbalanced training sets. *IEEE Transactions on Neural Networks*, 4(6):962–969, 1993.
30. Martin F. Moller. A scaled conjugate gradient algorithm for fast supervised learning. *Neural Networks*, 6:525–533, 1993.
31. D. J. Montana and L. Davis. Training feedforaward neural networks using genetic algorithms. In *Proceedings of Eleventh International Joint Conference on Artificial Intelligence (IJCAI-89), Detroit, MI*, pages 762–767. Morgan Kaufmann, Palo Alto, CA, 1989.

32. Taek Mu and Hui Cheng. Contrast enhancement for backpropagation. *IEEE Transactions on Neural Networks*, 7(1):515–524, 1996.
33. A. Van Ooyen and B Nienhuis. Improving the convergence of the back propagation algorithm. *Neural Networks*, 5:465–471, 1992.
34. Alexander G. Parlos, B. Fermandez, Amir Atiya, J. Muthusami, and Wei K. Tsai. An accelerated learning algorithm for multilayer perceptron networks. *IEEE Transactions on Neural Networks*, 5(3):493–497, 1994.
35. S. J. Perantonis and D. A. Karras. An efficient constrained training algorithm for feedforward networks. *IEEE Transactions on Neural Networks*, 6(6):237–149, Nov 1995.
36. J. Pujol and R. Poli. Efficient evolution of asymmetric recurrent neural networks using a pdgp-inspired two-dimensional representation. In *the First European Workshop on Genetic Programming(EUROGP'98), Paris, Springer Lectre Notes in Computer Science*, volume 1391, pages 130–141, 1998.
37. J. Pujol and R. Poli. Evolving neural networks using a dual representation with a combined crossover operator. In *the IEEE International Conference on Evolutionary Computation (ICEC'98), Anchorage, Alaska*, pages 416–421, 1998.
38. J. Pujol and R. Poli. Evolving the topology and the weights of neural networks using a dual representation. *Special Issue on Evolutionary Learning of the Applied Intelligence Journal*, 8(1):73–84, 1998.
39. Amr Radi and Riccardo Poli. Discovery of backpropagation learning rules using genetic programming. In *1998 IEEE International Conference of Evolutionary Computational (ICEC'98), Anchorage, Alaska*, pages 371–375. IEEE, May 1998.
40. Amr Radi and Riccardo Poli. Genetic programming can discover fast and general learning rules for neural networks. In *Third Annual Genetic Programming Conference (GP'98), Madison, Wisconsin*, pages 314–323. Morgan Kaufmann, July 1998.
41. Martin Riedmiller. Advanced supervised learning in multi-layer perceptrons from backpropagation to adaptive learning algorithms. *Computer Standards and Interfaces Special Issue on Neural Networks*, 16(3):265–275, 1994.
42. Martin Riedmiller and Heinrich Braun. A direct method for faster backpropagation learning: The RPROP Algorithm. *IEEE International Conference on Neural Networks 1993 (ICNN93), San Francisco*, pages 586–591, 1993.
43. D. E. Rumelhart, G. E. Hinton, and R. J. Williams. *Parallel Distributed Processing.* MIT Press, Cambridge, MA, 1986.
44. Dilip Sarkar. Methods to speed up error back propagation learning algorithm. *ACM Computing Surveys*, 27(4):519–542, 1995.
45. Wolfram Schiffmann and Merten Joost. Speeding up backpropagation algorithm by using cross-entropy combined with pattern normalization. *International Journal of Uncertainity, Fuzziness and Knowledge-based Systems (IJUFKS)*,, 6(2):177–126, 1998.
46. Femando F. Silva and Luis B. Almeida. *Speeding Backpropagation*, pages 151–158. Advanced Neural Computers, Elsevier Science Publishers B.V. (North-Holland), 1990.
47. Sara A. Solla, Esther Levin, and Michael Fleisher. Accelerated learning in layered neural networks. *Complex System*, 2:625–640, 1988.
48. Alessandro Sperduti and Antonina Starita. Speed up learning and network optimization with extended back propagation. *Neural Networks*, 6:365–383, 1993.
49. Ramana Vitthal P. Sunthar and Ch.Durgaprasada Rao. The generalized proportional-integral-derivative (pid)gradient descent back propagation algorithm. *Neural Networks*, 8(4):563–569, 1995.
50. J. G. Taylor. *The Promise of neural networks.* Springer-Verlag, London, 1993.

Table 1. Summary of Table 3 where Yes = better than SBP and No = worse than SBP.

Rules	Problems			
	XOR	Encoder	character recognition	Display
$NLR_o + SBP$	Yes	Yes	Yes	Yes
$NLR_o + NLR_1$	No	No	Yes	Yes
$NLR_o + NLR_2$	No	Yes	Yes	Yes
$NLR_o + NLR_3$	No	Yes	Yes	Yes
$NLR_o + NLR_4$	No	Yes	Yes	Yes
$NLR_o + NLR_3(m)$	Yes	–	–	–
$NLR_o + NLR_4(m)$	Yes	–	–	–

Table 2. Performance of $NLR_o with NLR_h$ and SBP on two hard problems.

Vowel					
		Learning Epochs			Successful
Algorithm	η	Min.	Max.	Mean	Runs
SBP	0.08	124	273	256.9	100
$NLR_o + NLR_h$	0.08	120	200	165.8	100
Sonar					
		Learning Epochs			Successful
Algorithm	η	Min.	Max.	Mean	Runs
SBP	0.1	373	420	396.7	100
$NLR_o + NLR_h$	0.1	117	167	138.1	100

51. Tom Tollenaere. Super SUB:Fast adaptive back propagation with good scaling properties. *Neural Networks*, 1:561–573, 1990.
52. W.T.Zink T.P.Vogl, J.K. Zigler and D.L.Alkon. Accelerating the convergence of the backpropagation method. *Biological Cybernetics*, 59:256–264, Sept. 1988.
53. Michael K. Weir. A method for self determination of adaptive learning rate in back propagation. *Neural Networks*, 4:(371–379), 1991.
54. D. Whitley and T. Hanson. Optimizing neural networks using faster, more accurate genetic search. In J. D. Schaffer, editor, *Third International Conference on Genetic Algorithms, Georg Mason University,*, pages 391–396. Morgan Kaufmann, 1989.
55. M. Spears William, K. A. De Jong, T. Baeck, David Fogel, and Hugo de Garis. An overview of evolutionary computation. In *Proceedings of the European Conference on Machine Learning*, pages 442–459, 1993.
56. Merten Joost Wolfram Schiffmann and R. Werner. Optimisation of the backpropagation algorithm for training multilayer perceptrons. Technical report 16/1992, University of Koblenz, Institute of Physics, 1992.
57. Byoung-Tak Zhang. Accelerated learning by active example selection. *International Journal of Neural Systems*, 5(1):67–75, 1994.

Table 3. Performance of the discovered learning rules on four different problems.

		XOR			
		Learning Epochs			Successful
Algorithm	η	Min.	Max.	Mean	Runs
SBP	0.96	101	870	163.95	100
$NLR_o + SBP$	0.96	50	197	63.39	100
$NLR_o + NLR_1$	0.96	44	1000	832.54	18
$NLR_o + NLR_2$	0.96	1000	1000	1000	0
$NLR_o + NLR_3$	0.96	16	1000	926.8	16
$NLR_o + NLR_4$	0.96	2	1000	688.26	17
$NLR_o + NLR_3(m)$	0.96	49	1000	161.68	89
$NLR_o + NLR_4(m)$	0.96	58	88	70.95	100
		Encoder			
		Learning Epochs			Successful
Algorithm	η	Min.	Max.	Mean	Runs
SBP	0.4	44	303	118.67	100
$NLR_o + SBP$	0.4	15	108	36.85	100
$NLR_o + NLR_1$	0.4	500	500	500	0
$NLR_o + NLR_2$	0.4	15	105	50.66	100
$NLR_o + NLR_3$	0.4	10	118	34.74	100
$NLR_o + NLR_4$	0.4	16	78	34.37	100
		Character Recognition			
		Learning Epochs			Successful
Algorithm	η	Min.	Max.	Mean	Runs
SBP	0.3	179	358	226.54	100
$NLR_o + SBP$	0.3	34	76	51.29	100
$NLR_o + NLR_1$	0.3	43	94	61.26	100
$NLR_o + NLR_2$	0.3	71	331	149.35	100
$NLR_o + NLR_3$	0.3	54	160	83.21	100
$NLR_o + NLR_4$	0.3	40	108	64.31	100
		Display			
		Learning Epochs			Successful
Algorithm	η	Min.	Max.	Mean	Runs
SBP	0.8	130	500	250.514	87
$NLR_o + SBP$	0.8	46	204	79.069	100
$NLR_o + NLR_1$	0.8	46	180	79.94	100
$NLR_o + NLR_2$	0.8	71	331	149.35	100
$NLR_o + NLR_3$	0.8	41	108	66.81	100
$NLR_o + NLR_4$	0.8	46	116	72.6	100

Evolution of Ship Detectors for Satellite SAR Imagery

Daniel Howard, Simon C. Roberts, and Richard Brankin

Software Evolution Centre
Systems & Software Engineering Centre
Defence Evaluation and Research Agency (DERA)
Malvern, Worcestershire WR14 3PS, UK
dhoward@dera.gov.uk

Abstract. A two-stage evolution scheme is proposed to obtain an object-detector for an image analysis task, and is applied to the problem of ship detection by inspection of the SAR images taken by satellites. The scheme: (1) affords practical evolution times, (2) is structured to discover fast automatic detectors, (3) can produce small detectors that shed light into the nature of the detection. Detectors compare favorably in accuracy to those obtained using a SOM neural network.

1 Introduction

A characteristic of Genetic Programming that separates it from other AI approaches is its ability to produce a tangible function, rule, or computer program. In the field of Computer Vision, GP can be used to produce an explicit rule or function of pixel data to detect the presence of a class of object in a digital image. And it may be possible to determine the principles of detection, i.e. work out how the detector does its job, by inspecting the detector.

The high computing requirement of GP however, is a relative disadvantage that is usually mentioned in the literature [1]. Strategies for tackling problems in this area have considered computing times. For example, Tackett [2] used image features, and Poli [3] used pre-computed statistics of pixel information in the search; others have tried to control the bloating behavior of GP, e.g. [4].

The subject of this paper is a staged GP strategy [5–9] that overcomes excessive computing times to allow solution on a home computer. When tested very near a hard real world setting it has produced simple detectors, and it has been possible to interpret them to understand the object detection strategy.

2 Two-stage evolution strategy

The two-stage GP strategy uses two separate GP searches or stages to discover two object detectors. An object detection test can be carried out at any pixel in a digital image by applying both detectors.

R. Poli et al. (Eds.): EuroGP'99, LNCS 1598, pp. 135–148, 1999.
© Springer-Verlag Berlin Heidelberg 1999

Detectors work on the grey level pixel values of a digital image. They can be algebraic formulae involving the values at pixels belonging to a small region surrounding the pixel undergoing the test. A return value that exceeds a threshold indicates that an object is located at the pixel undergoing the test.

The first GP stage works on a set of test points that is made up of all known 'object' pixels in a training image plus a small random sample of 'non-object' pixels from the training image. The fittest detector from this first GP stage is then applied to all pixels in the training image to discover the set of all false alarms or misclassified object pixels. The misclassification will occur because it will not usually be possible to represent the 'non-object class' by a random sample of non-object pixels. The second GP stage works on a set of test points consisting of all known object pixels in the image plus these false alarms. Total evolution time for the two-stage GP strategy is small because the number of pixels in both sets of test points is very much smaller than the total number of pixels in the training image.

The first and second detectors (the fittest detector of the first stage and the fittest detector of the second stage) are combined using AND and this fused detector is applied to any image to detect objects. In practice, it is the first detector part of this fused detector that performs most of the work because an image normally contains an enormous number of non-object pixels and only few object pixels. In this case, it becomes efficient to manipulate the first GP stage to produce a detector that is small and therefore cheap to implement, e.g. involves few terms, few types of terminals, cheaper functions. This can not compromise the overall power and generality of the search because the job of the first detector is much easier than that of the second detector. The unconstrained second GP stage must discriminate objects and false alarms that look very much alike.

In conclusion, advantages of using the two-stage GP strategy are:

1. fast evolution times because it involves a minority of pixels;
2. fused detector that can maximise the speed of processing of images;
3. first stage could be tuned for sensitivity and the second for specificity, e.g.[6].

3   Problem Domain

Sensors on satellites can be used to compose images of the Earth's surface. Both ERS-1 (ERS stands for: European Remote Sensing) and RADARSAT satellites are equipped with synthetic aperture radar (SAR) to produce images that a photographic interpreter (PI) can visually inspect to detect the presence of objects.

For instance, a human PI can detect the presence of ships in the vastness of the oceans from visual inspection of low-resolution SAR images. It is an example of a task that can be made less tedious and more timely by a software tool that can automatically scan the image to indicate the location of ships.

4   Experiments on ERS-1 SAR images

The first part of this study considered a set of five 50 meter and 100 meter resolution images of the English Channel taken by ERS-1 between July 1992 and November 1992. The ERS-1 satellite uses a 5.3GHz (C-band) SAR instrument with along track resolution of 30 meters and cross track resolution of 27 meters, with SAR data processed to give the required image resolution. Each ERS-1 image corresponds to a ground region of approximately 100 square km.

The images are shown in Figure 1 and more information is given in Table 1. Four of the images were acquired when the satellite was traveling southwards, i.e. with descending orbits. The wind direction was mainly south-westerly. Orientation of the satellite relative to the ships in the channel has an effect because detection is highest when the ships are broadside the satellite beam. The label given to each image is the corresponding satellite orbit number. A number of interesting features can be seen in these images including ships, sand banks, and current flows. The first experiment involved the 100 meter resolution images. Image 5664 was used to evolve the automatic ship detectors, serving as the training image for both stages of GP. Images 6666 and 5084 were used as test images to help to generalise the evolved detectors. Images 5163 and 7167 were used to validate the generality, i.e the blind test.

4.1   Definition of Truth

For the experiment using the 100 meter resolution images, a ship 'truth' for each image was required in order to evolve, test and validate the ship detectors. A unique pixel was designated for a given ship in this truth. HMCG radar data was available to construct some of this truth but most of it was deduced by visual inspection of 50 meter resolution images that corresponded to the 100 meter resolution images.

However, at close inspection, the images around the ship locations in this truth revealed that, at least to the human eye, some of the ships were clearer while other designated ships did look like areas of ocean. This raised the question as to whether certain pixels in the 100 meter resolution image could be safely designated as ships.

Table 1. Characteristics of ERS-1 SAR images of the English Channel.

image	date of acquisition	orbit type	wave height (m)	wind speed (knots)	wind direction (degrees)
5664	15/8/92	descending	0.9	10	220
6666	24/10/92	descending	1.4	19	265
5084	5/7/92	ascending	2.0	22	15
5163	11/7/92	descending	0.7	14	215
7167	28/11/92	descending	1.1	8	310

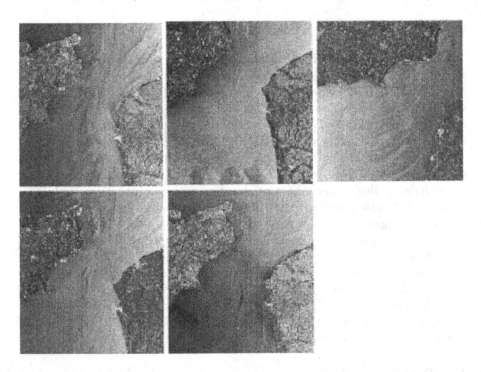

Fig. 1. 100 meter resolution ERS-1 SAR images of the English Channel. Top row: (left) training image 5664; (middle) test image 6666; (right) test image 5084. Bottom row: (left) validation image 5163; (right) validation image 7167.

To address this question we extracted small sub-images centered on the ship pixels in both the 50 meter and 100 meter resolution images, and transformed the pixel values in these sub-images to provide a better indication of the contrast between the ship and its local environment. The transformation consisted of a simple shift in the mean and standard deviation of the pixel values in each sub-image, followed by normalising the pixel values in the localised sub-image. Transformed sub-images taken from a 100 meter resolution image and its equivalent 50 meter resolution image are displayed in Figure 2. Note that corresponding sub-images represent the same geographical area, hence there are four times as many pixels in the 50 meter sub-images. Clear ships are indicated by bright sub-image centres and uniformly darker surroundings. The figure shows that it is possible to grade the ships in terms of their distinction, such that lower grades identify more distinct ships. Five grades of object were distinguished with grade 1 the clearest and grade 5 the faintest. Referring to the grade 5 sub-images, it can be seen that the ships in the 50 meter resolution sub-images are not distinguishable in the corresponding 100 meter resolution sub-images.

Note that relatively bright pixels often appear much more distinct in the normalised sub-images than in the overall image. For example, Figure 2 also displays a number of differently graded ships that appear in a segment of image

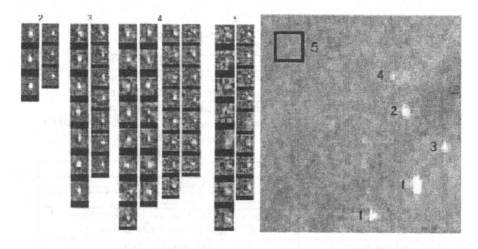

Fig. 2. Ship truth grading. Left: the columns indicate the subjective ship grading; the image strips on the left are taken from one of the 100 meter resolution SAR images while the strips on the right are from the corresponding 50 meter resolution SAR image; note that for grade 5 ships in the truth it becomes difficult to justify that the 100 meter resolution image contains the ships. Right: ship truths shown *in-situ* on a portion of one of the 100 meter resolution SAR images; note that the ship of grade 5 is practically indistinguishable from many of the ocean pixels.

5664. The grade 1 to 4 ships are clearly visible, but the grade 5 ship (in the box) is indistinguishable from the general ocean clutter. As a result of the above observations, only the clearer ships (grades 1 to 4) in image 5664 were used to evolve detectors.

4.2   GP implementation

A steady-state GP algorithm was implemented. Each pixel from the truth was surrounded with a square box or sub-window of pixels. This box was large enough to include a ship and some of the ocean that surrounded it, and at the same time small enough never to include more than one ship - ships can be close to each other. Statistics were computed from the sub-window and fed as primitives to the GP algorithm. Simple mathematical operations, see Table 2, were chosen for the internal nodes of the GP tree. Figure 3 helps to explain the statistics chosen for the GP primitives, e.g. I_{9x9} is the average of the pixel values inside the 9 by 9 box surrounding and including the pixel; V_{9x9} is the standard deviation of the pixel values in the 1 pixel deep perimeter; P_{9x9} is the corresponding perimeter average; $D_{3x7} = I_{3x3} - P_{7x7}$ and pix is the value at the pixel.

Arbitrarily, it was decided that the evolved detector operating over the ocean pixels should return a positive real number to denote a ship detection, and zero or a negative value to denote an ocean pixel, giving only four possible returns: a false alarm or FP or false positive is a positive return for an ocean pixel; a ship

Table 2. GP parameter settings

Parameter	Setting
function set	addition, subtraction, multiplication, protected division, min, max
terminal set	integer (range: -127 to 128, step: 1), negative real (range: -1.00 to -0.005, step: 0.005), positive real (range: 0.005 to 1.00, step: 0.005), pixel statistics
tournament size	4, 6, 8
speciation (mating radius)	200, population size
no. of random seeds	20
no. of training sub-images	first detector: 5059 second detector: 59 + FP from first detector (see section 2)
population size	first detector: 5000 second detector: 200, 500, 1000, 2000, 5000
max generations	first detector: 10 second detector: 30
max tree size (nodes)	first detector: 20second detector: 1000
termination-criteria	exceed max generations or an individual achieves zero fitness

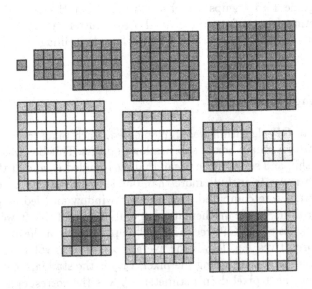

Fig. 3. GP primitives examples; from left to right, top row: pix, I_{3x3}, I_{5x5}, I_{7x7}, I_{9x9}; middle row: V_{9x9} or P_{9x9}, V_{7x7} or P_{7x7}, V_{5x5} or P_{5x5}, V_{3x3} or P_{3x3}; bottom row: D_{3x5}, D_{3x7}, and D_{3x9}. The statistic is computed using the pixel values in the shaded areas.

missed or FN or false negative is a negative return for a ship pixel; TN and TP are oceans and ships classified correctly.

4.3 Justification for the two-stage strategy

Each image contained $O(10^6)$ pixels. In the first GP stage, $O(10^3)$ ocean pixels were selected at random together with all clear ships in the truth, i.e. grades 1 to 4. When the champion detector from the first stage was applied to the entire training image, this resulted in $O(10^2)$ false detections which was small in comparison to the number of ocean pixels in the entire image but significant with respect to the number of ships - also $O(10^2)$. Hence, the evolution times for discovering second detectors though the dominant factor were not excessive.

Over 99% of the returns from the first detector were negative so that the second detector only applied to a very small number of pixels - the TP and FP from the first detector. Hence, the second detector did not influence total CPU time of detection to any appreciable extent, even though it had the potential to be a more complex detector.

The second detector was studied to show that it could do much more than to simply lift the detection threshold of the first detector in an attempt to eliminate the FP. The interested reader can find this study in reference [7].

It is also interesting to note that a few of the initial random seeds managed to discover very short second detectors.

4.4 Optimisation of GP parameters

The GP method involves a number of free parameters. These can be varied so that the evolved detector can optimise the objectives of accuracy, or how well the evolved detector can generalise across multiple images; convergence, or the computing time required to evolve the most accurate detectors; and performance, or how fast the detector can identify ships in service, which is in turn related to the detectors simplicity. As stated, the maximum size of the detector in the first evolution stage was restricted to produce simple and fast detectors. Preliminary experimentation investigated this parameter by restricting the maximum tree size to between 10 and 300 nodes. The same solution was derived whenever the size was greater than 100 nodes. The evolved detector always had less than 50 nodes and it commonly had less than 20 nodes. In order to encourage a simple solution, the maximum size of the first detector was set to 20 nodes. In addition, the first detector processed a minimal number of pixel statistics. Three statistics were first investigated: I_{3x3}, P_{7x7} and V_{7x7}. However, it was found that the value of the centre pixel was also required in order to hit small, faint ships. For all GP runs, the first detector was allowed to evolve for exactly 10 generations.

The maximum size of the detectors in the second evolution stage was set to 1000 in order to allow large trees to evolve whilst retaining practical computing times. All of the pixel statistics were available in this stage and the selection weighting for each node (function or terminal) was the same. The population of second detectors evolved for 30 generations. Each evolutionary stage processed 59 ships (grade 1 to 4) from the training image. The first stage was also trained with 5000 randomly selected ocean pixels. Each evolutionary parameter configuration was run using 20 random seeds to govern the various random selections, e.g. initial population, tournament selection, crossover point selection, etc. However, each run used the same 5000 training ocean pixels.

4.5   Procedure to assess generalisation

The accuracy of the evolved detectors was established by calculating a figure of merit (FOM) as follows:

$$FOM = \frac{TP}{ships + FP} \qquad (1)$$

where TP is the number of true positives or ship hits, FP is the number of false positives or false detections that result from the application of a fused detector to an image, and $ships$ is the total number of ships in the truth and including grade 5 ships. The FOM and the two test images were used in a procedure that was automated as follows. For each run corresponding to a choice of GP parameters, i.e. a given random seed, population size, tournament size, etc.:

1. Save a list of the ten best unique detectors at each generation of the second evolution stage and then fuse each one of these with the first detector.
2. Compute the FOM over both test images for each fused detector.
3. Select the fused detector with the highest averaged FOM, provided that this detector has $FOM > 0.5$ for both images, i.e. it generalises well across both images.

Figure 4 demonstrates why this procedure is needed by displaying FOM resulting from a run in this investigation. The figure shows that FOM always increase for the training image, but over-training occurs at a certain generation (the 14th in this case) and FOM consequently drops for other images.

4.6   Fitness measure optimisation

Three fitness measures were investigated (this work is fully described in [7]). One of them was very similar to that used by Poli in [3]. However, the one that produced the best results we called: 'modified metric' fitness measure, f_{MM}, the only of the fitness measures to account for the ship grading, SG:

$$f_{MM} = \frac{\sum_{hits}(5 - SG)}{\sum_{ships}(5 - SG) + FP} - 1 \qquad (2)$$

The impetus for introducing SG into the fitness was that the measures that did not include it occasionally caused obvious ships to be missed, even grade 1 ships. In these cases, the detector performed well on the 6666 image (which includes many grade 4 ships) but produced poor results for the 5084 image. Hence, the

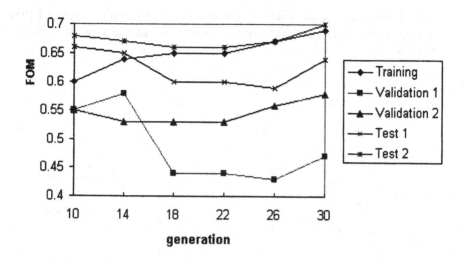

Fig. 4. Variation of FOM with generation.

detector was probably focusing on hitting small, faint ships at the expense of missing large, bright ships. Such detectors were never evolved using f_{MM}.

Unlike the other measures that did not involve SG, f_{MM} gives a better distinction between the fitness of each individual. It is possible that false alarms are discouraged by a measure that rewards the detection of clearer ships, thus more consistently producing accurate detectors that generalise across all images.

4.7 Summary of evolution study

While [7] gives a full account of our investigations it is worth noting some of the main conclusions of the study:

1. Effective and simple first detectors could be evolved by restricting the terminal set to only 4 pixel statistics and the maximum tree size to 20 nodes.
2. Small effective fused detectors could be evolved, i.e. both the first and second detectors comprising less than 20 nodes.
3. The evolution of detectors was fairly insensitive to the random seed in terms of accuracy but certain random seeds did lead to parsimonious detectors, i.e. a very small second detector.
4. The convergence rate decreased with tournament size but lower convergence rates more reliably produced good detectors. (See Figure 5) A tournament size of 6 produced a reasonable trade-off between convergence rate and reliability for a population size of 5000 individuals.
5. Large population sizes more reliably produced good detectors, due possibly to the consequent greater starting diversity with which to evolve detectors. (See Figure 6) However, larger population sizes lead to longer evolution times. A population of 2000 individuals gave a reasonable trade-off between

reliably evolving a good detector and run-time. The results suggested that a population larger than 5000 may be needed for tournament sizes greater than 6.

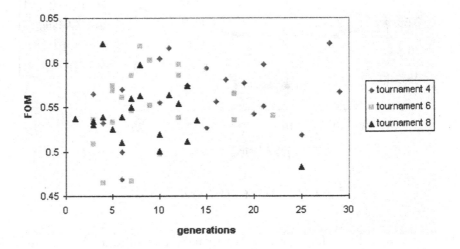

Fig. 5. Effect on *FOM* of varying the tournament size.

4.8   Comparison to Kohonen Self-Organising Map

The GP results in Table 3 were obtained by applying an accurate fused detector to all five images. This GP run used a population of 5000 individuals and a tournament size of 4. The first detector in the fused pair trained in 10 generations and had 17 nodes. The second detector trained in 28 generations and had 123 nodes.

The performance of this fused detector pair was compared to results by Foulkes at DERA who tested a number of algorithms including multi-layer perceptron neural networks and self-organising maps. The best results in his report, obtained with a Log-Median Kohonen net [11] pg. 21, are displayed side by side to those of the best GP detector. The comparison is fair in the sense that both DERA teams invested a considerable amount time on this problem and used the same image for training the automatic detectors. Comparing these results there is no case where the GP method has fewer TP and more FP. However, the converse is not true. It cannot be concluded that GP is a superior method based on these tests alone, but it can be concluded that the detectors produced by the two-stage GP method are very accurate.

As explained in Section 4.1, certain ships in the truth are extremely faint being essentially indistinguishable from some of the ocean pixels at 100 meter image resolution. Thus, it is important to note that the exclusion of these ships

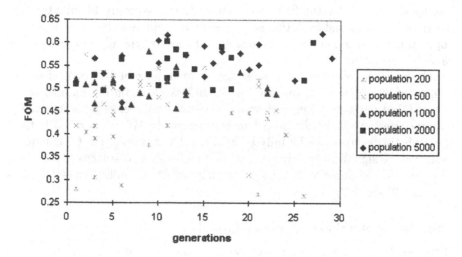

Fig. 6. Effect on *FOM* of varying the population size.

from training data in image 5664 did not affect the accuracy of the detectors. There was also evidence to suggest that by excluding grade 5 targets from the training data, evolution time was curtailed and evolution convergence was improved.

Table 3. Comparison between GP and the SOM.

image	truth	best SOM			GP		
		TP	FP	FOM	TP	FP	FOM
5664 (training)	77	44	2	0.56	56	0	0.72
6666 (test)	33	18	1	0.53	22	1	0.65
5084 (test)	55	20	8	0.47	22	1	0.59
5163 (valdidation)	71	55	11	0.67	48	1	0.67
7167 (valdidation)	58	46	6	0.72	41	1	0.69

4.9 Estimates of computer run-time

All work was carried out on a 300MHz Pentium II PC with 128MB of RAM under Windows NT. Three types of run-time should be distinguished:

1. run-time required to evolve detectors for a given random seed;
2. run-time required to discover the optimal detector;
3. run-time required to process one image, i.e. to automatically detect the ships in the image.

The total run-time for the first evolution stage was typically 14 minutes. The run-time for the second evolution stage was more variable as it depended on the population size and number of training sub-images. It typically ranged between 25 and 60 minutes.

The run-time required to discover the optimal detector will depend on the number of test images, on the number of random seeds, on the number of detectors saved per generation, and on the maximum number of generations. The optimal detector can be discovered in approximately 170 hours of CPU time. However, this process can be fully parallelised. Furthermore, the CPU requirement may be significantly reduced with techniques such as stochastic sampling. The CPU time required to detect ships in an image of one million pixels is always less than 40 seconds.

4.10 Interpretation of detector formulae

GP differs from other artificial intelligence techniques that carry out parameter regression by encoding sets of solution parameters. Symbolic regression evolves and executes computer programs that are themselves candidate solutions to the problem. GP, thus, provides us with the formula for the ship detector.

Formulae for all champion detectors are reported in [7]. When simplified, nearly all the first detectors produced in the experiments had relatively few statistics and, to a first approximation, had the following type of formulation:

$$pixel\ value - local\ mean - local\ variance - constant \tag{3}$$

This is equivalent to local spot detection and, in the absence of further information sources - such as intuition, past experience, geographical and scenario knowledge by analysts - could be considered to be a rough approximation to the human eye approach to ship detection. Second detectors had the tougher job of eliminating the false detections without sacrificing the number of hits. They did not do this by a simple scaling of the detection threshold for the first detector. The situation was rather more complicated. For example, the following was the formula for a remarkably simple, and yet successful second detector, a different version of spot detection:

$$D_{3x5} * pix - 11 * V_{9x9} - P_{5x5} \tag{4}$$

From the numerical analysis carried out in [7] it can be deduced that the leading term is $D_{3x5} * pix$: for a hit, the stronger a ship the greater the value of D_{3x5} (the difference of local means) and hence the larger the contribution to the detector; for a false detection, the smaller was the value of D_{3x5} and hence the greater contribution of the term $-P_{5x5}$.

4.11 Work on the 50 meter resolution imagery

A limited investigation was carried out over the 50 meter resolution version of these images. The following first detector emerged from that investigation:

$$min[min(pix, 0.32) - 0.25, I_{5x5} - P_{13x13} - 0.695] \tag{5}$$

The detector knows that pixel values that are less than 0.25 are oceans, and the rest are subjected to a version of spot detection.

5 Experiments on RADARSAT images

Such an insight into the structure of the ship detection allowed Brankin [10] to handcraft a version of the spot detector to hunt for ships in a 10-m resolution image of the Scottish coastline taken by a different satellite, i.e. the RADARSAT satellite.

The RADARSAT satellite also has a 5.3GHz SAR instrument whose sensor can be used in a number of different modes giving an along-track resolution of 10 meters for fine beam mode and 100 meters for wide scan mode. The area covered being 50x50 km for fine beam mode and 500x500 km for wide scan mode. The images used in this study were ScanSar narrow beam with a nominal spatial resolution of 50 meters and an area coverage of 300x300 meters. RADARSAR ScanSar narrow has a far higher signal to noise ratio compared to ERS-1 imagery, making the problem easier. These images are two orders of magnitude larger than those considered in the ERS-1 experiments and so require the fastest possible detector.

It turned out that when a simple threshold detector was combined with a spot detector all ships in the truth of the images involved were detected. Those investigators who used neural networks had spent time training a detector to achieve the same task.

6 Conclusions

This investigation has shown that a GP approach to automatic ship detection in SAR imagery can successfully evolve detectors which generalise well across multiple images, minimise computational effort during image processing, and require only a minimal time to evolve. At least as far as accuracy is concerned the results compare very favorably with those obtained on the same problem by rival techniques such as Kohonen neural networks.

Unlike artificial neural networks, GP works directly with the computer program, in this case the formula for the detector. Through the procedure implemented here, small formulae are obtained that shed light on the workings of the detector. The principles of detection can be gathered from analysis of these formulae. This results in an interaction between investigator and method that can guide the definition of the problem and the nature of its solution.

The GP study carried out here involved a huge search space, but it was automated to discover outstanding detectors from a large number of very competitive detectors.

References

1. Winkeler J. F. and Manjunath B. S.: Genetic Programming for Object Detection. In Koza, Deb, Dorigo, Fogel, Garzon, Iba and Riolo (editors). Genetic Programming 1997: Proceedings of the Second Annual Conference.
2. Tackett W. A.: Genetic Programming for feature discovery and image discrimination. Proceedings of the Fifth International Conference on Genetic Algorithms. Morgan Kaufmann, 1993.
3. Poli R.: Genetic Programming for Image Analysis. In Koza, John R., Goldberg, David E., Fogel, David B., and Riolo, Rick L. (editors). Genetic Programming 1996: Proceedings of the First Annual Conference Cambridge, MA: The MIT Press.
4. Harris C. and Buxton B.: Evolving edge detectors with Genetic Programming. In Koza, John R., Goldberg, David E., Fogel, David B., and Riolo, Rick L. (editors). Genetic Programming 1996: Proceedings of the First Annual Conference Cambridge, MA: The MIT Press.
5. D. Howard: Application of Genetic Programming to target detection and CFD problems. DERA Malvern technical report DERA/CIS/SEC/TR980322, 1998.
6. Roberts S.C. and Howard D.: Evolution of Vehicle Detectors for Infrared Line Scan Imagery Proceedings of First European Workshop in Evolutionary Image Analysis and Signal Processing EvoIASP, Gothenburg, Sweden, 1999.
7. Roberts S.C., Howard D., Brankin R.: Genetic evolution of automatic ship detection in SAR imagery. DERA Malvern report DERA/CIS/SEC/TR980323, 1998.
8. Howard D., Roberts S. C., Brankin R.: Advances in Engineering Software, vol. 30(5) (1999) 303-311.
9. Howard D., Roberts S. C., Brankin R.: Genetic Programming for Target Detection, Journal of Defence Science, March 1999.
10. Brankin R.: Automatic ship detection in 10-m resolution SAR imagery: an investigation. DERA Malvern technical Report DERA/CIS/SEC/TR980324, 1998.
11. Foulkes S.B.: Ship detection in ERS-1 and Radarsat SAR images using a self-organising neural network. DERA Malvern technical report DERA/LS1/TR980309, 1998.

Automatic Generation of Affine IFS and Strongly Typed Genetic Programming

Anargyros Sarafopoulos

School of Media Arts & Communication
National Centre for Computer Animation Bournemouth University
Talbot Campus Fern Barrow, Poole, Dorset BH12 5BB, UK
asarafop@bournemouth.ac.uk

Abstract. Iterated Function Systems (IFS) are recursive systems that have applications in modeling, animation and, Fractal Image Compression. IFS can be represented as arrays of floating point constants or, as shown in this paper, hierarchical data structures and therefore are good candidates for evolutionary applications. This paper describes a Strongly Typed Genetic Programming (STGP) approach to the automatic generation and evolution of 2D affine IFS, and affine maps in general. We explain the nature of the encoding used in conjunction with STGP, and demonstrate with examples its application to the inverse problem for IFS.

1 Introduction

Fractal objects are objects whose geometry and natural beauty is often a result of their self-similar structure. Affine IFS provide a method for generating fractals and are based on a recursive application of affine transformations/maps on sets of points on the Euclidean space. This method of generating fractals is due to J. Hutchinson [6]. IFS were later successfully used in modeling, animation and, fractal image compression. Barnsley [2, 3] was the first to indicate that IFS can be used for fractal image compression and developed an interactive system for the generation and solution of *inverse problem for IFS* (see section 6).

Because of their nature, as sets of floating point numbers, IFS are directly evolvable, and have been used in conjunction with evolutionary algorithms. Angeline [1] describes a system based on an extension of the concept of affine IFS, which is applied for the interactive evolution of „Fractal Movies" using Evolutionary Programming (EP). Other researchers have used Genetic Algorithm (GA) for the resolution of the inverse problem for IFS and in conjunction with fractal image compression [12, 13]. Cretin and Lutton [4] have applied Genetic Programming (GP) to the resolution of the inverse problem for „mixed-IFS", that is, IFS which are not affine. Other methods for evolving fractals, such as Lindenmayer Systems have also been investigated using GP [7].

We notice that, although evolutionary methods such as GA and EP have been applied for the generation of affine-IFS, there is not direct application (to the author's knowledge) of GP to the evolution of affine IFS. This paper proposes a system for the evolution of sets of affine transformations. We describe our STGP architecture for the

R. Poli et al. (Eds.): EuroGP'99, LNCS 1598, pp. 149-160, 1999.
© Springer-Verlag Berlin Heidelberg 1999

evolution of affine-IFS (IFS-STGP), and subsequently demonstrate its application on the resolution of the inverse problem for IFS.

2 Modeling Affine IFS

An affine transformation is defined as linear transformation followed by a translation. A 2D affine transformation is defined as:

$$w(x) = L(x) + T = \begin{bmatrix} a & b \\ c & d \end{bmatrix} \begin{bmatrix} x_1 \\ x_2 \end{bmatrix} + \begin{bmatrix} e \\ f \end{bmatrix}. \tag{1}$$

A transformation on a metric space is called contractive or a contractive mapping if there is a constant $0 \le s < 1$ such that:

$$d(f(x), f(y)) \le s \cdot d(x, y) \forall x, y \in R^2. \tag{2}$$

Where $d(x, y)$ denotes the distance between points x, y. Any such number s is called a *contractivity factor* for f. This means, that points in the space when affected by the transformation are placed always closer together. Consider the process of repeatedly applying f to a set of points in space. The process will eventually lead to all points being crunched into a single point in space, the *fixed point* of the transformation. The Contraction Mapping Theorem [2] states that if f is contractive then it posses exactly one *fixed point* xf and moreover for any point, the sequence:

$$\{ f^{\circ n}(x) : n = 0, 1, 2, \dots \}. \tag{3}$$

Converges to xf, that is:

$$\underset{n \to \infty}{Lim} f^{\circ n}(x) = xf, \forall x. \tag{4}$$

A (hyperbolic) iterated function system consists of a complete metric space (in this case 2D Euclidean space) together with a finite set of *contractive* mappings Wn, with respective contractivity factors Sn, for $n = 1, 2, \dots N$.
The notation for the IFS is $\{ Wn, n = 1, 2, \dots N \}$. The contractivity of the IFS is given by $MAX\{ Sn, n = 1, 2, \dots N \}$. This paper deals with fractals, which are black and white pictures, drawings, „black-on-white" subsets of space. Therefore, it becomes natural to introduce space H. Space H is the space of „black-on-white" drawings on a flat surface, or more formally, the complete metric space whose elements are compact subsets of 2D Euclidean space. In order to, correctly, define space H we need a distance measure between points in H, this is given by the *Hausdorff* metric.

$$d_H(A, B) = \max[\max_{x \in A}(\min_{y \in B} d(x, y)), \ \max_{y \in B}(\min_{x \in A} d(x, y))]. \tag{5}$$

Let $\{ Wn, n = 1, 2, \dots N \}$ be an iterated function system with contractivity s, then the transformation W given by:

$$W(B) = \bigcup_{n=1}^{N} w_n(B).$$ (6)

is a contraction mapping on the metric space H [2]. Which means that there is a unique fixed-point A that belongs to space H given by equation 4. The fixed-point A is called the *attractor* of the IFS, and it is the fractal object we've been looking for. There are two well-known methods of constructing IFS fractals the Photocopy Algorithm and the Chaos Game Algorithm [3, 4].

3 Encoding and Random Generation of Affine Maps

If the coding of an IFS is an array of floating point constants, generating random IFS could be as simple as generating sequences of random numbers, however we thought that there are more „intuitive" ways of representing affine maps. By definition an affine map (see equation 1) is a linear map followed by a translation. We insisted on a representation that could emphasize this fact. Also, it is well known that the set of linear transformations forms a *group*, that is, if f and g are linear maps so is $f(g)$, and if f is a linear map so is its inverse.

Thus we can compose linear transformations to make new linear transformations. This leads to the question of finding a set of elementary transformations out of which all transformation can be generated by composition. The most general linear transformation can be generated by composition of a *scaling* with a *rotation* and a *skew*. It is possible therefore to use these three primitive maps in order to generate by composition any workable mapping. We thought that this provides an interesting method for the automatic generation of linear maps. This method allows hierarchical structure and the composition of affine maps as Lisp Symbolic Expressions (S-expressions). It is interesting that contractive maps also form a *semigroup* and therefore combinations of contractive linear maps are linear contractive maps. It follows that all contractive maps can be generated by composition of a small set of elementary contractive maps.

Table 1. Elemetary contractive transformations used in the expirements described in this paper.

evaluation	arguments	
Scale	$a, d \in [0, 1)$	$(x_1 \cdot a, x_2 \cdot d)$
scale ∘ rotation	$a, d \in [0,1), \vartheta \in [0,2\pi)$	$(x_1 \cdot a \cdot \cos\vartheta - x_2 \cdot a \cdot \sin\vartheta, x_1 \cdot d \cdot \sin\vartheta + x_2 \cdot d \cdot \cos\vartheta)$
rotation ∘ scale	$\vartheta \in [0,2\pi), a, d \in [0,1)$	$(x_1 \cdot a \cdot \cos\vartheta - x_2 \cdot d \cdot \sin\vartheta, x_1 \cdot a \cdot \sin\vartheta + x_2 \cdot d \cdot \cos\vartheta)$
scale ∘ skew-x	$a, d, b, \in [0,1)$	$(x_1 \cdot a, x_1 \cdot a + x_2 \cdot a \cdot d)$
scale ∘ skew-y	$a, d, c, \in [0,1)$	$(x_1 \cdot a, x_1 \cdot cd + x_2 \cdot d)$

The 2D *contractive elementary maps* used for the generation of IFS codes in the experiments described in this paper are shown in table 1. Function parameters are constrained so that all transformations are contractive. To ensure that a linear map A

of the type *scale ∘ skew* is contractive we calculate the contractivity of the map and adjust the parameters recursively until, the contractivity constrains hold true. The contractivity factor is calculated by taking the *norm* of the linear transformation A, the norm of linear transformation is defined as:

$$\| A \| = \max \{ \frac{\| Ax \|}{\| x \|} : x \in R^2, x \neq 0 \} . \tag{7}$$

The norm of a point $\|x\|$ is defined to be its distance from the origin $O\ (0,\ 0)$.

4 Strongly Typed Genetic Programming

In GP population individuals are defined as hierarchical Lisp Symbolic Expressions. S-expressions are composed of two types of functions, functions that accept arguments and called *non-terminal functions*, and functions take no arguments called *terminals*. For brevity we use the term *function* to mean *non-terminal function*. One important constrain of GP is that S-expressions have to satisfy the property of *closure* [8]. That is, all functions have to accept arguments and return values of the same type. This allows for legal crossover recombination and mutation of S-expressions. Montana [9] has introduced STGP by extending the GP paradigm to overcome the problem of closure. That is, functions in STGP can accept arguments and return values of different data types. Generation, crossover and mutation are constrained so syntactic correct S-expressions are produced.

5 STGP Architecture

We used STGP instead of GP, because expressing the structure of affine IFS involves more than one data type. An IFS is itself is a list of affine-maps, affine maps are made of linear transformations and translations (see equation 1). In the 2D case, linear maps are made as composition of 2D elementary transformations, and elementary transformations and translations can be expressed as arrays of floating point numbers. STGP allows us to use separate data types for different types of terminal floating-point ephemeral constants. Discrimination among constants is based on their functionality, so we differentiate between scale ratios, skew ratios, angles of rotation, and translation constants. The IFS were constrained to contain at least three affine maps, so the *output type* is MAP_LIST_3, *which* is a list of at least three affine maps. The number of data types used in the simulation is shown in table 2.

Table 3 lists the set of non-terminal functions used in the simulation. The set of data types and functions mirror the hierarchical structure for the generation of affine IFS as described above. The functions that represent linear transformations (that contain scale rotation or skew) follow the principle outlined in section 3. f_map_list is used in a fashion similar to the common Lisp function PROGN. It creates lists of affine maps, and allows generation of S-expressions with variable number of affine transformations. Matrix composition functions are used in order to allow for complex combination of linear maps. f_linear_composition_2/3 take as arguments two/three linear maps and combine them by post multiplying their corresponding matrixes. Table 4 lists the terminal set of functions in STGP. This set reflects the functionality of the floating-point constants in the system. Allowing for different types of constants, disables crossover between types which are not related such as the combination of rotation angles with scaling ratios, skew ratios or translation constants. The values of these constants are within the range outlined in table 1. Translation constants are constrained within the range [-0.5, 0.5]. The attractors of the generated IFS exist in a 1x1 square space centered at the origin.

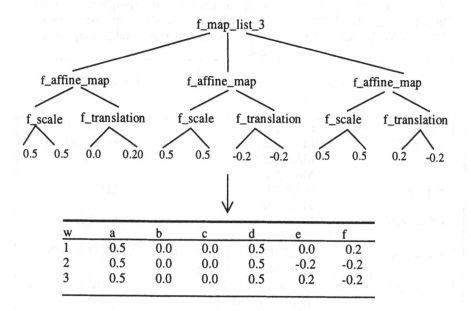

Fig. 1. *S-expression* representing an IFS that contains three affine (*f_affine_map*) transformations. Each affine map is made of a scale transformation (*f_scale*) and a translation (*f_translation*). Function (*f_map_list_3*) is the root of all S-expressions in the simulation and it represents a list of three affine maps. The *S-expression* is converted to an array format before fitness evaluation. Column *w* contains the number of affine maps, each row contains the coefficients *a*, *b*, *c*, *d*, *e*, and *f* (see equation 1) of the corresponding map.

For the generation of a random population of expressions the methods outlined by Montana [9] were used. The S-expressions are subsequently interpreted into a typical IFS form, a table of floating point constants, as shown in figure 1. The attractor of the IFS can then be rendered using the photocopy (or other) algorithm.

The hierarchical IFS representation allows for the generation of IFS with a variable number of affine maps, it also allows for modification of the maps in the IFS by composition of linear transformations and translations, rather than by simply adjusting the IFS parameters. This is similar to the way a human designer would adjust a 2D/3D model by stretching, rotating, and translating co-ordinates in space. It is also in line with systems for the interactive resolution of the inverse IFS problem and systems for the interactive generation of affine IFS in general [3].

Table 2. Types used in the STGP representation of affine IFS

types	functionality
MAP_LIST_3	a list of at least three affine maps, this is the output or return type of S-expressions
MAP_LIST	a list of n affine maps, where n = 1,2, ..., N
LINEAR_MAP	a linear transformation
TRANSLATION	translation or shift along the x and y axis
EPHEMERAL_CONST_T	translation ephemeral floating point constant
EPHEMERAL_CONST_S	scale ratio, ephemeral floating point constant
EPHEMERAL_CONST_SK	skew ratio, ephemeral floating point constant
EPHEMERAL_CONST_ANGLE	angle (in radians), ephemeral floating point constant

Table 3. Functions used in the STGP representation of afine IFS

functions	arguments	return type
f_map_list_3	MAP_LIST MAP_LIST MAP_LIST	MAP_LIST_3
f_map_list	MAP_LIST MAP_LIST	MAP_LIST
f_affine_map	LINEAR_MAP TRANSLATION	MAP_LIST
f_translation	EPHEMERAL_CONST_T EPHEMERAL_CONST_T	TRANSLATION
f_trn_composition	TRANSLATION TRANSLATION	TRANSLATION
f_linear_composition_2	LINEAR_MAP LINEAR_MAP	LINEAR_MAP
f_linear_composition_3	LINEAR_MAP LINEAR_MAP LINEAR_MAP	LINEAR_MAP
f_scale	EPHEMERAL_CONST_S EPHEMERAL_CONST_S	LINEAR_MAP
f_scale_rotation	EPHEMERAL_CONST_S EPHEMERAL_CONST_S EPHEMERAL_CONST_ANGLE	LINEAR_MAP
f_rotaton_scale	EPHEMERAL_CONST_ANGLE EPHEMERAL_CONST_S EPHEMERAL_CONST_S	LINEAR_MAP
f_scale_skewx	EPHEMERAL_CONST_S EPHEMERAL_CONST_S EPHEMERAL_CONST_SK	LINEAR_MAP
f_scale_skewy	EPHEMERAL_CONST_S EPHEMERAL_CONST_S EPHEMERAL_CONST_SK	LINEAR_MAP

Table 4. Terminals used in the STGP representation of affine IFS

Terminals	return type
t_ephemeral_const_scale	EPHEMERAL_CONST_S
t_ephemeral_const_trns	EPHEMERAL_CONST_T
t_ephemeral_const_skew	EPHEMERAL_CONST_SK
t_ephemeral_const_angle	EPHEMERAL_CONST_ANGLE

6 Inverse Problem , Collage Theorem and Fitness Measures

We test our IFS-STGP system, against the inverse problem for IFS. According to this problem we are asked to find an affine IFS whose attractor is a given image. Barnsley [2] has demonstrated what is known as the *collage theorem*. According to the collage theorem given a black and white image $L \in H$, an IFS $\{W1, W2, W3, ... Wn\}$ with contractivity factor s and a number E grater tan zero, we get:

$$h\left(L, \bigcup_{n=1}^{N} w_n(L) \right) \leq E \Rightarrow h(L, A) \leq E / (1 - s) . \tag{8}$$

where $h(\ )$ is the Hausdorff distance, and A is the attractor of the IFS. Equivalently:

$$h(L, A) \leq (1 - s)^{-1} \cdot h\left(L, \bigcup_{n=1}^{N} w_n(L) \right). \tag{9}$$

The theorem tells us that in order to find an IFS whose attractor is close to or looks like L we need to minimize the right term of equation 9. In other words, we need to find a collage of the images of L under the transformations, which is near to L. We can use the right term of equation 9 as a fitness measure. However, calculating the Hausdorff distance is computationally expensive. Previous work on the inverse problem has rarely used the Hausdorff metric, instead several alternative methods have been proposed. The most obvious is taking the pixel difference between the target image and the attractor, but this lacks sensitivity to the actual shape of the target and produces poor results. An alternative to pixel difference proposed by Nettleton and Garigliano [10] is an algorithm that increments an individual's fitness when points under transformation fall into the target shape, and decrements the fitness when points under transformation miss the target shape. The above distance measure can be taken between the attractor and the target or between the collage image and the target. Cretin and Lutton [4] propose another approach based on pixel difference between *distance images* [5] of the target and the attractor. However, they state that it does not perform well when images contain many linear elements.

The fitness function described by Nettleton is calculated using the code listing that follows. Notice that *(fitness)* stores standardized fitness values as described by Koza [8]. The *INCREMENT* parameter varies randomly between runs in the range [2, 20].

```
fitness := pixels_in_target_shape;
FOR y=0 TO target_height DO
  FOR x=0 TO target_width DO
    IF      collage[y][x]=1 AND target[y][x]=1 THEN
        fitness := fitness -1;
      ELSE IF collage[y][x]=1 AND target[y][x]=0 THEN
        fitness := fitness + INCREMEN;
      ELSE
        fitness := fitness
```

7 Results

We use the fitness function described by Nettleton [5], which we name the Nettleton Fitness (NF). When using Nettleton Fitness, the major advantage is that calculations involved are less intensive. However, this function is less sensitive to the target shape than the Hausdorff Fitness and can leave the system trapped in local minima. The NF is taken between the collage shape and the target shape. We found that by adjusting the '*INCREMENT*' parameter (shown in the program listing above) we can obtain better or worse results depending on the target shape, so we modify the *INCREMENT* between separate runs in the range from 2 to 20 inclusive. For the results presented in this paper, the images of a filled square (box problem) and a Barnsley fern (fern problem) are used as target shapes. Both images share the same resolution of 64x64 pixels. In this paper we do not present the S-expression trees because it is impossible to visually interpret them or analyze, instead we present the tabular notation for IFS derived from the S-expressions as shown in tables 5 and 6.

7.1 Drawing a Box Using NF

The box problem was easy and the system produced 100% correct results in all runs. That is, the system produced collages that completely covered the target shape. However because of rounding off errors during the calculation of the collage the attractor of the IFS is not a 100% match of the target shape but a close approximation. This approximation becomes more and more inaccurate as the contractivity of IFS moves closer to 1 (see equation 8). In order to avoid deceptive fitness evaluations, S-expressions with contractivity above a given threshold are removed form the population. In the box problem the *contractivity threshold* was set to 1.0. We used a population of 50 individuals for 301 generations and 10 runs. The maximum tree depth was set to 8 and mutation probability was set to 0.02.

The solution of the problem shown in figure 2 is a set of transformations that create a collage that completely covers the target shape. Note that the coefficients of the linear of transformations 1, 2, 4 and 5 shown in table 5 are variations of a single linear transformation.

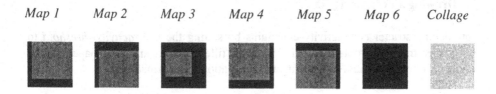

Fig. 2. Mappings providing a solution for the box collage problem. *Gray color* represents the target shape under the transformations, and the dark gray/*black color* the target shape itself. Maps *3* and *6* are redundant and can be ignored without affecting the solution. The *light gray* square is the collage shape.

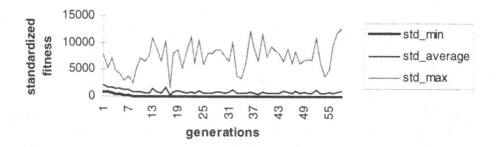

Fig. 3. *Standardized fitness* graph for the Box collage problem. The *std_max* curve, marked with triangles, varies along a wide range. *std_min* curve, marked with filled diamond shapes, converges quickly and reaches a solution at generation 57.

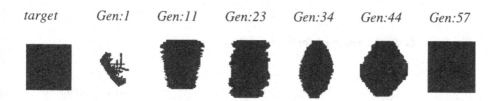

Fig. 4. Box collage problem, from left to right: original image (*target*) and best images of generations (*Gen:*) *1, 11, 23, 34, 44* and finally the solution at generation *57*. The images are generated using the photocopy algorithm. Notice that the solution (*Gen:57*) is very similar but not exactly the same as the *target*. This is due to deceptive fitness evaluation. Fitness evaluation becomes more and more inaccurate as the contractivity of IFS approaches 1.0.

7.2 Drawing a Fern Using NF

Introducing stricter contractivity constrains by setting the *contractivity threshold* to 0.5 makes the box problem harder. However, filled squares and box shapes can be easily represented by uniform scaling and translation transformations.

Table 5. Parameters of the IFS that solves the Box problem.

w	a	b	c	d	e	f
1	-0.93	0.0	0.0	0.84	0.0313	0.0782
2	-0.93	0.0	0.0	0.84	0.0313	-0.0539
3	0.611	0.0	0.0	0.557	-0.076	0.0269
4	-0.93	0.0	0.0	0.84	-0.0328	0.0734
5	-0.93	0.0	0.0	0.84	-0.0342	-0.0412
6	-3.91E-07	-0.00043	-8.38E-08	1.65E-05	-0.0717	0.0542

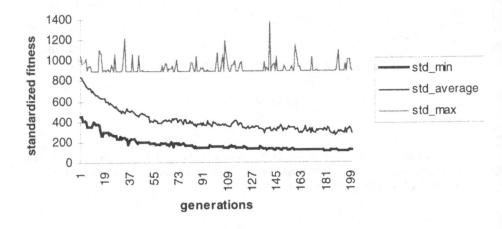

Fig. 5. *Standardized fitness* graph for the Fern collage problem

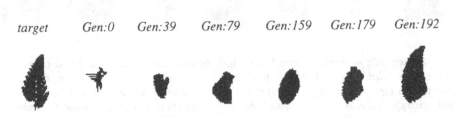

Fig. 6. The fern collage problem, from left to right: original image and best images of generations 0, 39, 79, 159, 179, and finally the best of generation 192. The shapes are rendered using the photocopy algorithm.

We test our IFS-STGP system against amore complex model, the shape of a fern. The system did not manage to produce a 100% correct solution for this problem. The best solution is shown in figure 6. For the fern problem the *contractivity threshold* was set to 0.85. We used a population of 200 individuals for 200 generations and 10 runs. The maximum tree depth was set to 8 and mutation probability was set to 0.02. Table 6 lists the coefficients of the best solution. Although there is a well-known solution that consists of 4 transformations, the number of affine maps used by the fittest evolved solution is 10.

Table 6. Parameters of the best solution for the fern problem

w	a	b	C	d	e	f
1	0.0	0.1	0.1	-0.3	0.0	-0.1
2	0.834	-0.1	0.099	0.834	0.012	-0.03
3	0.145	0.0	0.0	0.064	-0.015	0.029
4	0.196	-0.0496	-0.067	-0.145	-0.0554	0.0183
5	0.837	-0.099	0.099	0.837	-0.0104	0.0194
6	0.16	0.073	0.0	0.547	-0.03	0.055
7	0.839	0.0427	-0.042	0.819	0.0142	0.0967
8	0.83	-0.1	0.1	0.84	0.0	-0.1
9	0.1	0.2	0.5	-0.2	0.0	0.0
10	0.83	-0.1	0.1	0.84	-0.05	-0.06

8. Conclusions

We have demonstrated a representation that allows the evolution of affine transformations based on the hierarchical combination of small numbers of primitive maps. We tested our system against the inverse problem for IFS with results that compare well with those reported in the literature [3, 10]. The inverse problem for the fern is substantially more difficult than the box problem since more than one basic linear transformation is needed to solve it. We are thinking of extending both the fitness evaluation methods as well as introducing stricter type constrains, for example each affine map may define a separate data type.

References

1. Angeline, J. P. Evolving Fractal Movies, Genetic Programming 1996: Proceedings of the first Annual Conference, Pages 503-511, MIT Press, (1996)
2. Barnsley, M. F. Fractals Everywhere, Academic Press, (1988)
3. Barnsley, M. F., and Hurd, L. P. Fractal Image Compression, AK Peters, (1993)
4. Cretin, G. Lutton, E. Levy-Vehel, J. and Roll C. Mixed IFS: Resolution of the Inverse Problem Using Genetic Programming, Artificial Evolution, volume 1063 of LNCS, Springer Verlag, (1996) 247-258
5. Borgefors, G. Distance Transformation in arbitrary dimension. Computer Vision, Graphics, and Image Processing 27, (1984) 231-345

6.   Hutchinson, J. E.: Fractals and Self Similarity. Indiana University Journal, Vol. 35, No. 5, (1981)
7.   Jacob C.: Evolving Evolution Programs: Genetic Programming and L-Systems, Genetic Programming 1996: Proceedings of the first Annual Conference, MIT Press (1996) 107-115
8.   Koza, J. R.: Genetic Programming: On the Programming of Computers by Means of Natural Selection, MIT Press (1992)
9.   Montana, D. J.: BBN Technical Report #7866:Strongly Typed Genetic Programming. Bolt Beranek and Newman, Inc. 10 Moulton Street, Cambridge, MA 02138, USA, March 25 (1994)
10. Nettleton, D. J. and Garigliano, R.: Evolutionary algorithms and the construction of fractals: solution of the inverse problem. Biosystems (33), Elsevier Science (1994) 221-231
11. Redmill, D. W. Bull, D. R. and Martin, R. R. : Genetic algorithms for fast search in fractal image coding. In R. Ansari and M. J. Smith, editors, Visual Communications and Image Processing '96, volume 2727, SPIE Proceedings (1996) 1367-1376
12. Saupe, D. and Ruhl, M. 1996: Evolutionary fractal image compression. In Proceedings ICIP-96 (IEEE International Conference on Image Processing), volume I, Lausanne, Switzerland, September (1996) 129-132
13. Vences, L. and Rudomin, I.: Fractal Compression of single images and image sequences using genetic algorithms, The Eurographics Association (1994)

Reactive and Memory-Based Genetic Programming for Robot Control

Björn Andersson, Per Svensson, Peter Nordin, and Mats Nordahl

Complex Systems Group, Institute of Physical Resource Theory, Chalmers University of Technology, S-412 96 Göteborg, Sweden, Email: nordin,tfemn@fy.chalmers.se

Abstract. In this paper we introduce a new approach to genetic programming with memory in reinforcement learning situations, which selects memories in order to increase the probability of modelling the most relevant parts of memory space. We evolve maps directly from state to action, rather than maps that predict reward based on state and action, which reduces the complexity of the evolved mappings. The work is motivated by applications to the control of autonomous robots. Preliminary results in software simulations indicate an enhanced learning speed and quality.

1 Introduction

The field of autonomous mobile robotics attracts an accelerating interest. Autonomous robots that use legs instead of wheels are useful both in environments created for humans and in more natural terrain. Humanoid robots are particularly interesting, since man is the standard for almost all interactions in the world, and most environments, tools and machines are adapted to our abilities, motion capabilities and geometry.

An autonomous mobile robot system demands high performance both of its mechanical components and control software. The many degrees of freedom in a light mobile robot create new problem domains in control and navigation where conventional methods often fall short. Control of autonomous robots is a promising application area for evolutionary algorithms.

We have attempted to use genetic programming (GP) to control autonomous robots. In particular, this article describes a new approach, called *reactive GP with memory*, to using genetic programming in a reinforcement learning [8] situation, where an explicit world model is used as part of the learning algorithm.

In the work on robots, this algorithm is part of a larger software structure for learning, control and planning based on genetic programming. This hierarchical structure consists of three layers: a reactive layer, a model building bayer, and a reasoning layer. These layers represent different levels of control and consciousness.

- The first layer is a *reactive layer* based on on-line evolution of machine code. This assumes that all fitness feedback is obtained directly from the physical robot, which means that the evolved programs often spend most of their time

R. Poli et al. (Eds.): EuroGP'99, LNCS 1598, pp. 161-172, 1999.

waiting for feedback from the physical environment during their evaluation. This limits the speed of learning, and the constant movement also shortens the life span of the hardware. On the other hand the method is simple, and operates without any need to introduce a priori assumptions about the problem domain. This layer is used for reactive behaviours like balancing.

- The second layer is a *model building layer*, which works with memories of past events. The system tries to evolve a model of the environment as well as the robot itself. The model could for example map sensor inputs and actions to a predicted reward. The best model at a certain instant is then used to determine the action which results in the best predicted fitness given current sensor inputs. In this way, the genetic programming system can run at full speed without having to to wait for feedback from the environment, instead fitting the programs based on memories of past events. The model building layer is also used for basic control tasks.

- The third layer, the *reasoning layer*, is a symbolic processing layer for higher brain functions that require reasoning, such as as navigation, safety, and energy supply. This layer is built on genetic reasoning, a method where evolution is used as inference engine [5].

The algorithm introduced in this article is primarily relevant for the model building layer. In earlier work, we have used genetic programming to evolve a model of registered memory events [6]. This model was then used to find the action with the best predicted outcome. The problem with this approach is the balance between exploration and exploitation, in that the GP system spends a lot of effort trying to model the entire memory space, while we are primarily interested in the parts with high predicted rewards. So while a symbolic model of the memories may seem to correspond very well to the actual memories it may not accurately model the important region of best reward, where we would prefer the system to spend most of its time. This region is often minute compared to other recorded reward signals. However, if the structure of the best reward is lost then it is usually impossible for the agent to make reasonable decisions. The effect of the phenomenon in realistic applications is that we either fail to map the important part of the memory space, or at least spend too much time mapping its less interesting regions.

In this paper we present novel work on how to select memories in order to increase the probability of modelling the relevant parts of memory space. The basic principle is to increase the probability of storing memory instances with a favorable reward value. The approach also differs from previous work on genetic programming with memory by evolving maps directly from state to action, rather than maps that predict reward based on state and action. This reduces the complexity of the evolved mappings. Preliminary results in software simulations indicate an enhanced learning speed and quality.

2   Methods

The machine code genetic programming approach used in all experiments below is called Automatic Induction of Machine Code GP (AIMGP) [5]. AIMGP is about 40 times faster than conventional GP systems due to the lack any interpreting steps. In addition is the system compact, which is beneficial when working with a real robot.

2.1   Genetic Programming with Memory

Genetic programming with memory (e.g., [5, 6] can be described as two processes running in parallel. One process is responsible for the evolution of a model of the environment, given a finite number of memories of past events. Here the environment means not only the physical environment in which the robot resides, but rather the relationship between sensors, motor values and rewards in a physical environment. We evolve functions that predict the reward (or punishment) associated with an action in a specific situation. The fitness of the individuals describes how well their predictions correspond to the memories of previous events. The memories consist of three different parts:

1. The situation encountered (described for example by servo angles and sensor values).
2. The action taken (for example the modified servo angles).
3. The resulting reward (or punishment, i.e., negative reward)

An action-selection process is also needed. Given the state of the environment (including both sensor readings and motor settings), the action-selection procedure uses the model of the best individual to choose the action that gives the highest predicted reward. When this action has been performed, the memory-table is updated with this new experience.

The motivation for this approach is a desire to reduce the time needed to evolve control programs for physical robots. Using stored memories of rewards in previously encountered situations allows the evolutionary part of the program to run continuously without having to wait for the slow movements of the robot. The individuals are no longer control programs that return actions, but rather models that predict how good different actions are in various situations.

A critical factor for the performance of the algorithm is the size of and update procedure for the memory table. To increase the speed of evolution, we would like to keep the memory size small. On the other hand there is a minimum number of memories needed to accurately model the environment, depending on its complexity. The choice of update procedure for the memory-table is also important. The algorithm needs to forget as well as learn. The simplest way of learning new memories and discarding old ones is simply to keep a finite window of size N to the past, and to discard the oldest memory when a new situation is encountered. This procedure may encounter problems, e.g., in situations where an action is performed repeatedly, which leads to all memories becoming identical. In this situation, the selective pressure may benefit individuals which simply predict a constant reward, leading to the extinction of more complex and globally accurate models.

A better way to select memories is to try to keep memories that are representative of the environment. We have tried a simple algorithm which keeps the table sorted, and discards the memory whose reward value is most similar to that of its neighbours. This results in a homogenous distribution of memories according to their associated reward, but of course it does not guarantee an appropriate distribution of memories in the sensor-action space. A more complex strategy that probably would give better results would be to save memories depending on their position in the sensor-action space [7].

2.2 Reactive Genetic Programming with Memory

The most important new result in this paper is that we have developed a reactive GP method which combines the advantages of genetic programming with and without memory. It uses memories to avoid the need to wait for the robot's movements, but the individuals are functions that return an action rather than models that predict reward. This allows the evolutionary process can run at maximum speed, and at the same time avoids the complications associated with having to evolve a very complex world model.

In the beginning memories are collected from random movements. During the run, old memories are replaced by memories of new actions if the new memories meet certain conditions. The existing memories are searched for the one where the situation most closely resembles the current situation, where the metric is defined as the Euclidean distance in the situation-space (defined in terms of sensor values and other state variables) If the closest memory has a worse reward value than the new one it is replaced. The distance between situations is defined as the Euclidean distance in the situation-space.

The memories are defined in the same way as in the GP with memory approach. That is, they consist of a situation (described by sensor values, servo angles and so on), an action (described, e.g, by the new servo angles) and an associated reward value.

The fitness for the individuals depends on how well their actions resemble the actions in similar situations stored in the memory-table. In this case, the metric is the Euclidean distance in the space of actions.

3 Experiments

In this article we only consider a simple software simulation of a robot in an artificial environment (our real robot experiments will be described elsewhere). The state of the robot is given by its position (x and y), velocity, angle and rotation-rate. Its environment consists of four walls and a number of circular obstacles. The program controls the robot by setting its velocity and rotation rate. Time is divided into discrete intervals.

The environment used in the experiments is shown, e.g., in Figure 8 below. The walls are 30 units long; the obstacles have a diameter of 10 units. The properties of the robot are given in Table 1.

Table 1.: Properties of the simulated robot.

Property	Value
Diameter	1 unit
Max velocity	1 unit/tick
Max rotation rate	0.5 rad/tick

The robot has five sensors around its edge. Sensor S_0 point in the forward direction, while S_1 and S_7 point in 45 degree angles away from it, see Figure 1. The sensors return a value $(5 - r)/5$, where r is the distance to the closest wall or obstacle in its direction, see Figure 2, for distances up to 5 units, then a value of 0.

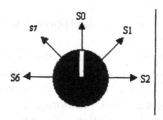

Fig. 1.: The simulated robot and its sensors.

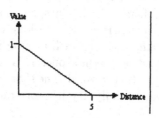

Fig. 2.: The value returned by a sensor as a function of the distance to the closest object.

The reward function is defined as described in Table 1. The negative reward (punishment) is given by the sum of the contributions in the table, with the collision term included only if the robot has run into a wall or an obstacle.

Table 2.: Reward for the simulated robot.

Event	Negative Reward
Collision	100
Low speed	$(Velocity_{max} - Velocity)/velocity_{max}$
Sensors	$100(S_0 + 0.3(S_1 + S_7))^2$
Rotation rate	$50|Rotation|/Rotation_{max}|$

This function is designed to encourage movement, and to discouraged rotation, so that the robot tries to move in a straight line. In the vicinity of a wall or obstacle non-zero values for the sensors S_0, S_1 or S_7 give negative reinforcement, so that walls and obstacles are avoided.

GP With Memory

Our first experiments used a conventional approach to genetic programming with memory.

The rewards used in memories are described in Table 2. The individuals' fitness is the square error - the sum of the squares of the differences between the individual's predicted reward and the memories of real reward.

The memory-table contains 1000 memories. Each memory consists of the current world-state (or current situation), the action-vector and the resulting reward. The situation-vector consists of outputs from the distance sensors represented as 3 real values in the interval [0, 1]. The action-vector consists of 2 real values, also in the interval [0, 1]. The first value represents the chosen velocity and the second represents the turn-rate. The last part of the memory vector is the reward that the action resulted in, represented as a positive real value.

The memory-table was divided into two parts, a long-term memory of 800 entries sorted according to their reward values, and a short-term memory of 200 entries. When a new entry is inserted into the long-term memory, the existing memories are searched for the memory with a reward closest to its own neighbours, which is then replaced by the new one. This results a constant distribution of memories according to their reward. The short-term memory contains the last 200 events encountered. Initially, the memory-table is filled with memories of random movements.

The results of this experiment showed the need for improvement of this simple model. The first problem was that the evolved functions tried to map the whole fitness-landscape. However, the only interesting areas are the minima and their surroundings. The individuals became rather good at predicting the fitness at a large scale, but they do not manage to map all the details in the fitness landscape. We tried a few different approaches to solve this problem. First, we tried giving the memories different weights depending on their associated reward. Low reward value (positive reward) resulted in a higher weight. However, we did not notice any significant improvements.

After that, we tried introducin a cut-off at some fitness value in order to increase the significance of the memories close to the minimum. The individuals used this, e.g., by putting a plane at the cut-off point - this gave them pretty good fitness but depleted the gene pool of instructions that give a diverse behaviour. The system simply tried to get memories of actions where the outcome was easy to predict, e.g., running straight into the wall. We also tried different proportions of long- and short-term memories. While we saw that the long-term memory was more important, the results were not satisfactory and conclusive.

To be able to study the results in greater detail we plotted the reward values for all possible actions in two situations: (1) The robot is located in an open area and cannot feel any walls with its sensors and (2) the robot is facing a wall.

These 3-D plots show only three of the function's six dimensions since three sensor values are defined by the situation. There are many other possible situations and the individuals have to adapt to all possible actions in each of them. This is why the approximation in a single situation often looks very inadequate. What we see is that the evolved functions adapt to the large scale features of the real function while the minimum, which is important, is not likely to be accurately predicted.

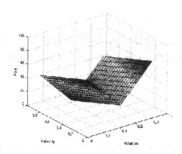

Fig. 3.: Real reward value as a function of velocity and rotation
for situation 1.

In Figure 3 and Figure 4 we see that the individual has incorporated the fact that the reward value is better for high speeds, but the dependence on rotation is completely ignored and therefore the minimum is not in the right place.

In figures Figure 5 and Figure 6 we see that the individual has discovered that not turning away from the wall would result in a large negative reward,

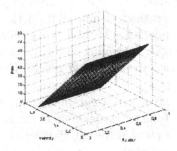

Fig. 4.: Evolved reward value as a function of velocity and rotation for situation 1.

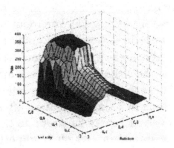

Fig. 5.: Real reward value as a function of velocity and rotation for situation 2.

and it even knows which direction is best to turn in. However, while the real reward function has a minimum around velocity 25 and rotation 22, the evolved function's minimum is for velocity 0.

GP Without Memory

This was a purely reactive experiment. The population consisted of 100 individuals and after one generation of 100 tournaments the best individual was inspected. It almost completely avoided colliding with the walls and obstacles (it hit something only 9 times during 250 runs of 4 ticks each). It used a wall-following tactic. After only 13 generations a "bouncing" approach was discovered, see Figure 8.

A comparison with the results of the previous section shows that GP with memory cannot compete in its present form. This led us to try to combine the two methods in a new way, where the individuals look the same as in the reactive experiment (they take a description of the situation as input and return an action) but we save memories of good actions (where fitness is below some

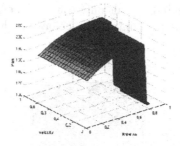

Fig. 6.: Evolved reward value as a function of velocity and rotation for situation 2.

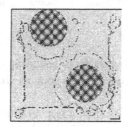

Fig. 7.: The route of the best individual after the first generation.

threshold) and use them to train the population on-line while the robot is moving.

Reactive GP with Memory

In order to compare the performance of the different approaches, the combination of GP with memory and reactive individuals was tested on the same simulated environment as GP with and without memory.

We used a population size of 1000 individuals. The program size was limited to 256 instructions, with an initial value of 80. We use a memory-table of size 1000. No short-term memory was used in these experiments.

The experiments showed the feasibility of the reactive GP with memory approach.

Several different forms of behavior were seen in the experiment:

The individuals often seem to prefer the bouncing behaviour when they are trained with the new algorithm. In a bouncing strategy, the robot continues in a straight line at maximum speed until the sensors pick up a wall or an obstacle. Then it turns away from the object and continues in a new direction. This makes it appear to be bouncing around in the environment. This approach is optimal in the sense that the fitness is 0 between the bounces. Figure 8 shows an example of this behaviour. Since the individuals only consider the short-term consequences of their actions this is the most intelligent behaviour that can be expected.

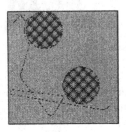

Fig. 8.: The route of a bouncing individual.

The appearance of this behavior is encouraging, since it gives an optimal reward in the short-term perspective. As soon as after 4 generations the bouncing behaviour started to emerge.

A perfect bouncing individual was not seen until the 11th generation. This behaviour was periodically suppressed by individuals that were good at predicting the memories but bad at controlling the robot (these strategies are somewhat less interesting, since they spend most of their time trying to go through a wall and are not included among the figures). Gradually we saw more and more bouncing and by the 40th generation the bouncing behaviour was completely dominant and perfected. After 51 generations the first individual that was capable of entirely avoiding collisions appeared.

In Figure 9 we can clearly see that the behaviour of the robot improves significantly over time. Initially it collides almost all the time (198 collisions out of 200 possible in the third generation for example). The absence of collisions in the first generation is due to the fact that the robot was just spinning around in a small circle.

We can divide the individuals into different classes. Those that cause many collisions (more than 100) are mostly individuals that only take into consideration that it is good to go fast and straight and therefore plunge straight into a wall. Those that perform moderately well (30 to 100 collisions) are attempting a bouncing strategy, but do not master it in all situations. The good individuals (up to 30 collisions) are bouncing, but may be overly optimistic in some situations close to the walls or obstacles and thus end up colliding.

The number of generations needed to get adequate control programs using the reactive GP with memory approach is slighly greater than the purely reactive on-line method without memory. However, measured in terms of time, not generations, the new approach is superior. If each evaluation of an individual on the robot takes a second then one generation of 100 tournaments involving

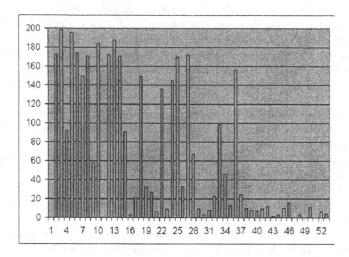

Fig. 9.: The number of collisions over time when the robot is controlled by the best individuals during 53 generations.

4 individuals each takes close to 7 minutes and the run discussed above over 13 generations would take almost 90 minutes. Reactive GP with memory is much faster and the time consumption is reduced by at least a factor of 20.

4   Summary and Conclusions

Genetic Programming for on-line control is a promising but challenging research area. The disadvantage of comparatively slow feed-back from the environment can be addressed by the evolution of a world model. However, this increases the complexity of the task and it can be difficult to find adequate solutions. The mixure of reactive and memory based approach presented in this paper shows a promising middle way with both fast fitness calculations and effective convergence.

Acknowledgement

Peter Nordin gratefully acknowledges support from the Swedish Research Council for Engineering Sciences.

References

1. W. Banzhaf, P. Nordin, R. E. Keller, F. D. Francone: Genetic Programming - An Introduction. Morgan Kaufmann, San Francisco, CA, (1998).

2. I. Harvey, P. Husbands, D. Cliff : Issues in Evolutionary Robotics. School of Cognitive and Computing Sciences, The University of Sussex, England, U.K, (1992).
3. N. Jakobi, P. Husbands and I. Harvey: Noise and the Reality Gap: The use of Simulation in Evolutionary Robotics In Advances in Artificial Life: Proc. 3rd European Conference on Artificial Life, Moran, F., Moreno, A., Merelo, J., Chacon, P. (eds.) Springer-Verlag, Lecture Notes in Artificial Intelligence 929 (1995) pp. 704-720.
4. P. R. Merlyn: Toward a Humanoid Robot: Artificial Intelligence and the Confluence of Technologies. SRI Consulting, http:// future.sri.com/ BIP/datalog/ dldesc/2031.html, (1996).
5. P. Nordin: Evolutionary Program Induction of binary Machine Code and its Application. Krehl Verlag, Mnster, Germany.
6. P. Nordin, W. Banzhaf,M. Brameier: Evolution of a world model for a miniature robot using genetic programming. Robotics and Autonomous Systems, Elsevier Science B.V. **25**, (1998), pp 105-116.
7. M. Salganicoff: Tolerating Concept and Sampling in Lazy Learning Using Prediction Error Context Switching. In Artificial Intelligence Review 1,1Kluwer Academic Publishers, Netherlands. (1997) , p. 133-155.
8. S. Sutton, A.G. Barto: Reinforcement Learning - An Introduction. MIT Press, Cambridge MA, (1998).

Distributed and Persistent Evolutionary Algorithms: A Design Pattern

Alessandro Bollini and Marco Piastra

Università di Pavia, Dipartimento di Informatica e Sistemistica
Via Ferrata 1, 27100 Pavia, Italy

Abstract. In the scenario of distributed processing for evolutionary algorithms the adoption of object-oriented database management systems (ODBMS) may yield improvements in terms of both robustness and flexibility. Populations of evolvable individuals can be made persistent across several evolutionary runs, making it possible to devise *incremental* strategies. Moreover, virtually any number of evolutionary processes may be run in parallel on the same underlying population without explicit synchronization beyond that provided by the locking mechanism of the ODBMS. This paper describes a design pattern for a genetic programming environment that allows combining existing techniques with persistent population storage and management.

1 Introduction

Evolutionary computing is quickly gaining acceptance as a viable approach to many problems of industrial interest, such as signal processing, process control, planning and data mining. However, as larger and more complex problems are tackled, practical considerations suggest that the current generation of genetic programming environments, which were designed mainly as research tools, could be improved on.

Evolutionary approaches to real-world problems usually imply large search spaces and complex fitness evaluation functions, which are likely to require the evolutionary environment to interact with other systems, in order to perform numerical simulations or to retrieve training data. Besides the need for large computational resources, such applications set a new specific requirement for the evolutionary environment, that is the ability to manage very large populations in a way that is at the same time efficient and flexible. Parallel and distributed genetic programming environments (see [12] for a review) have been shown to provide high performance at a reasonable cost, but usually force a specific model of population partitioning.

In this paper we address the requirements related to the management of large populations, discussing the overall architecture of evolutionary computing frameworks with a twofold goal:

- *decoupling* population storage and management from the definition of the evolutionary processes acting on the population,

R. Poli et al. (Eds.): EuroGP'99, LNCS 1598, pp. 173–183, 1999.
© Springer-Verlag Berlin Heidelberg 1999

– achieving *persistence* of population states within and across the boundaries of individual evolutionary runs, regardless of their specific settings.

In our opinion, concurrent object-oriented databases management systems (ODBMS) could support decoupling and persistence quite effectively: in order to integrate them with evolutionary frameworks, we propose an extension to the current set of design patterns for genetic programming, in the line of [9] (from a conceptual point of view the same pattern could be applied to any form of evolutionary algorithm: however, we feel that genetic programming is likely to reap the greatest benefits because of the complexity of the data structures being manipulated and of the large computational requirements of its usual applications). This approach complements existing distributed and parallel designs in an orthogonal way, making them more flexible and easier to implement. In fact, provided their interactions are structured according to the pattern described in Sect. 3, multiple evolutionary processes running in distinct high-performance processors could access the centralized, persistent population in a very efficient way, allowing at the same time the most convenient partitioning model (demetic, panmictic, niched, ...) to be adopted without any concern for the thorny issues related to concurrent access and consistency (Sect. 2). This architecture is quite robust against process failures, supports populations larger than the physical transient memory of the co-operating systems and introduces the capability to safely suspend and resume evolution at any time.

All of these features are eventually going to be required as more computation-intensive problems are considered, but persistent populations could support many interesting forms of *incremental* evolution as well. Evolutionary runs are usually considered as independent episodes and little or no support is currently provided for integrating them into a complex scenario of multiple evolutionary paths. Practical wisdom and previous work in areas such as the evolution of object-oriented programs [8, 2] suggest that complex evolutionary experiments should be split into smaller steps and finely tuned through an incremental procedure, possibly by checking out several alternative evolutionary paths and comparing the intermediate results. Persistent populations make such strategies viable and provide a well-defined interface for the tools required to analyze and manage intermediate populations after each evolutionary step is completed.

The following sections give an overview of the issues related to object-oriented persistence and present an overall design pattern for an evolutionary algorithms environment supporting persistent populations. Although the proposed design pattern is independent, to a certain degree, of the features of specific programming languages and ODBMS, we consider a concrete reference architecture based on Java and ObjectStore by Object Design [10], which is also freely available in a pure Java, single-user version.

2   Object-Oriented Persistence

Besides making it possible to store populations persistently, a database management system (DBMS), may provide a fundamental advantage for distributed evolutionary programming systems by introducing a transaction-based access mechanism to persistent storage. First of all, this mechanism protects the current status of an evolutionary run from both software and hardware failures. In addition, the combination of transaction and data locking offered by a multi-user DBMS makes it possible to devise an overall design pattern where the synchronization of distributed and concurrent processes is entirely delegated to the DBMS itself, thus avoiding the need to make each process aware of the global arrangement of the distributed system. However, the software integration of a DBMS may well require some substantial provisions for translating data structures in their persistent forms and vice-versa. The run-time computational burden for such a translation may be substantial, but this problem, which is usually reported in literature as deriving from the so-called "impedance mismatch" between data formats [4], is specifically addressed by ODBMS designs.

According to the ideas first introduced by Atkinson [1], programming languages could be made much more effective and powerful by adding the capability to manipulate persistent data structures in a transparent manner, i.e. by making the persistence of data structures orthogonal to the manipulation constructs in the programming language. Current object databases are inspired to this principle and achieve a substantial degree of orthogonality between persistence of data structures (i.e. objects) and language constructs.

From the standpoint of software engineering, the ODMG standard [4] fosters the uniform and seamless integration of the Java programming language with DBMS technology. In keeping with the ODMG scenario, Java objects of nearly any class should be exchangeable with the DBMS in both directions by just adding a minimum of extra provisions. The potential benefit should be evident: application algorithms need not be altered in dramatic ways in order to handle persistent objects. In particular, it will be shown how orthogonality makes the *persistent* extension compatible with most genetic programming strategies described in the literature.

2.1 Java-ODBMS Integration

According to the ODMG standard, every manipulation on persistent objects has to take place within a *transaction*, whose begin and commit points are explicitly stated in the program. Furthermore, physical pointers are not allowed in Java programs, as well as any other kind of external manipulation of the object heap. As a result, unless a special Java virtual machine is used, persistent objects have a different life cycle from transient ones and that must be taken into account in software design. In ObjectStore, during a transaction, persistent objects may either be *hollow* when first referenced or *active*, when fully fetched. Outside a transaction, persistent objects may either be *stale* or *retained*.

At stage (a) in Fig. 1, the persistent object X is *active*, that is fully fetched and practically indistinguishable from any other Java object in the virtual machine. Object X contains a reference to another object Y which has not been involved in the computation process up to this point. The latter is *hollow*, in the sense that it exists as a reference but its contents have not been actually fetched

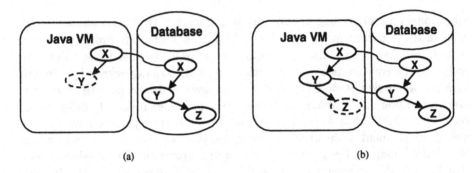

Fig. 1. A typical scenario occurring in an ObjectStore transaction.

yet. Note that both X and Y belong to a more complex data structure in the database, which also include object Z. At stage (b), object Y becomes involved in the ongoing process (e.g. a method has been invoked on it): this causes a sort of object fault [7] causing object Y to become *active*, i.e. fully fetched. Since object Y contains a reference to object Z, the latter is pre-fetched as an *hollow* object and the process continues. As we see, persistent objects are fetched incrementally and on-demand. When *active*, persistent objects behave exactly as any other Java object.

Active and *hollow* persistent objects may be seen as local, transient copies of the objects in the database. Clearly, in order to maintain consistency, the presence of such objects in the Java virtual machine entails locking somehow the persistent memory in the database to prevent other ongoing processes from altering the scenario depicted in Fig. 1. In order to give other processes a chance to work with persistent objects, the transaction must eventually be either committed or rolled back. When a transaction ends, persistent objects become either *stale* or *retained*. A *stale* object is a useless data structure just waiting to be garbage collected and any attempt to use it causes an exception. On the other hand, a *retained* objects is still usable but no longer representative of what is stored in the database. Objects may be *retained* either as *read_only* or *update*, but regardless of their state when a new transaction is started, *retained* objects are restored to the contents of the database.

Large sets of persistent objects in an ODBMS are arranged in collections. Persistent collections can be almost treated like any other persistent object: the ODMG standard defines an API for them which is very close to that of the usual, transient collections. However, their actual implementation is substantially different from that of transient ones, as different is the set of goals to be met. In particular, persistent collections must behave gracefully with respect to performance: for instance, it should not be necessary to completely fetch a huge collection in order to access an object within it. Moreover, persistent collections are designed to contain very large amounts of objects, in the range of tens of thousands or more. As such, they need to support searching strategies which go quite beyond the mere enumeration of elements. Typical ODBMS support indexing and some of them support the implementation of application-specific, custom indexing mechanisms as well.

2.2   The Basic Access Pattern

As first described in Sect. 1, the population in the evolutionary framework being proposed is stored in a shared ODBMS. Each evolutionary process is a Java program, explicitly designed to take advantage of the ODBMS integration described above. All of the evolutionary processes acting in parallel on a persistent population access it according to the basic pattern described in the UML sequence diagram in Fig. 2. The first and third steps of the pattern involve purely transient computations, while the second and fourth ones are carried out within database transactions.

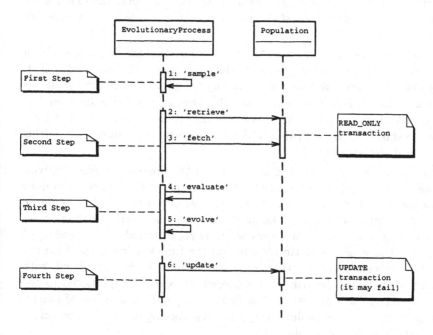

Fig. 2. The basic access pattern.

Each run in an experiment is considered as the multiple iteration of this pattern. Basically, each iteration starts with the sampling (1) of a collection of individuals from the population.

Then, the sample must be retrieved (2) and fetched (3), that is all the persistent objects composing it must be looked up in the indexes maintained by the DBMS and made *active*. In keeping with what we have seen before, this must be done within a transaction, that can be made *read_only* as no changes are made to the population database. Then, the transaction is committed and the persistent objects are *retained* (not shown). This means that, after the second step, the whole sample of individuals is fully loaded in the Java virtual machine as a set of Java objects.

The third step is entirely carried out without interacting with the persistent population. First, the individuals in the sample are evaluated (4) and then selected for genetic manipulation and substitution (5). Very likely, this step may be computationally intensive, however there is no interaction with other evolutionary processes working in parallel. During the fourth step, the population is updated by substituting selected individuals with the offspring produced by the genetic operators (6). This operation has to be done within an *update* transaction, as it involves altering the population database. It is worth remarking that no actual selection (in the DBMS sense) takes place during this last step; in fact, the Java ODBMS integration maintains a direct association between *retained* objects and their database counterparts. In this way, the identification of substitution candidates is straightforward. At the completion of the fourth step, all persistent objects are made *stale* and de-allocated by the garbage collector at some later point.

The pattern represents an *optimistic* schema for database interaction [3]. In each episode, an evolutionary process fetches a sample and then works on it. Other evolutionary processes are free to modify the population in the meantime; in particular, another process might substitute one of the individuals fetched in the sample. However, this causes a clash only if the process in point later attempts to substitute an individual which has already been substituted. In this case the third step should fail.

As an alternative, a pessimistic schema could be adopted; i.e. every individual in the sample is locked on fetch in the second step and the lock is maintained until the fourth step completes. Thus, the success of the fourth step would be guaranteed. Intuitively, however, the pessimistic schema entails a risk of access conflicts among evolutionary processes which is proportional to the product of the number of processes, the sample size and the time window going from the second step through the completion of the fourth step. On the other hand, with the optimistic schema, the risk of access conflicts is only proportional to the number of evolutionary processes. Provided the population is orders of magnitude larger than the set of evolutionary processes working in parallel, the actual collision rate becomes negligible.

The Java-ODBMS integration makes it possible to retain across transactions a sort of direct database pointer to the fetched objects, so that any subsequent access can be done directly without using indexes. In this way, in the fourth step, an early check for potential failures is implicitly performed while accessing the individual to be substituted; if the individual does no longer exist, an exception is raised by the ODBMS and the the transaction is simply rolled back without any further action.

On the positive side, the basic access pattern entails no explicit need for synchronization, as it would happen with transient, distributed processes. In fact, the set of evolutionary processes working in parallel are synchronized implicitly by the locking mechanism in the ODBMS. Furthermore, the locality of accesses to individual objects which is typical to the ODBMS approach helps keeping the interactions to a minimum, although some form of spurious interaction due to the use of indexes is unavoidable.

More important, quite apart from the suspend-and-resume capability, the approach presented does not entail a "topology problem" [12] for the set of evolutionary processes, as there is no direct network connection established among them. As a global consequence, evolutionary processes may be either added or taken away at any point in time, unless the ODBMS itself fails.

3   The Overall Design Pattern

In order to describe the software design of the approach we will use the popular approach of design patterns, as first introduced in [6]. More precisely, the description of the proposed solution is organized in a layered schema including a *framework* and a *toolkit*.

A framework is defined in [6] as a set of co-operating classes that make up a reusable software design for a specific software domain, whereas a toolkit is a collection of reusable and related classes designed to implement useful, general-purpose functions. This way of thinking is particularly suited to the overall design of the *persistent evolutionary algorithms* (EA) implementation.

3.1   The Persistent EA Framework

Figure 3 contains a (simplified) UML class diagram describing the Persistent EA Framework, where the parts to be specialized are depicted in grey. The main class is EvolutionaryProcess, i.e. an aggregation of two main components, Selector and Operator, and two side components, Retriever and Updater. Selector and Operator are *transient* abstract classes, as they do not deal directly with the persistent Population. Every interaction with the latter is rather seen through a Sample, which is basically a limited collection of individuals representing the operational context for each iteration episode.

A Selector also contains a Sampler, which implements a specific sampling policy. Due to the substantial independence from persistence management, Selector and Operator may implement any kind of policy for the EvolutionaryProcess that fits the basic access schema in Fig. 2. On his own, the class EvolutionaryProcess contains only the immutable implementation of the basic access schema.

More precisely, the first step takes place when the EvolutionaryProcess asks the Selector to define its sampling request for the episode. The Selector forwards the request to the Operator to define the Sample cardinality. Then the Selector calls the Sampler to define the individuals to be retrieved from the Population (see also the next section).

During the second step, the EvolutionaryProcess passes the sampling request to the Retriever. The latter implements the actual policy for retrieving the individuals with the requested features. It is clear that such an implementation depends on how the population is actually arranged, but this does not affect

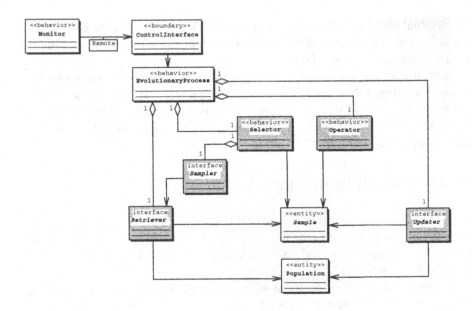

Fig. 3. The UML class diagram for the Persistent EA Framework.

the framework directly. The step ends when a Sample of individuals has been retrieved and fully fetched.

In the third step, the control is first passed over to the Selector, which perform the evaluation of individuals, and then to the Operator which combines some of the individuals in the Sample to produce an offspring of new individuals. At the end of the step, the Sample is enriched by these new individuals and the candidates for substitution are properly marked.

The final fourth phase is managed by the Updater, which first checks whether the substitution can be performed (otherwise the transaction is rolled back) and then performs the actual update of the Population.

The clean separation between transient algorithms (Selector and Operator) and the persistence managers (Retriever and Updater) yields a substantial independence of the two design dimensions. Designers of evolutionary experiments need not be concerned with the low-level details of the ODBMS interface. On the other hand, the role of the two persistent components is highly standardized and thus suitable for a generic and reusable implementation in the toolkit.

To make it feasible the remote control and monitoring of the whole set of EvolutionaryProcess being run in an experiment, the framework is completed by a ControlInterface, which is a network interface – e.g. RMI or CORBA – to the control set of the former.

3.2   The Persistent EA Toolkit

The main design function of the Persistent EA Toolkit is to support the sampling strategies defined in the transient Sampler. The separation of roles between

Sampler and Retriever follows the above mentioned line of isolating transient algorithms from the management of persistence.

More precisely, the Sampler encapsulates (on the transient side) the details about how a sample of individuals can be identified in the persistent population. The Retriever encapsulates (on the persistent side) the way the population is actually arranged and indexed in the database. Since it does not seem advantageous to define a generic interface between these two components, the basic design assumption is that the Sampler and the Retriever are mutually dependent to a certain extent and have to be implemented accordingly. On the other hand, the interface between the Selector and the Sampler can be conveniently defined in a general way, as the requests made by the former to the latter are basically limited to the indication of the sample size.

On the persistent side, the management and indexing of the population is jointly performed by the Retriever and the Updater, which are thus to be implemented in pairs. The Retriever and the Updater also encapsulate the transaction boundaries and expose only atomic operations to the other transient components.

The indexing policy deserves a few more observations, as it represents a crucial aspect of the actual implementation. In the line of principle, an ODBMS supports a fairly flexible indexing policy. A typical ODBMS contains a built-in implementation of the most common persistent indexing algorithms (e.g. hashing, B^+-Tree [5]) but it also contains the raw ingredients for implementing a specific indexing strategy on a particular data collection. Clearly, with the framework in question, the indexing strategy is strictly dependent on the sampling policy being adopted for a particular application.

In the simplest case, samples are drawn from a uniform probability distribution over the entire population, as it may happen with a panmictic tournament approach. In such a case, the required data structure is a persistent array – usually available in an ODBMS – which allows accessing the individuals in a population through an integer index. Each cell in the persistent array contains a database pointer to the corresponding individual; a substitution can be performed in a straightforward way by changing the content of a cell. Note that no index maintenance is required in this case and thus the overhead is minimal.

In a more complex case the sample is drawn from a univariate distribution depending on an individual attribute – e.g. fitness – or a multivariate distribution, as it could be convenient with Pareto optimization. In particular, the implementation of the fitness proportionate selection algorithm requires an *ad hoc* indexing policy. Note however that the required indexing strategy is very similar to the techniques adopted for spatial data structures. More precisely, the fitness proportionate selection algorithm can be seen as the uniform point sampling from a line segment that is partitioned into intervals being proportional to the fitness of each individual. Each interval corresponds to a specific individuals and all intervals are non-overlapping. Some effective techniques for this kind of indexing strategy are discussed for instance in [11] and can be found in many multimedia database implementations.

The above-mentioned dependency between the Sampler and the Retriever in the design pattern derives from the capabilities of the different implementations of the latter. In particular, the way the sample is defined, i.e. in terms of desired features, depends on the kind of Retriever being actually used.

4   Conclusions

As the field of evolutionary computing matures, a clear trend toward more complex data structures is becoming apparent. Genetic programming differentiated itself from mainstream genetic algorithms because of the adoption of complex genomes based on dynamic data structures and in the near future both practical and theoretical developments are likely to require even more complex and integrated structures. On one hand, real-world problems, such as the image analysis tasks we work on, require a tight integration of the evolving structures with problem-specific ancillary data at the level of the single individual. On the other one, extensions of the basic evolutionary paradigm, such as culture-aware frameworks [13], require a global integration at the level of the whole population, to support for instance non-genetic transmission of information among individuals and generations.

In our opinion, the overall architecture and the related design pattern presented in this paper provide a way of supporting both kinds of integration without interfering with the definition of the evolutionary processes and suggest some considerations worth further investigation. The same tools introduced to store and manage persistent populations could also be easily exploited to manage problem-specific data structures, such as training and test sets, which for real-world problems can grow quite large and troublesome. At a more abstract level, persistent populations provide the required technical foundations for exploring the definition of shareable *genetic libraries*, that is intermediate populations containing pre-evolved solutions to basic domain-specific tasks (to be used as building blocks in the solution of complex problems) or pools of partially evolved solutions (to be used as parting point for a series of related experiments).

References

1. M. Atkinson. Programming languages and databases. Technical Report CSR-26-78, Department of Computer Science, University of Edinburgh, August 1978.
2. Wilker Shane Bruce. Automatic generation of object-oriented programs using genetic programming. In John R. Koza, David E. Goldberg, David B. Fogel, and Rick L. Riolo, editors, *Genetic Programming 1996: Proceedings of the First Annual Conference*, pages 267–272, Stanford University, CA, USA, 28–31 July 1996. MIT Press.
3. R. C. G. Cattell. *Object Data Management*. Addison-Wesley, Reading, MA, USA, 2nd edition, 1994.
4. R. C. G. Cattell, D. K. Barry, and D. Bartels, editors. *The Object Database Standard: ODMG 2.0*. Morgan Kaufmann, San Mateo, CA, USA, 1997.
5. D. Comer. The ubiquitous B-Tree. *ACM Computing Surveys*, 11(2), 1979.

6. E. Gamma, R. Helm, R. Johnson, and J. Vlissides. *Design Patterns: Elements of Reusable Object-Oriented Software*. Addison-Wesley, Reading, MA, USA, 1994.

7. T. Kaehler and G. Krasner. LOOM: Large object-oriented memory for Smalltalk-80 systems. In S. B. Zdonik and D. Maier, editors, *Object-Oriented Database Systems*. Morgan Kaufmann, San Mateo, CA, USA, 1990.

8. William B. Langdon. Data structures and genetic programming. In Peter J. Angeline and K. E. Kinnear, Jr., editors, *Advances in Genetic Programming 2*, chapter 20, pages 395–414. MIT Press, Cambridge, MA, USA, 1996.

9. Tom Lenaerts and Bernard Manderick. Building a genetic programming framework: The added-value of design patterns. In W. Banzhaf, R. Poli, M. Schoenauer, and T. C. Fogarty, editors, *Proceedings of the First European Workshop on Genetic Programming*, LNCS, Paris, 14-15 April 1998. Springer-Verlag.

10. Object Design Inc., Burlington, MA, USA. *ObjectStore: Java API User Guide*, release 3.0 edition, 1998.

11. H. Samet. *The Design and Analysis of Spatial Data Structures*. Addison-Wesley, Reading, MA, USA, 1990.

12. Chong Fuey Sian. A Java based distributed approach to genetic programming on the Internet. Master's thesis, Computer Science, University of Birmingham, 1998.

13. Lee Spector and Sean Luke. Cultural transmission of information in genetic programming. In John R. Koza, David E. Goldberg, David B. Fogel, and Rick L. Riolo, editors, *Genetic Programming 1996: Proceedings of the First Annual Conference*, pages 209–214, Stanford University, CA, USA, 28–31 July 1996. MIT Press.

Evolving an Environment Model for Robot Localization

Marc Ebner

Eberhard-Karls-Universität Tübingen
Wilhelm-Schickard-Institut für Informatik
Arbeitsbereich Rechnerarchitektur
Köstlinstraße 6, 72074 Tübingen, Germany
ebner@informatik.uni-tuebingen.de

Abstract. The use of an evolutionary method for robot localization is explored. We use genetic programming to evolve an inverse function mapping sensor readings to robot locations. This inverse function is an internal model of the environment. The robot senses its environment using dense distance information which may be obtained from a laser range finder. Moments are calculated from the distance distribution. These moments are used as terminal symbols in the evolved function. Arithmetic, trigonometric functions and a conditional statement are used as primitive functions. Using this representation we evolved an inverse function to localize a robot in a simulated office environment. Finally, we analyze the accuracy of the resulting function.

1 Motivation

Robots are usually equipped with a variety of sensors that can be used to sense their environment. Information from these sensors can be used to create an internal model of the environment. Such models can be very helpful to the robot in moving from one place to another. Sometimes, however, it may be necessary that the robot relocalizes itself if it has lost track of its current position. This may happen if the robot performs a movement due to an external force that is not sensed by the internal sensors or if odometry errors accumulate. We are exploring the use of an evolutionary method to evolve a representation of the environment that can be used for robot localization. Before we describe our evolutionary approach to robot localization we give a brief review about existing approaches.

2 Background

A detailed overview about traditional methods for self localization of a mobile robot is given by Talluri and Aggarwal [16]. They classify the different methods into four categories: landmark-based methods, methods using trajectory integration and dead reckoning, methods using a standard reference pattern, and

R. Poli et al. (Eds.): EuroGP'99, LNCS 1598, pp. 184–192, 1999.
© Springer-Verlag Berlin Heidelberg 1999

methods using a priori knowledge of a world model which is matched to the sensor data. Often, the world model is constructed using sonar sensors, a laser range finder or from a set of images. Basic methods for map learning are reviewed by Thrun et al. [18]. The information from different types of sensors may be fused to create a three dimensional map of the environment [21].

Talluri and Aggarwal [14, 15, 17] used visual information to locate a mobile robot in an outdoor environment. Image features are used to search for the current position in a model of the environment. Burgard et al. [5] used position probability grids to estimate the absolute position of a mobile robot equipped with sonar sensors. Yamauchi and Beer [23] incrementally built a topological map of the environment using information from the robot's odometry. Kurz [11] constructed a topological map from ultrasonic range data using a self-organizing feature map. Von Wichert [19] and von Wichert and Tolle [20] developed a self-organizing visual environment representation for a mobile robot. Geometric moments calculated for image segments are used to relocate the robot inside a topological map created from an omnidirectional view of the environment. Crowley et al. [6] used principal components of range data for position estimation of a mobile robot. First, training scans are used to generate a lookup table mapping eigenvalues of the range data to possible robot positions. The acquired range data projected into eigenspace is used as an index into this table and a number of candidate poses are extracted. A Kalman filter is used to reject invalid hypotheses as the robot moves. Beetz et al. [3] also used an active method for relocalization for a mobile robot. Whenever the robot has lost track of its position it performs an action which will minimize the uncertainty taking a cost criteria to perform the action into account. For an experimental comparison of two localization methods, Markov localization and scan matching, see Gutmann et al. [7].

Balakrishnan and Honavar [1] followed a biologically motivated approach to spatial learning for robot localization. They developed a computational model of the hippocampus. Their simulated mobile robot incrementally constructs a neural model of the experienced environment. Sensor readings that have not been experienced previously are remembered together with position information obtained from dead reckoning. Later, if similar sensor readings are experienced, the position information is recalled and used to correct possible localization errors. Yamada [22] evolved behaviors for a mobile robot to recognize different types of environments.

Our approach to robot localization is completely different from traditional methods. We are trying to evolve a function that estimates the robots position given the current sensor readings. Thus the whole system is under evolutionary control. We try to evolve an internal representation of the environment. Nordin and Banzhaf [12, 13] previously evolved a world model using genetic programming with linear genotypes [2] for robot control. They evolved a function which estimates the expected fitness for possible motor commands given the current sensor readings. A planning process searches the space of possible motor commands using the evolved function to predict the expected fitness of the action.

The best action is executed on the real robot. The resulting actual fitness of this action is stored along with sensor readings and motor commands in a memory buffer. This memory buffer is used by a learning process to evolve the function to predict fitness values before the action is executed.

Fig. 1. Where in the map shown on the left is the robot located given the shown sensor readings? The correct location is shown on the right.

3   Evolving an environment model for robot localization

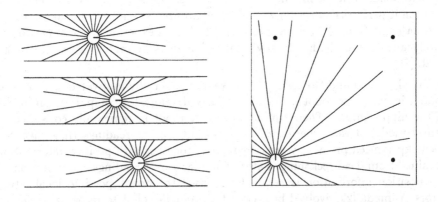

Fig. 2. Two examples for ambiguous sensor readings. If the robot travels through a long corridor it will get the same sensor readings for all points along a line parallel to the corridor [5]. If the robot is in a large room it will not be possible to tell in which corner the sensor readings were taken. In addition to the actual position of the robot three other positions are also possible.

In our experiments it is assumed that the robot perceives its environment using a laser range finder or a ring of sonar sensors. The environment is perceived like a floor plan. Robot simulators usually use a floor plan to calculate distance information for the sensors. There exists a mapping M from the robot's position P to sensor values S.

$$M : P \xrightarrow{\text{World}} S$$

To localize a mobile robot using the sensor information we are trying to invert this mapping. That is, we are trying to find a mapping M^{-1} which estimates the robot position P for the current sensor values S (Figure 1).

$$M^{-1} : S \xrightarrow{\text{Model}} P$$

Of course, it is often not possible to find an inverse mapping as the examples in Figure 2 show. Without any point of reference this task cannot be solved. Points of reference that are usually available include doors, windows or objects which are distributed inside a room such as a desk and some chairs. The location of these objects can be used to disambiguate the sensor readings.

Traditional methods usually rely on some type of matching method to locate the robot inside the world model using the current sensor readings. Often these methods only locate the robot inside a model up to some prespecified grid resolution. Differently from these traditional methods, we are trying to evolve an inverse function which converts sensor readings into a map location. If it is indeed possible to find such a function it would be possible to continuously localize the robot for all possible sensor readings. On a real mobile robot the method could be used to associate sensor readings with position information obtained using the robot's odometry. The evolved inverse function represents the robot's model of the world. It could later be used to relocate the robot if odometry information becomes inaccurate or is completely absent due to a system malfunction.

4   Symbolic regression using genetic programming

To evolve the inverse mapping from sensor readings to robot localizations we are using genetic programming [8, 10, 2]. Koza [9] has shown that genetic programming can effectively be used to search for a function described by a finite number of mappings. To apply genetic programming to the task of robot localization we first have to define the set of input variables.

The task of finding a function which maps raw range values to position in the environment is a very difficult task due to the number of variables. Therefore we preprocess the raw range values. This preprocessing has to have a number of requirements. Its major purpose is to perform a data reduction to reduce the size of the search space. Relevant features of the environment should be amplified and no valuable information should be lost. In addition, the reduced set of variables should vary smoothly with a change in position of the robot. Because we are trying to estimate the position (x and y coordinates) of the robot the resulting set of variables should be independent of the robot's orientation.

In our experiment we calculated the moments of the distribution of range values [4]. The following set of terminals was used.

- Moments $M_x = \frac{1}{n} \sum_{i=1}^{n} (\text{Range}(i))^x$ (x={1,2,3,4}),
- Central moments $CM_x = \frac{1}{n} \sum_{i=1}^{n} (\text{Range}(i) - M_1)^x$ (x={2,3,4,5}),
- Moments of first derivative $DM_x = \frac{1}{n} \sum_{i=1}^{n} (\Delta\text{Range}(i))^x$ (x = {2,3,4,5}),
- and the ephemeral random constants RAND (range [0,1)), RAND10 (range [0,10)), and RAND100 (range [0,100)).

The following elementary functions were used:

- Arithmetic functions: +,-,*,/ where the division operation evaluates to 1 if the absolute value of the divisor is less than 10^{-10}.
- Trigonometric functions: SIN, COS, TAN, ASIN, ACOS, ATAN, ATAN2,
- and the conditional statement IFLTE.

where

$$\text{ASIN}(x) = \begin{cases} \frac{\pi}{2} & x > 1 \\ -\frac{\pi}{2} & x < -1 \\ \text{asin}(x) & \text{otherwise} \end{cases}, \text{ACOS}(x) = \begin{cases} 0 & x > 1 \\ \pi & x < -1 \\ \text{acos}(x) & \text{otherwise} \end{cases},$$

$$\text{TAN}(x) = \begin{cases} 0 & |\cos(x)| < 10^{-10} \\ \frac{\sin(x)}{\cos(x)} & \text{otherwise} \end{cases}$$

Provided that the sensors are placed dense enough the resulting moments are nearly independent of the orientation of the robot. For our experiments we have used 720 sensors. This is a typical number of sensor readings available from a standard laser range finder.

5   Experiments

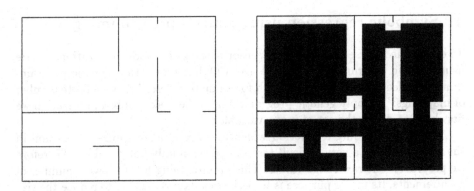

Fig. 3. Environment used during the experiments (left). Black areas show possible positions for fitness cases (right).

For our experiments we have used the simulated environment shown in Figure 3. The environment shows a floor plan of a section from a hypothetical office building with size 7.5m × 6m. The task is to evolve a representation of the environment using 1000 fitness cases (associations between sensor readings and robot location) which are distributed over the environment. The fitness cases are randomly distributed over the black areas shown in Figure 3. We evolved one individual for the x coordinate and another individual for the y coordinate. The error of the individual which tries to recall the x coordinate is calculated according to

$$\text{error} = \frac{1}{n} \sum_{i=1}^{n} \left(x_{\text{actual}} - x_{\text{estimated}} \right)^2 \tag{1}$$

where x_{actual} is the actual x coordinate of the robot, $x_{\text{estimated}}$ is the value estimated by the evolved individual and n is the number of fitness cases. The estimated position is truncated if it falls outside an area of a size twice as large as the original map. The error of the individual which calculates the y coordinate is calculated in the same way. The adjusted fitness of each individual is calculated as $\text{fitness}_{\text{adj}} = \frac{1}{1+\text{error}}$.

We performed five runs for each coordinate using different random seeds to initialize the first generation. A population size of 1000 individuals was used. Tournament selection with size 7 was used and crossover, reproduction and mu-

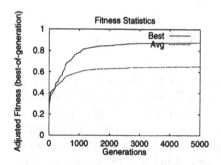
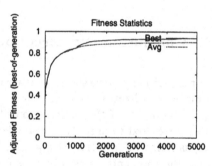

Fig. 4. Adjusted fitness for all generations averaged over 5 runs. The graph on the left shows the statistics for the x coordinate, the one on the right shows the statistics for the y coordinate.

tation probabilities were set to 85%, 10% and 5% respectively. The run was aborted after 5000 generations. Figure 4 shows the resulting fitness statistics averaged over five runs for the two coordinates. The task of evolving an inverse function for the y coordinate seems to be easier than the task for the x coordinate. The best individuals of the five runs were combined to form a single individual consisting of two trees. This individual was tested on 10 additional random fitness cases. The result of this test is shown in Figure 5. The robot is shown in the current location and the estimated position is marked with a small circle. The estimated location is very accurate for most locations but also differs by a large amount for some locations. To locate points where the error of localization was correct up to a certain error we used an additional 1000 fitness cases. Figure 6 shows locations where position estimation was accurate up to 1m (left) and locations where position estimation differed by more than 1m (right).

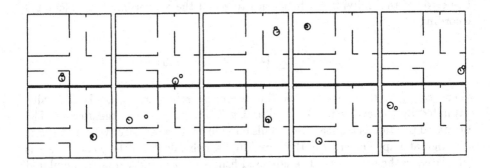

Fig. 5. Generalization results for 10 additional fitness cases. The robot is shown in the correct position. The estimated position is marked with a small circle.

6 Conclusion and directions for further research

Our experiments have shown that it is possible to evolve an internal world model for robot localization using genetic programming. To reduce the size of the search space moments of the distribution of sensor readings are calculated. The moments are used to amplify relevant features of the environment while maintaining as much information as possible. Using the genetic programming paradigm with the moments as terminals and arithmetic functions, trigonometric functions and a conditional statement as elementary functions we evolved a single function which approximates the inverse mapping from sensor readings to robot positions.

The estimated position could be filtered as the robot moves to improve the accuracy of the method. Also, other input representations might be more suitable for the task of robot localization. These could also be placed under evolutionary control.

7 Acknowledgments

This work was supported in part by a scholarship according to the Landesgraduiertenförderungsgesetz. For our experiments we used the lil-gp Programming System [24].

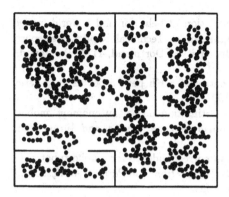 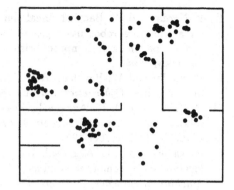

Fig. 6. 1000 additional fitness cases were used to locate points where position estimation was correct up to an error of 1m (left) and where position estimation differed by more than 1m (right).

References

1. K. Balakrishnan and V. Honavar. Spatial learning for robot localization. In J. R. Koza, K. Deb, M. Dorigo, D. B. Fogel, M. Garzon, H. Iba, and R. L. Riolo, editors, *Genetic Programming 1997: Proceedings of the Second International Conference on Genetic Programming, 1997*, pages 389–397. Morgan Kaufmann, 1997.
2. W. Banzhaf, P. Nordin, R. E. Keller, and F. D. Francone. *Genetic Programming - An Introduction: On The Automatic Evolution of Computer Programs and Its Applications.* Morgan Kaufmann Publishers, San Francisco, California, 1998.
3. M. Beetz, W. Burgard, D. Fox, and A. B. Cremers. Integrating active localization into high-level robot control systems. *Robotics and Autonomous Systems,* 23:205–220, 1998.
4. I. N. Bronštein und K. A. Semendjajew. *Taschenbuch der Mathematik.* Verlag Harri Deutsch, Thun und Frankfurt/Main, 24th edition, 1989.
5. W. Burgard, D. Fox, D. Hennig, and T. Schmidt. Estimating the absolute position of a mobile robot using position probability grids. In *Proceedings of the 14th National Conference on Artificial Intelligence,* pages 896–901. AAAI Press/MIT Press, 1996.
6. J. L. Crowley, F. Wallner, and B. Schiele. Position estimation using principal components of range data. *Robotics and Autonomous Systems,* 23:267–276, 1998.
7. J.-S. Gutmann, W. Burgard, D. Fox, and K. Konolige. An experimental comparison of localization methods. In *International Conference on Intelligent Robots and Systems, Victoria, B.C.,* October 1998.
8. J. R. Koza. *Genetic Programming, On the Programming of Computers by Means of Natural Selection.* The MIT Press, Cambridge, Massachusetts, 1992.
9. J. R. Koza. *Symbolic Regression - Error-Driven Evolution.* In J. R. Koza. *Genetic Programming I: On the Programming of Computers by Means of Natural Selection,* pages 237–288. The MIT Press, Cambridge, Massachusetts, 1992.
10. J. R. Koza. *Genetic Programming II, Automatic Discovery of Reusable Programs.* The MIT Press, Cambridge, Massachusetts, 1994.
11. A. Kurz. Constructing maps for mobile robot navigation based on ultrasonic range data. *IEEE Transactions on Systems, Man, and Cybernetics – Part B: Cybernetics,* 26(2):233–242, April 1996.

12. P. Nordin and W. Banzhaf. Real time evolution of behavior and a world model for a miniature robot using genetic programming. Technical Report SysReport 5/95, Department of Computer Science, University of Dortmund, 44221 Dortmund, Germany, 1995.

13. P. Nordin and W. Banzhaf. Real time control of a Khepera robot using genetic programming. *Cybernetics and Control*, 1997.

14. R. Talluri and J. K. Aggarwal. Position estimation for an autonomous mobile robot in an outdoor environment. *IEEE Transactions on Robotics and Automation*, 8(5):573–584, October 1992.

15. R. Talluri and J. K. Aggarwal. Image/map correspondence for mobile robot self-location using computer graphics. *IEEE Transactions on Pattern Analysis and Machine Intelligence*, 15(6):597–601, June 1993.

16. R. Talluri and J. K. Aggarwal. Position estimation techniques for an autonomous mobile robot – a review. In C. H. Chen, L. F. Pau, and P. S. P. Wang, editors, *Handbook of Pattern Recognition and Computer Vision*, chapter 4.4, pages 769–801. World Scientific Publishing Company, 1993.

17. R. Talluri and J. K. Aggarwal. Mobile robot self-location using model-image feature correspondence. *IEEE Transactions on Robotics and Automation*, 12(1):63–77, February 1996.

18. S. Thrun, A. Brücken, W. Burgard, D. Fox, T. Fröhlinghaus, D. Hennig, T. Hofmann, M. Krell, and T. Schmidt. Map learning and high-speed navigation in RHINO. In D. Kortenkamp, R. P. Bonasso, and R. Murphy, editors, *Artificial Intelligence and Mobile Robots: Case Studies of Successful Robot Systems*, pages 21–52, Menlo Park, California, 1998. AAAI Press/The MIT Press.

19. G. von Wichert. Vismob: Aufbau und Nutzung selbstorganisierender, bildbasierter Umweltrepräsentationen für mobile Roboter. In P. Levi, T. Bräunl, and N. Oswald, editors, *Autonome Mobile Systeme 1997*, pages 84–94, Berlin, 1997. Springer-Verlag.

20. G. von Wichert and H. Tolle. Towards constructing and using selforganizing visual environment representations for mobile robots. In M. Á. Salichs and A. Halme, editors, *3rd IFAC Symposium on Intelligent Autonomous Vehicles, March 25-27, 1998, Madrid, Spain*, pages 712–717, 1998.

21. P. Weckesser and R. Dillmann. Modeling unknown environments with a mobile robot. *Robotics and Autonomous Systems*, 23:293–300, 1998.

22. S. Yamada. Learning behaviors for environment modeling by genetic algorithm. In P. Husbands and J.-A. Meyer, editors, *Proceedings of the First European Workshop on Evolutionary Robotics, Paris, April 1998*, pages 179–191, 1998.

23. B. Yamauchi and R. Beer. Spatial learning for navigation in dynamic environments. *IEEE Transactions on Systems, Man, and Cybernetics – Part B: Cybernetics*, 26(3):496–505, June 1996.

24. D. Zongker and B. Punch. *lil-gp 1.01 User's Manual (support and enhancements Bill Rand)*. Michigan State University, March 1996.

Adapting the Fitness Function in GP for Data Mining

J. Eggermont, A.E. Eiben, and J.I. van Hemert

Leiden University, P.O. Box 9512
2300 RA, Leiden, The Netherlands
{jeggermo,gusz,jvhemert}@cs.leidenuniv.nl

Abstract. In this paper we describe how the Stepwise Adaptation of Weights (SAW) technique can be applied in genetic programming. The SAW-ing mechanism has been originally developed for and successfully used in EAs for constraint satisfaction problems. Here we identify the very basic underlying ideas behind SAW-ing and point out how it can be used for different types of problems. In particular, SAW-ing is well-suited for data mining tasks where the fitness of a candidate solution is composed by 'local scores' on data records. We evaluate the power of the SAW-ing mechanism on a number of benchmark classification data sets. The results indicate that extending the GP with the SAW-ing feature increases its performance when different types of misclassifications are not weighted differently, but leads to worse results when they are.

1 Introduction

In constraint satisfaction problems (CSP) a set of variables is given together with their domains and a number of constraints on these variables. The task is to find an instantiation of the variables such that all constraints are satisfied. A commonly used approach to constraint satisfaction problems in evolutionary computation is the use of penalty functions. Thus, an evolutionary algorithm (EA) operates on populations consisting of vector instantiations as candidates and the fitness of an arbitrary candidate is computed by adding up the penalties for violating the given constraints. Formally, the fitness function f is defined as:

$$f(x) = \sum_{i=1}^{k} w_i \cdot \chi(x, i) \ . \tag{1}$$

where k is the number of constraints, w_i is the penalty (or weight) assigned to constraint i, and

$$\chi(x, i) = \begin{cases} 1 \text{ if } x \text{ violates constraint } i \\ 0 \text{ otherwise} \end{cases} \ . \tag{2}$$

One of the main drawbacks to this approach is that the penalties, or weights, for constraints need to be determined in accordance with the hardness of the

R. Poli et al. (Eds.): EuroGP'99, LNCS 1598, pp. 193–202, 1999.
© Springer-Verlag Berlin Heidelberg 1999

constraints. After all, the EA will primarily 'concentrate' on satisfying those constraints that carry the highest penalties. Nevertheless, to determine how weights should be assigned to constraints appropriately, might require substantial insight into the problem, which might not be available, or only at substantial costs.

In the Stepwise Adaptation of Weights (SAW) mechanism this problem is circumvented by letting the EA defining the weights itself. In a SAW-ing EA the weights are initially set at a certain value (typically as $w_i = 1$) and these weights are repeatedly increased with a certain step size Δw during the run. The general mechanism is presented in Figure 1.

> *On-line weight update mechanism*
>   set initial weights (thus fitness function f)
>   **while not** termination **do**
>   **for** the next T_p fitness evaluations **do**
>   let the EA go with this f
>   **end for**
>   redefine f and recalculate fitness of individuals
>   **end while**

Fig. 1. Stepwise adaptation of weights (SAW)

Redefining the fitness function happens by adding Δw to the weights of those constraints that are violated by the best individual at the end of each period of T_p fitness evaluations. This mechanism has been successfully applied to hard CSPs, such as graph 3-coloring [4, 5], 3-SAT [1, 3], and randomly generated binary CSPs [6, 9]. Extensive tests on graph coloring and 3-SAT [2, 8, 13] showed that algorithm performance is rather independent from the values of T_p and Δw, thus they need not to be fine tuned.

Looking carefully at the SAW-ing mechanism one can observe that its applicability is not restricted to constrained problems. The basic concept behind SAW-ing is that the overall quality of a candidate solution is determined by 'local scores' on some elementary units of quality judgment, like constraints in a CSP. Then, the quality of a candidate solution (the fitness used in an EA) can be defined as a weighted sum of these local scores, where the weights should reflect the importance, respectively hardness of the elementary units of quality judgment.

A classification problem, as perceived in the rest of this paper, is defined by a data set consisting of data records, where each of the records is assigned a label, its class. The task is to find a model that takes a record as input and gives the class of the record as output. A natural way of comparing models is by their classification accuracy on the whole data set, the perfect model would generate the right class for every (known) record. It is obvious that this problem fits the above description: the overall quality of a candidate solution (the accuracy of a model on the whole data set) is determined by local scores on some elementary units of quality judgment (data records). Thus, an evolutionary algorithm searching for a good model classifying the given records in a data set D could use any suitable representation of such models and the fitness function can be defined similarly to Equation 1 as follows.

$$f(x) = \sum_{r \in D} w_r \cdot \chi(x, r) \,. \tag{3}$$

where $\chi(x, r)$ is now defined as

$$\chi(x, r) = \begin{cases} 1 \text{ if } x \text{ classifies data record } r \text{ incorrectly} \\ 0 \text{ otherwise} \end{cases} \tag{4}$$

More generally, the following formula can be used.

$$f(x) = \sum_{r \in D} w_r \cdot error(x, r) \,. \tag{5}$$

where $error(x, r)$ is a measure of misclassification, generalizing the simple good/no-good characterization by $\chi(x, r)$ in Equation 4.

2   A Library for Evolutionary Algorithm Programming

All experiments reported here are performed using our Library for Evolutionary Algorithm Programming (LEAP). This library differs from the many libraries for programming evolutionary algorithms that have been build as a toolkit, i.e., a loosely connected set of building blocks, that put together in the right way provides a user with a functioning program. The problem with a toolkit is that it is often difficult to learn and to maintain. Also most of them are aimed at one specific area within evolutionary computation.

By using a *framework* instead of a toolkit we can overcome these problems. A framework does not supply the user with loosely connected building blocks, instead it provides an almost running algorithm. The user only has to put in the last pieces of the puzzle and maybe has to change the parts of the framework that are not appropriate for the problem. The framework will then provide a running evolutionary algorithm using the provided pieces, substituting the changed parts.

When additions are made to the library, programs made with it can easily make use of these additions, by only changing some lines of code in a specific and predetermined place. As long as the new method is compatible with the old one, in a high level specification sense, the library will produce a new evolutionary algorithm without much extra work. A selection mechanism could easily be tested on different kind of algorithms, thus providing an easy way of sharing techniques between different areas of research.

A preliminary version of LEAP can be downloaded from its Internet site[1]. The library is programmed in c++, using the Standard Template Library (STL)[2]

---

[1] LEAP: http://www.wi.leidenuniv.nl/~jvhemert/leap/
[2] Available at: http://www.sgi.com/Technology/STL/

and comes equipped with a programmers manual [10]. It has been build using techniques from the paradigm Design Patterns [7]. A more detailed description of LEAP can be found in [9].

3   An adaptive GP for data classification

The adaptive GP we study in this paper deviates in two aspects from the usual GP for data classification. The first, and most important modification is the usage of the SAW-ing mechanism that repeatedly redefines the fitness function. The second modification concerns the representation. Namely, here we apply a representation based on so-called atomic expressions as leaves and only Boolean operators in the body of the trees. This implies some changes in the implementation of the mutation operator. The most important parameters of our GP are summarized in Table 1, for more details we refer to [9].

Table 1. Main parameters of the adaptive GP

Parameter	Value
Function set	{and, or, nand, nor}
Atom set	attribute greater or less than a constant
Initial maximum tree depth	5
Maximum number of nodes	200
Initialization method	ramped half-and-half
Algorithm type	steady-state
Population size	1000
Parent selection	linear ranking
Bias for linear ranked selection	1.5
Replacement strategy	replace worse
Stop condition	perfect classification or 40000 fitness evaluations
Mutation type	1. subtree replacement 2. subatomic mutation
Subatomic d parameter	0.1
Mutation probability	0.1
Crossover	swap subtrees
Crossover probability	0.9
Crossover functions:atoms ratio	4:1
SAW-ing update interval T_p	100
SAW-ing Δw parameter	1
SAW-ing initial weights	1

3.1   Representation and mutation using atoms

In the design of the representation we are deviating from the idea of having a function set of real valued operators and a special operator in the root of the tree that chooses the class depending on the values given by the subtrees [11]. Instead, we process numerical information at the leaves of a tree, transform it into Boolean statements, and apply only Boolean functions in the body of the tree. This is meant to increase the readability of the emerging models.

An *atom* is syntactically a predicate of the form *operator(var, const)*, built up from the following three items:

1. a variable indicating a field in the data set,
2. a constant between 0 and 1, and
3. a comparing operator, denoted by $A_<$ and $A_>$.

Evaluating an atom *operator(var, const)* on a record r within this syntax amounts to determining whether the value standing in the field *var* of r is smaller (for $A_<$) or larger (for $A_>$) than the given constant *const*, returning a Boolean value as answer. Notice that our GP fulfills the closure property because atoms produce a Boolean output after processing the numerical arguments. In this representation the conditional part of a rule could look like:

$$(A_>(r_1, 0.347) \textbf{ nor } A_<(r_0, 0.674)) \textbf{ and } A_>(r_1, 0.240)$$

which, in turn, is represented by the tree in Figure 2.

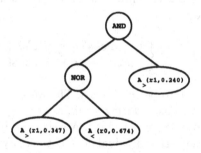

Fig. 2. Representation of a classification rule as a tree.

The new representation also gives rise to a new operator, called subatomic mutation. Every time an individual is selected for a mutation, we first choose a node in the tree to work on. If this node is part of the function set, a subtree mutation will be performed. If this node is a leaf (an atom), we choose with equal chance if this will be a subtree mutation or a subatomic mutation. A *subatomic mutation* works by first selecting, with equal chance, if the operation will be performed on the variable or on the constant. In case of a variable we just randomly select a new variable. In case of the constant c a small number Δc $(-d < \Delta c < d)$ is generated which is then added to the constant as follows[3]:

$$c' = \begin{cases} 0, & \text{if } c + \Delta c < 0, \\ 1, & \text{if } c + \Delta c > 1, \\ c + \Delta c, & \text{otherwise.} \end{cases}$$

---

[3] The values for all records are between 0 and 1 in the data sets we consider.

3.2 SAW-ing method for GP

As explained in the introduction, extending a GP with the SAW-ing technique can be done by using a fitness function in the spirit of Equation 3 or 5. The test suite we use for the experiments consists of binary classification problems, where exactly two disjoint classes are present. Denoting these classes by A and $\bar{A}$, it is thus sufficient to evolve models (classification rules) for class A only in the form of

$$condition(r) \longleftrightarrow class(r) = A,$$

where r is a record and the candidate solutions (trees in the population) represent the expression $condition(\cdot)$. Due to the Boolean typing of our trees, we can directly interpret a tree x on a record r as true or false. According to the above formula we have that a tree x classifies r into A iff x evaluates to true on r. To simplify explanations later on we introduce the notation $class(r)$ for the real class of r and

$$predicted(x, r) = \begin{cases} A, \text{ if } x \text{ is true on } r, \\ \bar{A}, \text{ if } x \text{ is false on } r. \end{cases}$$

for the class where a tree x classifies r into. With this notation we redefine χ from Equation 4 to become:

$$\chi(x, r) = \begin{cases} 1 \ predicted(x, r) \neq class(r) \\ 0 \ predicted(x, r) = class(r) \end{cases}$$

and the fitness function is to be minimized. The weights w_r used in the fitness function are initially set to one. During a run, after every T_p evaluations the GP is interrupted and the weights are changed. A weight w_r belonging to record r is increased with Δw if the best individual does not classify r correctly. After this phase all individuals have to be re-evaluated using the new fitness function.

Note that the stop condition of our algorithm is based on counting the number of fitness evaluations. This is in accordance with the common practice of generate-and-test style search methods. Because each newly created candidate solution is immediately evaluated, the number of evaluations equals the number of points visited in the search space. Using the SAW-ing technique, however, an extra overhead of re-evaluations is created and it could be argued that we should count the re-evaluations too. We do not do this for two reasons. Firstly, it is the number of points visited in the search space that we really want to count. Secondly, we can minimize the re-evaluation overhead by simply caching the classification results for each individual. That is, the first time an individual is evaluated it is assigned an additional bit-vector with the length of the number of records. In this vector we store the result of each classified record. This enables us to skip the time consuming evaluation of the individual x on each r when x is re-evaluated, instead we can suffice with looking up the values from this vector.

The algorithm using the SAW-ing mechanism will be called GP+SAW and the one without GP.

4   Experiments and results

We have compared the GP and GP+SAW techniques to other data classifying algorithms on four different data sets from the Statlog[4] [12] data set. All the experiments involve an n-fold cross validation. The results are obtained by averaging the classification error or misclassification cost over the n folds. We compare our GP and GP+SAW with four algorithms selected from the Statlog project. All the selected algorithms were best in one of the data sets, and showed a reasonable performance in the others. Also the default performance is reported, which is calculated by using the very simple classifying rule of always going for the safe prediction. For example in heart disease it is safe to say everyone has a heart disease.

The first experiments involve the Australian Credit Approval and Pima Indians Diabetes data sets. The Australian Credit Approval data set has 690 records and a 10-fold cross validation is performed. The Pima Indians Diabetes set has 768 records, and here a 12-fold cross validation is performed. When running the algorithms GP and GP+SAW we used the fitness function according to Equation 3 and the definition of χ above. The comparison is based on the average percentage of wrongly classified records in the test sets. The results in Table 2 show that the performance of GP+SAW is better than GP. For the Diabetes data set GP+SAW even manages to beat one (NaiveBay) of the Statlog algorithms.

Table 2. Classification error for the test phase on the Australian Credit Approval and Pima Indians Diabetes data sets

algorithm	Australian	Diabetes
Cal5	0.131	0.250
Discrim	0.141	0.225
LogDisc	0.141	0.223
NaiveBay	0.151	0.262
GP	0.246	0.283
GP+SAW	0.242	0.258
Default	0.440	0.350

The German Credit and Heart Disease data sets have respectively a size of 1000 and 270 records. Here the experiments consist of a 10-fold and a 9-fold cross validation test. The results are compared using a measure called the Average Misclassification Cost. This is calculated by using a cost matrix, which assigns a cost to each pair of true (rows) and predicted (columns) values. The cost matrix for these two data sets is the same:

class	good/absent	bad/present
good credit/heart disease absent	0	1
bad credit/heart disease present	5	0

[4] Available at: http://www.ncc.up.it/liacc/ML/statlog

According to this table we ran the algorithms GP and GP+SAW on these two problems using the fitness function in Equation 5 and the definition of $error(x, r)$ as follows.

$$error(x, r) = \begin{cases} 0 \ predicted(x, r) = class(r) \\ 1 \ predicted(x, r) = A \ \text{and} \ class(r) = \bar{A} \\ 5 \ predicted(x, r) = \bar{A} \ \text{and} \ class(r) = A \end{cases}$$

where class A stands for 'good credit' and 'heart disease absent', respectively.

Results show that for the German Credit data set, GP has a reasonable performance, obtaining a classification cost close to the best. However for the Heart Disease data set, both GP and GP+SAW have an inferior performance, although still better than the Default measure.

Table 3. Average Misclassification Costs for the German Credit and Heart Disease data set

algorithm	German	Heart
Cal5	0.603	0.444
Discrim	0.535	0.393
LogDisc	0.538	0.396
NaiveBay	0.703	0.374
GP	0.579	0.456
GP+SAW	0.943	0.537
Default	0.700	0.560

5   Conclusions and further research

The basic motivation for this study comes from the observation that the composition of the fitness function in a penalty based EA for CSPs is very similar to that of an EA (GP) for data classification. It is thus a natural question to investigate whether the SAW-ing mechanism, which can substantially increase the performance of an EA on CSPs, can lead to improvements on data classification problems as well.

Regarding the results of our experiments two cases can be distinguished. In case of the Australian Credit Approval and the Pima Indians Diabetes data sets GP+SAW clearly outperforms GP alone. This confirms that SAW-ing forms a useful extension of the standard machinery, leading to better results at low costs. On the German Credit and the Heart Disease data sets, however, the outcomes are reversed. When looking for an explanation of this result it immediately occurs that the latter two problems differ from the first two, because a cost matrix biases the measurement of misclassifications. It could be hypothesized that this 'skewed' measurement interferes negatively with the re-weighting mechanism of SAW-ing, misleading the GP+SAW algorithm. Namely, the SAW-ing mechanism

increases the weights of misclassified records, regardless to the low (1) or high
(5) contribution of this misclassification to the fitness value (to be minimized).

Current research is concerned with further investigation of the German Credit
and the Heart Disease problems. The first experiments support the hypothesis
that the inferiority of GP+SAW is caused by the 'skewed' measurement of misclassifications. Evaluating the outcomes of the experiments disregarding the cost
matrix during validation, counting only the percentage of misclassifications as a
result, yields better results for GP+SAW as can be seen in Table 4.

Table 4. Classification error for the test phase for the German Credit and Heart
Disease data set

algorithm	German	Heart
GP	0.382	0.278
GP+SAW	0.351	0.270

Although these outcomes are not anymore comparable with the benchmark
techniques from Statlog, they provide evidence that SAW-ing can increase GP
performance on the third and fourth data sets too. Presently we are working on
a modified version of the SAW-ing mechanism that does take the cost matrix into
account when re-defining weights of records. We are also testing the GP and the
GP+SAW algorithms on large real world data sets from finance.

Future research is divided into two main parts. The first part concerns the
implementation of the traditional GP approach to data classification tasks, and
its comparison with the present variant where we use an atom-based representation and a steady-state population model. The second part is the development of LEAP, where the main focus will be on the extension of the func-
tionalities and the possible integration of LEAP with another library called EO
(Evolvable|Evolutionary objects)[5].

References

1. Th. Bäck, A.E. Eiben, and M.E. Vink. A superior evolutionary algorithm for 3-
   SAT. In V. William Porto, N. Saravanan, Don Waagen, and A.E. Eiben, editors,
   Proceedings of the 7th Annual Conference on Evolutionary Programming, number
   1477 in LNCS, pages 125–136. Springer, Berlin, 1998.
2. A.E. Eiben and J.K. van der Hauw. Graph coloring with adaptive evolutionary
   algorithms. Technical Report TR-96-11, Leiden University, August 1996. Also
   available as http://www.wi.leidenuniv.nl/~gusz/graphcol.ps.gz.
3. A.E. Eiben and J.K. van der Hauw. Solving 3-SAT with adaptive Genetic Algorithms. In *Proceedings of the 4th IEEE Conference on Evolutionary Computation*,
   pages 81–86. IEEE Press, 1997.

---

[5] Available at http://geneura.ugr.es/~jmerelo/EO.html

4. A.E. Eiben and J.K. van der Hauw. Adaptive penalties for evolutionary graph-coloring. In J.-K. Hao, E. Lutton, E. Ronald, M. Schoenauer, and D. Snyers, editors, *Artificial Evolution'97*, number 1363 in LNCS, pages 95–106. Springer, Berlin, 1998.
5. A.E. Eiben, J.K. van der Hauw, and J.I. van Hemert. Graph coloring with adaptive evolutionary algorithms. *Journal of Heuristics*, 4(1):25–46, 1998.
6. A.E. Eiben, J.I. van Hemert, E. Marchiori, and A.G. Steenbeek. Solving binary constraint satisfaction problems using evolutionary algorithms with an adaptive fitness function. In A.E. Eiben, Th. Bäck, M. Schoenauer, and H.-P. Schwefel, editors, *Proceedings of the 5th Conference on Parallel Problem Solving from Nature*, number 1498 in LNCS, pages 196–205, Berlin, 1998. Springer.
7. E. Gamma, R. Helm, R. Johnson, and J.Vlissides, *Design Patterns: elements of reusable object-oriented software.* Addison-Wesley, 1994.
8. J.K. van der Hauw. Evaluating and improving steady state evolutionary algorithms on constraint satisfaction problems. Master's thesis, Leiden University, 1996. Also available as http://www.wi.leidenuniv.nl/MScThesis/IR96-21.html.
9. J.I. van Hemert. Applying adaptive evolutionary algorithms to hard problems. Master's thesis, Leiden University, 1998. Also available as http://www.wi.leidenuniv.nl/~jvhemert/publications/IR-98-19.ps.gz.
10. J.I. van Hemert. *Library for Evolutionary Algorithm Programming (LEAP).* Leiden University, LEAP version 0.1.2 edition, 1998. Also available at http://www.wi.leidenuniv.nl/~jvhemert/leap.
11. J.R. Koza. *Genetic Programming.* MIT Press, 1992.
12. D. Michie, D.J. Spiegelhalter, and C.C. Taylor, editors. *Machine Learning, Neural and Statistical Classification.* Ellis Horwwod, February 1994.
13. M. Vink. Solving combinatorial problems using evolutionary algorithms. Master's thesis, Leiden University, 1997.

Evolving Fuzzy Rule Based Classifiers with GA-P: A Grammatical Approach

Santiago García, Fermín González, and Luciano Sánchez

Departamento de Informática. Universidad de Oviedo. Spain,
{carbajal, fermingm, luciano}@lsi.uniovi.es

Abstract. Genetic Programming can be used to evolve Fuzzy Rule-based classifiers [7]. Fuzzy GP depends on a grammar defining valid expressions of fuzzy classifiers, and guarantees that all individuals in the population are valid instances of it all along the evolution process. This is accomplished by restricting crossover and mutation so that they only take place at points of the derivation tree representing the same non-terminal, thus generating valid subtrees [13].
In Fuzzy GP, terminal symbols are fuzzy constants and variables that are chosen beforehand. In this work we propose a method for evolving both fuzzy membership functions of the variables and the Rule Base. Our method extends the GA-P hybrid method [6] by introducing a new grammar with two functional parts, one for the Fuzzy Rule Base (GP Part), and the other for the constants that define the shapes of the fuzzy sets involved in the Fuzzy Rule Base (GA Part). We have applied this method to some classical benchmarks taken from the collection of test data at the UCI Repository of Machine Learning Databases [9].

1 Introduction

When applying GP to the design of fuzzy rule-based Systems the main open problems are the implementation of pure reinforcement learning, allowing rule chaining, and including the definition of the membership function in the genetic coding [7][2][12]. This last point was addressed in some GA related works (see [4] [11]), but these methods cannot be directly extrapolated to GP case.

L.M Howard and D.J. D'Angelo introduced GA-P in [6], an hybrid of traditional Genetic Algorithms and Genetic Programming able to effectively search for the values of the constants involved in GP expressions. In previous works, we adapted GA-P to imprecise, interval valued data [5] and compared it to genetically tuned fuzzy rule-based knowledge bases. Now we propose a method that we call Fuzzy GA-P to concurrently evolve the Fuzzy Rule Base and the membership functions. To test the viability of our method, we have applied it to a set of classification problems, and, in the future, will use it as a tool in some industrial applications [10].

Fuzzy GA-P describes Fuzzy Rule Based Classifiers using a grammar with two functional parts: the Rule Base (GP Part) plus the definition of the coefficients on which membership functions depend (GA Part). Both parts will evolve simultaneously by means of crossover and mutation operators designed for this

R. Poli et al. (Eds.): EuroGP'99, LNCS 1598, pp. 203–210, 1999.

representation. This way, we propose one solution to the problem of including the definition of the membership functions in the genetic coding of the individuals in Fuzzy GP.

2   Fuzzy Rule Based Classifiers based on a grammar

In [7] Andreas Geyer Schulz introduced a grammar for deriving Fuzzy Rule Bases and combined a genetic algorithm with a context-free language to evolve classifier systems. The method was called Fuzzy GP. In Fuzzy GP, constants are regarded as terminal symbols, so their value is not affected by the learning algorithm.

A Fuzzy Rule Based Classifier can be described in terms of a BNF grammar that generates a set of IF-THEN rules that assigns the input patterns to a number of classes depending on the fuzzy values of some input variables. A generic grammar for this type of classifiers could be:

```
S := <Rule_Base>;
<Rule_Base> := <Rules> ;
<Rules> :=  <Rule> | <Rule> <Rules>  ;
<Rule> := IF <Antecedent> THEN <Consequent> ;
<Antecedent>:= ( <Assert> )
            | ( <Operator> <Antecedent>  <Antecedent> );
<Operator> := OR | AND ;
<Assert> := <Input_Variable> = <Input_Fuzzy_Value> ;
<Consequent> :=  <Output_Fuzzy_Value> ;
<Input_Fuzzy_Value> := FUZZY_SET_1  | FUZZY_SET_2|...|FUZZY_SET_K;
<Output_Fuzzy_Value>  := Class_1  | Class_2 |...| Class_m  ;
<Input_Variable> := X1 | X2 |...| XN ;
```

This grammar can be used to generate an initial population of classifiers for any problem that can be described as a set of input variables, a number of linguistic variables that partition every universe of discourse, and a number of classes to classify the input patterns. For instance:

```
IF (AND(X4= LARGE)(X1 = SMALL)) THEN CLASS_1

IF (AND
    (X6 = MEDIUM)
    (OR
      (OR (X4 = MEDIUM)(X2 = LARGE))
      (AND(X1 = LARGE)(X4 = LARGE))
    )
  ) THEN CLASS_2

IF (X2 = SMALL) THEN CLASS_3
```

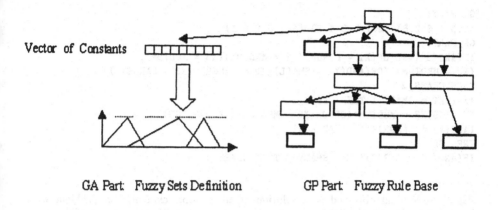

Fig. 1. A GA-P Fuzzy Rule Based Classifier. Individuals in GA-P comprise a chain of parameters and a tree. The tree defines a fuzzy rule bank. The chain of parameters codify the membership functions of the linguistic variables on which the rule bank depends.

3 A GA-P Grammar to evolve Fuzzy Rule Based Classifiers

GA-P techniques [6] can be adapted to work with grammatically directed Fuzzy Rule Based Classifiers Evolution. To do this, we introduce a new grammar structure with two functional parts, as we mentioned in section 1. One tree describes the surface structure of the rule bank and one vector is used to codify the constants that define the fuzzy memberships of the linguistic variables on which the rules depend. For example, the grammar shown in the last section will be adapted as follows:

```
<GA-P_Rule_Base> := <Vector_Of_Constants> <Rules> ;
<Vector_Of_Constants> := <T1> ... <TM>;
<T1> := <digit> "." <digit>;
 ...
<TM> := <digit> "." <digit>;
<digit> := "0"|"1"|"2"|"3"|"4"|"5"|"6"|"7"|"8"|"9";
<Rules> :=  <Rule> |<Rule> <Rules>  ;
<Rule> := IF <Antecedent> THEN <Consequent> ;
<Antecedent>:= (<Assert> )
               | ( <Operator> <Antecedent>  <Antecedent> );
<Operator> := OR | AND ;
<Assert> := <Input_Variable> =  <Input_Fuzzy_Value>  ;
<Consequent> :=  <Output_Fuzzy_Value> ;
<Input_Fuzzy_Value> := FUZZY_SET_1  | FUZZY_SET_2 | FUZZY_SET_K ;
<Output_Fuzzy_Value>  := Class_1  | Class_2 |... | Class_m  ;
<Input_Variable> := X1 | X2 |... | XN ;
```

```
GA_PART:
(0.3 1.6 2.5) (2.1 3.9 4.3) (4.1 5.2 6.1)
GP_PART:
IF(AND(OR(AND(OR(X1 = LARGE)(X3 = MEDIUM)(X5 = MEDIUM))
(X3 = MEDIUM))(OR(AND(X4 = SMALL)(X2 = LARGE))(X3 = LARGE)))
THEN CLASS_2
IF ( X1 = SMALL ) THEN CLASS_3
IF (AND(X3 = MEDIUM)(OR(OR(X2 = MEDIUM)(X5 = LARGE))
(AND(X1 = LARGE)(X3 = LARGE))))
THEN CLASS_2
IF(AND(X1 = LARGE)(X3 = SMALL)) THEN CLASS_1
```

Fig. 2. Individual obtained as a solution of an example classification problem with fuzzy GA-P algorithms. The first part of this individual codifies the shapes of the three Fuzzy Sets SMALL, MEDIUM and LARGE, and the GP-PART reflects the derivation of the grammar for a standard Fuzzy Rule Based Classifier. All inputs were normalized between 0 and 6 so that all variables share the same fuzzy partition.

Figure 1 illustrates the coding of a rule bank as a GA-P individual. Assuming triangular memberships, each group of three constants is interpreted as the left, right and modal point respectively of one of the fuzzy sets that appear in the Fuzzy Rule Base.

In Figure 2 an individual obtained as a solution of a classification problem with fuzzy GA-P algorithms is shown. The first part of this individual codifies the shapes of three Fuzzy Sets (SMALL, MEDIUM and LARGE) that form a fuzzy partition of the range of all input variables (in this case, the same fuzzy partition is shared by all inputs; the modifications needed for evolving a different partition for every variable are straightforward). GP-PART section reflects the derivation of the grammar for a standard Fuzzy Rule Based Classifier, what was called by Zadeh the "surface structure" of the fuzzy rules.

Before doing the fitness calculation for each individual, the memberships that define all fuzzy partitions are set to the values stored in the GA-PART. To ensure semantic correctness the following operations are performed:

1. The values of each group of three constants are reordered after every application of the crossover operation.
2. The modal points of all fuzzy sets in every partition must also be ordered so that linguistic labels assigned to the elements of the partition (i.e. "SMALL", "MEDIUM", "LARGE") make sense.

3.1 Modified crossover and mutation to preserve grammatical correctness

3.2 Crossover operator

It is important that during the evolution process, the new individuals generated are correct and complete derivations of the grammar that describes the general

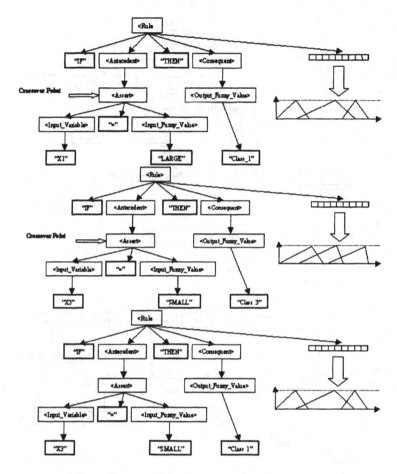

Fig. 3. Parents and offspring in GA-P crossover

structure of a Fuzzy Rule Based Classifier. So, the crossover operator must be adapted in a way that offspring produced by two syntactically valid parents will be in accordance with the grammar, too. This objective can be easily reached if we only let crossover take place in those points of the two parents that represent the same Non Terminal Symbol of the grammar. This Non Terminal Symbol will be part of the Rule Base, or part of the vector of constants. In the first case, a standard GP crossover operator is done, as shown in Figure 3. In the second case, we perform an one-point-crossover operation between the vectors of constants of the two parents [8], and the GP Part remains unchanged.

3.3   Mutation

To guarantee that mutation produces syntactically valid individuals, we only let this operator take place at points of the derivation tree that represent a Non-Terminal symbol of the grammar with more than one possible derivation. Then

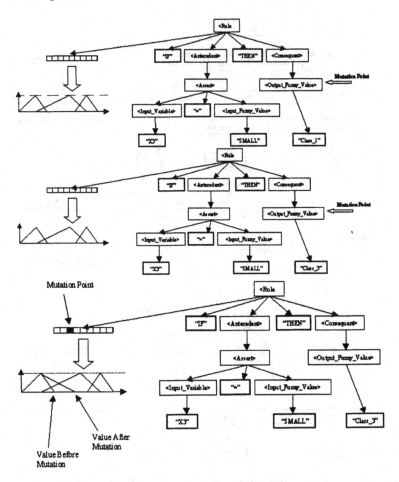

Fig. 4. Individuals before and after GP mutation (upper and center parts) and GA mutation (lower part).

mutation consists on the process of changing one derivation of a Non-Terminal for another.

Figure 4 shows how the mutation operator changes the first derivation of the Non Terminal Symbol <Output_Fuzzy_Value> by the third one, while ensuring that the individual is grammatically correct. In the same figure is also shown how mutation operates when the selected point lies inside the chain of parameters. In this last case, a standard GA mutation is applied.

4   Results

Seven standard classification problems were selected to compare Fuzzy GA-P with Geyer Schulz's Fuzzy GP [7]. The results of the experiments are shown

Problem	Train Fuz. GP	Train Fuz. GA-P	Test Fuz. GP	Test Fuz. GA-P
IRIS	97.63	97.45	95.6	95.1
PIMA	77.4	78.1	62.5	65.67
WINE	94	90	82.2	80
MONK1	100	97.3	98.5	95.1
MONK2	97.3	94.5	95.4	89.2
IONOSPHERE	96.3	89.3	86.9	80.2
SOYBEAN	83	91	73.1	76.9

Table 1. Comparison of numerical performance and complexity of the final model between Fuzzy GP and Fuzzy GA-P. Means of 50 runs.

Problem	Best Fuz. GP	Best Fuz. GA-P	Mean Fuz. GP	Mean Fuz. GA-P	Deviation Fuz. GP	Deviation Fuz. GA-P
IRIS	9	5	10.55	7.55	2.35	3.82
PIMA	8	6	8.45	8.70	0.73	3.34
WINE	11	7	13.1	9.80	2.34	3.38
MONK1	5	5	6.9	8.20	2.32	2.85
MONK2	11	9	12.15	10.70	2.03	2.23
IONOSPHERE	16	16	17.8	19.95	1.98	2.57
SOYBEAN	29	25	32.9	26.70	2.86	2.95

Table 2. Comparison of number of rules obtained using Fuzzy GP and Fuzzy GA-P. Means of 50 runs.

in tables 1 and 2. There are not significant numerical differences in the performance of both systems. Fuzzy GP and Fuzzy GA-P Results are not better than that ones obtained using pure GP of GA-tuned Fuzzy Systems. But there is a slight difference of complexity between Fuzzy GA-P and Fuzzy GP, which in turn produces models far more simple than GA-tuned Fuzzy Classifiers [4]. Since the objective of these kind of methods is to find an expression that makes sense linguistically while not being much less accurate than black-box models (i.e. neural networks, statistical classifiers or large GP expressions), we suggest that the ability of GA-P methods for searching numerical values contributes positively to the problem of finding a rule-based description of a classifier that is as short as possible.

5   Concluding remarks

Fuzzy GP is a kind of Evolutionary Fuzzy Rule-Based Systems that up to date has achieved less numerical accuracy than GA-based Fuzzy Rule Bank tuning procedures. On the other hand, the descriptions of the systems that Fuzzy GP produces are by far much simpler than GA-tuned fuzzy classifiers that use to be structured as a Mc Vicar-Gregor table. Fuzzy GP is capable to evolve models that do not depend on all input variables and its grammar can use linguistic connectives different from AND, which is the only connective allowed in most EFRBS.

In this work we have proposed one solution to an open problem in Fuzzy GP: evolving the memberships of the linguistic variables along with the structure of the rules. This evolution allows models with even simpler structure than Fuzzy GP, as our results show.

References

1. Blickle, T. "Evolving Compact Solutions in Genetic Programming: A Case Study". Parallel Problem Solving From Nature IV. Proceedings of the International Conference on Evolutionary Computation. Voigt, Ebeling, Rechenberg, Schwefel, eds. Springer-Verlag, LNCS 1141. pp 564-573, 1996.
2. Bonarini, A.: Elf: "Learning Incomplete Fuzzy rule Sets for an Autonomous Robot". Proceedings of the First European Congress on Intelligent Technologies and Soft Computing (EUFIT '93), ELITE Foundation, Aachen, D, 69-75. 1993.
3. Dietterich, T.G.: "Approximate Statistical Tests for Comparing Supervised Classifiers". Neural Computation, 1998.
4. Cordón, O., Herrera, F. "A three-stage evolutionary process for learning descriptive and approximate fuzzy logic controllers knowledge bases from examples". International Journal of Approximate Reasoning, vol 17, no. 4, pp 369-407, 1997.
5. Cordón, O. Herrera, F. , Sánchez, L. "Evolutionary Learning Processes for Data Analysis in Electrical Engineering Applicationes". Applied Intelligence, No. 10, pp. 5-24. 1999.
6. Howard L. M., D'Angelo, D. J.: "The GA-P: A Genetic Algorithm and Genetic Programming Hybrid". IEEE Expert. Vol 10, N. 3, June 1995.
7. Geyer-Schulz, A.: *Fuzzy Rule-Based Expert Systems and Genetic Machine Learning.* Studies in Fuzziness and Soft-Computing. Springer-Verlag. 1996.
8. Koza, J.: *Genetic Programming: on the Programming of Computers by Means of Natural Selection.* MIT Press, 1992.
9. Murphy, P.M,, Aha, D.W: UCI Repository of Machine Learning Databases. Mantained at the Department of Information and Computer Science, The University of California at Irvine, 1992.
10. Otero Rodríguez, J., García Carbajal, S. Sánchez Ramos, L.: "Fuzzy Control Applied to a Gas Transport Network In a Siderurgycal Environment". In Proceedings of 7th. International Conference in Information Processing and Management of Uncertainty in Knowledge-Based Systems I.P.M.U.'98. pp. 403-410. Paris. July, 1998.
11. Pérez Rodríguez, R.: *Fuzzy Rule Learning Using Genetic Algorithms.* Ph. D. Thesis. Department of Computer Science and artificial Intelligence. E.T.S. de Ingeniería Informática. University of Granada.
12. Valenzuela-Rendón, M.: "The Fuzzy Classifier System: A Classifier System for continuosly Varying Variables". Proceedings of the Fourth International Conference on Genetic Algorithms. Belew, Booker, eds. San Mateo, California. pp. 346-353. 1991.
13. Whigham, P.A.: *Grammatically Based Genetic Programming.* San Mateo, California. Morgan Kaufmann Publishers. 1991.

Evolving Neural Network Structures by Means of Genetic Programming

Wolfgang Golubski and Thomas Feuring

Universität–GH Siegen, FB 12: Elektrotechnik & Informatik
Hölderlinstraße 3, D–57068 Siegen, Germany
{golubski, feuring}@informatik.uni-siegen.de

Abstract. The goal of this paper is to present a more efficient way to automatically construct appropriate neural network topologies as well as their initial weight settings. Our approach combines evolutionary algorithms and genetic programming techniques and is based on a new network encoding schema where instead of a string like encoding the graph representation of neural nets is used. This way of "encoding" reduces the computational expense and leads to a greater variety of network topologies.

1 Introduction

Neural nets are known to be a powerful tool for a wide range of problems, such as classification, recognition and others. Their advantage is that they can be trained by using a set of input/output pairs. The underlying input/output relationship can be approximated by a suitable neural net during the training process.

It is well known that feedforward nets are universal approximators which means that a three layered feedforward net can approximate any continuous function on a compact domain. Since there are numerous of different network topologies and even more different weight initializations finding a suitable network topology is a quite complex optimization problem. But how can we find a suitable network topology with appropriate weight values? Currently, neural nets are essentially constructed by means of (1) backpropagation algorithms [7], (2) genetic algorithms [1, 3], or (3) genetic programming strategies [2]. Each approach has its own well known advantages but also some important disadvantages like the followings:

- *Backpropagation:* Many different network topologies have to be trained and tested before a suitable net is obtained. The training process highly depends on the initialized network weights. Each network topology has to be trained several time before it can be accepted. This procedure is obviously very time consuming so only a few network topologies can be trained and tested. Some experience is needed in order to find a "good" net. A second problem which occurs is that by permutation of the weights an identical net can be obtained. This results in an error surface having many global minima so that it usually appears rough in many dimensions. This can slow down Backpropagation.

R. Poli et al. (Eds.): EuroGP'99, LNCS 1598, pp. 211–220, 1999.

- *Genetic Algorithm:* Neural nets have to be coded into a string-like representation (of binary or real values) so that crossover and mutation operators can be used to optimize the net topology [10]. Directed search on the set of all weights of a net can be used for the task of finding a suitable network topology. So the initial net structure remains (nearly) unchanged.
- *Genetic Programming:* The coding process here (e.g. nets are encoded in grammar trees [4, 5], or in Lisp functions [8]) is the most difficult part because of its computational inefficiency. The networks to be encoded are different in their topology as well as in their number of weights. Again symmetry of the net weights can slow down the search for "good" nets.

To overcome these facilities we propose an approach [6] which combines the ideas of genetic algorithms and genetic programming. The net topology is no longer coded into a string representation but the graph of the net is used as a representation itself. Crossover operators as well as mutation operators can be defined on these graphs instead on strings or trees. Some advantages of this representation are that the process of evolving a suitable net is speed up since no coding and decoding is required and that the permutation problem can be reduced. Furthermore this approach can be seen as a generalization of other evolutionary based neural net creating approaches since we are using a more general coding scheme.

The main contributions of our paper are:

- A simple representation of neural networks by directed, weighted graphs where nodes represent neurons and the incoming arcs of the inner nodes are attached with real values called weights;
- Deriving recombination of neural nets by randomly selecting and exchanging subgraphs between neural nets;
- Defining various crossover operators;
- Presenting experimental results delivered by benchmarks on three test functions.

The paper is organized as follows. After this introduction we describe the basic structure of the neural nets to be examined in this paper. In Section 3 we focus on the basic structure of the genetic programming based algorithm used for evolving the neural nets. In that section we introduce different crossover and mutation operators. In the following section we present a detailed analysis of the tests performed and results obtained with our approach. Finally, some conclusions as well as some proposals for future works are given in Section 5.

2 Neural Nets

The neural nets we are interested in are feedforward neural nets consisting of an input layer, one or more hidden layers as well as an output layer, see Figure 1. At this stage of the project we are using exactly two or three hidden layers. Furthermore, all neurons of a layer are fully interconnected with all the neurons of the next layer.

Input   Second   Third   Output
Layer   Layer   Layer   Layer

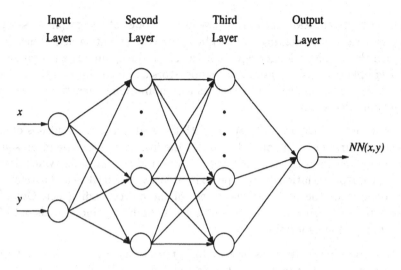

Fig. 1. Three Layered Neural Net.

The input neurons simply distribute the input data to all the neurons of the second layer. The later neurons compute the weighted sum of their inputs. This result is mapped by a transfer function to the output of the corresponding neuron. In ours tests we are using the sigmoidal function $s(x) = (1+\exp(-x))^{-1}$ to compute the output of the neurons. These outputs are sent via the directed arcs to the neurons of the third layer. These neurons act in much the same way as the neurons of the second layer. Finally, the output neurons compute the weighted sum of the outputs of the third layer neurons. Here the transfer function can be the identity function $i(x) = x$ if the desired output is not normed to the interval $[0, 1]$ or it can be a sigmoidal function as in the neurons of previous layers if the desired output is normed to $[0, 1]$.

3   Our Approach

Koza [9] used the idea of Genetic Algorithm [1] to evolve LISP programs. Hereby starting with a set of LISP programs new LISP programs are evolved by recombination until a sufficient good solution has been found. Programs are represented by their syntactic tree structure. Crossover operators operate on the tree structures by randomly selecting and exchanging subtrees between individuals which are selected according to a fitness function. This way a new tree representing a new program is generated. In contrast to evolutionary algorithms no mutation operators are used in the genetic programming approach.

In our method we combine the genetic algorithm concept with the genetic programming ideas by using graphs instead of trees. Since feedforward nets as shown in Figure 1 and 2 look like directed weighted graphs this structure is obviously a suitable candidate for representing neural nets. This way we reduce the computational expense needed for coding and decoding of neural nets. In the graph representation each arc between two nodes of the graph is associated with a real value representing the weight of the corresponding neural net. In our approach the graph no longer represents a certain program but a neural net. So, crossover operators as well as mutation operators can be defined on these graphs. This is why our approach can be seen as a combination of genetic programming and genetic algorithms.

The whole evolution process starts with the evaluation of the fitness of all individuals (neural nets). As an indicator for the fitness we used the mean squared error on a given training set consisting of input and output pairs, which describe the input output relation to be approximated by a neural net. Therefore, the smaller the error the better is the fitness of the corresponding net. Out of the fittest nets the (λ, μ) selection process, selects the best μ individuals out of the λ members of the generation.

The recombination process now builds a temporary generation by applying a crossover operator to the previously selected individuals (of the previous generation). In order to build the temporary generation we randomly choose 10% or 20% (reproduction rate) of the μ fittest neural nets to become members of the temporary generation. Since the population size of the temporary population is λ the remaining neural nets are constructed by recombination. So, first two "parents" are chosen randomly from the μ selected members. Then the crossover operator first chooses the hidden layer which is recombined in the exchange process. Now two subgraphs (consisting of nodes and the arcs to these nodes) of the chosen layer of both parents are randomly taken and exchanged in order to produce two temporary individuals. Both are taken into the temporary generation. The process of choosing parent nets is repeated until the temporary population consists of λ individuals. Two different crossover operators are used in our experiments. The first one is non-restrictive which means that the subgraph to be exchanged can consist of a randomly chosen number of nodes according to the number of nodes of the corresponding layer. Figure 2 describes this situation. In this Figure the second layer is chosen for the recombination process. A three node subgraph (Parent A) and a one-node subgraph (Parent B) are selected in the second layers and exchanged to produce Child 1 and Child 2. For Child 1 the three-node subgraph is substituted by a one-node subgraph. Since the number of input neurons is identical we only have to focus on how to change the arcs from the substituted subgraph to the nodes of the third layer. Since the third layer of Parent A only has three nodes but there are four arc in the chosen one-node subgraph of Parent B we randomly delete one arc and use the remaining three to connect to one-node subgraph with the three nodes of Parent A to obtain Child 1. For Child 2 we proceed similarly except that for each of the nodes of the three-node subgraph a new arc (and a weight) is randomly generated. Finally, both children are taken into the temporary generation. We call this a non-restrictive crossover operator since the graph can grow rapidly. Since we are interested in small nets, we have tested two versions of the crossover strategies: one where the randomly chosen part is only restricted by the number of neurons in its layer (the non restrictive) and one where the randomly chosen part cannot

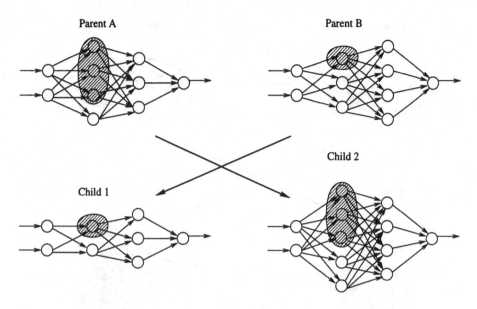

Fig. 2. Crossover Operator (non restrictive).

be greater than two neurons (the restrictive version). For this crossover operator only one-node or two-node subgraphs can be chosen for the parent graphs (see Figure 3). This way the growth of the nets is reduced. Therefore, this crossover operator is denoted as restrictive. The most important parameter adjustments are summarized in Table 1.

Table 1. Parameter Adjustment

Parameter	Version 1	Version 2
Population size	1000	1000
max. generation	200	200
Recombination rate	80%	90%
Reproduction rate	20%	10%
Number of fittest nets	72	72
Fitness type	MSE	MSE
Fitness threshold	0.01	0.01

After recombination and reproduction step a mutation process follows. According to a predefined mutation rate the mutation process builds a new member of the new generation by adding to each weight a value $\exp(\tau * N(0,1))$ where $N(0,1)$ stands for a normally distributed random variable having expectation value zero and standard deviation one and τ is an additional parameter which is set to $n^{-0.5}$, where n is the number of network weights needed for the corresponding net (see [1]).

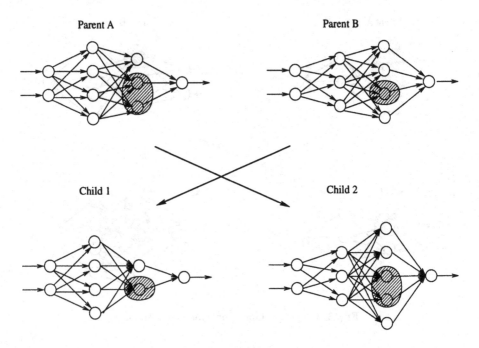

Fig. 3. Crossover Operator (restrictive).

Now again the selection operator finds the best members of the population, which are used by the recombination operator to produce a temporary generation and the mutation operator which mutates each temporary element in order to construct the next generation. This evolution process of the neural net structures continues until a given number of generations is reached, or a given fitness level is obtained.

This concept was implemented and tested using different benchmark data sets as well as different settings. All results obtained by this approach are discussed in detail in the following section.

4   Results

The application of our implemented algorithm is currently going on. We present results of three test functions (sin, Rosenbrock, Schaffer (see [10])) which were trained 5 times using two (NN2L, rNN2L) and three (NN3L, rNN3L) hidden layers and crossover operator without (NN2L, NN3L) and with limited (restrictive) (rNN2L, rNN3L) growth, altogether in two parameter versions (v1 and v2). E.g. rNN3Lv2 names the neural net evolution having three hidden layers, using the restrictive crossover operator based on the parameter settings of version 2.

4.1 Successful Runs

A test run is classified as successful if within 200 evolution steps the mean squared error is less than 0.01. The number of successful runs versus unsuccessful runs are given in Table 2 and 3. In the most cases the 2 hidden layer nets show better results than the 3 hidden layer nets but the schaffer example indicates that sometimes a 3 hidden layer net leads to a better net.

Comparing unrestricted, growing, crossover (NN2L, NN3L) and its restricted version (rNN2L, rNN3L) we surprisingly observe that the restricted crossovers show significantly better results than its counterpart.

Table 2. Successful Runs for the Different Crossover Operators and Net Sizes for the Parameter Version 1

	NN2Lv1	NN3Lv1	rNN2Lv1	rNN3Lv1
sin	2:3	3:2	4:1	2:3
rosenbrock	2:3	0:5	4:1	0:5
schaffer	1:4	1:4	0:5	3:2

Table 3. Successful Runs for the Different Crossover Operators and Net Sizes for the Parameter Version 2

	NN2Lv2	NN3Lv2	rNN2Lv2	rNN3Lv2
sin	2:3	0:5	5:0	3:2
rosenbrock	3:2	3:2	5:0	3:2
schaffer	4:1	5:0	1:4	4:1

4.2 The Sizes of the Best Nets

Considering the topological size, see Table 4 and 5, of the evaluated nets the restrictive crossover is the more appropriate one. The non restrictive version leads to an unlimited growth of the net sizes, see the results of NN3L. But again like above the schaffer-function is a good example that greater net structures are thoroughly rich in meaning.

4.3 The Number of Generation Steps Needed

Similar to the results above, see Table 4 and 5, we obtain that the restrictive version is superior to the non-restrictive one according to the number of generation steps of the evolution process needed to get a succesful run. E.g. rNN2Lv2 and NN2Lv2 applied to sin shows that 4 of 5 test runs of rNN2Lv2 finish more faster than the best NN2Lv2 run does.

Table 4. Results about the Net Sizes (Number of Neurons in the Hidden Layers) of the Best Successful Nets and the Number of Generation Steps needed

	NN2Lv1	NN3Lv1	rNN2Lv1	rNN3Lv1
sin	10-2 [187]	14-2-9 [173]	12-2 [128]	8-2-2 [88]
	18-2 [121]	23-2-25 [158]	8-9 [106]	15-10-5 [138]
		39-2-25 [177]	16-4 [162]	
			13-8 [112]	
rosenbrock	11-6 [175]		7-2 [145]	
	30-2 [94]		12-3 [94]	
			12-9 [112]	
			15-8 [167]	
schaffer	23-2 [187]	17-2-2 [83]		10-2-2 [133]
				9-5-2 [107]
				13-8-2 [139]

Table 5. Results about the Net Sizes (Number of Neurons in the Hidden Layers) of the Best Successful Nets and the Number of Generation Steps needed

	NN2Lv2	NN3Lv2	rNN2Lv2	rNN3Lv2
sin	52-2 [187]		14-8 [142]	14-13-7 [180]
	60-2 [155]		9-19 [96]	9-6-10 [141]
			15-6 [166]	12-7-11 [181]
			18-10 [147]	
			19-8 [151]	
rosenbrock	30-2 [165]	25-5-2 [102]	13-13 [152]	8-9-16 [156]
	45-12 [155]	12-25-2 [89]	17-14 [128]	10-9-4 [148]
	73-3 [112]	38-2-13 [193]	20-11 [90]	13-13-8 [130]
			10-2 [80]	
			15-13 [132]	
schaffer	11-2 [167]	8-2-2 [67]	14-5 [152]	8-3-2 [125]
	9-2 [90]	8-2-2 [132]		8-6-5 [57]
	11-2 [138]	16-7-2 [169]		11-2-2 [89]
	27-2 [118]	14-2-2 [116]		11-6-2 [134]
		14-7-2 [67]		

4.4   Parameter Version 1 vs Parameter Version 2

Here the unique winning adjustment is version 2 with a higher recombination rate (90%). All runs of the test functions except NN3Lv2 applied to sin show better results with respect to successful runs and the number of generation steps needed. A comparison of the net sizes shows a complex picture. Sometimes the algorithm using parameter version 1 delivers smaller nets and sometimes the parameter version 2 algorithm evaluates smaller nets than its competitive parameter version.

5   Considerations about the Computational Expense

In this section we want to compare the computational expense of training a layered neural net with backpropagation and obtaining a neural net with out genetic programming based approach. The following considerations are very roughly since they will ignore the fact that network sizes occurring in our genetic programming based approach are different. However this assumption will simplify the following discussion.

In both approaches the same computational expense is needed for evaluating the error of a given network since in both nets a feedforward pass is performed. The weight updates using the backpropagation algorithm is more expensive than the corresponding forward pass. Since the recombination and mutation processes are also more time consuming than a forward pass (two passes through each individual have to be performed) we estimate both update methods to be nearly the same (from a computational expense point of view).

If we further assume that 1000 elements are evaluated in the genetic programming based approach we end up with the following comparison. One generation in our approach is roughly as expensive as 1000 backpropagation steps for a given network with a given weight initialization. So, if we would net 200 generations for finding a suitable net topology ending up with an error of 0.001, we could need 200.000 backpropagation steps in order to find a suitable net. Of course, using the backpropagation algorithm would lead to testing different networks with different weight initializations. Depending on how lucky the user is he could find a good net with a smaller error than 0.001 within 200.000 steps. Since some experiences are needed to find a good net it might also take some longer to find a good net. The point here is that using our approach there would be no need for a user to "search" for a suitable net. So, with our approach this human resource is saved.

Let us mention one final point. Our approach only leads to a got initialization of the most suitable network. The resulting net can easily be trained by a second order descent methods like the quickprop algorithm. This method leads to a faster descent as the backpropagation. Since the quickprop only guarantees local convergence (the algorithm converges only if the error is sufficiently close to the minimum) it is not suitable (from a theoretical point of view) to use this algorithm instead of the backpropagation.

6   Conclusions and Further Works

We presented a genetic programming based neural net topology initialization approach and showed results on three test functions applied to different crossover strategies and two genetic parameter adjustments. The tests are very promising even if the sizes of the nets obtained by the program could be smaller. The restrictive crossovers show better results than the unlimited growing crossovers and a higher recombination rate is much better than a smaller one.

Currently we are working on (1) an extension of the exchanging subgraphs property to yield a crossover operator where subgraphs consisting of neurons of two succeeding layers are participated; (2) a direct comparison of backpropagation strategies and our approach and (3) a hybrid extension of our algorithm where after a fixed number of population steps a fixed number of backpropagation steps should help to improve the overall quality of the evolved nets.

References

[1] Bäck, T.: "Evolutionary Algorithms in Theory and Practice : Evolutionary Strategies, Evolutionary Programming, Genetic Algorithms". Oxford University Press, New York, 1996.

[2] Banzhaf, W., Nordin, P., Keller,R.E., Francone, F.D.: "Genetic Programming: An Introduction". Morgan Kaufmann Publishers, 1998.

[3] Fogel, D.B.: "Evolutionary Computation: Toward a New Philosophy of Machine Learning". IEEE Press, Piscataway, 1995.

[4] Gruau, F.: "Neural Network Synthesis using Cellular Encoding and the Genetic Algorithm". PhD-Thesis, University of Grenoble, France, 1994.

[5] Gruau,F., Whitley, D., Pyeatt, L.: "A Comparison between Cellular Encoding and Direct Encoding for Genetic Neural Networks", Proc. of Genetic Programming 1996, Stanford University, pp. 81–89.

[6] Golubski, W., Feuring, T.: "Genetic Algorithm based Neural Network Initialization: Part 1", to appear: International Conference on Computational Intelligence for Modelling Control and Automation 1999, Vienna, Feb. 1999.

[7] Haykin, S.: "Neural Networks - A Comprehensive Foundation". Macmillan College Publishing Company, New York, 1994.

[8] Koza, J.R., Rice, J.P.: "Genetic generation of both the weights and architecture for a neural network", In Proceedings of International Joint Conference on Neural Networks, Seattle, Los Alamitos, CA: IEEE Press, Volume II, pp. 397-404, 1991.

[9] Koza, J.R.: "Genetic Programming II". Cambridge/MA: MIT Press, 1994.

[10] Whitley, D.: "Genetic Algorithms and Neural Networks". in: Periaux, J. and Winter, G. (eds) "Genetic Algorithms in Engineering and Computer Science", 1995.

Genetic Reasoning: Evolutionary Induction of Mathematical Proofs

Peter Nordin, Anders Eriksson, and Mats Nordahl

Chalmers University of Technology
Department of Physical Resource Theory
S-41296, Göteborg, Sweden
{nordin,tfemn}@fy.chalmers.se

Abstract. Most automated reasoning systems rely on human knowledge or heuristics to guide the reasoning or search for proofs. We have evaluated the use of a powerful general search algorithm to search in the space of mathematical proofs. In our approach, automated reasoning is seen as an instance of automated programming where the proof is seen as a program (of functions corresponding to rules of inference) which transforms a statement into an axiom. We use genetic programming as the general technique for automated programming. We show that such a system can be used to evolve mathematical proofs in complex domains, i.e. arithmetics. We extend our previous research by the implementation of an efficient and stable C-language system in contrast to earlier work in Prolog.

1 Introduction

We present an approach to reasoning that uses a genetic search heuristic to navigate and search in the space of true statements. An algorithm inspired by natural selection and survival of the fittest is used to search for proofs.

To use a genetic process as the architecture for mentally related activities could, at first, be considered awkward. As far as we know today, genetic information processing is not directly involved in information processing in brains, though the idea of genetics as a model of mental processes is not new. William James, the father of American psychology, argued in 1879, just 15 years after Darwin published *The Origin of Species*, that mental processes could operate in a Darwinian manner [6]. He suggested that ideas "compete" with one another in the brain, leaving only the best or fittest. Just as Darwinian evolution shaped a better brain in a couple of million years, a similar Darwinian process operating within the brain might shape intelligent solutions to problems on the time scale of thought and action. This allows "our thoughts to die instead of ourselves".

Genetic Programming uses the mechanisms behind natural selection for *evolution of computer programs*. This application contrasts with other evolutionary algorithms, which often optimize real numbers or vectors of real numbers. GP differs from most other evolutionary techniques and most other "soft-computing" techniques in that it produces symbolic information (i.e. computer programs) as

R. Poli et al. (Eds.): EuroGP'99, LNCS 1598, pp. 221–231, 1999.

output. It can also process symbolic information as input very efficiently. Despite this unique strength genetic programming has so far been applied mostly in numerical or boolean problem domains.

In this paper we exploit GP's strength in processing purely symbolic information through search in the domain of proofs.

Genetic Programming is a method for automated programming. A formal proof of a statement could be seen as a computer program and a theorem prover could be considered as an application of automated programming. The proof program is a list of inference functions transforming a statement into an axiom (or into a statement known to be false, i.e. a contradiction). Rules of inference are seen in this notion as functions from theorems to theorems, like in, for instance, the programming language *ML*. The inference rules are rules which match a part of a formula and rewrite it as something equivalent, or equally true. To give an example, the formula $X + 0$ could be replaced by X, as one of the axioms of Peano arithmetic tells us. This rule describes a function from theorem to theorem. In the same way the reverse is true and X could be replaced by $X + 0$ (but this is considered as another function).

This simplest form of a theorem prover systematically applies rules of inference to construct all possible valid logical deductions. This was what the pioneering AI research tried in the 1950s, with a most notable example being the Logic Theory Machine of Alan Newell and Herbert Simon [10]. In practice, however, such a method can only find very short proofs. The combinatorial explosion will quickly exhaust any computer resources. Different, more efficient variants of representation and search methods have been introduced later, like the *resolution* method pioneered by, for instance, Robinson in the early 1960s, [14, 5]. These methods were more adapted to machine reasoning than to human reasoning, hence their implementations were more efficient. Still they needed to be governed by strategies and heuristics optimizing the order in which clauses were resolved etc. Resolution theorem provers are useful against the combinatorial explosion but they cannot eliminate it entirely. They can still only produce proofs of modest length.

The disappointment with some of these reasoning systems lead to the conclusion that more human knowledge needs to be put into the reasoning process, or, as Bledsoe put it [2]:

> The word "knowledge" is a key to much of this modern theorem-proving. Somehow we want to use the knowledge accumulated by humans over the last few thousand years, to help direct the search for proofs.

This knowledge is included as heuristics, weights and priorities in the theorem prover. If it is an *interactive theorem prover* it can have its heuristics modified by a human during execution. Regarding search algorithm, most systems rely on a hill-climbing algorithm, back-tracking or a best-first heuristic [17].

In our research we are investigating a different approach. Instead of using explicitly added heuristics to guide the search we apply a more powerful and robust general search algorithm. The hypothesis is that the robustness of genetic search could free the reasoning system from some of the burdens of carrying specialized heuristics. The search could then be more autonomous and act more "intelligently" when it produces solutions to problems with less a priori knowledge.

2   Genetic Reasoning

In order to apply GP to reasoning and automated theorem proving (ATP) we need to design an appropriate fitness function, function set and choose a theorem representation. In this paper, our goal is to handle statements about arithmetics in a logic as powerful as first order logic.

The function set is made up of functions representing rules of inference. One such function could be the rule $X + O$ *can be replaced by* X. All functions we use are unary-functions – they take one statement as input and produce another equivalent statement as output. This means that the tree representation of the individuals in GP collapses into a linear list representation[1] and that recombination will exchange linear segments of the individual genome, see figure 1.

The actual statement that should be proven true or false is represented by a

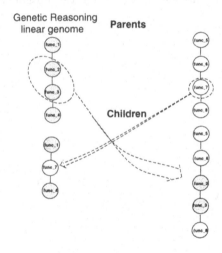

Fig. 1: Crossover in Genetic Reasoning.

tree. Universal quantification is indicated by leaving variables free. Existential quantification is represented by a Skolem function, as common in several approaches to ATP. The natural numbers are built into our system in the form of the *zero (0)* symbol and the successor function. Figure 2 shows how the (false) statement $3 = 2 + 0$ would be represented.

The inference functions in the genome are then applied in turn to this structure.

---

[1] Note that in this application the genome structure is linear while the fitness case input is a tree structure. It is sometimes the other way around in other GP applications.

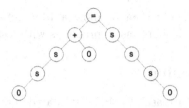

Fig. 2: Representation of the statement $3 = 2 + 0$.

When all inference functions have been applied – when the individual "program" has terminated – the result will be another tree structure representing an equivalent statement. Let us say that we call the rule "$X + O$ can be replaced by X" $func_1$. If this function is part of the genome it will try to match a subtree in the statement and, if it finds a match, will replace it with X, see figure 3.
In figure 3 the function matches a sub-tree in the statement and the statement

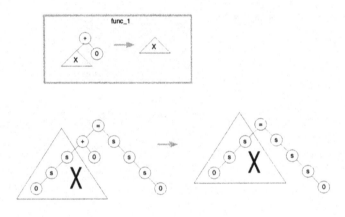

Fig. 3: Application of $func_1$ to the statement $3 = 2 + 0$.

can be transformed. With this transformation the size of the statement structure is reduced, but there exists an equal number of functions in the function set that increase the size of the structure. If a function *does not* match any sub-tree in the statement then the structure is left untouched. This procedure provides syntactic closure and also gives the opportunity of temporary storage of unused material in the genome. The phenomenon of unused genetic material appearing in the genome is called *introns* in biology and may play an important role in the efficiency of genetic search, see [11, 12].

2.1   The Fitness Function

We are interested in proving that an expression is a conclusion that follows from a body of knowledge, a set of axioms. Expressions are sentences in a formal language. The set of sentences in the language is defined by the generative hull of a set of production rules and a set of sentences.

In general, proving a statement can be formulated as a minimization problem. Otter, a well known theorem prover, uses this principle to find proofs in first order logic and to reason with equality [9]. In this scheme, the user may provide a problem specific cost function. In our work, we have chosen to implement a simple strategy, which simply counts the number of symbols (not including parentheses) in the sentences. This is the default strategy used by Otter, and it is not hard to guarantee that solutions to the optimization problem determine the truth value of a statement by choosing appropriate production rules. We start with the statement sentence, and use the production rules to transform it. Thus, at every time we have only a single sentence (called *state*).

The fitness function is very simple in our genetic reasoning system. It is just the number of nodes in the statement structure (figure 2). The two simplest and shortest statements are the Boolean constants **t** and **f**, each represented by only one node. These truth-values are short-hand for an axiom or a contradiction, respectively. So the genetic system will try to simplify any expression down to the statement of either true or false, represented by the nodes **t** and **f** which carry the highest fitness values.

Genetic search has been proven to perform robustly in a wide variety of highly multi-modal search domains where local optima easily can trap local hill-climbing approaches. So, the pressure towards simplifying a statement does *not* mean that the system will try to constantly shorten the structure. The concept of a population of solution candidates helps the search to avoid local optima. The selection criterion does not monotonically select the best individuals from generation to generation but reproduces individuals probabilistically with a large variation in fitness.

2.2   Representation

We represent sentences as text strings. A sentence may be a ground symbol or zero or more sentences enclosed by parentheses. A ground symbol is either a variable (lower-case letters) or a constant (capital letters). This is essentially the syntax of S-expressions in the Lisp language, and gives a simple way to represent tree structures in strings.

The production rules are represented as sentences on the form (ab) or $(a\&b)$, where the rule head a and the rule body b are sentences. In the latter case, b is expected to be a production rule. This implements conditional matches. We also implemented a special production rule, which finds and replaces every occurrence of the first variable in a sentence with the rule body. This is a form of variable instantiation, which is very useful in some proofs.

2.3 Genetic Search

The individuals are simply linear sequences of production rules with variable length. The user specifies a subset of production rules as the function set or simplification set. Each individual evaluation is started using the investigated statement as *the state*. The individual is then applied to the state, and the rules of the simplification set are iterated until no match is found.

At start-up, a population is created by selecting the length and production rules randomly. We usually let length vary between half and three quarters of the maximum length of the individuals.

We use steady state replacement with a tournament selection of four individuals. This value was chosen *ad hoc*, but seems to work well over a wide range of problems [1].

To create the offspring, either crossover or simple copying is selected according to a specified probability. The crossover method, homologous or normal, is selected randomly. In homologous crossover, the crossover points (two in each individual) are identical in both individuals. In normal crossover, the crossover points are selected independently. If a child is too large, one of the parents is copied instead.

Mutations of the children occur with a specified probability and intensity. A number of positions are selected and replaced randomly according to the intensity.

Finally, the fitness value of the individuals are evaluated and stored. The original PROLOG version of the system uses a logic similar to that of the automated reasoning system Nqthm [3]. It is a quantifier-free first order logic with equality. The rules of inference are from propositional logic and equality. The C-language implementation described in this paper does not yet implement all features of the PROLOG system, such as induction.

Functions defining all boolean arithmetic operations are built-in ($\wedge, \vee, \neg, \rightarrow$). The boolean constants **t** and **f** representing an axiom, and a contradiction, respectively are also built-in. There are if-then-else functions as well as equality.

The natural numbers and arithmetics are defined by the Peano axioms and the symmetry relation.

It is possible to add functions defining abstract data types and lemmas to support a specific application.

2.4 Implementation

Our previous work has been performed with a prototype in PROLOG. The built-in features of PROLOG, such as pattern matching and list handling, simplify implementation significantly. However, it seemed difficult to find a PROLOG system that was stable enough for very long iterative runs. The PROLOG system also proved inefficient in some part of the algorithm, especially those where the built-in features constituted no benefit such as the evolutionary algorithm.

Instead, we have implemented a dedicated system in the C language. The system takes a text file containing the production rules, the state sentence, and the parameters for the genetic programming method. All memory allocation occurs at start-up, and no dynamic memory handling occur during the genetic search. Thus, the system does not have any problem with memory leakage or garbage collection. This is possible since only the statement-sentence changes its state, and it is therefore sufficient to keep two constant length buffers (whose lengths are specified in the input file), and swap them.

All sentences are represented as simple character strings. This limit the number of constants allowed, but it is easy to extend this implementation to handle multi-character symbols, or (whichever is faster) to use more bits per symbol.

Matching with the simple matching procedure is fast. The match of a rule head against a single sub-sentence takes time proportionale to the lengths of the strings, and there are no problems with variable names. In effect, the two expressions matched have separate name spaces, and no variable renaming or other checks are needed. There are no recursive calls in the procedure.

Unification is implemented essentially as in [16, page 103]. Both sentences are explored in parallel, with recursive calls to check variable bindings. This operation is often much slower than the simple matching, but may also be considerably more powerful since it may bind free variables in the state sentence. Variable bindings are stored in arrays in the simple match case and as pointers to sub-sentences in the unification case. This allows for rapid access with almost no overhead. A stack with the names of the bound variables is used so it is not necessary to clear the whole array after every match, only the current bindings.

3   Results

We present some examples of algebraic simplification, where we have chosen a standard axiomatization of the real numbers. The axiomatization is not complete. For example, inequality and the axiom of choice are not represented. Nevertheless, it is sufficient for our purposes in this paper. The production rules and their representation are listed in table 3.

3.1   Identities one and two

These problems are two identites from basic algebra, $a * 0 = 0$ and $N * N = 1$, where N represents the number -1 (as can be seen in table 3). To prove these identities, one has to expand the initial expressions significantly before it is possible to apply a greedy approach, and only go "downhill". Thus, simple descent algorithms may find these tasks hard when dealing directly with production rules. At the cost of a vastly expanded search space, evaluating fitness after several steps allows for hill climbing before descending to a lower fitness. The average and median number of generations needed to find the optimal solution is shown in table 1, based on ten runs. The initial population is called generation zero. An example of a proof is shown in table 2. Of 24 steps, only 11 matches. This demonstrates that it is very easy for the system to construct introns.

3.2 Identity three

This problem does not require expansion as the earlier problems, but it is difficult because it demands several operations without any fitness feedback. The average and median number of generations needed to find the optimal solution is shown in table 1. Considerably larger individuals and populations were necessary to solve this problem. The fitness as a function of generation number for ten runs is shown in figure 4. Though convergence of the best fitness varies, the median fitness of the same run does not deviate much from the best fitness.

We also tested to reduce the search space, by only allowing production rules for manipulating sums and eliminating zero, i.e. rules 0 and 2 to 5 in table 3. Though we tried different population sizes, the system failed to find any solution.

In a third set of runs, we allowed the same set of production rules as above, and added rules 15 to 17. This makes it very easy for the system to form introns in order to protect good parts of the individual (for a discussion of the role of introns in genetic programming, see [11, 1]). However, even with these changes, no solution was found.

Table 1: Problem overview. The problem column contain the sentence to be minimized. The table contains the median and average generation where the best solution was found (from ten runs).

No.	Problem	Median	Average	Pop. size	Max. ind. size
1	(*A0)	1	2.6	50	100
2	(*NN)	1	2.5	50	50
3	(+A(+(+B(N*A))C))	34.0	33.5	200	100

4   Future Work

One possible application area is the autonomous robot field. We plan to use genetic reasoning as a central part of an evolutionary control architecture which will be the basis for several humanoid robotics experiments. The software architecture is built mainly on evolutionary algorithms and specifically Genetic Programming. Evolution is thus used to induce programs, functions and symbolic rules for all levels of control. Three hierarchical layers are used for control: Reactive Layer, Model building Layer and Reasoning Layer.

The third layer is a symbolic processing layer built on genetic reasoning used for higher "brain functions" requiring reasoning. The objectives of this layer are to administrate high level tasks such as navigation, safety, and energy supply.

Table 2: Sample proof. Only matching rules are shown. The rows
under the horizontal line show the steps in the final simplification process. The leftmost column shows the line
count of the individual. Some proofs are shorter, but it
is typically not the shortest proofs that are found.

Line	Production rule	Resulting state
	Initial state	`(*A0)`
1	`(a(*a1))`	`(*(*A0)1)`
3	`((*a1)a)`	`(*A0)`
9	`(0(+a(*Na)))`	`(*A(+a(*Na)))`
10	`(a(+a0))`	`(+(*A(+a(*Na)))0)`
14	`(a(*a1))`	`(*(+(*A(+1N))0)1)`
16	`((*a(+yx))(+(*ay)(*ax)))`	`(*(+(+(*A1)(*AN))0)1)`
18	`((*a1)a)`	`(+(+(*A1)(*AN))0)`
19	`((+a0)a)`	`(+(*A1)(*AN))`
21	`((*a1)a)`	`(+A(*AN))`
22	`((*ay)(*ya))`	`(+A(*NA))`
24	`(a(+a0))`	`(+(+A(*NA))0)`
	`((+a0)a)`	`(+A(*NA))`
	`((+a(*Na))0)`	`0`

Table 3: Replacement rules used in the runs. The simplification
set normally consists of rules 0, 5, 7, and 14. Note that
a is bound by the first match in rule 14, so the second
part of the rule is only applied to sentences matching
the binding.

Nr.	Mathematical equation	Representation
0	$a + 0 = a$	`((+a0)a)`
1		`(a(+a0))`
2	$(a + b) + c = a + (b + c)$	`((+(+ab)c)(+a(+bc)))`
3		`((+a(+bc))(+(+ab)c))`
4	$a + b = b + a$	`((+ab)(+ba))`
5	$a + N * a = 0$	`((+a(*Na))0)`
6		`(0(+a(*Na)))`
7	$a * 1 = a$	`((*a1)a)`
8		`(a(*a1))`
9	$(a * b) * c = a * (b * c)$	`((*(*ab)c)(*a(*bc)))`
10		`((*a(*bc))(*(*ab)c))`
11	$a * b = b * a$	`((*ab)(*ba))`
12	$a * (b + c) = a * b + a * c$	`((*a(+bc))(+(*ab)(*ac)))`
13		`((+(*ab)(*ac))(*a(+bc)))`
14	$a \neq 0 \rightarrow a * a^{-1} \rightarrow 1$	`((¬(=a0))&((*a(/a))1))`
15	first variable $\rightarrow 0$	`(#0)`
16	first variable $\rightarrow 1$	`(#1)`
17	first variable $\rightarrow N$	`(#N)`

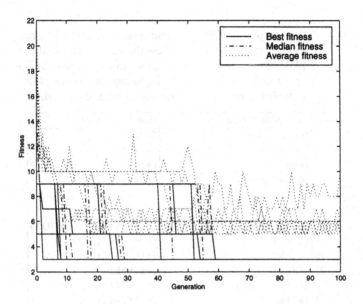

Fig. 4: Fitness, in ten independent runs.

5   Summary and Conclusions

We have demonstrated that automated reasoning could be seen as an instance of automated programming. In this spirit we have evaluated the use of a robust genetic search algorithm to search the space of proofs. The system has been able to avoid local minima in its search and has found proofs of statements from complex domains such as arithmetics. The system uses no heuristic or human knowledge to guide its search, instead it relies on the performance of the search algorithm. We believe that this technique has applications in many automated reasoning and machine learning domains, for instance in robot planning. A special purpose system makes the approach more reliable, efficient and reliable.

Acknowledgement

Peter Nordin gratefully acknowledges support from the Swedish Research Council for Engineering Sciences.

References

1. Banzhaf, W., Nordin, P., Keller R.E., Francone, F.D. (1998) Genetic Programming - An Introduction. Morgan Kauffmann, San Fransisco, and d-punkt, Heidelberg, Germany.
2. Bledsoe W. W., (1977) Non-Resolution Theorem Proving, In *Artificial Intelligence*, Vol. 9, pp 2-3.

3. Boyer R.S., Moore J.S. (1979) Proving Teorems about LISP-Functions, In *J.ACM*, Vol. 22, pp 129-144.
4. Boyer R.S., Yu Y. (1992) Automated Correctness Proofs of Machine Code Programs for a Commercial Microprocessor, In *Automated Deduction - CADE-11* Kapur D. (Ed), pp. 416-430.
5. Bundy A., (1983) The Computer Modeling of Mathematical Reasoning, Academic Press, London, pp. 74-77.
6. James W. (1890) The principles of psychology Vol.1. Originally published: Henry Holt, New York 1890.
7. Koza, J. (1992) *Genetic Programming*, MIT Press, Cambridge, MA
8. Lowerre, B.T., Reddy, R.D. (1980) The Harpy Speech Understanding System. In *Trends in Speech Recognition.* Lea, W.A. (Ed.) Englewood Cliffs, Prentice-Hall, New York.
9. McCune W.W. (1994) Otter 3.0 Reference Manual and Guide. Argonne National Laboratory, Argonne, USA.
10. Newell, A., Shaw J.C., and Simon H. (1957) Empirical Explorations of the Logic Theorem Machine: A case study in Heuristic, in *Proceedings of Western Joint Computer Conference* Vol. 15.
11. Nordin J.P., Banzhaf W. (1995a) Complexity Compression and Evolution, in *Proceedings of Sixth International Conference of Genetic Algorithms, Pittsburgh, 1995,* L. Eshelman (ed.), Morgan Kaufmann, San Mateo, CA
12. Nordin, J.P. ,F. Francone, Banzhaf W. (1995b) Explicitly Defined Introns in Genetic Programming. In *Advances in Genetic Programming II,*(In press) Kim Kinnear, Peter Angeline (Eds.) , MIT Press USA.
13. Nordin, J.P. , Banzhaf W.(1995c) Controlling an Autonomous Robot with Genetic Programming. In proceedings of: *1996 AAAI fall symposium on Genetic Programming,* Cambridge, USA.
14. Robinson J.A., (1965) A Machine Oriented Logic Based on the Resolution Principle, In *J.ACM*, Vol. 12, No. 1, pp. 23-41.
15. Rosenblom, P. (1987) Best First Search. In *Encyclopedia of Artificial Intelligence,* Shapiro, S. (Ed) Vol. 2, Wiley, New York.
16. Russel S., Norvig P. (1995) Artificial Intelligence: A modern approach. Prentice-Hall, Inc.
17. Winker S., Wos L., (1978) Automated Generation of Models and Counterexamples and its application to Open Questions in Ternary Boolean Algebra, In Proceedings of 8th international symposium Multiple-Valued Logic, Rosemont, Ill., IEEE and ACM, pp. 251-256, New York

How to Invent Functions

J. Roland Olsson

Chalmers University, Department of Computer Science
S-412 96 Gothenburg, Sweden
rolsson@cs.chalmers.se

Abstract. The paper presents the abstraction transformation which is a fundamental method for creating functions in ADATE. The use of abstraction turns out to be similar to evolution by gene duplication which is emerging as the most important theory of "building blocks" in natural genomes. We discuss the relationship between abstraction and its natural counterparts, but also give novel technical details on automatic invention of functions. Basically, abstraction is the reverse of the inlining transformation performed by optimizing compilers.

1 Introduction

This paper describes a general and effective technique, called abstraction, for inventing new functions on-the-fly during automatic evolution of programs as in ADATE [8, 9]. In 1991, we invented and designed abstraction for use in ADATE, but expect that abstraction is useful also in other evolutionary computation paradigms such as GP [5] and possibly also EP [3].

Modern genetics research has shown that the genetic operators employed by nature are quite sophisticated and that a model only including for example point mutation and crossover is much too simple. Since natural evolution is the most successful form of evolutionary computation so far, it is natural to compare proposed genetic operators with their counterparts in nature. Therefore, we will below discuss if abstraction and substitution in ADATE have roles similar to gene families, repetitive DNA and RNA editing through substitution [4].

In order to explain abstraction in an easy way, we will actually start by describing how it would operate on DNA. The later sections of this paper give technical descriptions of abstraction as a program transformation and show that it is a fundamental and mathematically elegant operation.

As more and more genes are sequenced, it becomes increasingly clear that Susumo Ohno's theory of evolution by gene duplication [7] is correct. It is beyond the scope of this paper to delve into current genome research where new gene families are discovered quite often. For example, Tadashi Imanishi [2] has a list of 425 families in the human genome, where the genes in each family are so homologous that they very likely share a common origin.

We will now introduce abstraction by studying the process where a sequence of DNA is copied to a new location in the genome and then diverges from the original through mutations.

R. Poli et al. (Eds.): EuroGP'99, LNCS 1598, pp. 232–243, 1999.

For example, assume that we somewhere in the genome have the subsequence of base pairs

$$\text{GGATTCTGG},$$

which would be translated to the three amino acids glycine, phenylalanine and tryptophan. Assume that this sequence is copied and then mutated by changing the first T to C and that the complete genome becomes

$$\ldots\text{GGATTCTGG}\ldots\text{GGACTCTGG}\ldots,$$

where the right-most subsequence is a mutated copy of the left-most subsequence.

Such repetitive and almost equal building blocks can be described using a function definition where the parameters indicate the variation between the different copies of a block. The building block in the above genome, for instance, corresponds to the function definition

$$f(x) = \text{GGA}x\text{TCTGG},$$

which allows the complete genome to be written as

$$\ldots f(\text{T})\ldots f(\text{C})\ldots,$$

where the original subsequence is $f(\text{T})$ and the mutated copy is $f(\text{C})$.

Note that a human genome may contain a million calls to a function like f if f represents a so-called short interspersed element (SINE), some of which occur about a million times in the human genome! This function is then a small help function that is useful over and over again. However, the role of SINEs is still unclear.

Let us now repeat the above copy-and-mutate process using function invention from the beginning. To simplify this introductory presentation, assume that the function to be invented has exactly one parameter and that an actual argument is only one base pair i.e., A, C, T or G.

Given that the function definition is to be based on the subsequence GGATTCTGG, there is one possible function definition for each of the nine positions in the subsequence. These possibilities are

$$f(x) = x\text{GATTCTGG}$$
$$f(x) = \text{G}x\text{ATTCTGG}$$
$$f(x) = \text{GG}x\text{TTCTGG}$$
$$f(x) = \text{GGA}x\text{TCTGG}$$
$$f(x) = \text{GGAT}x\text{CTGG}$$
$$f(x) = \text{GGATT}x\text{TGG}$$
$$f(x) = \text{GGATTC}x\text{GG}$$
$$f(x) = \text{GGATTCT}x\text{G}$$
$$f(x) = \text{GGATTCTG}x$$

An abstraction is carried out by choosing one of these nine alternatives and then rewriting the "genome" accordingly. Using functional programming notation [12], we can for example obtain the "genome"

$$\textbf{let}$$
$$\textbf{fun } f(x) = \texttt{GGA}x\texttt{TCTGG}$$
$$\textbf{in}$$
$$\dots f(\texttt{T}) \dots$$
$$\textbf{end}$$

We say that GGAxTCTGG is the body of f whereas the original GGATTCTGG is the pre-body of f.

Note that abstraction is an equivalence-preserving operator which means that it does not change fitness. In the simple example above, the number of possible abstractions is linear in the length of the pre-body, but in practice, the number of possibilities is occasionally quadratic or even cubic in the size of the pre-body. Since ADATE sometimes may need to examine a substantial fraction of all possible abstractions, we require that an abstraction shows its fitness advantage as soon as possible so that irrelevant abstractions are eliminated quickly.

In ADATE, this quick demonstration of usefulness is accomplished by one or more REQ and R transformations [9] that immediately follow an abstraction.

Very roughly speaking, this would correspond to the insertion of $f(\texttt{A})$, $f(\texttt{C})$, $f(\texttt{T})$ or $f(\texttt{G})$ somewhere in the above "genome", for example yielding

$$\textbf{let}$$
$$\textbf{fun } f(x) = \texttt{GGA}x\texttt{TCTGG}$$
$$\textbf{in}$$
$$\dots f(\texttt{T}) \dots f(\texttt{C}) \dots$$
$$\textbf{end}$$

Note that this genome is equivalent to the one obtained through the above copy-and-mutate process that did not use abstraction, but the copied sequence is now easer to identify and reuse since it is the body of a function. Since functions produced by ADATE often are recursive, a copy-and-mutate operator could not replace abstraction.

In ADATE, abstraction is a fundamental and highly useful program transformation that has proven its value over and over again since we introduced it in 1991. Most of the examples on the ADATE web site [10] would not work without it. During large scale program evolution, abstraction is essential for at least the following two reasons.

1. The user of an automatic programming system should not be required to define all needed help functions. Instead, the user should define a small

number of primitives whereas the system automatically constructs a possibly large number of help functions.

2. The system can construct a help function exactly where it is needed and avoid having a too large scope for the function.

Scope restriction is important when human beings write programs but much more so in automatic programming based on combinatorial search. If many irrelevant functions are available at a given position in a program, combinatorial search for program improvements at that position becomes harder.

A form of scope restriction actually seems to exist in DNA since repeats often occur in localized regions. One of several examples in [4] is the clustering of multiple copies of genes encoding ribosomal RNA in humans. One can speculate that the probability that a copy will become located at a given position is inversely proportional to the distance between that position and the position of the original. Such probabilistic scoping could also be useful in ADATE, GAs and GP. Note that ADATE already has a variant of such a scoping scheme, but its usefulness has not yet been experimentally verified since synthesized programs are too small.

2   Abstraction Applied to Functional Program "Genomes"

Abstraction is in principle applicable to practically all kinds of "genomes", including binary strings as in GAs, machine code as in Peter Nordin's work [6] and functional programs as in ADATE. We will now use a small and pedagogical example to show how abstraction operates on functional programs.

Assume that we want ADATE to synthesize a function max3 that finds the greatest of three integers, which is a simple program indeed. The specification contains a number of input-output pairs where each input is a tuple with three integers and the corresponding output is one of these three. The only primitive in the specification is <.

Using ADATEs a-little-bigger-a-little-better population management [11], the following program will typically become a permanent member of the population

```
fun max3( X, Y, Z ) = if X < Y then Y else X
```

ADATE would actually use case-analysis instead of an if-expression, but we use if here to improve readability.

Assume that the entire body of max3 is chosen as the pre-body of an abstraction of arity (number of parameters) one, two, three or four, which gives many alternatives, for example

```
fun max3( X, Y, Z ) =
  let
    fun g( V ) = if V < Y then Y else X
```

```
in
  g( X )
end
```

This abstraction and most others are not useful, but the following is.

```
fun max3( X, Y, Z ) =
  let
    fun g( V1, V2 ) = if V1 < V2 then V2 else V1
  in
    g( X, Y )
  end
```

ADATE has substituted V1 for X and and V2 for Y. An almost trivial R transformation [9] then inserts g(_, Z) and yields the following 100% desirable program

```
fun max3( X, Y, Z ) =
  let
    fun g( V1, V2 ) = if V1 < V2 then V2 else V1
  in
    g( g( X, Y ), Z )
  end
```

Thus, it was easy for this abstraction to very quickly prove its usefulness.

This example shows that abstractions can be substitutive which means that a number of equal subexpressions are replaced with one and the same parameter. These equal subexpressions can be arbitrarily big and need not consist of a single variable as above.

Since substitution is a very fundamental operation in mathematics and computer science, we were not surprised to find that it also occurs in natural genetics. Simply speaking, DNA is transcribed to messenger RNA (mRNA) which is translated into proteins. However, RNA is edited in complex and still mysterious ways [4] before it is translated to proteins. For example, editing can use so-called guide RNA (gRNA) templates and seems capable of performing operations similar to systematic substitution and possibly more advanced operations that remain to be discovered.

From a computer science point of view, abstraction is related to inlining [1] which is a common transformation in compilers that expand a function call by replacing it with a properly instantiated copy of the body. Abstraction tries to find the function definition by reversing this process.

3   The Algorithm for the Abstraction Transformation

A naive algorithm for abstraction is quite simple and would just produce all alternative abstractions of a given arity and consider them all to be equally important. For a given pre-body represented as an expression tree consisting of s nodes, there is never more than $\binom{s}{a}$ non-substitutive alternative abstractions if a function of arity a is to be invented. Even if a typically is very small and the number of alternatives due to various constraints is considerably less than $\binom{s}{a}$, the number of alternatives grows sufficiently quickly with s to motivate heuristics that give more weight to abstractions that are more likely to be useful.

3.1 Weighted Search

ADATE iteratively deepens [8] a so-called cost limit l that says how many children programs that are to be produced from a given parent program. An abstraction is assigned a cost c which indicates that l/c programs are to be based on the abstraction. For example, if $l = 5000$ and an abstraction has cost 50, this abstraction will be allowed 100 children to prove its usefulness. Thus, an abstraction that heuristically seems to be more likely to lead to a fitness improvement should be assigned a lower cost.

There are many choices that need to be made before an abstraction is fully specified e.g., the arity, the pre-body and the subexpressions to parameterize. The cost of an abstraction depends on the sequence of choices that the abstraction algorithm had to make before producing it. This sequence represents a root-to-leaf path in an implicit decision tree with the original program in the root and programs containing invented functions in the leaves.

Each branch in the decision tree is labeled with a weight that is multiplied with the cost limit of the parent node to obtain the cost limit of the child node. Like a probability, a weight is a number between zero and one. The sum of all weights on the out-going branches of a node is one.

If $w_1, w_2, \ldots, w_{\#w}$ are all the weights along a root-to-leaf path, the cost of the abstraction corresponding to the leaf is $1/w_1/w_2/\ldots/w_{\#w}$.

Example. Assume for a moment that there only is a choice between arity one and arity two and that arity one has weight 0.7 whereas arity two has weight 0.3. If the initial cost limit is 10000, ADATE would produce a total of 7000 programs based on abstractions of arity one and a total of 3000 programs based on abstractions of arity two. □

An important and difficult question is how to determine the weights. One approach is to have a large set of different examples, at least a few hundred, and repeatedly run ADATE on the set with different weights to see how the total run time for the set changes. It would be possible to automatically optimize the weights in this way, but enormous CPU resources would be required since even a single run on a single example may take a few days on a single processor.

Our approach was to study the relative frequency with which a given branch seems to result in a fitness improvement, but the weights we obtained should be considered as ad hoc values that are unlikely to be optimal. Since we used only 12 examples , the statistical sample was so small that we "equalized" or "smoothed" the weights which means that for example arity eight is assigned a small weight even though it does not appear in any of the experiments.

3.2   Positions and Substitutions

In order to identify a node in an expression tree, ADATE uses a so-called position which is a list of natural numbers [i_1, i_2, ..., $i_{\#i}$] specifying how to walk to the node if you start at the root. Each i_k specifies that the next node to walk to from the current node is child number i_k. The left-most child has number 0. For example, the position of Y in g1(X, g2(Y, Z)) is [1, 0].

We say that the position of a pre-body is a *top* position whereas the position of a subexpression to be parameterized is a *bottom* position. For example, the first abstraction in section 2 uses the top position [] and the bottom position [0, 0].

Recall that a single parameter may replace several equal subexpressions in the pre-body through substitution. For example, in the second abstraction in Section 2, the bottom positions for V2 are [0,1] and [1] . The list of positions associated with a given parameter is said to be an *alternative*. Note that the number of alternatives to be chosen equals the arity.

If two alternatives [$P_1, \ldots, P_{\#P}$] and [$Q_1, \ldots, Q_{\#P}$] are chosen, no P_i is allowed to be a prefix or a suffix of any Q_k since this would lead to an attempt to parameterize the same subexpression occurrence more than once.

Assuming that the pre-body contains n equal subexpressions $E_1, \ldots, E_n$, the number of alternatives only containing positions of E_i's is 2^n, which means that trying all possible substitutions may cause combinatorial explosions. However, we have only observed substitutions that replace all E_i's with a common ancestor and never so far seen any use for substitutions restricted to arbitrary subsets of E_i's.

Therefore, ADATE only considers substitutions that replace all occurrences in a given subtree. With this heuristic, it can be shown that the maximum number of extra alternatives due to substitution is $s - \log_2(s + 1)$, where s is the size of the pre-body i.e., the number of nodes in the pre-body.

```
case As of nil => nil | cons( A1, As1 ) =>
case As1 of nil => As | cons( A2, As2 ) =>
case Bs of nil => As | cons( B1, Bs1 ) =>
case g1( As1, Bs1 ) of nil => nil | cons( C1, Cs1 ) => Cs1
```

Fig. 1. A sample pre-body.

Example. Figure 2 shows all 18 alternatives produced by ADATE for the pre-body in Figure 1. The four last alternatives are substitutive i.e., replace two or more equal subexpressions. The last alternative, for example, replaces the two last occurrences of As. □

The choice of arity, the choice of top position and the choice of alternatives are discussed in the following three subsections.

```
[ [0] ]                [ [1] ]                    [ [2] ]
[ [2,0] ]              [ [2,1] ]                  [ [2,2] ]
[ [2,2,0] ]           [ [2,2,1] ]                [ [2,2,2] ]
[ [2,2,2,0] ]         [ [2,2,2,0,0] ]            [ [2,2,2,0,1] ]
[ [2,2,2,1] ]         [ [2,2,2,2] ]              [ [0], [2,1], [2,2,1] ]
[ [1], [2,2,2,1] ]    [ [2,0], [2,2,2,0,0] ]     [ [2,1], [2,2,1] ]
```

Fig. 2. The alternatives for the pre-body in Figure 1.

3.3   The Choice of Arity

In the current version of ADATE, the weights of arities are chosen according to the following list of (arity, weight) pairs.

```
val Arity_weights =
[ ( 8, 0.02 ), ( 7, 0.02 ), ( 6, 0.02 ), ( 5, 0.02 ), ( 4, 0.04 ),
  ( 3, 0.08 ), ( 0, 0.20 ), ( 2, 0.28 ), ( 1, 0.32 ) ]
```

For example, arity zero is assigned the weight 0.20. An arity zero abstraction is a special case where the invented function actually becomes a local constant with the same value as the pre-body.

Please note that ADATE does not need to introduce all parameters immediately and can increase arity as needed using the embedding transformation [8,9]. The newest version of ADATE also uses abstraction to increase the number of parameters of an existing function. Combinatorially, this is much cheaper than the embedding transformation in [8,9]. However, we do not have space here for a discussion of embedding.

3.4   The Choice of Top Position

Recall that a cost limit l says how many programs that are to be produced. If there are many choices of top positions and many alternatives for each choice, the cost of an abstraction may become too high and exceed l. Therefore, it is often necessary to only try a subset of all possible top positions. Like most ADATE transformation algorithms, the abstraction algorithm has a built-in "small-is-beautiful" preference, meaning that a smaller pre-body typically is preferred to a bigger. For a given arity, we will now describe what subset of top positions that ADATE chooses.

An abstraction is sometimes coupled to a previous transformation [8,9] which means that not all positions in the program are to be allowed as top positions. The abstraction algorithm is given a top_pos_ok predicate as argument. This predicate says if a given position is allowed and is the first constraint on the positions to be chosen.

For a given top position P, assume that $n_a(P)$ is the number of legal combinations of a alternatives where a is the arity. The cost of an abstraction is chosen to $n_c \cdot n_a(P)$, where n_c is the total number of chosen top positions. Basically, n_c

is increased as long as $n_c \cdot n_a(P) \leq l$ for all chosen P. The specific algorithm is as follows.

All positions that satisfy the top_pos_ok predicate are classified into three groups, namely chosen positions, candidate positions and other positions. A position is said to be chosen iff ADATE has decided to use it as a top position. A candidate position is such that all its children have been chosen. Initially, there are no chosen positions and only the leaves are candidates.

As soon as a position P becomes a candidate, $n_a(P)$ is computed and stored in a priority queue organized in order of increasing ($n_a(P)$, $s(P)$) where $s(P)$ is the pre-body size.

Assume that n_c is the current number of chosen positions. The first position P in the queue is chosen repeatedly until $n_c \cdot n_a(P) > l$. The reason that the priority queue uses $s(P)$ as a secondary key is primarily that $n_a(P)$ is independent of P when the arity is zero.

3.5   The Choice of Alternatives

The choice of alternatives uses fairly simple heuristics and weighting but still requires a carefully designed algorithm to avoid bad combinatorial properties.

A simple heuristic rule is that the size of the body except alternatives must be at least two. Another rule is that a bottom position never is allowed to specify a so-called dont-know constant [9].

However, the most important heuristics is weighting based on the usage of parameters. The main principle is to discriminate against bodies containing if-tests that do not depend on any parameter. Since ADATE uses case instead of if, we will formulate this principle for case-expressions.

A case-expression in a body is considered to be *static* if it has at least two activated rules and the expression it analyzes does not depend on any parameter of the function being invented. Let C be the set of all case-expressions in a body that do not occur in a function definition local to the body. The body and the abstraction that introduced it are classified as static if C is empty or at least one case-expression in C is static. An abstraction that is not static is said to be *dynamic*.

The weight 0.7 is allocated to dynamic abstractions whereas 0.3 is allocated to static abstractions. If there are no abstractions of one kind (static or dynamic), the weight 1.0 is allocated to the other kind.

For a given top position, dynamic abstractions are synthesized by "covering" a dependency graph that models the relationship between case-expressions. The graph is directed, acyclic and has exactly one node for each case-analyzed expression such that the corresponding case-expression has at least two activated rules.

Static abstractions could be produced by ensuring that the graph is not covered, but this is unnecessary since static abstractions in general are substantially easier to produce than dynamic abstractions. Therefore, it is sufficient with a straightforward combinatorial search that produces all abstractions and eliminates the dynamic ones.

Example. Consider the pre-body in Figure 1. The four nodes in the dependency DAG correspond to the case-analyzed expressions As, As1, Bs and g1(As1, Bs1). For example, there is an edge from Bs to g1(As1, Bs1) since the latter expression directly depends on the former. The edges in the DAG are (As, As1), (As, g1(As1, Bs1)) and (Bs, g1(As1, Bs1)). □

An abstraction is dynamic iff it *covers* all roots of the DAG without eliminating all case-expressions from the body. We say that a bottom position covers a root iff it is an ancestor or a descendant of the root.

ADATE does not actually produce the DAG. Instead, it finds the roots directly for a given top position using a preorder traversal, remembering the case-rule variables introduced so far. A case-analyzed expression is a root iff it doesn't contain any of these variables. The preorder traversal does not enter *Decs* in a sub-expression of the form

let *Decs* in *E* end

How to Choose Bottom Positions for Dynamic Abstractions

A *root alternative* is such that it covers at least one root i.e., contains at least one position which is an ancestor or a descendant of at least one root.

Example. The pre-body in Figure 1 has two roots, namely As at position [0] and Bs at position [2,2,0]. In Figure 2, the five root alternatives are

[[0]]   [[2]]   [[2,2]]   [[2,2,0]]
[[0], [2,1], [2,2,1]]

Assuming that the arity *a* is three, the following table shows some combinations of root alternatives and other alternatives. Note that each combination of root alternatives eliminates all roots from the body.

Root choices	Other choices
[[0]] [[2,2]]	[[1]]
[[0]] [[2,2]]	[[2,0]]
[[0]] [[2,2]]	[[2,1]]
[[0]] [[2,2,0]]	[[1]]
[[0]] [[2,2,0]]	[[2,0]]
[[0]] [[2,2,0]]	[[2,1]]
[[0]] [[2,2,0]]	[[2,2,1]]

□

ADATE first chooses root alternatives so that each root is covered and then chooses other alternatives. Note that one or more of the root alternatives are allowed to be redundant in the respect that they are not needed to cover all roots.

Deciding if a cardinality *a* subset of the alternatives suffices to cover all roots is an instance of the NP-complete MINIMUM COVER problem. Therefore, it is difficult to find an algorithm with a run time that is polynomial in *a* in the worst case and that decides if it is possible to cover all roots using an arity-*a* abstraction on a given pre-body.

If there are n root alternatives and ancestor-descendant relationships are ignored, the number of possible choices of root alternatives is $\binom{n}{a}$. If both the pre-body and the number of roots are big and the roots are not localized to a small part of the pre-body, there might not be any covering choice of roots.

If it is not possible to finish, the algorithm for making root choices tries to detect this early. If the arity left is a', the algorithm checks the number of roots taken out by each remaining alternative and computes the sum for the a' alternatives that take out most roots. If the number of uncovered roots exceeds this sum, it is impossible to finish.

4   Conclusions

The experimental data available through [10] show that function invention through abstraction is both indispensable and effective in ADATE. Therefore, it was fascinating to discover that nature already uses similar tricks and that these are in the process of being unraveled through ongoing gene sequencing efforts. In particular, sequencing has uncovered vast amounts of repetitive DNA and the prevalence of homologous genes sharing a common ancestor gene, which shows the importance of gene duplication in natural evolution.

The weighted iterative-deepening search presented above is unlikely to be optimally adapted to the statistical properties of functional programming e.g., the initial arity of a function when the function is first conceived. However, we believe that the average number of abstractions produced before finding one that is useful is within a small factor, say three, of the optimum on a large set of examples.

Since our first publications on ADATE [8,9], the implementation of abstraction has been refined with substitution and built-in production of dynamic abstractions, which is particularly important for large pre-bodies. We have also expanded the range of initial arities and successfully employed abstraction mechanisms to perform embedding.

Abstraction is fundamental in ADATE and very likely in most forms of large scale evolution, including the development of life on Earth.

References

1. A. W. Appel, *Modern compiler implementation in ML*, Cambridge University Press, 1998.
2. T. Endo, T. Imanishi, T. Gojobori and H. Inoko, Evolutionary significance of intra-genome duplications on human chromosomes, *Cell*, number 205, December 31, 1997, pp. 19–27.
3. D. B. Fogel, *Evolutionary Computation: Toward a New Philosophy of Machine Intelligence*, IEEE Press, 1996.
4. W. S. Klug and M. R. Cummings, *Essentials of genetics*, Prentice-Hall, 1999.
5. J. R. Koza, *Genetic programming: on the programming of computers by means of natural selection*, MIT Press, 1992.

6. J. P. Nordin, *Evolutionary program induction of binary machine code and its applications*, Krehl Verlag, Münster, 1997.

7. S. Ohno, *Evolution by gene duplication*, Springer-Verlag, 1970.

8. J. R. Olsson, Inductive functional programming using incremental program transformation and Execution of logic programs by iterative-deepening A* SLD-tree search, Research report 189, Dr scient thesis, ISBN 82-7368-099-1, University of Oslo, 1994.

9. J. R. Olsson, Inductive functional programming using incremental program transformation, *Artificial Intelligence*, volume 74, number 1, March 1995, pp. 55–83.

10. J. R. Olsson, Web page for Automatic Design of Algorithms through Evolution, http://www-ia.hiof.no/~rolando/adate_intro.html (current Nov. 23, 1998).

11. J. R. Olsson, Population management for automatic design of algorithms through evolution, *International Conference on Evolutionary Computation*, 1998.

12. Å. Wikström, *Functional Programming Using Standard ML*, Prentice Hall International, 1987.

Automatic Parallelization of Arbitrary Programs

Conor Ryan and Laur Ivan

Dept. of Computer Science and Information Systems
University of Limerick, Ireland
{conor.ryan|laur.ivan}@ul.ie

Abstract. We describe the latest version of the Paragen system, a tool for the automatic transformation of serial programs into functionally identical parallel ones. Previous papers on this work have described means of converting either sequences of instructions or individual loops, and here we describe how the two tasks can be melded into a single, seamless operation.

1   Introduction

In the past few years, the speed of network communication has increased dramatically, to the extent that technologies such as ATM or Gigabit Ethernet offer data transmission at speeds approaching that of those normally associated with the speed found within multi-processor computers. Systems such as Beowulf exploit this speed by linking together several modest computers on a fast network operating as a single parallel computer, at a fraction of the cost of supercomputers.

Unfortunately, the migration from single processor machines to parallel machines tends to be a painful one. A simple recompilation of code is unlikely to provide much speed up, and, in some cases, can even result in a program taking longer to execute. To take advantage of these kind of architectures, one must modify the code, a painstaking activity that requires intimacy with both the code and the architecture, while still retaining a modicum of uncertainty.

The most practical way to adapt a program to a parallel architecture is to rewrite areas of the program that are most likely to take advantage of this new architecture. It is, however, a non trivial task to identify these areas, and existing tools, e.g. KAP Fortran, are semi-automated at best, and generate extremely conservative parallel code. That is, a piece code may only undergo a single simple transformation to convert it to parallel, and if it contains any constructs not programmed into the compiler, it is left alone.

The benefit of using GP to apply transformations is that it is able to build up complex chains of transformations which can be applied to a piece of code. These transformations are capable of elaborate behaviour, such as relocating lines of code, or "massaging" loops into places that are conducive to the performance of subsequent transformations. That parallelisation is something of a black art is one of the things that makes it attractive for GP, for, although many transformations are well known, there are no simple deterministic algorithms for their application.

R. Poli et al. (Eds.): EuroGP'99, LNCS 1598, pp. 244–254, 1999.
© Springer-Verlag Berlin Heidelberg 1999

Our system, the Paragen system, has two libraries of transformations, each of which has been reported on seperately[Ryan 97]. This paper describes how the system can correctly choose the proper type of transformation, and even use one set of transformations to set up the code so another transformation may subsequently perform.

2 Parallelization Issues

The parallelization of sequential code usually raise two major problems:

Data dependency problems occur when the original sequential code is compiled for execution on a parallel system. Two instructions are data independent if neither uses variable(s) modified by the other, or if none of them modifies the same variable(s) used by the other one [Lewis 92]. In other words, considering **x.M** the set of modified variables and respectively **x.U** the set of used variables of the instruction **x**, then two instructions are *data independent* if:

$$((A.M \cap B.U) \cup (B.M \cap A.U) \cup (A.M \cap B.M)) = \phi \tag{1}$$

Load balancing refers to the amount of instructions executed by one of the processors within the parallel architecture. If a sequence can be executed in parallel over several processors, then it would be useful if all the processors spent the same amount of time executing portions of that sequence. The ideal case is when all the processors finish at the same time, if, for example, one had data independent instructions, identical from execution time point of view, and 4 processors, groups of 3 instructions can be executed on each processor. Unfortunately, this is usually not the case, as in most of situations, the number of instructions is not a multiple of number of processors. Furthermore, it is unlikely that all instructions can be executed in the same amount of time.

3 Parallel Architectures

Paragen is designed to be language independent. This language independence is achieved by virtue of the fact that Paragen only requires information about the instructions, and not the actual instructions themselves.

Current work is concentrated on transforming the original source into an MPI implementation in order to be executed on a machine working with this protocol, specifically, Beowulf machines.

The MPI standard provides a powerful set of functions. For example, its version 2.0 allows the *parallel file I/O* and *remote memory access*. There are several implementations of this standard:

- **LAM** (Local Area Multicomputer) - set of MPI daemons running on a farm of workstations, PVM-like.
- **MPICH** (MPI Chameleon) - full implementation of MPI 1.1 using rsh for spawning processes.

– **AFMPI** (Aggregate Function MPI) - subset of MPI 2.0 - for *AFAPI* (Aggregate Function API) capable network hardware. AFAPI is a fully abstract program interface that seeks to provide the most important aggregate communication functions. The MPI implementation, which is based on it, is used for low-latency communication between systems.

Beowulf was selected for its capability to emulate various parallel topologies [Almasi 89], allowing the testing and adjustment of Paragen's parameters according to the requested topology.

4 Environment

Unlike most GP implementations, Paragen does not evolve programs. Rather it is an embryonic system which progressively applies a set of evolved transformations to a serial program. Paragen's design was based on several of the OCCAM laws [Burns 88]. The key law is:

$$SEQ(A, B) = PAR(A, B) \qquad (2)$$

if there are no data dependencies between A and B.

This rule, combined with the associativity rule:

$$SEQ(A, B, C) = SEQ(A, SEQ(B, C)) \qquad (3)$$

can be combined in order to obtain complex execution flows. For example, a result may be:

$$SEQ(ABCDEFG)=PAR(SEQ(A,SEQ(PAR(B,C),PAR(D,E))),SEQ(F,G)) \qquad (4)$$

In general, however, the areas of a program which stands to benefit most from parallelization are those that contain loops. Paragen has two distinct sets of transformations which can be applied, one for loops and the other for ordinary, atomic instructions.

Paragen uses a "bottom-up" technique for processing the program. This means it processes from the highest nesting level blocks ({...} in C/C++) towards the the main program as an entity (considered to have the nesting level 0). We define the smallest entity used by Paragen during one step **Atom**. We define two categories of atoms. "*Instruction Atoms*' can be as simple as a trivial instruction (a=b+c;) or as complicated as an entire {...} block. The "*MetaLoop Atoms*" can be a single loop or a set of consecutive loops.

Also, we define two working modes:

– *Atom Mode* works at atom level. This is essentially concerned with groups of simple instructions. This is the default mode for Paragen, and it remains in this mode until it encounters a metaloop, whereupon it enters loop mode.
– *Loop Mode* is designed to transform (if possible) the loops or the sequences of loops.

The atom and loop mode are interlaced. A Paragen step begins with processing the original chain of instructions in atom mode. When a MetaLoop atom is encountered on one of the tree leaves, Paragen switches to loop mode and processes that atom. The final fitness function will be the aggregate result of the atom and the loop mode fitnesses.

5   Atom Mode

While in atom mode, Paragen processes the atoms for a specific nesting level. For example, if we have:

```
 0:  // ---------------------- level 0
 1:  a=a+1;
 2:  if(i=0) {
 3:      // ------------------- level 1
 4:      for(j=1;j<10;j++) {
 5:          // --------------- level 2
 6:          a++;
 7:      } // for --------------- (end of level 2)
 8:      a-=10;
 9:      b++;
10:  } // -------------------- if (end of level 1)
11:  b--;
```

then for the level 0 the sequence processing will generate the following atoms:

```
A01:  Instruction Atom ("a=a+1")
A02:  If Atom ("if(i=0){...}")
A03:  Instruction Atom ("b--")
```

but for level 1, the result will be:

```
A11:  Loop Atom ("for(...){...}")
A12:  Instruction Atom ("a=-10")
A13:  Instruction Atom ("b++")
```

Paragen works at nesting block level. This means it seeks data dependencies within the level, not outside the level. For example, the data dependency between a=a+1; (level 0) and a-=10; (level 1) is recognized as a data dependency between a=a+1; and if(i=0){...}.

The transformations for atom mode are arranged in the traditional tree structure used in GP, but are evaluated in normal order to permit forking within the parallel program [Ryan 97].

There are several classes of atom mode transformations:

- **Pxx** and **Sxx** class, which splits the input chain according to the percent **xx**. The **Pxx** class effectively fork the execution of a program.

- **Fxxx** and **Lxxx** class, which splits the input chain into two program segments, one containing either the first or last instruction, and the other containing remaining instructions. The segment with the single instruction is scheduled relative to the other segment, which may be subject to further transformations. The relative scheduling can be in parallel or in sequence, depending on the form of the transformations, i.e. xxx can be *PAR* or *SEQ*.
- **SHIFT** class, which delays the execution of the input chain with *one time-step*.

Each atom mode transformation is an internal node in a tree. They take as input the current *program segment* which they perform their transformation on, before passing it onto the next transformation(s) in a tree. The program segment starts as the entire function to be parallelized, and progressively gets smaller as the transformations are applied.

The leaves of each individual are either **NULL** or **PARNULL** transformations. **NULL** simply leaves the instructions in the current program segment as they were, while **PARNULL** causes all remaining instructions to be executed in parallel.

For example, the **Pxx/Sxx** class splits the input chain in two, according to a percentage parameter (eg. P40 means P and the percentage is 40%). "P" states that the instructions transmitted to the left and the right subtrees will be executed in parallel, whilst "S" means that the instructions passed to the right subtree will be executed after the chain of instructions transmitted to the left subtree have finished. For example, if we have an execution chain of 5 instructions [ABCDE], then after applying a Pxx with xx=40 (P40) operator, the result will be:

Operation	Input	Output
P20	[ABCDE]	[AB]
		[CDE]

so [AB] and [CDE] are to be executed in parallel and [AB] will be passed to the left subtree and [CDE] will be passed to the right subtree for further transformations.

Changing P40 to an S40 will result in the beginning of the [CDE] sequence after [AB] was finished.

5.1 Fitness in Atom Mode

There are two distinct parts to the fitness function, speed and correctness. While it is difficult to measure exactly how long a program will take to execute, it is a relatively simple matter to measure the speed of similar programs relative to each other. The correctness issue, is, however, a far more complex issue. Any program produced by this system must be 100% correct, otherwise it will simply be unusable.

The correctness measure is calculated by using a method we term "Directed Data Dependency Analysis as described in [Ryan 98]. Essentially, this system uses the transformations applied to the program to direct analysis to the parts that require analysis. Any atoms which have had their order of execution changed are examined for dependency clashes and, should any occur, the individual is punished.

6   Loop Mode

Loop mode is Paragen's key benefit for most of the programs need parallelization because of their iterative sequences. These loops have quite a different approach for parallelization: the purpose is not to parallelize what's inside the loop, but the loop itself. The ideal case is to transform a sequential loop **for** ...**endfor** into a parallel loop **parfor** ...**endparfor**. It means each iteration will be executed on a different processor. Unfortunately this is not the case in most of the situations because of *cross-iteration data dependencies*. A cross-iteration data dependent instruction is an instruction which needs variables results computed in previous iteration.

We have identified several categories of loop transformations:

- single loop transformations - loop transformations for which the domain is the current loop within the metaloop,
- multiple loop transformations - loop transformations which are to be applied to several consecutive loops,
- loop order alteration transformations - loop transformations which alter the loops' execution order within the metaloop.

The multiple loop transformations are the reason for the metaloop's existence, and it is in these that the power of Paragen lies. No other parallel compiler is capable of rearranging instructions to encourage more sympathetic transformations.

Because the loop transformations cannot be applied to the atoms, they are kept in a seperate, linear, genome. A linear genome is employed because, as will be seen later on, the loop mode is called as needed by atom mode, and the latter already has the ability to fork its execution.

A significant operator for this category is **Loop Fusion** operator. Given:

```
PARFOR(i=0;i<100;i++)
  a[i]=x[i]*i;
PARFOR(j=0;j<100;j++)
  b[j][0]=m[j]-j;
```

after applying the Loop Fusion, the result is:

```
PARFOR(i=0;i<100;i++) {
  a[i]=x[i]*i;
  b[i][0]=m[i]-i;
}
```

This particular operator is very useful for decreasing the communication overhead between tasks. A legacy of adopting nesting levels to navigate the programs is that the two instructions within the loop can also be operated on by atom mode, thus reducing the time taken even further.

So far, we have identified 28 individual loop transformations, however, due to space constraints we will only describe Fusion.

6.1 Loop Mode Fitness Function

While in Loop Mode, Paragen tries to apply all the operators included in the chromosome to the given MetaLoop. For now, the fitness function is relatively simple and counts the number of successes for the applied operators, thus, loops which are successfully transformed increase the fitness of an individual. The decision to reward useful transformations rather than punish unsuccessful ones was taken because there is always the possibility that a loop cannot be parallelised, because of the dependencies it contains.

7 Example Individual

Figure 1 shows a simple individual that we wish to apply to the following program:

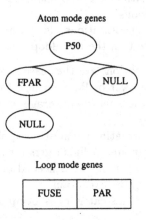

Fig. 1. A sample indivudal.

```
1: a=1;
2: for (b=0;b<200;b++)
     d[b]=b+a;
3: for (c=0;c<200;c++)
     e[c]=c+a;
```

```
4: a=10;
5: for (c=0;c<10;c++)
    f[c]=f[c]*3;
```

The five instructions are broken into four atoms, as described below:

Atom	A	B	C	D
Instruction(s)	1	2,3	4	5

Instructions 2 and 3 are in the same metaloop atom because they are adjacent loops. Evaluation begins with the tree, and the system is in atom mode, furthermore, the program segment is the entire program, that is, [ABCD]. All transformations follow this basic algorithm:

1. Test if the first atom contains a loop
2. If so, switch to loop mode
3. Else, apply transformation

In the case of P50, the first item is a=1; which clearly is not a loop, so the P50 is applied, yielding two new program segments, [AB] and [CD]. [AB] is sent to the left side of the tree while [CD] goes to the right hand side. The next transformation is FPAR, which again runs through the simple algorithm described above. Again, the first item is a=1;, so FPAR is applied, which results in [B] being sent to the following transformation, the NULL transformation, which performs the same check as before.

In this case, the first item *is* a loop, so the system enters loop mode. The first transformation in the loop genes is FUSE, as described earlier, this first tests if there are two loops available, and, upon getting a satisfactory answer, checks if they are already parallel loops. As they are not, the system attempts to convert them and, if successful, it will fuse them. It turns out that both loops can be parallelised, so the fusion is a success.

The metaloop doesn't require any further processing, so the system return to atom mode and then applies NULL to its atom, [B], which causes execution of that particular branch of the tree to execute.

Evaluation continues with the right hand side, which applies NULL to [CD]. When it performs the loop test, it won't detect any loop, as C is simply an atom, so evaluation ends there. Notice that the final loop is not detected as there weren't enough transformations, so it does not get modified.

In terms of atoms, execution is now of the form:

```
PAR-BEGIN
    a=1;
    parfor (b=0;b<200;b++)
        BEGIN
        d[b]=b+a;
        e[b]=c+a;
        END
```

```
   a=10;
PAR-END
for (c=0;c<10;c++)
  f[c]=f[c]*3;
```

From careful examination of the code, one can see immediately see that there is a dependency clash between the two statements:

```
a=1; and
a=10;
```

As with any GP run, it is only to be expected that such mistakes will be made by individuals as the population evolves. Of course, it is necessary that the fitness function can automatically detect these, and, to this, we employ a system we describe as Directed Data Dependency Analysis [Ryan 97]. We use the individual to direct us to parts of the program that may require analysis, that is, any part of the program that had the order of instructions modified.

When doing this, we start at the most deeply nested transformations, and work out. The most deeply nested is FPAR, which caused [A] and [B] to be executed at the same time. There are no dependency clashes between these two atoms, so the fitness is not affected, and we work back up through the tree. The other transformation that altered the order was P50, which caused [AB] and [CD] to be executed at the same time. However, this is not enough information, as we must keep track of the changes caused by subsequent transformations, i.e. in this case, FPAR. The overall effect is that both [A] and [B] are now executed at the same time as [C] which does cause a dependency clash, so the individual is punished.

8   Results and Examples

To illustrate the performance of Paragen, we apply the atom mode transformations to two problems. The first contains 9 data independent instructions, which gives a best case of one time step if the program were to be run in parallel. The second problem contains the same 9 instructions, but these are repeated, generating a total of 18 instructions, giving 9 data dependencies. This program can be executed in two time steps assuming that all data dependencies can be avoided.

Figure 3 shows the same 9 instructions repeated twice, parallelized within 1200 iterations, the result being 2 timesteps.

Although it is not feasible to compare Paragen to other systems, i.e. there are no other automatic parallelisation tools, and comparing to humans is an unreliable measure, we believe these results show some interesting properties of Paragen. Any human who had examined the first test case would parallelise the second very easily, but, even though it doesn't use pattern detection, Paragen is able to generate a solution to the second problem almost as quickly as the first.

In both of these test cases, the simplest individual would use **PARNULL**, as this forces all instructions to execute in parallel. In fact, for the first problem,

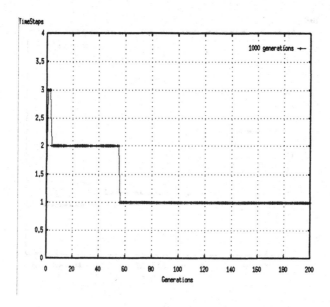

Fig. 2. Time required for execution of a program with nine instructions.

the perfect individual would contain just the **PARNULL** transformation! To avoid making the problem too easy, we disabled that transformation for these experiments.

9 Conclusions and Future Work

We have described the current version of our parallel compiler, Paragen. Paragen can take programs consisting of both loops and atomic statements, and convert them into parallel. This is achieved by having two libraries of transformations, one peculiar to loops, the other to atoms, and by permitting Paragen to seamlessly switch between different modes.

The next step is to examine the performance of Paragen on some standard benchmark code, both code that was written with a view to being parallelized and code that requires substantial rewriting to run in parallel. We believe that in the latter case, Paragen will prove to be a valuable tool.

References

[Almasi 89] Almasi G., Gottlieb A. (1989): *Highly Parallel Computing.* The Benjamin/Cummings Publishing Company Inc.

[Burns 88] Burns, A. (1998): *Transforming Occam Programs.* In *Programming Occam 2.* Addison-Wesley

[Davis 91] Davis, L.V. (1991): *Handbook of Genetic Algorithms.* Van Nostrand Reinhold

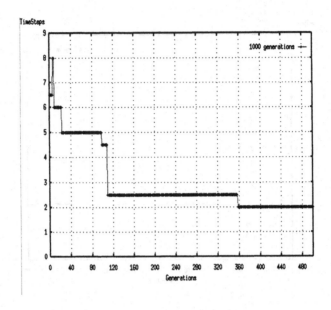

Fig. 3. 18 instructions containing 9 data dependencies

[Koza 92] Koza, J. (1992) : *Genetic Programming.* Cambridge : M.I.T. Press

[Lewis 92] Lewis, T. (1992) : *Introduction to Parallel Computing.* Prentice Hall

[Chaudhuri 89] Chaudhuri P. (1992): *Parallel Algorithms. Design and Analysis.* Prentice Hall of Australia

[Ryan 98] Ryan, C and Ivan, L. (1998): *Automatic Parallelization of Loops in Sequential Programs using Genetic Programming.* GP 98

[Ryan 97] Ryan, C. and Walsh, P. (1997): *The Evolution of Provable Parallel Programs.* Genetic Programming 1997

[Ryan 96] Ryan, C. and Walsh, P. (1996): *Paragen: A novel technique of the Autoparallelization of Sequential Programs using Genetic Programming.* In Genetic Programming. MIT Press

[WATCOM] Watcom Corp. (1993): *User's Guide.* Watcom Corp. Canada

[WATCOM] Watcom Corp. (1993): *Linker.* Watcom Corp. Canada

Evolving Controllers for Autonomous Agents Using Genetically Programmed Networks

Arlindo Silva[1], Ana Neves[1], and Ernesto Costa[2]

Centro de Informática e Sistemas da Universidade de Coimbra

[1] Escola Superior de Tecnologia, Instituto Politécnico de Castelo Branco, Av. do Empresário, 6000 Castelo Branco – Portugal
{arlindo, dorian}@dei.uc.pt
[2] Departamento de Engenharia Informática, Universidade de Coimbra, Polo II – Pinhal de Marrocos, 3030 Coimbra – Portugal
ernesto@dei.uc.pt

Abstract. This article presents a new approach to the evolution of controllers for autonomous agents. We propose the evolution of a connectionist structure where each node has an associated program, evolved using genetic programming. We call this structure a Genetically Programmed Network and use it to successfully evolve control systems with very different architectures, by making small restrictions to the evolutionary process. Experimental results of applying this method to evolve neural networks, distributed programs and rule-based systems capable of solving a common benchmark problem, the Ant Problem, are presented. Comparison with other known genetic programming based approaches, shows that our method requires less effort to find a solution.

1 Introduction

One of the many questions still without answer in the emergent field of evolutionary robotics concerns the choice of the most appropriate architecture to be evolved as the control system for autonomous robots [17]. The same problem poses itself in other areas where there is a need to evolve controllers for autonomous agents, e.g. in artificial life. In the literature, we can find several approaches to this problem, the most promising of which seem to be:

1. **Neural Networks** - This is undoubtedly the architecture more often chosen (and more strongly defended) to be evolved as the control system for autonomous agents: [5], [10], [12]. The topology of the networks, however, varies substantially between approaches, and so does what is really evolved: connections' weights; weights and connections; weights, connections, and number of neurons, etc...
2. **Programs** – Several authors propose the use of extended versions of genetic programming (GP) [14] to evolve programs capable of controlling the robot. [3] suggests the use of GP with a high level *behavioural language*. [2] uses GP to evolve assembly code, which maps sensorial inputs into actuator actions.
3. **Rule Based Systems** – [8] and [11] use several forms of classifier systems, or rule based systems, where the rules are genetically evolved to obtain valid controllers.

R. Poli et al. (Eds.): EuroGP'99, LNCS 1598, pp. 255-269, 1999.
© Springer-Verlag Berlin Heidelberg 1999

In this paper we propose a new approach to controller evolution, based on a connectionist structure we call Genetically Programmed Network (GPN). A GPN is constituted by a set of nodes, where each one node has an attached program, several connections between these nodes, a set of inputs and a set of outputs (see Fig. 1).

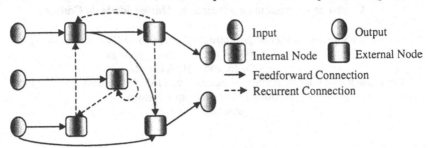

Fig. 1. A Genetically Programmed Network. Every node has an associated program, generated by genetic programming.

The nodes are the computing elements in the network and each one uses the attached program to compute its output based on data flowing in from its connections. Connections act as a mean of data transportation between the networks' inputs and nodes, from node to node and from nodes to the network's outputs. The network's inputs receive information from the agent, e.g. sensorial information, and make it available (by the existing connections) to the nodes in the network. Outputs present the result of the network computation to the agent to be used as a new command.

Programs are evolved using genetic programming in an evolutionary process that will, hopefully, produce a GPN capable of controlling the agent in a way it can achieve its goals. Genetic programmed networks are described in detail in section 2 and the evolutionary process used to evolve valid controllers from a GPN population is explained in section 3.

Section 4 describes the application of GPN to a benchmark problem, the Ant Problem. Controllers based on three different architectures (distributed programs, recurrent neural networks and rule-based systems) are successfully evolved using GPN. GPN based approaches are shown to require less effort to find a solution than other approaches known to us. In section 5 we draw some conclusions about these first results and we outline ongoing and future work in section 6.

2 Genetically Programmed Networks

Genetically Programmed Networks were primarily designed to be used as controllers for intelligent agents. The role of the agent will be that of using its sensors to gather information about the environment, and its actuators to act on it, while the GPN generates commands for the actuators based on the sensorial information available and its current internal state. In this article we will use the word *agent* while referring to the entity being controlled by the GPN. When the term *environment* is used, it is the environment where this entity dwells that is being mentioned.

2.1 GPN General Structure

A Genetically Programmed Network is constituted by (Fig. 1):
- A set of inputs, whose values are received from the agent.
- A set of outputs, whose values are computed by the GPN and should be interpreted by the agent as a command.
- Two sets of nodes: internal nodes and external nodes.
- A set of connections, which link the previous components into a network.

Every node in the GPN is constituted by (Fig. 2):
- A set of inputs.
- One output only.
- A genetically evolved program.

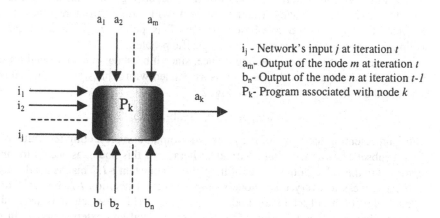

i_j - Network's input j at iteration t
a_m - Output of the node m at iteration t
b_n - Output of the node n at iteration t-1
P_k - Program associated with node k

Fig. 2. A GPN node accepts inputs from the connections with other nodes and GPN inputs and computes its own output.

A node's input values at a certain iteration t can have three origins:
1. They can be the values of the inputs from the agent to the network at iteration t.
2. They can be the output values of other nodes in the network at iteration t.
3. They can be the output values of other nodes in the network at iteration t-1.

The structure of a particular GPN is partially defined at the start of the evolutionary process, since the networks' inputs and outputs, as well as the number of internal and external nodes are set *a priori*. Connections are developed as the programs associated with each node are evolved, so the structure will also be dependent on the evolutionary process.

2.2 GPN Behavior

The desired behavior of a GPN is to compute, based on the inputs presented by the agent, an answer, codified in its outputs, which the agent can understand as a command. This command, or a sequence of commands, should lead the agent to perform as well as possible in some problem the environment poses to it. This behavior is achieved by executing the programs associated with the network's nodes. These programs define the connections between nodes and compute each node output based on the inputs available.

2.2.1 The Programs

The program associated which each node can be evolved using any variant of GP. The approach to GP we use is adapted from [13] and it uses C++ instead of Lisp for extra speed and flexibility. What is particular to GPN is the terminal and function set. While in GP, typically, both of these sets are specifically chosen for the problem which is being solved, in GPN the restrictions are mainly architectural. What this means is that we choose terminals and functions accordingly with the architecture we want to evolve, i.e. evolving a neural network will require different functions and terminals than evolving a rule-based system. This point will be made clearer in section 4 when we apply our method to a specific problem.

The terminal set is of extreme importance, since it must contain a terminal for each input available to the node the program is associated with. This way, a terminal set T can have the following terminals (see Fig. 2):

$$T = \{i_1, i_2, ..., i_l, a_1, a_2, ..., a_m, b_1, b_2, ..., b_n, ...\} \tag{1}$$

with i_j representing the value of the jth network input, a_j representing the value of the jth of a subset of m nodes whose outputs at iteration t this node has access to, and b_j representing the value of the output of the jth node at instant $t-1$. This means that every node has access to every other node's output value at iteration $t-1$, but only to the output value of a subset of all nodes at instant t. This distinction is particularly relevant when it comes to differentiate between internal and external nodes. In fact, while external nodes can have a terminal set

$$T_e = \{i_1, i_2, ..., i_l, a_1, a_2, ..., a_m, b_1, b_2, ..., b_n, ...\}, \tag{2}$$

internal nodes have a terminal set

$$T_i = \{i_1, i_2, ..., i_l, b_1, b_2, ..., b_n, ...\}, \tag{3}$$

which means they don't have access to any other node's output at iteration t.

Another difference between our system and GP is the fact that we use two function sets. Beside the usual function set F, whose members are all the functions that can be a node in the program, we use a special function set called the root set R. The members of this set are the functions that can be chosen to be the root node in the program's tree.

2.2.2 Establishing Connections

Lets first look at what happens when any program associated with some node includes in its code one of the above terminals. The value of a network's input or of other node's output becomes available to some computation being done in this program, so we can say that a **connection** has been established between the node associated with the program an the input or node corresponding to the included terminal. Depending on the terminal we can have two types of connections:

1. **Feedforward connections** – when a i_j or a_j, terminal is included in a program, this program will have access to the values of the correspondent network's inputs and node's output in the same iteration t the program is being run. This creates connections similar to the ones in feedforward neural networks. In our approach this connections are allowed from network's inputs to any node and from internal nodes to external nodes. This is guaranteed by the different terminal sets available to the programs associated with external and internal nodes. The main importance of feedforward connections in GPN is that they allow the establishment of **functional** relations between nodes, i.e. internal nodes can perform some computations obtaining intermediate values that external nodes can then use in more complex computations.

2. **Recurrent connections** – when a b_j terminal is included in a program, it will have access to the output value of the node correspondent to that terminal in the iteration prior to the one in which the program is being run. This way, a **recurrent** connection is established from the node associated with the terminal to the node associated with the program that includes the terminal. These connections are similar to the ones allowed in recurrent neural networks or in cellular automata and they can exist between any two nodes in a network. Their extreme importance in GPN comes from the fact that they allow **temporal** relations to be established between nodes. This means that a sequence of n recurrent connections between nodes can be used in a GPN to keep available a value computed n iterations ago. The evolutionary process creates recurrent connections between nodes to implement the memory needed to keep track of previous system's states.

The process of establishing connections in a GPN gives us the first difference between internal and external nodes: forward connections can only be established from internal nodes to external ones. It also explains two of the most interesting features of GPN: the easy way of creating temporal and functional relations between nodes and the implicit way this relations are created, which frees the evolutionary process of maintaining any explicit representation for connections between nodes.

2.2.3 Running the GPN

Programs evolved using genetic programming are the processing elements in a GPN. To run the GPN all the programs associated with the network's nodes must also be run. In an ideal, parallel, implementation of a GPN, all programs, or, at least, subsets of programs, could be run simultaneously. Like most connectionist structures it seems that the most natural implementation for a GPN would be a distributed one. In a sequential implementation, internal nodes are the first ones to be run, so that their outputs are available to propagation by forward connections to external nodes. External nodes are then run sequentially and their output copied to the network's outputs. This procedure emphasizes the other major difference between internal and external nodes: each external node has an associated network's output and the output value of the ith external node at iteration t corresponds to the value of the ith network's output. This implies that the number of network's outputs and external nodes is always the same.

3   Evolving Genetically Programmed Networks

To successfully evolve a GPN, we must devise a representation scheme for the individuals, as well as the operators that will act on them.

A GPN individual has **n chromosomes**, one for each node in the network. Since the chromosomes correspond to the programs associated with the networks' nodes, it follows that each individual I_i (a GPN) is simply represented by a sequence of programs:

$$I_i = \{P_1, P_2, ..., P_n\}, \tag{4}$$

with P_n the program associated with the network's n^{th} node. Order is important, since, like in the biological model, the genome operators are designed to act on chromosomes with the same *position* in the individuals they belong to.

3.1 Operators

The three main operators used in GP are also needed to evolve GPNs, therefore we must define reproduction, crossover and mutation in a way they can be applied not only to a program but also to a GPN, a sequence of programs. What we did was, basically, to define the three operators at two different levels: at individual level and at program level. At individual (GPN) level we than have:

- **Reproduction** – reproduction is an asexual operator which, given a certain individual returns an exact copy as its child. To achieve this, program reproduction must be applied to every program associated with the individual's nodes. The resulting programs will be associated with the correspondent nodes in the new individual.
- **Crossover** – crossover is a sexual operator which, given two individuals, produces two children by recombination of the original individuals. Applying crossover to two individuals implies applying program crossover to every pair of correspondent programs in these individuals.
- **Mutation** – mutation introduces random changes into an individual. To produce a mutated child of a given individual program, mutation is applied to every program in the parent before it is copied to the correspondent node in the child.

At program level, operators are defined in a way similar to GP:

- **Program Reproduction** – the program reproduction operator returns an exact copy of the parent program as the child program.

- **Program Crossover** – The program crossover operator takes two programs and returns two children resulting from the recombination of the parents. To do this, a sub-tree is identified in each of the parents, with its root node randomly chosen. These sub-trees will then be swapped in the new programs. When crossover is not possible (e.g. one of the children would be larger than the maximum size allowed) copies of the two parents are returned as the children, and crossover degenerates into program reproduction.
- **Program Mutation** – A mutated child program is obtained by substituting a randomly chosen sub-tree of the program for a new, randomly generated, sub-tree.

3.2   The Initial Population

An initial population composed of n individuals with m nodes will imply the generation of $n*m$ programs. Since that at this stage in our study of GPNs we don't allow the individuals' number of nodes to vary, neither inside a population nor during the evolutionary process, this number remains constant during evolution. The generation of this initial set of programs is done using what [14] calls the „grow" method: a restriction is made on the tree's maximum depth and, while this depth is not reached, nodes are randomly chosen from the reunion of function and terminal sets. When the maximum depth is reached, nodes are randomly chosen from the terminal set alone, which causes the tree's depth to be no greater then the maximum depth allowed. This method creates trees of different sizes and shapes and revealed itself appropriate to be used with our approach.

3.3   Selection and Evolution

Tournament selection, usually of size $n=4$, was used in our experiments. Candidates for reproduction are chosen after entering a tournament between n individuals randomly chosen from the current population. The individual with the best raw fitness is considered to be the winner and is copied into a mating pool with the same size as the population. After the mating pool is full, reproduction is applied to 10% of the individuals, mutation to 5% of the individuals and crossover to the remaining ones. The individuals resulting from the operator application are copied into a new population. The process ends at a limit generation (the initial population generation is considered to be generation 0) or when an individual with some goal fitness is found.

4 Experimental Results

4.1 The Ant Problem

As a first test to the method described in the previous sections we needed a relatively simple control problem, extensively studied in literature and preferably having been the object of approaches using evolutionary techniques. A problem that fulfils these requirements is the usually called Ant Problem. Originally presented in [6], this problem consists in developing a controller capable of guiding an artificial ant in a toroidal 32×32 cell world so that the ant correctly follows a discontinuous trail of sugar. The ant has a rudimentary sensor, which informs it if there is sugar in next cell in the direction of its movement. The ant can perform four actions: turning left or right while remaining in the same cell, moving one cell in the current direction or doing nothing. The total number of actions the ant can perform to follow the complete trail is usually limited.

We can find many evolutionary approaches to this problem. [6] uses a genetic algorithm (GA) to evolve both neural networks and finite automata capable of following the „John Muir" trail, [1] and [18] use, respectively, a GA and Parallel Distributed Genetic Programming (PDGP) to evolve neural networks capable of following the same trail. The variant of this problem we will try to solve is called the „Santa Fé" trail and it has been extensively used as a benchmark problem for GP. It was first presented in [14], and is harder, with more levels of deception than the „John Muir" trail. [15] presents an extensive study of the program space for this problem in GP, and compares the effort needed to find a solution with random search, GP and several other search techniques. Effort is defined, as in [14], to be number of individuals that need to be evaluated to ensure a solution is found, with probability z, and can be computed using the following equations:

$$R(m,i,z) = ceil\left(\frac{\log(1-z)}{\log(1-P(m,i))}\right)$$

$$P(m,i) = \frac{S(i)}{n} \qquad (5)$$

$$I(m,i,z) = m \times R(m,i,z) \times (i+1)$$

with $P(m,i)$ the cumulative probability of success at iteration i with a population m; $S(i)$ the number of successful runs at iteration i, n the total number of runs; $R(m,i,z)$ the number of runs needed to find a solution at iteration i, with a population m and probability z; and $I(m,i,z)$ the number of individuals that must be evaluated to guarantee that a solution is found with probability z. Table 1 presents, for comparative purposes, values of $I(m,i,z)$ for several approaches. Most of these values were taken from [15]. The value for evolutionary programming (EP) was taken from [4]. Results from GPN based approaches are also presented in the same table.

Method	I(m,i,z)	GPN Based Method	I(m,i,z)
GP	450,000	Dist. Program	81,600
Sub-Tree Mutation	426,000	Rule Based System	86,700
PDGP	336,000	Neural Network	59,500
Strict Hill Climbing	186,000		
EP	136,000		

Table 1. Comparative results over the number of individuals that must be evaluated to find a solution with probability 0.99 for the „Santa Fe" trail.

From Table 1 we can see that the best non-GPN results are those obtained by [4]. These are obtained using a form of evolutionary programming with three mutation operators to evolve programs capable of solving „Santa Fe" trail problem. In [16] better results are obtained, but the problem is somewhat changed: the ant is only allowed to see the next n sugar cubes, and the next n are only inserted when the previous n are collected.

4.2 Using GPN to Solve the Ant Problem

In this section we will present three different approaches to the described problem by using GPNs to evolve a distributed program, a rule-based system and a neural network, all capable of leading the ant trough the „Santa Fe" trail. We use a small population of only 100 individuals to allow the realization of a substantial number of runs. The fitness of an individual is the number of sugar pieces eaten after 400 commands. The results are averaged over 200 runs of 51 generations each. We use size 4 tournament as the selection method, and apply crossover to 85% of the mating pool, reproduction to 10% of the mating pool and mutation to the remaining 5%.

4.2.1 Evolving a Distributed Program

In our first attempt to use a GPN to solve the Ant Problem will try to evolve what we call a distributed program. This is the simplest way of using GPN, since it doesn't involve any particular restriction to induce the evolution of some desired architecture. Our first step in solving the problem will be the definition of the networks inputs and outputs. We chose to use 2 inputs with the values 10 when there is sugar in front of the ant and 01 when there is not. We use three outputs, each one corresponding to an available action: **move, turn right, turn left** (like in most GP based approaches **doing nothing** is not used). The action performed corresponds to the output with larger value. The next step concerns the decision on the number of internal and external nodes. As already described there must be an external node for each output, sob there are three external nodes. Since our method does not yet allow the number of internal nodes to be evolved, we also have to decide on it. After some empirical study we chose to use 6 internal nodes. The above parameters, which concern GPN topology, were kept constant over all experiments presented in this paper.

To allow the evolution of the GPN we must now define the function set F, the root set R and the terminal sets T_i and T_e. What we want the GPN to involve into is a program, distributed over the several nodes of the network as smaller subprograms. These programs must have access to each other output values and to the networks inputs so they can, working co-operatively, compute a valid output in response to the present inputs and system state. An important feature of the GPN is the way the system state is kept. Much like recurrent neural networks, GPN implement a memory of the system current state by allowing the establishment of recurrent connections between nodes, i.e. programs can access the outputs of other programs in the previous iteration. To allow the subprograms to access input values and other programs' output in the previous iteration, we must include, in the terminal set, terminals corresponding to this data. We could also allow feedforward connections, i.e. allow the external nodes' programs to access the output of the internal nodes' programs in the current iteration. Since this doesn't seem necessary to solve our problem, will keep the correspondent terminals out of terminal set by now. This implies that the terminal set for internal (T_i) and external (T_e) nodes will be the same. The function set must have the functions needed to compute the output values. Since binary output values are enough for the problem at hand, we will only include logical, comparative and an *if* function in the function set. Finally, we must define the root set, which corresponds to functions that can be the root of the program tree. Since we don't want to make any particular restrictions to the tree's root, the root set will have the same elements as the function set. Terminal, function and root set for evolving a distributed program capable of leading the ant through the „Santa Fe" trail are presented in Table 2.

$T_i = \{i_1, i_2, a_1, a_2, ..., a_9\}$
$T_e = \{i_1, i_2, a_1, a_2, ..., a_9\}$
$F = \{and, or, not, >, <, ==, !=, if\}$
$R = \{and, or, not, >, <, ==, !=, if\}$

Table 2. Terminal, function and root sets for evolving a distributed program capable of solving the Ant Problem.

It is important to note that none of this terminals or functions are problem dependent or have any kind of secondary effect, as is usual in GP. Using the above settings 200 independent runs were carried out and in each run a population of 100 genetically programmed networks was evolved for 51 generations. The obtained results and the topology of a successful distributed program are presented in Fig. 3.

The results obtained with this approach are substantially better, in terms of the number of individuals that must be processed so that a solution is found with 99% probability, than the ones obtained using other methods. From Table 1 we can see that „standard" GP needed to evaluate 450,000 individuals, while [4], using EP, has the best results known to us, with 136,000 individuals. Using genetic programming to evolve genetically programmed networks as distributed programs we need only to evaluate 81,600 individuals.

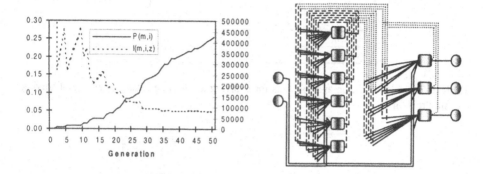

Fig. 3. Results for evolving a GPN as a distributed program and topology of a successful individual. The cumulative probability of success, $P(m,i)$, is *0.255* at generation *50*, and the smaller number of individuals that need to be processed, $I(m,i,z)$, with $z=0.99$ is *81,600* achieved at iteration *50*.

4.2.2 Evolving a Rule Based System

To fulfil our initial goal of allowing GPNs to be evolved to different architectures we will evolve a rule-based system capable of solving the Ant Problem. This system will be composed by a set of rules of the form:

if *<condition>* **then** *<conclusion1>*

else *<conclusion2>*

The evolution of such a system is simply done by applying some changes to the terminal, function and root sets used in the previous point to evolve a distributed program. The main change is the removal of the *if* function from function set while the root set is modified to have only the same *if* function. This will produce programs with the structure of the above rule, where *condition, conclusion1* and *conclusion2* will be subprograms composed of the instructions in the function set. The *knowledge* produced by a rule is the result of the subprogram executed as the rule conclusion. To allow this *knowledge* to be used by other rules in the same iteration, forward connections are allowed from internal nodes to external ones, and the T_e set is changed accordingly. Recurrent connections are also allowed so the rules can use the *knowledge* produced by other rules in the previous iteration. Terminal, function and root sets used in this experience are presented in Table 3.

For the same 200 runs, we obtained the results presented in Fig. 4. The topology of a successful rule based system is presented in the same figure. The results are still better than the ones of all other non-GPN approaches but don't improve on the ones obtained when evolving the distributed program based solution.

$T_i = \{i_1,\ i_2,\ a_1,\ a_2,\ ...,\ a_9\}$
$T_e = \{i_1,\ i_2,\ a_1,\ a_2,\ ...,\ a_9,\ b_1,\ b_2,\ ...,\ b_6\}$
$F = \{and,\ or,\ not,\ >,\ <,\ ==,\ !=\}$
$R = \{if\}$

Table 3. Terminal, function and root sets for evolving a rule-based system capable of solving the Ant Problem

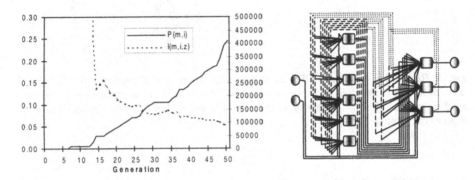

Fig. 4. Results for evolving a GPN as a rule based system and topology of a successful individual. The cumulative probability of success, $P(m,i)$, is *0.245* at generation *50*, and the smaller number of individuals that need to be processed, $I(m,i,z)$, with $z=0.99$ is *86,700* achieved at iteration *50*.

4.2.3 Evolving a Recurrent Neural Network

To evolve a recurrent neural network, the changes we have to make to the terminal, function and root sets are more substantial. The most important task is that of finding a way to evolve the connections' weights, since the way of evolving the connections themselves is inherent to our approach. The method we use to evolve the weights in connections is based in the attachment of a random number between 0 and 2.5 to every terminal appearing in a program. As the only functions in the function set are *add* and *subtract*, each program its no more than a linear combination of the node's available inputs multiplied by different values each time they appear. This means that, for each terminal, the evolutionary process will try to find a correct combination of values so that a correct weight for the correspondent connection is produced. We already mentioned that the function set has only two members: *add* and *subtract*, but we haven't said anything about the root set. This has only one element, the transference function *transf*. *Transf* has only one argument and returns this argument if its value is between 0 and 1, returns 0 if the value is less or equal to 0, and returns 1 if the value is more than 1. We could also have used several transference functions, leaving to the evolutionary process the selection of the most appropriate ones. Terminal, function and root sets used in this experience are presented in Table 4. The *w* before the terminals means they have an associated weight.

| $T_i=\{wi_1, wi_2, wa_1, wa_2, ..., wa_9\}$ |
| $T_e=\{wi_1, wi_2, wa_1, wa_2, ..., wa_9, wb_1, wb_2, ..., wb_6\}$ |
| $F=\{add, subtract\}$ |
| $R=\{transf\}$ |

Table 4. Terminal, function and root sets for evolving a recurrent neural network capable of solving the Ant Problem

For the same 200 runs, we obtained the results presented in Fig. 5. The topology of a successful neural network is presented in the same figure. These were the best results obtained by us, only needing to evaluate 59,500 individuals to find, with a probability of 99% a neural network capable of correctly guiding the ant to collect all the 89 sugar cubes on the „Santa Fe" trail.

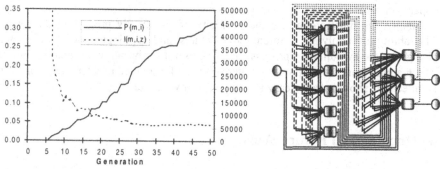

Fig. 5. Results for evolving a GPN as a recurrent neural network and topology of a successful individual. The cumulative probability of success, $P(m,i)$, is 0.315 at generation 50, and the smaller number of individuals that need to be processed, $I(m,i,z)$, with $z=0.99$ is $59,500$ achieved at iteration 34.

Results obtained in the three GPN based approaches are summarized in Table 1, together with the best non-GPN results.

5   Conclusions

In this article we described a new method to generate several forms of distributed programs, and applied it to the evolution of controllers for simple agents. This method is based on a connectionist structure, which we call Genetically Programmed Network, where each node has an associated program, evolved using genetic programming. Each GPN individual has several nodes, so its genome is a sequence of chromosomes, each one corresponding to a program. By manipulating the function, terminal and root set of the programs, we showed that it was possible to evolve GPNs into controllers with very different architectures.

As an example, we applied the described method to a commonly used benchmark problem, the „Santa Fe" trail problem, and evolved populations of GPNs into distributed programs, rule based systems and neural networks all capable of solving the given problem. By comparing our results to the ones of several other approaches to this problem, we concluded that the number of individuals we need to be evaluated so that a solution is found, with a probability of 0.99, was substantially less using GPN than in the best of those approaches. We believe this can be justified by the highly connectionist nature of our approach, which allows that both functional and temporal relations between nodes can be easily created by forward and recurrent connections. Memory mechanisms needed to solve problems where the previous state of the system must be remembered, can easily be implemented by recurrent (delayed) connections between nodes. Forward connections are expected to allow the straightforward evolution of communities of small programs with distributed functionality, which should be easier to evolve than a larger, isolated, program capable of providing the same functionality.

Finally, we must emphasize the plasticity of genetically programmed networks. The ability of evolving different architectures and topologies, with only minor changes to the evolutionary process, could be useful for bringing us some insight into which architecture would produce better solutions for a given problem. New or hybrid architectures should also be easy to evolve and investigate.

6   Ongoing and Future Work

In this work we have chosen to explore the polymorphic possibilities of the GPN, evolving several solutions with different architectures for the same problem. To prove this method is of real interest, we must apply it to a range of other problems, and we must be able to evolve yet more different control architectures. This is part of the ongoing work on GPN. Another important point concerns the current limitation of our system to a fixed number of internal and external nodes. We hope to deal with this limitation in the near future.

Acknowledgements

This work was partially funded by the Portuguese Ministry of Science and Technology under the Program PRAXIS XXI.

References

1.   P. Angeline, „Evolutionary Algorithms and Emergent Intelligence", PhD Thesis, Ohio State University, 1993.
2.   W. Banzhaf, P. Nordin, and M. Olmer, „Generating Adaptive Behavior for a Real Robot using Function Regression within Genetic Programming", *Genetic*

Programming 1997: Proceedings of the Second Annual Conference, pp. 35-43, Morgan Kaufmann, 13-16 July 1997.

3.   R. Brooks, „**Artificial Life and Real Robots**", *Towards a Practice of Autonomous Systems: Proceedings of the First European Conference on Artificial Life*, MIT Press, Cambridge, MA, 1992, pp. 3-10.

4.   K. Chellapilla, „**Evolutionary programming with tree mutations: Evolving computer programs without crossover**", *Genetic Programming 1997: Proceedings of the Second Annual Conference*, pages 431-438, Morgan Kaufmann, 13-16 July 1997.

5.   D. Cliff, P. Husbands and I. Harvey, „**Analysis of Evolved Sensory-Motor Controllers**", *Cognitive Science Research Paper*, Serial N° CSRP 264, 1992.

6.   R. Collins and D. Jefferson, „**Antfarm: toward simulated evolution**", *Artificial Life II, Santa Fe Institute Studies in the Sciences of the Complexity*, volume X, Addison-Wesley, 1991.

7.   J. Donnart and J. Meyer, „**A Hierarchical Classifier System Implementing a Motivationally Autonomous Animat**", *Proceedings of the Third Int. Conf. on Simulation of Adaptive Behaviour*, MIT Press/Bradford Books, pp. 144-153.

8.   M. Dorigo and U. Schnepf, „**Genetics-Based Machine Learning and Behaviour Based Robotics: A New Synthesis**", *IEEE Transactions on Systems, Man, and Cybernetics*, 23, 1, 141-154, January 1993.

9.   M. Dorigo and M. Colombetti, „**Robot Shaping: Developing Autonomous Agents through Learning**", *Technical Report TR-92-040*, International Computer Science Institute, April 1993

10.   D. Floreano and F. Mondada, „**Automatic Creation of an Autonomous Agent: Genetic Evolution of a Neural-Network Driven Robot**", *From Animals to Animats III, Proc. of the 3rd Int. Conf on Simulation of Adaptive Behaviour*, MIT Press/Bradford Books, 1994.

11.   J. Grefenstette and A. Schultz, „**An Evolutionary Approach to Learning in Robots**", *Proc. of the Machine Learning Workshop on Robot Learning, 11th International Conference on Machine Learning*, July 10-13, 1994, New Brunswick, N.J., 65-72.

12.   I. Harvey, P. Husbands and D. Cliff, „**Issues in Evolutionary Robotics**", *Proceedings of SAB92, the Second International Conference on Simulation of Adaptive Behaviour*, MIT Press Bradford Books, Cambridge, MA, 1993.

13.   M. Keith, „**Genetic Programming in C++: Implementation Issues**", *Advances in Genetic Programming*, pp. 285-310, MIT Press, 1994.

14.   J. Koza, „**Genetic programming: On the programming of computers by means of natural selection**", Cambridge, MA, MIT Press, 1992.

15.   W. Langdon and R. Poli, „**Why Ants are Hard**", Technical Report CSRP-98-04, The University of Birmingham, School of Computer Science, 1998.

16.   W. Langdon, „**Better Trained Ants**", Technical Report CSRP-98-08, The University of Birmingham, School of Computer Science, 1998.

17.   S. Nolfi, D. Floreano *et al*, „**How to Evolve Autonomous Robots: Different Approaches in Evolutionary Robotics**", *Artificial Life IV*, pp. 190-197, MIT Press/Bradford Books, 1994.

18.   J. Pujol and R.Poli, „**Efficient Evolution of Asymmetric Recurrent Neural Networks Using a PDGP-inspired Two-dimensional Representation**", *Proceedings of EuroGP'98, First European Workshop on Genetic Programming*, April 1998, Springer.

Concurrent Genetic Programming, Tartarus and Dancing Agents

Adrian Trenaman

NUI Maynooth, Co. Kildare, Ireland
Phone: +353-1-7083354, `trenaman@cs.may.ie`

Abstract. Evolutionary approaches such as genetic programming have often been applied to the automatic design of controllers for autonomous agents in virtual worlds. This paper applies a multi-tree genetic programming representation to the Tartarus world. Agent-controllers are evolved whose behaviour is the emergent effect of the interleaved evaluation of the program trees. Agents with good fitness and of very low complexity are evolved, and it is found that this technique evolves agents that exploit the characteristics of the runtime scheduler to provide an implicit rather than explicit form of state in the form of a "fixed dance".

1 Introduction

Artificial life holds as its manifesto that life-like behaviour can be realised through the emergent interaction of populations of semiautonomous entities [8]. Typically, the behaviour observed is characterised by such verbs as *flocking* or *swarming*, verbs that apply specifically to group behaviour. Adopting *Minsky's Society of Mind* approach, the individual itself becomes a population of semiautonomous entities, and the collective group behaviour becomes the behaviour of the individual [9]. This individual is usually referred to as an agent (though in Minsky's parlance the term agent refers to the semiautonomous entities that constitute the individual).

This computational model (shown in Figure 1) is adopted here, where agents are evolved whose behaviour is the emergent effect of a number of processes. Each process receives input from the environment through sensors, and can store and retrieve information from a shared memory area. Clearly, this model demands that we design the processes, the interaction between them, and the structure of the shared memory. Designing emergent behaviour and appropriate internal representations is hard, as discussed by Brooks in [2], and so we wish to apply an evolutionary approach to this task. The Tartarus problem is used as a benchmark, and is described further in Section 2. Tartarus was chosen because it is a problem that requires controllers capable of more than just reactive behaviour for good performance. Controllers must use some form of internal state to achieve good fitness, and so in using this benchmark we examine if this emergent paradigm can achieve such behaviour. This paper investigates two important issues: the efficacy of incorporating an explicit state mechanism into the

R. Poli et al. (Eds.): EuroGP'99, LNCS 1598, pp. 270–282, 1999.

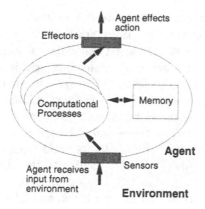

Fig. 1. The agent is made up a number of processes, receiving input from sensors and sending output to effectors that perform the agents actions. The processes can read and write to a shared memory area, thus allowing them to build and maintain internal representations.

agent architecture; and the effect of increasing the number of semiautonomous entities within the agent.

The processes within the agent are implemented as genetically evolved program trees [7], and the shared memory structure used by these trees is linear indexed memory. Interaction between the processes is achieved through the interleaved execution of the genetic programs and their use of shared memory. The trees are effectively evaluated in parallel, and so we call this technique "concurrent genetic programming". The interleaved execution is facilitated by a round-robin scheduler that allows each genetic program in the agent to evaluate a number of functions and terminals before passing control on to the next program in the agent. Further details of this scheduler are presented in Section 3.

A set of experiments to test the efficacy of this approach are described in Section 4, results of which are presented in Section 5. The approach evolves agents with good fitness, however it is found that the use of indexed memory does not offer a significant advantage over agents who do not use indexed memory. Instead the agents evolve to exploit the interleaved execution of their constituent processes and produce state in the form of a sequence of moves, or rather, a "dance". We conclude in Section 6 that evolutionary approaches that exploit this form of implicit state may be better suited to Tartarus than the explicit state approach used here. Finally, some ideas for future work are presented in Section 7.

2   Tartarus

Teller introduced the Tartarus world as a problem requiring the intelligent use of state for good performance [10]. The world is a 6×6 grid bounded by an impenetrable wall, in which 6 blocks are randomly placed in the inner 4×4

locations. A single agent is also placed in this central area, and its task is to push the blocks to the perimeter locations. Starting with a random position and direction (either N, S, E or W) the agent can choose to turn left, turn right or move forward into the cell it is facing. Turning left or right is performed in steps of 90 degrees, so the agent can only face (and move) in the directions North, South, East and West. If the agent attempts to move forward into a cell with a block in it, if will do so only if the block can be moved into the next cell in that direction. If this next cell contains a block or the wall then the move is unsuccessful and the agent remains in place. The agent senses its world using 8 sensors that return the contents of the 8 neighbouring cells, relative to the direction of the agent. This arrangement is shown in Figure 2. The sensors return one of three values: 0 for an empty cell, 1 for a cell containing a block, and 2 for the wall. The agent is not given its position in the world, nor is it given the size of the world: it must perform using the immediate sensory information alone. Every move the agent makes uses up one unit of energy, regardless of whether the move is successful or not, and the agent must move as many blocks to the perimeter as possible within 80 moves. The agent is awarded 2 points for every block in a corner and 1 point for every block in one of the 16 remaining perimeter cells. A number of "impossible worlds" exist in Tartarus, characterised by the appearance of a square of 4 blocks, which clearly cannot be moved giving the "push one block at a time" restriction. Agents are *not* tested in worlds containing such configurations, however, it is conceivable that such configurations could occur during the agent's work.

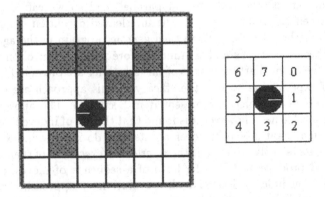

Fig. 2. A typical initial configuration for Tartarus (left). The agent senses its environment through 8 sensors numbered relative to the agent's orientation as shown on the right.

Tartarus is an interesting problem because agents without internal state perform very poorly at it. A simple strategy such as "If a block is ahead, push it" will be ineffective as there may be no feedback from the environment to let the agent know that this move has been successful. Such an agent could expend all of its energy pushing the same block against the same wall cell. To perform well an agent must use some internal state to allow more than just reactive behaviour.

Teller originally used the Tartarus problem to demonstrate the efficacy of linear indexed memory as an explicit state mechanism [10]. Agents, controlled by genetic programming trees with indexed memory, were evolved that performed well at Tartarus. Teller used genetic programming trees without indexed memory as a base-line, and these scored poorly yielding about 0.5 points per board. His best agents (using indexed memory and a single automatically defined function) scored about 4 points per board, thus demonstrating that those agents using indexed memory performed significantly better than those without. In one set of experiments, agents were evolved with access to indexed memory but *without* access to sensor information. Surprisingly, agents with good fitness were evolved, indicating that agents could evolve to use memory effectively while not storing or using the information they received from the environment.

Ashlock and Joenks [1] have proposed a different base-line for Tartarus, in which internal state is provided implicitly. The agent is controlled by a fixed sequence of a actions, which is repeated over and over until the agent runs out of energy. In this manner, the agent executes a "fixed dance", where implicit state is formed via sequencing of actions. Strings of actions of length 4, 5, 8, 10, 16, 20, 40 and 80 (all factors of 80) were evolved, and it was found that strings of length 16 and 20 performed best, giving a fitness of approximately 3 points per board. A variable length string representation was also tried, and it produced an agent with an average score of 4.866 using the following "dance": FLFFLFLFFFFRFLFLFLFFRF. Finally, using a novel representation called ISAc lists, where agents are controlled by a number of If-Statement-Action sequences, the authors evolved agents with scores in the region of 7 points.

A variation of Tartarus has been used elsewhere by Honovar and Balakrishnan [12] to investigate the evolution of sensor configurations. They modified the problem by using more time steps (216) and allowing the agent to evolve its own sensor configurations, beyond the immediate-neighbour sensor set-up described by Teller. Using a neural network approach on this modified world they achieved fitness in the range of 3.5 to 4.5 points per board, however, given the increased number of time steps it is hard to compare these with other results.

Previous work by the author [11] used a variation of Tartarus in which agents turned in steps of 45 degrees (thus allowing movement along diagonals) and only 5 blocks on the board. Agents where evolved with a multi-tree representation (where each tree constituted a genetic program). These program trees were evaluated by assigning each a thread, producing an agent behaviour as an emergent effect of the interaction and co-operation of the threaded processes. Using this approach multithreaded programs with access to indexed memory were evolved that scored up to 5 points per board. Multithreaded programs without access to indexed memory also performed well, leading to the conclusion that the agents evolved an implicit form of state due to the interleaving of program execution.

This variation of Tartarus, which we shall refer to from here on as Diagarus, may be easier to solve than the original Tartarus problem. This may be due to the lack of clutter on the board and the use of diagonal moves: agents evolved wide circular path strategies that cleared blocks to the perimeter. A significant drawback of this thread-based implementation was that the agents evolved were not robust, as their fitness was dependent on the dynamics of the runtime thread scheduler which were not recorded and which changed under observation.

This paper sets out to develop robust agents using the concurrent genetic programming approach, using a different experimental set-up with a fully deterministic round-robin scheduler, described in the next section.

3   Concurrent Genetic Programming

The essence of concurrent genetic programming is the concurrent evaluation of number of genetic programming trees to produce an emergent collective behaviour. Concurrency is achieved through the use of a round-robin scheduler and a function unique to this approach, the Yield function.

When the CGP runtime scheduler evaluates each program, it does so by giving each an amount of *program energy*. Program energy corresponds to the granularity of concurrency. Each genetic program is executed by traversing the program tree in an infix manner and evaluating the terminals and functions as they are encountered: the scheduler allows each tree to proceed in this manner for a number of functions and terminals equal to the energy. When the energy is "used up", the scheduler gives energy to the next tree, which is evaluated in a similar fashion. If a program completes its evaluation with energy left over, this energy is discarded and the next program in the agent is evaluated. When the last program in the sequence has expends its energy, execution resumes at the first program in the sequence. This program resumes evaluation at the last point of execution before it lost energy.

When any one of the genetic programs produces a result, the CGP runtime-scheduler halts execution and returns this result. This result may then be used, for example, to decide the next action of an agent. In the meantime, the CGP interpreter maintains the program-state of each of the genetic programs, ready to resume execution if required. The scheduler will continue evaluation of the genetic programs until the user decides not to continue, for example, when the agent has reached a certain level of fitness or has made a maximum number of moves.

To allow agents to evolve their own scheduling schemes around that of the round robin scheduler, we introduce the Yield function to the function set. When the Yield function is encountered, it discards the remaining program energy and allows the scheduler to move on to the next program in the sequence. For all the experiments in this paper program energy is 1, and so the agent's are evaluated as fine-grained concurrent processes. In this scenario, Yield acts as a no-op. It is possible to vary program energy to investigate a wider range of concurrent scheduling strategies, but this is outside the scope of this paper and left for future work.

The random creation of concurrent genetic programs proceeds much in the same was as the random creation of conventional genetic programs. A concurrent genetic program is created by specifying an initial depth and a growth type (either FULL or GROW) and each tree in the individual is grown with this initial depth and growth type. The ramp-half-and-half method is used to create the initial population, where trees are created alternatively using the FULL and GROW growth method, and the maximum depth for initial trees varies in the range 1 to some maximum depth.

There are a number of different strategies that can be used for the crossover and mutation of multi-tree individuals, a number of which are identified by Haynes [5]. Bruce [4, 3] uses a scheme where one of the trees in an individual is selected at random and crossed with the corresponding tree in the other parent. In this work, we use what Haynes has called "TeamAll" crossover, where a new individual is created by performing conventional genetic programming crossover on each corresponding set of trees in the parents. Mutation is applied by selecting one tree in an individual at random and applying conventional genetic programming crossover to this tree. Of course, other schemes exist for crossover and mutation, for example, mutating all the trees in an individual or allowing crossover between different trees in the parents, however, the current scheme was chosen for its simplicity.

This representation provides a general framework for the evolution of parallel controllers for agents, both for virtual worlds such as Tartarus and for real-world robotics. It raises a number of questions: first, does the technique work? That is, does concurrent genetic programming provide a rich program solution-space and does it provide an efficient search technique with which to navigate this space? If so, how does performance vary if we use more or less program trees in our individuals? In the next section, we describe a set of experiments designed to shed light on these questions.

4   Experiments

This section describes a set of experiments where concurrent genetic programming was applied to the Tartarus problem (described above in Section 2). The make up of the agents is that shown in Figure 1, where the computational processes are genetic programs, and the memory is linear indexed memory. In these experiments program energy is set to 1, and so the individuals are evaluated in a fine-grained pseudo-parallel fashion. The Yield terminal is in the function set, allowing the agents to perform a no-op.

For simplicity, we allow all the trees in an individual to use the same function and terminal sets. We use the same functions, terminals and indexed memory as Teller [10]. The agent senses its environment through 8 sensor terminals, labelled Sense0 to Sense7. Also in the terminal set are the integers 0–19.

(Or X Y)	Returns the MAX(X,Y).
(Not X)	Returns 1 if $X = 0$, 0 otherwise.
(Less X Y)	Returns 1 if $X < Y$, 0 otherwise.
(Add X Y)	Returns $X + Y$.
(If-Then-Else X Y Z)	Returns Y if $X > 0$, Z otherwise.
(Sub X Y)	Returns $X - Y$, floored to 0.
(Eq X Y)	Returns 1 if $X = Y$, 0 otherwise.
(ReadSM X)	Returns the contents of memory at position X.
(WriteSM X Y)	Returns contents of memory at position Y and then sets the contents of memory at position Y to X.
(Yield X)	Informs scheduler to continue evaluating next tree. When evaluation of this tree resumes the argument X is evaluated and this is returned.

Table 1. Function set shared by all trees in an individual

The programs can write to a shared memory location using ReadSM and WriteSM. ReadSM takes one integer argument, used as an index to specify which element in memory should be returned. WriteSM takes two integer arguments, the first a value and the second an index, and places the value into the indexed position in the linear memory element. WriteSM returns the previous contents of this memory location. These and the other functions are described briefly in Table 1.

When a program tree evaluates, that is, when its root node produces a result, this result is an integer value in the range 0–19. This is wrapped to produce a move forward, turn left or turn right using the following wrapper: if the result is in the range 0–6 then turn left, 7–13 then turn right, 14–19 then move forward.

On each generation, 40 Tartarus boards are generated randomly (omitting invalid boards as described in Section 2) and these are used to test the agents. By testing individuals against a different set of boards in every generation we ensure that individuals are exposed to a wide variety of initial board configurations. Raw fitness is calculated as the sum of the scores for each board, and so the maximum fitness is 400.

To examine the effect of different numbers of program trees on performance we vary the number of trees in the individual, creating agents with one, two and four trees. To examine the efficacy of indexed memory as a shared memory mechanism we evolve agents with and without access to the indexed memory functions Read and Write. This gives a total of 6 (3 × 2) experiments. Each experiment is run 20 times with different seeds: clearly, more runs would carry greater statistical significance, however, 20 was chosen to minimise the amount of computational time required produce the results, while giving some indication of the average performance under the different parameters.

Objective	To examine the application of concurrent genetic programming to the Tartarus as described in Section 2.
Fitness Cases	Individuals are measured against 40 worlds randomly generated in each generation.
Raw Fitness	The sum of points earned in the 40 fitness cases. The maximum raw fitness for Tartarus is 400; *Standardised* fitness is 400 - raw fitness.
Wrapper	When a program within an individual completes evaluation, its result is in the range 0–19. If the result is in range 0–6 then the agent turns left, 7–13 then the agent turns right, 14–19 then the agent moves forward.
GP Parameters	Population size = 800, maximum generations = 50, creation type is ramp-half-and-half, tournament selection is used with tournament size = 7, crossover occurs at 90%, reproduction at 9% and mutation at 1%.
CGP Parameters	Program energy set to 1 for multi-tree agents, infinity for single tree agents. Yield function allows agents to modify behaviour of scheduler.
Success Predicate	An individual scores 400 points for Tartarus.
Overall Individual Structure	Each program is made up of 1, 2 or 4 program trees.
Explicit Memory Constructs	A size 20 linear indexed memory is used, accessed using the functions ReadSM and WriteSM.
Terminal Set	Integers 0–19, sensors Sense0–Sense7
Function Set	Not, Or, IfThenElse, Less, Add, Sub, Eq, ReadSM, WriteSM, Yield

Table 2. Tableau describing concurrent genetic programming set-up for Tartarus.

A tableau summarising these genetic programming parameters is shown in Table 2.

5   Results

Results are summarised in Table 3, where we present the average and standard deviation of the maximum fitness over the 20 runs for each experiment. Also presented is the fitness of the best individual evolved for each experiment and its average score when evaluated after evolution on 5000 random boards. This last metric is the most telling, as it gives an indication of the utility of the evolved agents. The best agent produced by the two-tree experiment with memory scored 4.99 points. The best of the two-tree agents without memory scores 4.11 points, followed closely by the single-tree memory agents (similar to those evolved by Teller) scoring 4.00 points. The four-tree agents score just below 4 points, and the single-tree agents with no memory score a very poor 0.91 points.

The average best fitness per generation over the runs of each experiment is shown in Figure 3. The single-tree agents without memory perform very poorly, as expected. The single-tree agents with memory perform well, starting from an

Memory	Trees	Fitness	Mean	Std. Dev.	Score
No	1	345	359.30	5.23	0.91
	2	192	232.65	21.87	4.11
	4	213	223.90	6.96	3.75
Yes	1	219	249.55	15.65	4.00
	2	171	215.45	21.65	4.99
	4	213	228.75	7.87	3.85

Table 3. Results from the experiments. Each experiment was run 20 times, and fitness of the best individual over all runs is presented in the column labelled *Fitness*. This is the number of points the best individual scored over 40 boards. The mean and standard deviation of the maximum fitness over the 20 runs is presented in the next two columns. The *Score* column gives the average number of points scored by the best individual over 5000 boards.

initial low standardised fitness (in the region of 370) and progressing to better fitness. The multi-tree experiments start initially with a very high fitness at creation (between 250 and 300), exhibit some improvement and then rapidly bottom out. Initial fitness for the 4-tree agents is *better* than that of the 2-tree agents: the additional random program trees seem to boot-strap the evolutionary process with good initial random strategies.

The average complexity per generation over the 20 runs of each experiment is shown in Figure 4 (the complexity of a CGP agent is defined the number of nodes and terminals in all of its programs). Complexity of the one and two-tree agents grows as the number of generations increases. However, in the four-tree case, we observe an initial drop in complexity, presumably as the agents converge on simple "fixed-dance" solutions. In the case where agents have no memory, this initial drop in complexity is reversed and complexity soars. However, those agents with access to indexed memory fall further and only in later generations does this complexity begin to rise.

A four-tree agent of very low complexity is shown in Figure 5: despite its low complexity this agent scores 3.85 points. The agent uses only one sensor, `Sensor4`, however, this appears in a function call, (`less 16 Sensor4`), that will always evaluate to 0. The agent repeatedly sets the 14th position in memory to 0 and reads the constant value 0 from the 1st position in memory. We can conclude that the agent is *blind*, and uses memory only as a store of constant values in the range 0..19. The agent exploits the round-robin runtime scheduler to effect a fixed dance that gives the observed fitness.

Initial experience with the *Diagarus* variation of Tartarus, where agents are allowed move in diagonal lines and there is one less block on the board, give similar results: multi-tree agents without memory evolve strategies that can achieve reasonable fitness of about 3.8 points out of a maximum of 9. The rapid fall in the complexity of four-tree agents using memory and the bloat of four-tree agents without memory have also been observed in these runs. This suggests that the Diagarus problem is quite similar to Tartarus in terms of its difficulty and the solutions that the concurrent approach discovers.

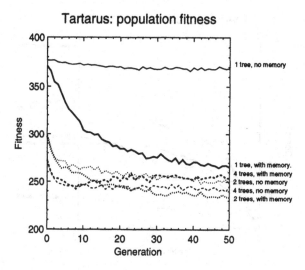

Fig. 3. Graph showing the average best fitness over the 20 runs of each experiment. The best fitness achievable is 0, while the worst is 400.

6   Conclusions

The results of Section 5 indicate that this concurrent genetic programming approach to the evolution of agents can produce agents of low complexity and good fitness for the Tartarus problem. The highest-scoring agent evolved used two trees and indexed memory, and its score of 4.99 points compares favourably against the fixed and variable-length action-string baseline for Tartarus proposed by Ashlock [1]. This agent also fares well in comparison to Teller's single tree agents with automatically defined functions. It has been shown that increasing the number of program trees yields higher fitness in the initial generations and faster convergence of the genetic algorithm on solutions that are of low complexity that effect a fixed dance rather than reflective behaviour.

The original aim of this work was to investigate the ability of this concurrent approach to evolve agents exhibiting an emergent behaviour that builds and maintains internal representations of the world. However, agents without explicit memory also perform very well. This, coupled with the good performance of the variable-length string strategies suggests that the formation of explicit internal representations is not required to solve Tartarus and may not be desirable in the first place. Although the best agent evolved does use indexed memory, this does not mean that the agent is building and using mental models of the world. Teller's observation of good "blind" agents using memory, along with similar "blind" agents observed here, suggest that the memory is used as a mechanism for producing sequential behaviour rather than as a repository for mental models.

The multi-tree representation used here exploits the interleaved evaluation of the program trees to form an implicit form of state in the form of sequential behaviour. In doing so, many runs converge on solutions that are analogous to those of the fixed and variable length action-string baseline. This suggests that it

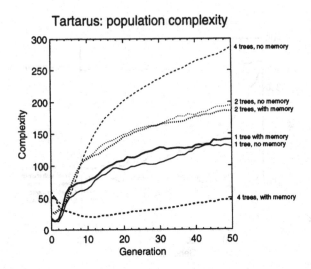

Fig. 4. Graph showing the average complexity of individuals over 20 runs for each experiment. A curious effect is observed for four-tree agents without memory: their complexity falls over time and only in later generations does it increase.

Tree 0: (writeSM (less 16 Sensor4) 14)
Tree 1: (Yield 17)
Tree 2: 15
Tree 3: (readSM 1)

Fig. 5. Four-tree agent of very low complexity scoring 3.85 points.

is more effective to evolve "dancing" agents rather than "thinking" ones for Tartarus, and offers a reason for why Ashlock's ISAc representation works so much better. The ISAc representation is based on sequential behaviour: agents are evolved with a *repertoire* of dance moves performed in a particular order, where the agent can improvise and skip certain moves depending on environmental conditions.

In summary, this paper has shown that the concurrent approach can evolve agents that perform well at Tartarus. The convergence on fixed-dance solutions as opposed to explicit representations is somewhat disappointing, however this stands testament to the ingenuity of the evolutionary approach in finding novel and unexpected solutions to problems.

7   Future Work

Although provision has been made in the runtime scheduler to investigate different levels of granularity of evaluation, the agents evolved in this paper were all evaluated in a fine-grained manner. Work in progress investigates the performance of agents with respect to the granularity of concurrency, from the fine-grained approach used here to more coarse-grained scheduling strategies.

To establish the generality of the approach as distributed AI technique, The approach is also being applied to another virtual-robotics problem, Ashlock's "Dozer" world. Dozer is similar to Tartarus but involves a larger board in which agents must group blocks together rather than push them to the perimeter.

The choice of indexed memory for explicit internal representation was made here as it provided a simple, unbiased mechanism by which an agent could develop its own mental models. However other memory structures, such as two-dimensional indexed memory, stacks, directed graphs or even simple scalar quantities may prove more effective. An investigation of these different mechanisms is left for future work. If this path is followed then care must be taken to ensure that the problems under investigation really do require internal state, and cannot be solved through the implicit state that this approach provides for free. Jacobi's T-Maze problem [6], in which an agent must make a decision (which way to turn at a T-junction) based on past event (a light shining on one side of the agent at the start of a corridor) may be a good starting point for such work.

Acknowledgements

The author wishes to thank Prof. David Vernon of NUI Maynooth for his continuous guidance in this work. Thanks are also due to the reviewers of an earlier version of this paper submitted to *Advances in Genetic Programming 3*.

References

1. Dan Ashlock and Mark Joenks. ISAc lists, a different representation for program induction. In John Koza et al., editors, *Genetic Programming: Proceedings of the Third Annual Genetic Programming Conference*, pages 3–10, Madison, Wisconsin, 1998. Morgan Kaufmann.
2. Rodney A. Brooks. Intelligence without representation. *Artificial Intelligence*, (47):139–159, 1991.
3. Wilker Shane Bruce. Automatic generation of object-oriented programs using genetic programming. In John R. Koza et al., editors, *Genetic Programming - Proceedings of the First Annual Conference*, pages 267–272, Stanford, California, July 1996. MIT Press.
4. Wilker Shane Bruce. The lawnmower problem revisited: Stack-based genetic programming and automatically designed functions. In John R. Koza et al., editors, *Genetic Programming - Proceedings of the Second Annual Conference*, pages 52–57, Stanford, California, July 1997. Morgan Kaufmann.
5. Thomas Haynes and Sandip Sen. Crossover operators for evolving a team. In John R. Koza et al., editors, *Genetic Programming - Proceedings of the Second Annual Conference*, pages 162–167, Stanford, California, July 1997. Morgan Kaufmann.
6. Nick Jacobi. Evolutionary robotics and the radical-envelope-of-noise hypothesis. *Adaptive Behaviour*, 6:131–174, 1997.
7. John R. Koza. *Genetic Programming: On the Programming of Computers by Means of Natural Selection*. MIT Press, Cambridge, Massachusetts, 1992.

8. Christopher G. Langton. Artificial life. In Christopher G. Langton, editor, *Artificial Life - Proceedings of an Interdisciplinary Workshop on the Wynthesis and Simulation of Living Systems*. Addison-Wesley, 1989.

9. Marvin Minsky. *The Society of Mind*. Simon & Schuster, New York, 1985.

10. Astro Teller. The evolution of mental models. In Kim Kinnear, editor, *Advances in Genetic Programming*, pages 199–220. MIT Press, 1994.

11. Adrian Trenaman. Concurrent genetic programming and the use of explicit state to solve problems in partially-known environments. In John R. Koza et al., editors, *Genetic Programming 1998: Proceedings of the Third Annual Conference*, Madison, Wisconsin, July 1998. Morgan Kaufmann.

12. Honovar V. and Balakrishnan K. On sensor evolution in robotics. In John Koza et al., editors, *Genetic Programming: Proceedings of the First Annual Conference*, pages 455–460, Stanford, California, 1996. MIT Press.

Author Index

Lecture Notes in Computer Science

For information about Vols. 1–1520
please contact your bookseller or Springer-Verlag